PIETY PROCLAIMED

An Introduction to Places of Worship in Victorian England

The age in which we live is a most eventful period for English art. We are just emerging from a state which might be termed the dark ages of architecture. After a gradual decay of four centuries, the style, – for style there was, – became so execrably bad, that the cup of degradation was filled to the brim; and as taste had fallen to its lowest depth, a favourable re-action commenced.

AUGUSTUS WELBY NORTHMORE PUGIN (1812-52):
An Apology for The Revival of Christian Architecture in England
(London: John Weale, 1843), 1.

First published 2002
by Historical Publications Ltd
32 Ellington Street, London N7 8PL
(Tel: 020 7607 1628)

ISBN 0 948667 77 X
British Library Cataloguing-in-Publication Data
A catalogue record for this book is available from the British Library

Typeset in Palatino by Historical Publications Ltd
Reproduction by G & J Graphics, London EC2
Printed by Edelvives, Zaragoza, Spain

PIETY PROCLAIMED

An Introduction to Places of Worship in Victorian England

JAMES STEVENS CURL

HISTORICAL PUBLICATIONS

In Memoriam

G. S. C. and S. C.

Deus, qui nos patrem et matrem honorare præcepisti,
miserere clementer animabus patris et matris meæ,
eorumque peccata dimitte, meque eos
in æternæ claritatis gaudio fac videre.
Per Christum Dominum Nostrum. Amen.

FRANCIS HENRY DICKINSON (*Ed.*) *Missale ad Usum Insignis*

et Præclaræ Ecclesiæ SARUM (the *Sarum Missal*)

(Burntisland: E. Prelo de Pitsligo, 1861-83), col. 873★

Contents

List of Illustrations

Throughout, captions will refer to the liturgical orientation of churches, whether or not the sanctuary is placed at the east end. Sources of illustrations are given in parentheses after each caption, with the year in which the picture was taken (where known) in square brackets. Abbreviations used are:

GB   The late Mr Gordon Barnes
MC   © Mr Martin Charles
CC   © Crown copyright. NMR.
JSC   © The Author, or from his collection
Eastlake   CHARLES L. EASTLAKE: *A History of the Gothic Revival. An Attempt to show how the Taste for Mediæval Architecture which lingered in England during the Two Last Centuries has since been encouraged and developed* (London: Longmans, Green, & Co., 1872)
EH   © Reproduced with the permission of English Heritage. NMR (National Monuments Record)
AFK   © Mr Anthony F. Kersting
GLPL   © Greater London Photograph Library, now the London Metropolitan Archive
NMR   National Monuments Record
V&A   Victoria and Albert Museum Print-Room

List of Colour Plates

List of Black and White plates

Preface and Acknowledgements

I have a good eye, uncle: I can see a church by daylight.
WILLIAM SHAKESPEARE (1564-1616): *Much Ado About Nothing* (1598-9), Act 2, Scene 1, line 86.

I am afraid he has not been in the inside of a church for many years; but he never passes a church without pulling off his hat. This shows that he has good principles.
SAMUEL JOHNSON (1709-84): Quoted in JAMES BOSWELL (1740-95): *The Life of Samuel Johnson* (1934 edition, revised 1964), Vol. I, 418.

The information on which this book is based derives from many sources, not least those quoted in the Select Bibliography and in the captions of the illustrations. No student of Victorian architecture (and I am not an exception) can afford to ignore the architectural magazines of the period, notably *The Builder*, *The Building News*, *The Architect*, *The Studio*, and, where churches are concerned, *The Ecclesiologist*.

A passion for visiting churches over many years has given me an abiding love for, and interest in, ecclesiastical buildings, and I have travelled in every county in England to attempt to assuage that passion. Mention of counties in England prompts a word of explanation as to the location of the exemplars I have selected from an embarrassment of riches: throughout, I have used the names of the old counties to describe the locations of the buildings mentioned. This I have done for the following reasons: first of all, I detest meaningless names like 'Avon', 'Cleveland', 'Cumbria', or 'Humberside' (which, in any case, appear to be ephemeral); secondly, the Penguin *Buildings of England* series is still arranged county by county in England; and, thirdly, the old county boundaries were related to diocesan boundaries, and they had profound *historical* meaning as well as documentary relevance.

At the beginning of the twenty-first century, however, it is becoming more and more difficult to get into churches: many (especially Victorian churches) are often locked (except for services or other functions), as vandalism and theft inexorably increase, and as insurance companies insist that steps are taken to protect the buildings and their contents. A church, often the finest building in an area, is *terra incognita* to the vast majority of a population which, if not actually antagonistic to the Churches, does not care about the buildings associated with them, bother to look inside them, or even give them a moment's consideration. Such a lack of curiosity or of any sense of enquiry seems to be endemic in these benighted times. There are even indications that *any* building that can be considered as architecture (with a personality, grandeur, power, emotional content, fine craftsmanship, scale, and quality) will be an object of loathing for those with no culture or sense of the significance of the past. This state of affairs has brought its own response from the Churches: 'redundant plant' is a familiar view of existing buildings, while increasing numbers of abandoned buildings (notably those of Nonconformist sects) have fallen victim to destructive vandalism or have been demolished. Many large Victorian churches in inner cities or towns have been destroyed, or are under threat, and, even today, the widespread prejudice against the Victorian period does not help the conservation of much fine fabric. Victorian churches are not, for the most part, mere copies (inaccurately referred to as 'pastiches' by some) of mediæval styles: they are often marvellously original buildings; some are frequently Sublime in their scale and breathtakingly moving in their impact on the eye and mind; not a few display craftsmanship second to none, and possess stained glass, fixtures, and furnishings of exquisite loveliness; and there are several churches that can be considered to be among the very first rank of works of architecture of any period. England has a treasure-house of Victorian churches, and England should awaken to that fact before it is far too late.

One of the problems, when considering Victorian churches, is that some commentators (despite much effort and many fine works of scholarship) have tended to regard works of the Gothic Revival from the late 1870s as the products of copyists suffering from a terminal decline of creativity. Many others look on the architecture of English late-Gothic Revivalists with blinkered eyes and total incomprehension. Some writers, seeking the origins of Modernism (one suspects in order to make it respectable by identifying spurious architectural precedents for it), saw mid-Victorian Gothic as original and pioneering, and somehow connected with an inevitable seamless Hegelian progression leading to the International Modern style (and style it was): such a distortion of truth would have astounded architects working in the 1860s and 1870s.

Another problem is that in the twenty-first century we live in a secular society. Few people understand churches, feel easy in them, or know how they once were used. I say 'once were used' because, in most cases, what goes on in churches bears little resemblance to the forms of service for which the buildings were designed. Both the Anglican and Roman Catholic Churches have embraced such radical changes to their liturgies in the last forty years or so that the original designs and layouts no longer make sense, as chancels are abandoned, church fabric is mutilated, and the architecture loses its meaning. The damage done since Vatican II has been colossal, and may prove to be terminal, at least as far as many church buildings are concerned, and possibly for the institutions as well.

It should also be remembered that, at the end of Queen Victoria's reign, just over a century ago, the Church of England was alive, well, vigorous,

and growing: it was central to national life; everywhere there were Anglican churches (many were very new or were being built, and the best, arguably, were better than any English churches built before); and it had over 20,000 clergymen. There was a great tradition of Anglican church-music; Anglicanism was immensely powerful in providing education, and its influence pervaded countless institutions; it provided a dignified, civilised, tolerant, and fundamentally decent presence throughout the land; and the buildings associated with it, new and old, for the most part were the best and the finest that the genius of the nation could provide. The literature of the *Bible* and the mellifluous texts of the old *Prayer Book* were familiar to many, and laid the foundations of education, a feeling for the English tongue, and the seemly dignity of ceremonial and worship. Our language owes much to the 'King James' *Bible*, yet few are familiar with it today: the disappearance of elementary Christian knowledge has eroded aspects of English identity, and there can be no doubting the growing impoverishment of the English tongue.

Things are different at the beginning of the twenty-first century: in the mistaken belief that spirituality is a 'product' and that it is necessary to appeal to the Mob, the Church of England has largely abandoned the austerely beautiful language of its liturgy (thereby jettisoning both dignity and the foundation of literate education), and has done immense damage to buildings that once gave consolation. Mystery and numinousness have been discarded in favour of fatuous and offensive advertising, absurd attempts to introduce a language akin to vulgar argot that will 'reach out' to the masses (clearly it will do no such thing), and the adoption of tenth-rate 'music' that lowers rather than elevates the spirits. When many are seeking spirituality, the Church cannot provide it, because the Church has lost its identity. The Roman Catholics have also largely abandoned their wonderful Latin liturgy, adopted forms of words that are banal in the extreme (even worse than some of the Anglican concoctions), damaged or demolished many of their buildings (most of which were Victorian), and turned to feeble tunes and twanging guitars in another excruciating attempt to 'reach out'. Triviality, wrong-headedness, and vulgarity prevail over depth, secure intellectual and æsthetic bases, and dignified ceremonial.

I have taught university students for nigh on a quarter of a century: I know that many of them long for spiritual experiences and respond to great architecture, how they react to authenticity, conviction, and straightforwardness, and how quickly they spot oleaginous frauds and bogus talking-down in some supposedly intelligible language. Indeed, I have seen the glazed expressions on faces when some unimpressive clergyman addresses them, and heard their hilarity and explosions of contempt afterwards. When the Churches are ashamed of their past, hopelessly uncertain about their future, lack authority, and adopt language, liturgical innovations, and infantile music that are dismal in the extreme, it is unsurprising congregations desert them in droves. This rapid, destructive, and appalling decline may well herald the end of much Christian observance, and threaten the survival of church buildings throughout the land (something many clerics would no doubt welcome).

Why write a book on Victorian churches in 2002, and how does such a book fit a climate (created by certain politicians) that is inimical to history (and especially to England's history) and that favours a *tabula rasa* as a more convenient foundation on which to impose a so-called 'multicultural' ideology (if it can be called that) owing nothing to the past? One of the objectives is to encourage greater awareness of the historic forces that lie behind a building or monument, and to foster the study of history and archæology through the study of sites, buildings, monuments, furnishings, and fittings, but the main reason for bringing out this volume is to attempt to show how rich and varied is England's nineteenth-century church architecture, to try to demonstrate the multifarious styles employed, and to give a flavour of the religious backgrounds that prompted the design and erection of churches, so that at least some encouragement can be given to their conservation. Thus the book touches on several themes: churches in their urban context; differences in liturgical approaches and how these

affected the design of buildings; patronage; architectural styles and architects; Pugin, Roman Catholic churches, and their influence on Anglican architecture; comfort and style for the church-goers; the architecture of Nonconformity; other religious buildings; and the different types of churches, including the working-class mission, the monumental buildings erected by single patrons, and the more spectacular exemplars. Space precludes a discussion of the tradesmen who worked on the buildings (a vast subject in itself), although a few important interior fittings and their creators have been identified. The story of Victorian churches does not begin with the Queen's accession to the Throne in 1837 any more than it ends with her death in 1901: this book therefore takes into account the background and history stretching back to the reigns of George IV and William IV, and ends in the Edwardian era a few years before the 1914-18 war.

Victorian churches survive in wide stylistic varieties, and these, too, have historical and archæological significance. The practised eye can detect influences drawn from many sources in the many buildings of the Gothic Revival, for instance, and these sources will include native English as well as Continental mediæval buildings: in some cases there are parts of Victorian churches that are direct quotations from mediæval originals, and in others the Victorian work gives a flavour of a certain style, but is freely treated.

In the works of architects such as Sir George Gilbert Scott (known as 'Great Scott' [1811-78]), George Edmund Street (1824-81), and George Frederick Bodley (1827-1907), their unquestioned scholarship is demonstrated, and it is abundantly clear that they knew their stuff. Rarely does Bodley fail to please, and it would be difficult to imagine a sensibility so blunted or unreceptive as to be incapable of being moved by the Bodley churches at Hoar Cross (1872-1900) and Clumber Park (1886-9), stunned by Scott's great building at Haley Hill, Halifax (1855-9), or excited by Street's powerful churches at Torquay (1861-5), or St James-the-Less, Westminster (1859-61). William Butterfield's (1814-1900) unforgettable churches, starting with All Saints, Margaret Street, London (1849-59), will invariably startle, with their strong, even violent colouring, but the originality of interpretation of Gothic, the bold and inventive use of materials, and the superb craftsmanship lavished on them cannot be doubted. And what of the overwhelming interiors of John Francis Bentley's (1839-1902) Westminster Cathedral (1894-1903), James Brooks's (1825-1901) great London churches, or Edmund Evan Scott's (d. 1895) Sublime St Bartholomew's, Brighton (1872-74)? Is there anything architecturally more noble in all England? And, for the lover of Victorian art, that treasure-house, William White's (1825-1900) St Michael's, Lyndhurst, Hampshire (1858-70), has to be one of the great architectural and artistic experiences. For the student of spatial effects, carpentry, and 'Rogue' Goths, Edward Buckton Lamb's (1806-69) extraordinary and elephantine churches at Leiston, Suffolk (1853), and Croydon, Surrey (1868-70), must be visited, while real archæological fragments may be seen within Thomas Henry Wyatt (1807-80) and David Brandon's (1813-97) marvellous church of Sts Mary and Nicholas, Wilton, Wiltshire (1840-6), and Sidney Howard Barnsley's (1865-1926) church of St Sophia (or The Wisdom of God), Lower Kingswood, Surrey (1890-1903).

The enthusiast can study excellent First Pointed (or Early English Gothic) at the Roman Catholic Cathedral in Norwich (1884-1910) without having to seek out mediæval work; can view splendid *Rundbogenstil* at Wilton without having to travel to Munich or Potsdam; can enjoy wonderful Second Pointed (or Decorated Gothic) in the fourteenth-century style at Cheadle, Staffordshire (1840-6), and see it as it is virtually impossible to see in any undamaged mediæval building; and even look at Byzantinesque work without having to go to Turkey or Greece. However, perhaps even more important, the churches of the last twenty-five years or so of Queen Victoria's reign are often wonderful things in themselves, and give a flavour of late Gothic that can be more enjoyable than mutilated work of the fifteenth and sixteenth centuries, especially where furnishings and fittings are concerned, for there are screens, font-covers, reredoses, and much else that are superior to similar artefacts surviving from the Middle Ages. This book, therefore, attempts to give proper weight to late-Victorian and Edwardian ecclesiastical design, and so does not stop with the Queen's death in 1901, but continues into the reign of King Edward VII for the simple reason that certain themes and trends reached fruition then, notably with the work of Comper and Temple Moore.

Stephen Dykes Bower (1903-94) wrote that the 'period when architects endowed their buildings with a recognisable style, predominantly Gothic, but in which horizons gradually expanded to embrace much that was not Gothic' could be belatedly admired, if not envied. It was 'after this broadening tendency had begun that the greatest perfection in Gothic itself was attained – notably represented by the work of Bodley and Garner, Pearson, Temple Moore, and others. The chief significance of an epoch that extended well into [the twentieth] century, producing such large and contrasting buildings as Bentley's Westminster Cathedral and Sir Giles Scott's Liverpool Cathedral, lay in the persisting ability to find inspiration in style and handle it with originality'. Quite so, and thus this brief survey attempts to include an appreciation of the late Gothic Revival, putting it firmly within the social and liturgical context without which it can make only limited sense. Pevsnerian bias against the glorious late Gothic Revival is, at least in part, redressed, for the masterly architects who created some of the very best churches and fittings (and whose influence continued through the work of Dykes Bower and his pupils) were not afraid of talking about, and creating, beauty in architecture, something the Relativists and their apologists have forgotten all about. In short, Victorian ecclesiastical architecture offers a whole range of superb examples of craftsmanship, styles, furnishings, monuments, and fittings, and a lot of it is still in a relatively unspoiled state, although much has been lost.

The student of Victorian churches should travel with Pevsner's *Buildings of England* books, arranged county by county, and should try to learn to recognise the main architectural styles (although not all Pevsner's judgements should be uncritically accepted). In order to get the most out of visits to churches some preliminary study of styles is therefore necessary, and an acquaintance with recurring elements to be found in ecclesiastical buildings will be of help. It is advisable to get to know the names used in Ecclesiology, and there are several useful glossaries in print, including the present writer's *Oxford Dictionary of Architecture* (Oxford: Oxford University Press, 2000), which has the fullest entries as well as biographies of many architects and descriptions of style. Published and other documentary sources are essential for an understanding of the subject, but there is no substitute for the experience of visiting and studying the buildings themselves.

I owe much to my understanding of Victorian churches to the years 1970-73 during which I was Architectural Editor of *The Survey of London*: by a happy chance the area on which I was obliged to work was the parish of Kensington, and I studied every ecclesiastical building within the parish, organising the drawings and photographic records as well as writing the descriptions. As most of the fabric of church buildings in Kensington is Victorian, I had a wonderful opportunity to absorb a great range of Victorian architectural responses to the problem of designing churches in a relatively compact area, and in a short space of time. I thank my former colleagues, Mr Ashley Barker, Mr Victor Belcher, Mr Peter Bezodis, the late Mr Frank Evans, Mr John Greenacombe, Mr Rodney Hubbuck, the late Mr John Sambrook, and Dr Francis Sheppard for all the exchanges of ideas and information during the very interesting period leading up to the publication of *Northern Kensington* (Volume xxxvii of *The Survey of London*) in 1973.

A word about the illustrations is necessary. In some cases (though not all) I have been obliged to use old photographs: the reasons for this are that often modern photographs are impossible because mature trees, later buildings, or (more usually) ghastly urban clutter (such as signs, lamp-posts, or overhead wires) now obscure the buildings. In other cases churches have been altered, 're-ordered', or damaged. I have been obliged to make reasoned assessments of the buildings I have selected for mention and/or

illustrations: omissions will attract criticism from some, while inclusions will bring opprobrium from others or from the same sources. In a short survey, however, it is not possible to include everything, and I have been very restricted by the requirements of my publisher: I have therefore tried to give as wide a range of buildings as possible within the limitations of my brief, for this is neither a gazetteer nor a catalogue.

For access to buildings all over England I record here my appreciation of countless clergymen, caretakers, church-wardens, and others who have given me time and enabled me to see what lies (almost inevitably these days) behind locked doors. I am also grateful to the staffs of the RIBA Library (notably Mr Trevor Todd) and Drawings Collection, of the Royal Archives at Windsor Castle, and of Lambeth Palace Library. The staff of Guildhall Library, City of London (including Mr Ralph Hyde [formerly Keeper of Prints and Maps], Mr John Fisher, and Mr Jeremy Smith), have been most helpful, as have Mrs Jill Palmer, Mr Martyn Everett, and Mr Alan Stevens of Saffron Walden Public Library (where the Town Library and collections of the Literary and Philosophical Society have been goldmines for information). Mr Martin Charles, Miss Iona Cruickshank, Mr Anthony F. Kersting, and Mr Rodney C. Roach helped with the illustrations, while Mr Ian Leith, Miss Lizbeth Gale, Miss Elizabeth Smith, and Mrs Anne Woodward (of the National Monuments Record, English Heritage), and Mr Christopher Denvir (of The Greater London Photograph Library – now the London Metropolitan Archive) rendered most valuable assistance, and have my thanks. Mr Charles's beautiful colour photographs (and some in black and white) embellish this book, and I am most grateful to him for making special journeys in order to provide the images I required. I am also indebted to Mr Eric Cartwright, Mr Warwick Pethers, and Dr Christopher Stell for advice and suggestions, and to Lady Freeman (Director of the Historic Chapels Trust) for invaluable help.

Inevitably, in a work of this nature, some quotations are necessary. Acknowledgement is given to Penguin Books Ltd. for permission to quote the occasional opinion of the late Sir

Nikolaus Pevsner (1902-83) from *The Buildings of England*: the main extracts are from *Cheshire* (1971), 344; *Cumberland and Westmorland* (1967), 75; *London 3: North West* (1991), 166 and 677; *London 2: South* (1983), 209-210; *North-East Norfolk and Norwich* (1962), 243-244; *Oxfordshire* (1974), 606-607; and *Suffolk* (1974), 329. I am grateful to Mrs Bridget Cherry for her good offices in this matter. I also thank John Murray (Publishers) Ltd. for permission to quote from the works of Professor Joseph Mordaunt Crook (*William Burges and the High Victorian Dream* [London: John Murray Ltd., 1981]) and of the late Lord Clark (*The Gothic Revival. An Essay in The History of Taste* [London: John Murray Ltd., 1962]): Mrs Deborah Gill was most helpful regarding these permissions. Dr Geoffrey Green, Managing Director of Messrs T. & T. Clark, kindly allowed me to quote from the late Reverend Dr Andrew Landale Drummond's *The Church Architecture of Protestantism: An Historical and Constructive Study* (Edinburgh: T. & T. Clark, 1934). Some of the material in the Select Glossary has been either quoted or derived from my *Dictionary of Architecture*, published by Oxford University Press in 1999: my thanks are due to Ms Vicki Rodger for arranging the necessary permission. For reasons not unconnected with the saving of space, footnotes have been eschewed: however, the Select Bibliography contains every work necessary in which to follow up the points made in the present book, and every author on whose texts this volume has drawn has been properly acknowledged in this way.

In addition to the persons mentioned above, I am grateful to the late Mr Gordon Barnes, the late Mr Stephen Dykes Bower, the late Mr A.H. Buck, Sir Howard Colvin, the late Mr Edmund Esdaile, the late Mr Basil Handford, the late Dame Penelope Jessel, Mrs Karen Latimer, the late Mr and Mrs Kit Norbury, Mr Anthony Rossi, the late Sir John Summerson, Mr Roger Towe, Professor David Watkin, and Mrs Kay Woollen for very many kindnesses. My elder daughter, Dr Astrid James, good-humouredly accompanied me in attempts (eventually crowned with success) to view the interiors of locked Butterfield churches. My younger daughter, Mrs Paul Teesdale, kindly investigated Christ Church, Streatham, for me. Dr Iain G. Brown, Assistant Keeper, Department of Manuscripts, National Library of Scotland, courteously and efficiently answered queries, for which I warmly thank him. I am indebted to Mr John Richardson, of Historical Publications Ltd., for his practical advice, and for agreeing to take on the project in the first place. Dr Stephen Johnson and other friends at English Heritage made valuable comments and suggestions from which this study has gained benefit. I am grateful to the Governing Body of Peterhouse, University of Cambridge, for granting me a Visiting Fellowship that enabled me to work on the text in the peaceful surroundings of the College. The book was typed, and prepared for submission, by Mrs Margaret Reed, of Woodhall Spa, Lincolnshire, who has my thanks. My wife, Professor Dorota Iwaniec, had to put up with the writing of the work, and, if she found the chaos tiresome, did not make this overt, and so I thank her for this and much else.

Finally, I remember with love and gratitude my parents, to the memory of whom this book is dedicated.

James Stevens Curl

Burley-on-the-Hill, Rutland; Peterhouse, Cambridge; Holywood, Co. Down; Broadfans, Dunmow, Essex; and Saffron Walden, Essex, 1993-2001

CHAPTER I

An Introduction to Denominations and Victorian Churches

Preliminary Remarks; The Established Church; Nonconformity; Roman Catholicism;
The Need for New Churches; The Fabric

'What is a church?' – Our honest sexton tells,
''Tis a tall building, with a tower and bells.'
GEORGE CRABBE (1754-1832): *The Borough* (1810), Letter 2, 'The Church', line 11.

For commonly, wheresoever God buildeth a church,
the devil will build a chapel just by.
THOMAS BECON (1512-67): *Catechism* (1560, Ed. J. AYRE, 1844), p.361.

Preliminary Remarks

It is as well, at the outset, to remind ourselves what is meant by the Victorian Age. It began when Princess Alexandrina Victoria of Kent (born 24 May 1819) succeeded to the Throne on the death of her uncle, King William IV (succeeded 1830), on 20 June 1837: it was to end with the Queen's death at Osborne House, Isle of Wight, on 22 January 1901. Victoria reigned for 63 years, 7 months and 2 days, some 4 years longer than King George III (25 October 1760 – 29 January 1820), and the age in which she was Queen is often perceived as that in which the Industrial Revolution, the railways, urban slums, and much else came into being. Yet the Industrial Revolution had begun some 80 years before Victoria ascended the Throne, and the first railways were operational in the reigns of her uncles, Kings George IV (1820-30) and William IV.

Unquestionably, the most spectacular changes to England during the Victorian period involved its urbanisation. At the beginning of the nineteenth century there were no towns in England and Wales (apart from London) with a population in excess of 100,000. By the time the Victorian Age began in 1837 there were 6 (including London), and in 1891 there were 24. In the half-century between 1841 and 1891 there was a remarkable increase in urbanisation: at the beginning of the period just over 17 per cent of the total population lived in towns of 100,000 inhabitants or more, but by its end the proportion stood at nearly 32 per cent, and the population of London in that time grew from just under 2 to nearly 4.25 million (a rise from just under 12 to just over 14.5 per cent of the total population of England and Wales). Victorian England was the first truly urbanised modern society, and by 1890 London had become a major world-metropolis. By 1901 the Census returns showed that more than three-quarters of the population lived in urban areas. That urbanisation was astonishingly successful: towns became magnets for the rural population, offering new opportunities for personal advancement unthinkable in the countryside, and in the course of Victoria's reign there was a great change from high to low birth- and death-rates in urban areas. Gross National Product dramatically increased; income per head more than doubled in the last half-century of the Queen's reign; and the Victorian legacy was one of unparalleled achievement and unimaginable creation of wealth by the standards of a century before. Even more remarkable was the civilising of the urban masses by means of education, sanitary reform, the provision of housing, and the stabilisation of society. Urban Man became literate and numerate; for the most part was far better housed than was the case in 1801; was less inclined to riot as part of a gin-soaked mob; and paid greater attention to hygiene, in the process becoming, as it were, potty-trained. And the part the Churches played in these undoubted advances must be stressed, for without the heroic efforts of countless clergymen and the laity it is doubtful if anything like stabilisation would have been achieved at all, let alone the extraordinary advances in adult literacy, conditions of housing, and general cleanliness: the great numbers of surviving Victorian churches and chapels are reminders of those heroic efforts, and can be regarded as memorials to the men and women who achieved an amazing transformation of conditions in only a generation or two.

The Established Church

At the beginning of the twenty-first century it is a fact that the majority of the populace of England knows little of what goes on in churches, let alone having any understanding of the denominational animosities that loomed large in Victorian times. Church leaders have admitted that Christianity has almost been eliminated from any relevance in the United Kingdom. In *Dover Beach* (1867), Matthew Arnold (1822-88) referred to the 'Sea of Faith' that

> Was once... at the full, and round earth's
> shore
> Lay like the folds of a bright girdle furled.

However, even then, when Victorian church-building was everywhere apparent, he could only hear

> Its melancholy, long, withdrawing roar,
> Retreating, to the breath
> Of the night-wind, down the vast edges
> drear
> And naked shingles of the world.

That ebbing of faith has not been reversed, and no flowing back of that sea is perceptible. Long ago the 'withdrawing roar' passed out of ear-shot, and the 'naked shingles' stretch as far as the eye can see. As the Sea of Faith has vanished, it is probably necessary to provide an outline of the main Christian religious groups for some

readers, and no apology is offered for doing so.

It should be fairly obvious to any observer that the finest legacy of ecclesiastical buildings left to us in England by the Victorians is that of the Anglican Church. The Anglican Communion of the Reformed Church of England (known until the Disestablishment of the Anglican Church of Ireland in 1869 [32 & 33 Vict., *c*.42] as the United Church of England and Ireland) claimed to be a fellowship within the One Holy, Catholic, and Apostolic Church of those constituted dioceses, provinces, or regional Churches in communion with the See of Canterbury: thus it claimed (and claims) to be part of the Catholic (Universal) Church, the authority of which stemmed from a supposed uninterrupted consecration of bishops from the time of St Augustine, Archbishop of Canterbury and Apostle of the English (died 604). However, the supreme authority of the Pope ceased to be acknowledged when the Monarch was declared to be Supreme Head of the Church of England in 1534 (26 Hen. VIII, *c*.1). So the Anglican Church, or the Church of England (otherwise known as The Established Church, the clergy, upholders, or members of which were and are known as Churchmen), was and is the State Church, headed by the reigning Monarch, and is subject in part to Parliament (a fact that has caused considerable anguish among not a few Churchmen).

Within the Anglican Church was a broad sweep of opinion and practice, from the 'High Church', 'Anglo-Catholic', 'Smells-and-Bells', 'Ritualistic', 'Tractarian', or 'Puseyite' groups (which sought to emphasise the 'Catholic' character of the Anglican Church, exalted the authority of the episcopate and the priesthood, believed in the saving Grace of the Sacraments, and regarded the Church of England as being in full continuity with the pre-Reformation Church *in* England) to the Low Church or Evangelical wing (which was more inclined to the Protestant view that repudiated papal authority).

A Protestant was the name given to those who separated from the Roman Catholic Communion in the sixteenth century in the famous Declaration of Dissent (essentially a protest) from the decision of the Diet of Speier (1529) which re-affirmed the Edict of the Diet of Worms denouncing the Reformation. However, the term 'Protestant' in relation to the Anglican Church has varied: in the seventeenth century it was applied to the Established Church of England, but in the nineteenth century the nomenclature began to fall from favour among those within the Anglican Communion who laid stress on the claims of Anglicans to be equally 'Catholic' with the Roman Church. Curiously, in the seventeenth century, Presbyterians, Quakers, or Separatists (those [also called 'Dissenters'] who withdrew from, or advocated separation from, the Established Church) were differentiated from 'Protestants' (who were seen primarily as Anglicans, and opposed to 'Papists').

The Evangelical party within the Anglican Church emphasised the importance of the Gospels, and was equated more closely with Protestant opinion: that school of Protestants maintained that the essence of the Gospels was the doctrine of Salvation by Faith in the Atoning Death of Christ, and tended to deny that Good Works or the Sacraments had any saving efficacy. Nineteenth-century Evangelicalism, in the words of 'George Eliot' (Mary Ann Evans [1819-80]), in *Middlemarch* (1871-2), 'cast a certain suspicion as of plague-infection over the few amusements which survived in the provinces': in short, it tended towards Sabbatarianism (the Christian view of Sunday as a Sabbath, in which the Fourth Commandment is strictly and joylessly observed), was very restrictive, and emphasised 'The Word' of the Gospels rather than rituals or Sacramentalism.

A Sacrament is the common name for certain visible solemn ceremonies or religious acts (also called 'efficacious signs'): before the Reformation there were Seven Sacraments (Baptism, Confirmation, the Eucharist, Penance, Holy Orders, Matrimony, and Extreme Unction), but Protestants generally only recognised Baptism and Holy Communion (or the Lord's Supper). The pre-Reformation view was that the Sacraments differed from other rites because they were channels by which supernatural Grace (the divine influence which operates in Man to regenerate and sanctify, to inspire virtuous impulses,

and to grant strength to endure temptation or tribulation) is imparted. The Protestant historical view of two Sacraments was based on the two Signs ordained by Christ (Baptism and the Eucharist), but neither was seen as conveying supernatural Grace. The Seven Sacraments, however, remained part of Roman Catholic beliefs.

Somewhere between the High and Low Church wings of the Anglican Church was Broad Church, which favoured a wide or liberal interpretation of dogmatic definitions and subscription to the Creed; and which emphasised the comprehensive, all-embracing, and tolerant nature of the Church in order to admit a variety of opinion on matters relating to belief, practice, and ritual. Unlike the High or Low Church parties, Broad Church devotees were not organised for purposes of proselytisation.

Now it is clear that the Evangelical wing of the Church of England required what was essentially an auditorium, with excellent acoustics and sight-lines so that the preacher of The Word could be seen and heard: chancels were not given emphasis, whilst the altar was a 'Communion-table', used on occasion, but not on a daily basis. Thus Anglican churches built for Low Church or Evangelical services tended to have plenty of seats, small chancels, wide, auditorium-like naves, and if there were transepts these would be for seats, and would not have chapels ranged along the eastern sides. Lady Chapels (for the veneration of Our Lady), of course, would be eschewed. In such churches the Gothic style of architecture was sometimes uneasily applied to the building, for nave-piers had to be slender (for visibility), and often supported galleries, so they were frequently made of cast iron. The architectural results were sometimes startling, rather than scholarly, and the churches were not infrequently somewhat ungainly in composition.

Churches for the Anglo-Catholic, High-Church, or Ritualist parties, on the other hand, were much more impressive, colourful, and often scholarly and imaginative in their interpretation of architecture. Naves, aisles, and chancels were usually separated visibly from each other, and chancels were large, often richly furnished, and fitted out with sedilia, piscinæ, reredoses, screens, and the like. In such churches the emphasis was on a setting for ritualistic ceremony rather than on static congregational worship. Chapels, notably Lady Chapels, were usual, while baptistries, chapels for the Reserved Sacrament (where part of the consecrated Host of the Eucharist is kept), and statues were more common than not. Anglican churches were usually orientated west-east, with the altar at the east end, but in tight urban sites this was not always possible.

Nonconformity

As far as the non-Anglican places of worship were concerned, most were for Nonconformists: indeed, there were far more church-buildings erected for Nonconformists than for Anglicans in the nineteenth century, and the Nonconformist churches were generally known as 'chapels'. It should be remembered that Nonconformists suffered grave disadvantages (as did the Roman Catholics) until Parliamentary enactments of the 1820s. For example, the *Corporation Act* (13 Cha. II, *st.* 2, *c.*1) of 1661 (which required all persons holding municipal offices to acknowledge the Royal Supremacy and to abjure resistance to the Monarch, whilst making ineligible for office all persons who had not within a year partaken of Communion as administered by the Anglican Church), the *Act of Uniformity* (14 Cha. II, *c.*4 of 1662), and the *Test Act* (25 Cha. II, *c.*2) of 1673 (which required office-holders to take Communion according to the usage of the Church of England) applied to Roman Catholics as well as to Protestant Dissenters. In 1828, however, these restrictive Acts were repealed ('Nonconformist Emancipation' – 9 Geo. IV, *c.*17), and Nonconformists (in the widest sense) could vote and hold office. Further restrictions on Roman Catholics were lifted (*Roman Catholic Relief Act*, otherwise 'Catholic Emancipation') in the following year (10 Geo. IV, *c.*7). Nevertheless, a certain social stigma attached to Nonconformists and Roman Catholics (whose places of worship were also referred to as 'chapels' to distinguish them from Anglican churches) until almost the end of Victoria's reign, although Roman Catholics

succeeded in achieving a fashionable status in certain instances and areas, especially when several distinguished Anglican clerics, eminent aristocratic families, or wealthy individuals converted to Rome.

Nonconformity and Independence carried their own penalties, and it was a feature of nineteenth-century Dissent that differences of opinion led to secessions: many branches, sects, and minorities often broke away from the main groups to found their own congregations. This led to the erection of many more buildings, usually quite small structures, but sometimes with pretensions to grandeur in order to cock a snook at the parent body.

Now all these groups of Nonconformist (in the sense, originally, of one who refused to conform to the discipline and ceremonies of the Church of England, and, later, of those who refused to conform or to subscribe to the *Act of Uniformity*) Protestant Dissenters had to raise funds to build their places of worship without State aid. The erection of chapels was therefore much more of local concern than was the case in the Anglican Church: Nonconformists and their ministers would form a committee that oversaw the planning and erection of the building, money being raised by donations, collections, borrowing, and, in some cases, the renting of pews (which led critics to declare that Dissent was mercantile in spirit, and preached the Gospel only to those who could pay for the privilege, the lower strata of society being left to rot in vice, ignorance, and Godless squalor). In the middle of the nineteenth century, however, some Nonconformist national bodies were set up to organise finance and to establish guide-lines for the design and management of chapels. Sometimes, chapels were private speculations by ambitious preachers or their supporters, but, more often, they were erected by groups of the like-minded of a particular denomination (or seceders from a denomination). Many chapels foundered through lack of support, internal wrangles, or other problems, and some preachers misjudged the responses their performances would bring. Certain Millenarians, for example, got the date of the Second Coming wrong, and it failed to occur: it would appear that support for those who miscalculated dwindled at once. As Dean Arthur Penrhyn Stanley (1815-81) put it in his *Christian Institutions* (1881), the 'whole history of early Millenarianism implies the same incapacity for distinguishing between poetry and prose'. Such dottiness in putting all on certainties which proved to be nothing of the sort undoubtedly occurred, but most Nonconformist preachers were more prudent, and avoided any sudden self-inflicted extinction of their following.

In terms of basic architectural requirements, the several denominations of Nonconformists did not differ greatly from each other. The congregation had to be seated as economically as was possible, and, because finance had to be raised entirely from private sources, this had to be achieved within a much tighter budget than that normally found in the Anglican Church. As preaching was the central element in Nonconformist observance, it was essential the minister should be seen and heard by the whole congregation, which, because of the static nature of the services, had to be seated in relative comfort (a similar demand for comfortable seating developed in Anglican churches of the Broad and Evangelical type, and reflected a desire to demonstrate improving social position and clout). The provision of galleries enabled a congregation to be housed within a smaller ground-area, and these galleries were usually placed on three sides of the building, supported on slender cast-iron columns, while the fourth side (opposite the entrance-doors) was occupied by a large arrangement including the pulpit, a platform or a rostrum, and (if prosperity permitted) the organ. Orientation was unimportant in Nonconformist architecture, so there was no requirement for the pulpit-end to be at the east: this had the advantage that Nonconformist chapels could be slotted into street-frontages, and any architectural show confined to the main façade. In a great many early Nonconformist chapels, the street-fronts (usually on the short side of a rectangular box) often betrayed the two-storey arrangement behind, and the fenestration had glazing-bars set within square- or semi-circular-headed openings. Simple pitched roofs terminated in pediments, and façades were of brick, stone, or stucco-faced: pediments frequently had a circular window placed in the tympanum, and a plaque with the date and the name of the denomination might be sited in the tympanum or somewhere else on the façade. In the case of the Wesleyan Methodists and the Presbyterians (see below), there was a certain emphasis on the 'Communion-table', but even it would be set below the pulpit and the architectural ensemble incorporating organ, platform, and, sometimes, choir. In this design, The Word was given visible precedence, and the Communion-rite was reduced in importance to a memorial or an allegory, rather than a symbol. However, this Nonconformist arrangement was really only a derivation of eighteenth-century Low Church Anglican church-interiors, before the Anglican Tractarian and Ritualist reforms obliterated so many of them (a few survive). Indeed, many features of early nineteenth-century chapels were essentially a continuation of the Classical Georgian tradition.

Roman Catholicism

Curiously, as has been mentioned above, the Roman Catholics (referred to in the past as, variously, 'Romanists', 'Romans', 'Catholics', or 'Papists', and meaning those recognising the spiritual supremacy of the Bishop of Rome as Pope, who are members of the Roman Catholic Church) were also lumped with Nonconformists in the last century. After all, English Roman Catholics were known as *recusants* (those who refused to attend Church of England services when it was legally compulsory to do so) and were regarded therefore as types of Dissenters. Early nineteenth-century Roman Catholic churches, as noted above, were known as 'chapels', and tended to be poor and unpretentious in architectural terms (not least so as not to draw attention to their existence), but, after 'Catholic Emancipation', and, especially after the restoration of the Hierarchy in England (see below), an undoubted triumphalism could be detected, and many Roman Catholic churches of the Victorian period are impressive buildings. There was an obvious desire on the part of the Roman Catholics to re-establish a central position in national life that had been lost in the sixteenth century, and, in order to demonstrate this, the physical presence of Roman Catholic churches in towns and cities was desirable. However, in many cases the numbers of the faithful were too small to justify the building of a great church, except in the north-western parts of England (where many members of the landed gentry were recusants and so set an example to their tenants and employees) and London, and, in any case, funds were all too often lacking (except when immensely rich Roman Catholics such as John, 16th Earl of Shrewsbury [1791-1852], stepped in to finance the erection of churches). In areas such as London's Kensington, private money and clerical ambitions helped to raise some fine structures, but in provincial towns many Roman Catholic churches are distressingly bare and unfinished-looking, reflecting the general shortage of cash and the social and economic standing of the bulk of the congregations. When there was plentiful money (either through private donations from pious Roman Catholics or through major fundraising for purposes of prestige and show), however, the results were often outstanding, as at Brompton Oratory, London, St Giles's, Cheadle, Stafford-shire, or Westminster Cathedral, London. High Anglican and Roman Catholic churches had many things in common, but generally speaking there was a refinement in the fittings in Anglican churches that was often missing in many Roman Catholic church interiors (as Pugin noted, again reflecting both social standing and sophistication of Taste). Roman Catholic churches erected from the 1850s onwards tended to draw heavily on Continental (especially French) models, and often sported canted apsidal chancels: they usu-ally had one or more chapels (one of which was, almost inevitably, the Lady Chapel), decked out with lavish finery. Unlike the majority of An-glican churches, however, Roman Catholic churches were not often orientated west-east with the altar at the east: this seems to have been because, from the time of the Counter Reforma-tion, such orientation ceased to be regarded as important, but, in addition, new churches were so often fitted within awkward urban sites that the west-east arrangement had to be abandoned.

In any case the range of chapels radiating from an apse in so many Continental churches left the majority of such chapels without the traditional orientation, and often Renaissance and Baroque churches in Europe (especially those based on the sixteenth-century church of *Il Gesù* in Rome) had altars in side-chapels set against liturgical north and south walls. So the traditional arrangement of placing altars in the east, even in chapels, had long been abandoned by the Roman Catholic Church.

The Need for New Churches

The French Revolution and the excesses of the Terror had caused revulsion in late-Georgian England. Rabid anti-clericalism that had been such a feature of events in France during the 1790s and early 1800s was perceived as extremely dangerous, and the authorities in England began to take note of the fact that new Anglican churches were few, notably in areas where there were large and growing populations. It was calculated that the population exceeded the seating available in Anglican churches by about two-and-a-half mil-lion. Godlessness (especially Godlessness involv-ing a rejection of Anglicanism) and Revolution were seen as connected, and fear of revolution-ary excess made the provision of new churches imperative to the Establishment. After all, Non-conformity had been instrumental in the over-throw and death of King Charles I, had been intimately concerned in the American Revolution, and, more recently, was closely involved in the dangerous rebellion in Ireland in 1798. Something had to be done, and Established religion was perceived as one of the means by which results could be achieved.

In the first part of the nineteenth century, then, religion (and especially the Anglican variety of religion) was seen as providing the framework by which the lower orders might be civilised. Anglican Churchmen also saw the building of churches as a bulwark against the growth of Non-conformity or Dissent. Contrary to popular belief, church-going was not universal in the Victorian period. The Anglican Church had ex-perienced moves away from it; there was a growth of indifference to religion; the Nonconformist sects attracted an enormous following (especially in Northern and Midland towns); and there was a new and growing challenge from the Roman Catholic Church: the Established Church was also hampered because in the rapidly-growing urban areas its traditional diocesan and parish organisations were ill-equipped to cope with new conditions, and, in any case, could only minister to, and seat, a tiny proportion of the population. In rural districts the influence of the Established Church was still strong in a social hierarchy where people 'knew their place', but in the urban milieu those hierarchies tended to break down, and the notion of 'social place' was diluted. In the 1851 Census it was demonstrated that the mass of the labouring population never attended church or chapel: in Birmingham in that year it would appear that something like 75 per cent of the population regularly 'abstained' from public worship, and the Churches began to talk openly of missionary activities at home rather than in India or Africa. The call to public worship in areas like London's East End or the teeming streets of Lambeth was largely ignored, while there were considerable numbers of working-men who were openly hostile towards religion. The scent of moral danger lay heavy on the smoky urban air.

The Fabric
As has been mentioned above, the Victorians and their predecessors were mightily concerned for the future of religion in urban areas, and much capital was to go into church-building. Town-dwellers in the early twenty-first century owe much to the enormous investment made in the fabric of nineteenth-century towns, especially those projects concerned with public utilities and those designed to ameliorate conditions. Capital was raised largely by voluntary and municipal efforts, and a very considerable amount of that capital was invested in buildings for religious purposes. In 1860 something like 7,500 new buildings were erected in London alone, peaking in 1880 at nearly 16,000: in the prosperous area of London's Kensington 200 buildings were put up in 1860, peaking in 1868 at nearly 1,000 in that year. Some 43 churches and chapels were erected

in the newly-expanded suburb of Kensington in some 20 years. Now this is phenomenal, and such patterns were not unusual throughout the country: this extraordinary activity in church-building on the part of Anglicans, Nonconformists, and Roman Catholics deserves our closest attention.

Much of the urban fabric of Victorian England is Sublime, in the sense of that eighteenth-century æsthetic category associated with vastness, ruggedness, power, terror, and the ability to stimulate the imagination and the emotions. An exaggerated scale, powerful, massive, unadorned fabric, and gloomy, cavernous repetitive structures would be classed as Sublime. Victorian buildings could astonish, and their huge size could overawe, impress, and subdue. In short, there appears to have been a relationship between religious rhetoric and Sublime architecture: this is amply demonstrated by the vast urban citadels of faith built by Tractarian Ritualists of the Church of England; in the larger, grandiose, Classical and Gothic chapels for Nonconformists in the northern towns; and in the huge, dim, cavernous Byzantinesque gloomths of the mighty Roman Catholic Cathedral in Westminster. Rhetoric was firmly embedded in High Victorian culture (as should be clear from any readings of the outpourings of religious harangues, published sermons, and tracts that appeared during that period), and was realised in an architecture for posterity as a *permanent* reminder, a monumental warning, and a symbolic presence. That permanence has been abandoned in the early twenty-first century; religious observance has again declined; and churchgoing is on the wane. A church is no longer regarded as essential to the success of a speculative housing development (as it was in Victorian England), or as a beacon of hope, bringing consolation, education, morality, and faith to the urban masses: indeed, many religious buildings have been abandoned by the very organisations that created them.

Anyone familiar with the towns and cities of England must be aware of the very great numbers of churches and chapels that are scattered through the urban fabric. Apart from the mediæval churches and the great cathedrals, there will be some impressive eighteenth-century churches and chapels, but throughout those urban areas developed during the Victorian period are many ecclesiastical buildings, often presenting a varied stylistic kaleidoscope of nineteenth-century Taste in both architectural and denominational terms. There are tall towers, often with spires, attached to large, bulky structures (frequently and impressively faced with stone), still dominating residential areas; huge brick churches like massive citadels rising up above the rooftops of London's Victorian suburbs; Gothic churches that look as though they had strayed from the countryside and become marooned in the morass of decaying houses or waste ground; plain chapels (often simple Classical preaching-boxes adorned with the date within the pediment); buildings drawing on round-arched forms, Byzantine, Romanesque, and Lombardic precedents; and strange stylistic hybrids that almost defy description. Many ecclesiastical buildings in urban areas today are in a poor state of repair, fall into the category of 'redundant plant' (a ghastly term used by philistine clergymen about churches that usually means

they will be vandalised or demolished), or have been adapted for uses that are wholly incompatible with their architecture or with the purpose for which they were built. To stand in the abandoned nave of a great Victorian polychrome Gothic church, where the dust and dirt lie thickly and soddenly on the floors and surfaces, the wind blows through the vandalised stained-glass windows, the rain drips through the damaged roof from which the lead has been stripped, and the once-lovely and finely-crafted fittings are smashed and overturned, can be a profoundly disturbing experience, for such places were built to resist the ravages of time: they were the products of faith, they were there to bring that faith to the people, and they were profoundly wonderful buildings for the very large part. And if their rhetoric resounded, and even resounds today, they are none the worse for that.

All in all, then, there was a considerable variety of religious buildings erected in the Victorian Age for large numbers of religious groups. This brief survey will describe the main themes and types, and will illustrate some outstanding examples.

CHAPTER II

The Religious Atmosphere in the 1830s and 1840s

Evangelicals and High Churchmen; Church Building; The Threat to the Established Order;
The Beginnings of Tractarianism; Attacks on Tractarianism, and the Newman Crisis;
Ecclesiology; The Anglican Response after 1833

[On Sunday July 14, 1833] Mr Keble preached the Assize Sermon in the University Pulpit. It was published
under the title of 'National Apostasy'. I have ever considered and kept the day as the start of the religious
movement of 1833.
JOHN HENRY NEWMAN (1801-90): *Apologia Pro Vita Sua* (1864). *See* the edition edited by
MARTIN J. SVAGLIC, subtitled *Being a History of his Religious Opinions by John Henry Cardinal*
Newman (Oxford: Clarendon Press, 1967), 43.

What is called the Oxford or Tractarian movement began… in a vigorous effort for the immediate defence of
the Church against serious dangers, arising from the threatening temper of the days of the Reform Bill.
RICHARD WILLIAM CHURCH (1815-90): *The Oxford Movement: Twelve Years, 1833-1845,* **i** (London:
Macmillan & Co., 1891), quoted also in *O.E.D.* (1933) in the entry on *Oxford*.

Evangelicals and High Churchmen

Threats to national security and the established order led to several momentous changes. Great Britain and Ireland were united by *Acts* of Parliament (39 & 40 Geo. III, *c.* 67 and 40 Geo. III, *c.* 38), which came into effect on 1 January 1801. As part of those *Acts* (passed by both the British and Irish Parliaments), the Churches of England and Ireland were also united, and Churchmen perceived this as an opportunity to strengthen Anglicanism and renew the spirituality of the nation. There was an upsurge of Anglican activity (especially in the sphere of church-building): the promotion of Anglicanism, and the creation of a visible Anglican presence in towns and cities, were primary concerns of constitutional loyalists.

In the first decades of the nineteenth century Evangelicals in London within the Established Church, prompted by the teachings of John Wesley (1703-91), became influential: they, like the Wesleyans, believed in teaching by example, in supporting temperance, in encouraging moderation, in doing good works, and in observing the 'Sabbath' (Sunday, in Evangelical Sabbatarian terms), in order to invigorate the nation's spiritual life, stability, and moral well-being.

Parallel with the increase of Evangelical clout was the rise of the so-called 'High and Dry' party of Sacramentarians: they perceived the Anglican Church as a visible organisation with a powerful rôle to play in raising the tone of society as a whole.

Sydney Smith (1771-1845) identified these two groups (consisting mostly of laymen, merchants, and intellectuals) as the 'Clapham Sect' (Evangelical) and the 'Hackney Phalanx' (High Church), named after the (then well-heeled) London suburbs in which the parish-churches had been rebuilt (in 1774-6 and 1793-7 respectively), thereby providing impetuses for renewed vigour in the life of those parishes.

At Clapham, John Venn (1759-1813), who was Rector from 1792 until his death, was at the centre of an important and influential group of Evangelical philanthropists which reached into the Establishment, politics, the Church, and the City of London, and was bound by faith, by philanthropic and missionary zeal, by its campaigns against drunkenness and vice, and by its desire to bring the Bible, decency, and morality into every home. It would be no exaggeration to claim that the Clapham Sect exerted an influence on national life far greater than its numbers might indicate: it was a prime mover in the abolition of the Slave Trade (William Wilberforce [1759-1833] was a member of the 'Sect'); it was in the vanguard of attempts to provide exemplary housing and adequate schooling for the working classes; it was of singular importance in bringing literacy, hygiene, and sobriety to the populations of the growing towns and cities; it was in the forefront of encouraging family life and decent living; and it was a powerful force in bringing Christianity to far-flung places in the world. It was the single most significant factor in creating what was to become the conscience of the Victorian Age.

The Hackney Phalanx, under the leadership of Joshua Watson (1771-1855 — brother of the Rector, John James Watson [1767-1839]) and Henry Handley Norris (1771-1850 — perpetual curate and later Rector of St John of Jerusalem, the parish-church of South Hackney [Clapton]), became the most important promoter of religious and philanthropic projects of the High Church party, and the rival and counterpoise of the Evangelical Clapham Sect. Most significantly, the Phalanx, through its influence with the Prime Minister (1812-27), Robert Banks Jenkinson (1770-1828), 2nd Earl of Liverpool (from 1808), secured the passing of the *Act for Promoting the Building of Additional Churches in Populous Parishes* (58 Geo. III, *c*. 45) in 1818.

Church Building

As early as 1803 *An Act to Promote the Building, Repairing, or Otherwise Providing of Churches and Chapels* (43 Geo. III, *c*.108) had been passed, amended in 1811 (51 Geo. III, *c*. 115), but 1818 was the key year for the future building of Anglican churches, with what became known as the first of the Church Building *Acts* (the second [59 Geo. III, *c*. 134], was passed in 1819). The Phalanx supported the formation of the Church Building Society (1817 — incorporated in 1828), the Church Building Commission (1818), and, ultimately, the Ecclesiastical Commission (1836) which provided the administrative structure within which the Anglican Church functioned during the Victorian period.

The Church Building *Act* of 1818 allowed for State finance to be made available for the erection of churches: the buildings put up as a result were known as Waterloo churches or Commissioners' churches, because they were built under the ægis of The Commissioners for Building New Churches appointed under the *Act* in the years following the Battle of Waterloo in 1815. 214 such churches were erected, and most were large and capacious to hold static congregations: some were Classical (especially the then fashionable Greek Revival) in style, but others (over 170) were 'Pointed', many being thin travesties of Gothic (with some honourable exceptions) consisting of rectangular preaching-boxes that could just as easily have been Classical late-Georgian auditory churches, but that paid lip-service to Gothic by acquiring pointed windows and insubstantial, unconvincing buttresses. The Commissioners, by the 1820s, however, were starting to recommend the adoption of the Gothic style, for Classical churches required handsome stone porticoes, and porticoes cost money. Subsequently, in 1824, *An Act to Make Further Provision and to Amend and Render More Effectual Three Acts Passed in the Fifty-Eighth and Fifty-Ninth Years of His Late Majesty and in the Third Year of His Present Majesty for Building and Promoting the Building of Additional Churches in Populous Parishes* (5 Geo. IV, *c*.103), was passed, consolidating earlier enactments.

The Phalanx, therefore, was of enormous importance in securing the means by which church-building could be promoted, but it was also a catalyst in the formation of the National Society for Educating the Poor, supported the Societies for the Propagation of the Gospel and for Promoting Christian Knowledge, and took a deep interest in the Church in the Colonies.

In the closing years of the Hanoverian period it should be remembered that religious and secular administrations within the Anglican Church were closely related. However, very often (especially in booming, expanding London), when more accommodation for worshippers was required, this took the form of proprietary chapels, erected by owners of land and/or developers (sometimes clergymen were active in creating such chapels) in areas where new houses were built in parts of existing parishes. Intended to increase the desirability of a residential district (and therefore ensure that rents could be kept at a satisfactory level), such chapels were supported by pew-rents, and their effectiveness depended on the charisma of the incumbent. Nevertheless, the very existence of proprietary chapels (often drab and basic preaching-boxes) could often inhibit the erection of new parish-churches because of the vested interests of the proprietors and the preachers.

The Tory post-Waterloo legislation of 1818 and 1819 (alluded to above) eased matters by providing public funds for new Anglican churches, long overdue in places (such as London) where there had been an expansion of the urban fabric. These enactments were passed against a background of fear: social unrest was endemic, and it was hoped that a programme of church-building would help to bring stability; Dissent was increasing, and was seen as disloyal and schismatic; the upheavals and new ideas of Revolutionary France had removed the old order in Europe and had been immensely destructive in terms of ecclesiastical fabric and organisation, all of which worried many people in England; and all the time the towns and cities inexorably grew as a result of migration from the land.

However, very soon, even before Queen Victoria came to the Throne in 1837, the position of constitutional loyalists, the links between Anglicanism and the State, and, indeed, the basis of the Union were to be systematically undermined.

The Threat to the Established Order

Secularism (the belief that the State, morals, and education should be independent of religion), Utilitarianism (the ethical theory evolved by Jeremy Bentham [1748-1832] that finds the basis of moral distinctions in the usefulness of actions, and the notion that only actions which bring happiness to the greatest number of people have moral worth), Nonconformity (explained above), and religious expediency were fast advancing in the 1820s, when yet more threats to the pre-eminence of Anglicanism became very real.

First of all (as noted above) came 'Nonconformist Emancipation' when the *Test* and *Corporation Acts* were abolished in 1828 under 9 Geo. IV, *c.* 17, and most restrictions on Dissenters were removed. Then, in 1829, came 'Catholic Emancipation' under 10 Geo. IV, *c.* 17, which enabled Roman Catholics to enter Parliament, belong to any Corporation, and hold high civil and military offices: it removed many of the more onerous aspects of the seventeenth- and eighteenth-century enactments against Roman Catholics. Not for the first or last time was Ireland to play a significant rôle in English affairs, in this instance as a direct result of the Union of the two Parliaments, for the voters of County Clare had obstinately insisted on electing Daniel O'Connell (1775-1847)—a Roman Catholic — as their Member of Parliament at Westminster. This forced Parliament's hand, and so 'Catholic Emancipation' became a reality.

Many were appalled at the time and later by these events. John Ruskin (1819-1900) declared in his *Seven Lamps of Architecture* (1849) that the 1829 *Act* was a national crime for which the Deity would inflict a special vengeance. However, 'Catholic Emancipation' led to a demand for new Roman Catholic churches, and in 1850 Pope Pius IX (*Pio Nono* [1846-78]), in a brief widely regarded as 'Papal Aggression', re-established the Roman Catholic Hierarchy in England and Wales. Set against widespread controversy over Ritualism in the Anglican Church, secessions to Rome, and the influx of destitute Irish fleeing from the Great Hunger occasioned by potato blight during the 1840s, this caused uproar, and Parliament in 1851 passed the *Ecclesiastical Titles Act* (14 & 15 Vict., *c.* 60) that prohibited the assumption of territorial titles by Roman Catholic archbishops, bishops, and deans. However, curiously, this *Act* was a dead letter, was never enforced, was wholly ineffective, and was repealed in 1871 (34 & 35 Vict., *c.* 53).

Now the events alluded to above give some idea of the apprehension with which the Roman Catholic Church was viewed at that time, when anti-Papist demonstrations were not uncommon. In these days of (largely) religious indifference among the English, the passions of the nineteenth century seem strangely remote. However, it was not simply a case of religious bigotry or sectarian animosities being activated that lay at the root of such reactions: the huge changes of the 1820s and 1830s were of a constitutional nature, as subsequent events have incontrovertibly shown.

During the last years of the reign of King George IV, over two hundred new Anglican district churches were built under the ægis of the relevant *Acts*, and were run by the vicars, vestries, and churchwardens of parishes. These churches functioned for religious reasons, and did not have the obvious commercial stigma of the proprietary chapels (which they largely superseded and made redundant). Furthermore, they had some free seats as well as rented pews, so answered some severe criticisms described below. Nevertheless, a profound and growing sense of unease prevailed in Church circles, for reasons that can only be outlined here.

Although State-supported works of church-building and extension were carried out on an impressive scale, the relationship between Anglicanism and that State was showing severe signs of becoming unravelled. Apart from the 'emancipation' of Nonconformists and Roman Catholics, Dissenters, Radicals, Utilitarians, and certain Whigs were vociferous in their demands for an end to payments to the Established Church (including Church rates and burial-fees), having succeeded, in any case, in virtually abolishing the secular powers of parish organisations. Then came the huge upheavals of Whig 'Reform' and events followed rapidly in what was to be, in fact, partial Disestablishment of the Anglican Church.

Unrest in Ireland over, among other things, the collection of tithes, led to the passing of an *Act* by the Whig Government led by Charles, 2nd Earl Grey (1764-1845), to facilitate the recovery of tithes in Ireland and for the relief of the clergy of the Established Church (2 & 3 Will. IV, *c.* 41). Prompted partly by the fear that revolution (which had toppled the monarchy of Charles X in France in 1830) would break out in the British Isles, the Government passed the momentous *Representation of the People Act* of 1832 (2 & 3 Will. IV, *c.* 45 and *c.* 88), which increased the number of parliamentary seats as well as the numbers

of parliamentary seats as well as the numbers allowed to vote: it also gave political power to groups which cared nothing for the delicate balance between Church and State that hitherto had prevailed.

This legislation was followed in the same year by the *Irish Tithe Composition Act* (2 & 3 Will. IV, *c.* 119) which began the process of commutation. In 1833 the *Church Temporalities (Ireland) Act* (3 & 4 Will. IV, *c.* 37) was passed by the Whig Government: it reduced two of the four archbishoprics (Tuam and Cashel) to bishoprics; united ten of the twenty existing bishoprics to adjacent sees; revoked the rights of churchwardens to levy church cess (an exaction) for the upkeep of ecclesiastical buildings; and permitted tenants on episcopal lands to purchase their holdings at a fixed annual rent. Purchase-sums and reserved rents, along with income from the suppressed sees, the tax on ecclesiastical livings, levies on the wealthier dioceses (Armagh and Derry), and the income and functions of the Board of First Fruits (the body set up in the eighteenth century to fund the building and repair of churches and glebes) were vested in Ecclesiastical Commissioners, who were empowered to use them for the building, upkeep, repair, and improvement of churches and other buildings. Although from an administrative/utilitarian point of view the *Act* provided a more efficient allocation of resources, it fatally weakened the Church of Ireland's position as a self-governing institution, and led to a *de facto* Disestablishment in 1869 under the *Irish Church Act* (32 & 33 Vict., *c.* 42), passed by the Liberal Government led by William Ewart Gladstone (1809-98), whose ambition was to 'pacify Ireland'. Another Liberal administration, under Herbert Henry Asquith (1852-1928), in which David Lloyd George (1863-1945) was a prime mover, disestablished the Anglican Church in Wales in 1914 (4 & 5 Geo. V., *c.*91), but this did not take effect until after the 1914-18 war.

Shortly after the *Church Temporalities (Ireland) Act* was passed, under the *Irish Tithe Arrears Act* (3 & 4 Will. IV, *c.* 100), a million pounds were advanced for the relief of tithe-owners on the security of arrears. Then the sinister *Poor Law Amendment Act* of 1834 (4 & 5 Will. IV, *c.* 76) was passed, a particularly inhumane piece of utilitarian legislation which effectively criminalised the poor by making the corpses of those who died penniless in workhouses available for dissection (the only legal supply of dead bodies had for a long time been those of persons executed for crimes). This offensive and cruel *Act* cut across all traditional Tory concerns, such as *noblesse oblige*, by which some poor were cared for by a high-minded Anglican landed aristocracy. Then, in 1835, came the *Municipal Corporations Act* (5 & 6 Will. IV, *c.* 76), which virtually removed all remaining secular authority held by the Established Church. Destruction of that authority and the erosion of Anglicanism in Ireland (culminating in the momentous *Acts* of 1833 and 1869) for what seemed to be reasons of appeasement and political expediency were powerful stimuli to the Oxford Movement (see below) and to the huge upsurge of spiritual, theological, and architectural revival.

The cumulative effects of these enactments were to alarm and enrage Churchmen, something that is usually interpreted as a reaction to loss of power, influence, and prestige. The main problem for the Churchmen, however, was none of those, but a perception that a collection of politicians had no right to interfere in or legislate for a body that was Catholic and bound by divine laws and orders. The Anglican Church, for so long as one with the State, was being sundered from that State, and its destinies were being increasingly controlled by a Parliament in which Radicalism, Whiggery, Expediency, and Nonconformity were overwhelming Anglican Tory constitutional loyalism.

Thereafter, the systematic erosion of the powers and status of the Anglican Church was to continue, and secular/political control over the Church drove many Churchmen to convert to Roman Catholicism or Nonconformity: some gave up on the Christian Churches and became non-attenders or agnostic. Those who seceded to Rome found the authority of the Papacy and the certainty of dogmas more congenial than seeing the State Church being humbled and dictated to by Whiggish politicians.

Although pacification of Ireland clearly was behind the two important Acts that spelled Disestablishment, peace did not break out: appeasement of Roman Catholics and (significantly for the running of Parliament) attempts to placate anti-Union members such as O'Connell, simply did not work. As many predicted, Disestablishment sent out clear messages, and the *Government of Ireland Act* of 1914 (4 & 5 Geo. V, *c.* 90 — the 'Home Rule Act') signalled the beginning of the end of the Union, so that at the close of the 1914-18 war the United Kingdom lost proportionally more of its land area than did defeated Germany.

The Beginnings of Tractarianism

The enactments of the 1830s, therefore, cannot be over-estimated in their long-term effects. It appeared that the towel was being thrown in as far as the Anglican Church was concerned, and that the process of dismantling it had been begun by the Whigs. Some Churchmen were outraged, and John Keble (1792-1866) was prompted to preach his celebrated sermon on 'National Apostasy' from the University pulpit, galvanised by the passing of the *Church Temporalities (Ireland) Act*. Like other dons at Oxford, Keble had been profoundly affected by 'Catholic Emancipation' and by the Reform Bill, and his famous sermon stimulated leading Oxford Churchmen to begin a systematic campaign to revive High Church principles and patristic theology: John Henry Newman (1801-90), in his *Apologia Pro Vita Sua* (1864), was emphatic in his assertion that Keble was the 'true and primary author' of the impressive and great revival of Anglicanism that began in Oxford, and so is known as the Oxford Movement. Newman also wrote that the Church needed, not Party men, but 'sensible, temperate, sober, well-judging persons, to guide it... between the Scylla and Charybdis of Aye and No'.

So Keble's well-aimed attack on Erastianism and Whiggery is generally regarded as the starting-point for the Oxford or Tractarian Movement: the 'Tractarians' (as they became known) argued that the Anglican Church possessed the 'privileges, sacraments, and a ministry, ordained by Christ', was part of the visible Holy Catholic Church, and had an unbroken connection with the early Christian Church through Apostolic Succession (the uninterrupted transmission of spiritual authority through a succession of bishops from the Apostles downwards). Furthermore, Anglicanism inculcated reverent views of the Sacraments, and several Oxford Movement Churchmen emphasised points of agreement in matters of doctrine with the Roman Catholic Church.

However, although Keble's sermon undoubtedly was an important catalyst in the revival of Anglicanism, and although it is commonly believed that nineteenth-century Anglican liturgical studies began with the founding of the Cambridge Camden Society in 1839, the work of John Mason Neale (1816-66), and the growth of Ecclesiology, the foundations had been laid earlier. The key figure was Charles Lloyd (1784-1829), who had noticed the similarities between the *Book of Common Prayer* and the Roman *Missal* and *Breviary*. When Lloyd became Regius Professor of Divinity at Oxford in 1822 he disseminated his views that the *Prayer Book* was essentially derived from early Christian and mediæval devotions (still at that time embodied in their Latin forms in the Roman service-books), and, at a time when many Anglicans were beginning to perceive the Church of England in historical terms of continuity with the pre-Reformation Church, Lloyd's teachings were significant. He taught his pupils (who included John Rouse Bloxam [1807-91], Richard Hurrell Froude [1803-36], Frederick Oakeley [1802-80], and Edward Bouverie Pusey [1800-82], all of whom [partly through his help] were to become powers in the Oxford Movement and in their professional lives), to be able to distinguish what aspects of Anglican texts and practices were early, mediæval, or reformed. Lloyd (who was consecrated Bishop of Oxford in 1827) gave his students a concept of historical connections, creating a powerful link with, and sympathy for, the pre-Reformation Church *in* England. Lloyd left copious notes and annotated works: these were collected, edited, and published, with new research, as *Origines Liturgicæ*; or *Antiquities of the English Ritual and a Dissertation on Primitive*

Liturgies in 1832 (the year *before* Keble's sermon), by William Palmer (1803-85). The book came out in a revised improved version in 1845, and there can be no doubting its importance in Anglican circles, any more than the impact of Lloyd's teachings on what was to become the Oxford Movement can be doubted, although this fact has received only limited recognition.

Also in 1832 was founded *The British Magazine and Monthly Register of Religious and Ecclesiastical Information* by Hugh James Rose (1795-1838) to propagate his High Church views on the restoration of ancient Anglican doctrines and practices. Rose, described as 'the Cambridge originator of the Oxford Movement', established connections with Newman, Palmer, Froude, Keble, and Arthur Philip Perceval (1799-1853) at Oxford in order to solicit contributions to his magazine. In July 1833 Froude, Palmer, and Perceval visited Rose at his rectory in Hadleigh, Suffolk, to discuss the worrying ecclesiastico-political situation. Soon afterwards Froude and Palmer founded the Association of Friends of the Church. The 'Hadleigh Conference' is regarded as an important landmark in the history of Tractarianism.

The first of a series of *Tracts for the Times* appeared in 1833, published until 1841. Authors included R. H. Froude, Keble, J. H. Newman, and E. B. Pusey, and the *Tracts* were issued with the intention (among others) of reviving doctrines and historical connections that had become clouded or submerged. Pusey, Regius Professor of Hebrew at Oxford from 1828, gave the Oxford Movement cohesion, respectability, and fame — so much so that the Tractarians and adherents of the Oxford Movement became known as 'Puseyites'. Under Pusey's influence the *Tracts* became solid doctrinal treatises, and his own contributions recalled the attention of Churchmen to the almost forgotten sacrificial aspect of the Eucharist as well as to the significance of the Sacrament of Baptism.

It should be remembered that Tractarianism aimed to secure for the Church of England a definite base of doctrine and discipline in the event of the very real threat of Disestablishment, or the equally real possibility that High

Churchmen would secede from the Anglican Established Church. Newman supplemented his contributions to the *Tracts* by giving regular sermons on Sunday afternoons in St Mary's, the University church in Oxford, and by 1839 his influence in Oxford was supreme. As Editor of *The British Critic* he greatly advanced the Oxford Movement.

Attacks on Tractarianism, and the Newman Crisis

The Oxford Movement came under severe fire after the publication of the *Literary Remains of Hurrell Froude* in 1838, for that work criticised many aspects of the Reformation, and encouraged some in their suspicions that Tractarians were crypto-Papists or worse. Then a real crisis developed. In 1841 Newman's *Tract XC*, dealing, *inter alia*, with the compatibility of the Thirty-Nine Articles (the revised articles of religion set down for the Reformed Church of England in 1563 and ratified by Parliament in 1571) with Roman Catholicism, was published, and the storm broke. Not only was publication of the *Tracts* ended, but Newman's arguments were dissected with devastating effect by Dr Nicholas Patrick Stephen Wiseman (1802-65), later Cardinal Archbishop of Westminster, but then Bishop of Melipotamus *in partibus Infidelium* (because Roman Catholic territorial titles had not then been assumed) and President of Oscott College: Wiseman also contributed several papers on the illogicality of the Tractarians' position in the *Dublin Review,* collected and published in 1841 as *High Church Claims.* Wiseman's writings also led Newman to perceive Anglicans as uncomfortably like semi-Arians (homoiousians, or those who held the Father and Son, in the Godhead, to be of like, but not the same, essence or substance). Newman was also attacked by Evangelicals, most effectively by Archibald Campbell Tait (1811-82), then a tutor at Balliol (who later became Archbishop of Canterbury), and others. Tait argued that the limits of honest interpretation had been transgressed, and that the reputation of the teaching body of the University of Oxford would be impaired unless protests were made.

Tractarians had faced earlier difficulties in 1838 when a Low Church group of Evangelicals devised a project to erect a Martyrs' Memorial to commemorate the three Anglican divines who had been burned at the stake in the reign of Queen Mary I (1553-58): these 'Protestant Martyrs' were Thomas Cranmer (1489-1556), Archbishop of Canterbury, Hugh Latimer (*c.*1485-1555), Bishop of Worcester, and Nicholas Ridley (*c.*1500-55), Bishop of London (the spot where the stake stood is marked in Broad Street, Oxford, to this day). An examination of the history of the Martyrs and of their theological, moral, and ecclesiastical positions left some uneasy. Based on one of the 'Eleanor Crosses', however, the Martyrs' Memorial was erected in 1841-3 to designs by George Gilbert Scott: approval was not universal.

When Michael Solomon Alexander (1799-1845), a Jew from the Grand Duchy of Posen and convert to Anglicanism, was appointed Bishop of the United Church of England and Ireland in Jerusalem in 1841 partly at the instigation of King Frederick William IV of Prussia (reigned 1840-61), this, to Newman, showed the Anglican Church 'courting an intercommunion with Protestant Prussia' (for Lutheran Orders were not recognised as valid) and with the 'heresy of the orientals, while it forbade any sympathy or concurrence with' the Church of Rome. Alexander entered Jerusalem with vast pomp in 1842, having travelled from Portsmouth in the perhaps unfortunately named steamship *Devastation.*

By the end of 1841, Newman's allegiance to the Anglican Church was on its deathbed, and in 1842, his confidence in himself broken, he withdrew from Oxford and passed 'three years of painful anxiety and suspense' before being received into the Roman Catholic Church in 1845. Benjamin Disraeli (1804-81) said of Newman's secession that it was a blow under which the Church of England still reeled years after the event, and Gladstone opined that it was not 'estimated at anything like the full amount of its calamitous importance'. Newman was ordained priest in Rome, and founded the Birmingham and London Oratories in 1847 and 1850 respectively. He was created Cardinal in 1879.

The Tractarians' attempts to revive an almost

lost belief in the historical continuity and liturgy of the Anglican Church had sustained a series of very damaging attacks and events, and the Oxford Movement attracted much opprobrium. The High Church party had been gravely embarrassed, but aspects of the Movement's ethos survived both in the emerging Anglo-Catholic party in particular and in the Church of England in general. Clergy began to take their responsibilities more seriously, and the dignity of their calling was given greater emphasis: High Church clergy carried out rubrical directions, and introduced changes into the forms of Divine Service that excited Protestant opposition and the condemnation of several bishops. It should be remembered that in the 1830s, all forms of Ritualism were suspect, chancels were often abandoned or (in post-Reformation churches) virtually non-existent, whilst vestments and even the Cross were unthinkable: clergymen wore severe black gowns, and congregations were of the static, non-participating kind (except for the saying of certain prayers, responses, and the Creed; participation in the psalms; and the singing of hymns).

However, it is important to understand that the Oxford Movement had begun with several express aims, one of which was to uphold the National Established Church against the claims of Rome, and another was to defend it against growing secularism and political interference. The case of Newman, though sensational in that the Anglican Church lost one of its greatest hopes, was by no means unique: many followed his example and seceded to Rome. The Revd. Anthony Symondson, S.J., has gone as far as to claim that the 'principles of the [Oxford] Movement could have no other logical termination than submission to the Holy See'.

Nevertheless, Tractarian ideals did not collapse, for in reality liturgical and aesthetic debate became more vociferous, and the Ritualistic controversies of the 1860s and 1870s were largely a result of the passion of the Tractarians to transform the setting, appearance, and liturgical essence of Anglican worship. Newman's secession did not destroy the High Church movement: on the contrary, it concentrated minds

and led to the evolution of a distinct strand within it. This was the remarkable flowering of Ritualism, with all that it implied in the way of architecture and artefacts, giving rise to Anglo-Catholic Anglicanism that drew on mediæval English liturgical traditions influenced by such works as Purchas's *Directorium Anglicanum*. By the end of the century, despite attempts to curb Ritualism by means such as the *Public Worship Regulation Act* of 1874 (37 & 38 Vict., *c*. 85), 'Smells and Bells', and with them a beautiful ritual carried out in appropriate settings, were established in many churches in England (and especially in London).

Ecclesiology

1833 was significant for the future of Anglicanism in many ways, not least because in that year the supreme jurisdiction in ecclesiastical matters within the Church of England was transferred to the Judicial Committee of the Privy Council, and alarm-bells rang ever more loudly in Church circles. After 1833, immensely influential architectural societies were established at the two ancient universities of Oxford and Cambridge. These were the Oxford Society for Promoting the Study of Gothic Architecture (later renamed The Oxford Architectural Society) and the Cambridge Society for the Study of Church Architecture (which was changed almost immediately to The Cambridge Camden Society [named after the antiquary and historian, William Camden (1551-1623)]). The Camden Society promoted the study of ecclesiastical architecture and of mutilated architectural remains by means of visits to churches, making collections of brass-rubbings, and publishing articles, criticisms, and illustrations. From its beginnings in *c*. 1836 (it was formally constituted in 1839) the Camden Society was far more than an antiquarian society: it was a pressure-group and a proselytising body which set out to encourage a study of mediæval art and architecture in order to promote the restoration of decayed churches and the building of new churches that would be scholarly, structurally excellent, and would provide suitable settings for a revived liturgy. Its ideals were set out in pamphlets such as *Hints for the Practical Study of Ecclesiastical Antiquities* (1839), *A Few Words to*

Church Builders (1841), and *Church Enlargement and Church Arrangement* (1842), but in 1841 appeared the first issue of the Society's journal, *The Ecclesiologist*, one of the most important architectural journals of the Victorian period that remained influential long after it ceased publication in 1868.

Ecclesiology is essentially the study of church forms and traditions, and of church-building and decorations: the Society provided a framework and a stimulus for the study of the arts, architecture, and liturgy of the Christian Church. Very quickly, the Cambridge Camden Society became identified with Tractarianism, and got itself into hot water as a result: by 1843 many off-shoots of the Oxford and Cambridge architectural societies began to dissociate themselves from the Cambridge society, and in 1844 Dr Francis Close (1797-1882), an Evangelical divine, and incumbent at Cheltenham, Gloucestershire, lambasted the two societies, stating that Romanism was taught analytically at Oxford and artistically at Cambridge, that *The Ecclesiologist* was identical in doctrine with *Tracts for the Times*, and that restoration of churches not only tended to, but actually was, Popery. The point was that the supporters of the two societies (who had become known as 'Ecclesiologists') not only studied and published architectural details and furnishings of mediæval churches, but explained what they meant to a Protestant population that knew nothing, or very little, of such things. However, Protestant opinion was suspicious of studies and explanations, fearing that such knowledge might have dire consequences. The Camden Society refuted these suggestions, but the accusation that *the 'Restoration of Churches'* was the *Restoration of Popery* (1844) came at the time of Newman's secession to Rome, and the damage was done. Those influential persons associated with the Society at once distanced themselves, and in 1845 it was moved that the Society should close. In fact it changed its name to The Ecclesiological Society, continued to publish *The Ecclesiologist*, but ceased to be associated with Cambridge and became a national Society based in London. It now closely equated morality with architecture, and exhorted architects, masons, carpenters, bricklayers, and all persons involved in church-building and restoration to live holy and serious lives. It became a powerful organ for architectural criticism, and could make or break reputations. Things had come to a dangerous pass.

The Anglican Response after 1833

Many Churchmen, in the early 1830s, prophesied the end of Anglicanism, but, apart from activities in Oxford and Cambridge associated with leading High-Church personalities and with Tractarianism, Evangelicalism was by no means played out. Abolitionists of slavery, led by Wilberforce, the Clapham Sect, the Church Missionary Society, and the Religious Tract Society were all active in promoting Evangelical activities, and were conspicuously successful in their efforts. In addition, the important figure of Charles Simeon (1759-1836), incumbent of Holy Trinity, Cambridge, Fellow of King's College, one of the founders (1797) of the Church Missionary Society, and friend of John Venn, brought the influence of the Clapham Sect to the University and town. Simeon's 'tenacious grasp of distinctive principles made him known beyond Cambridge, and he became an acknowledged leader' among Evangelical Churchmen. Indeed, in later life (the 1830s) he 'became an object of something like veneration, and exerted at Cambridge an influence still recognised more than a century after his death', as the *Dictionary of National Biography* put it.

Thus Evangelical and Ecclesiological influences were strong in Cambridge, and Simeon had a larger following at Cambridge than Newman had at Oxford, where Tractarian High Churchmen were dominant. However, despite the reactions occasioned by hostile legislation, many recognised that the Church of England was set to become one denomination among others, some of which had made considerable strides, and appeared as aggressive and threatening to the Established Church.

One of the key figures in the Anglican response to secularisation was Charles James Blomfield (1786-1857), Bishop of London from 1828, who was quick to recognise that if the Church were to have any chance of surviving, it would require a major reorganisation. Given the concessions made to Dissenters and Roman Catholics, and realising that it was impossible for Anglicanism as an institution to go on as it had done (as he confided in 1832 to William Howley [1766-1848], Archbishop of Canterbury [from 1828] — who had opposed Catholic Emancipation, the Reform Bill, and the Irish Church Bill), Blomfield craftily gained the ear of Sir Robert Peel (1788-1850), who helped him to achieve several objectives by lobbying and other means. Having prepared the political ground, as it were, Blomfield introduced proposals in the House of Lords in 1836 'for the creation of a fund to be applied to the building and endowment of additional churches in the metropolis', and was the moving spirit behind the establishment of the Ecclesiastical Commission (also 1836). Especially concerned with 'the better distribution of ecclesiastical revenues and duties, the prevention or diminution of pluralities and non-residence, and the augmentation of poor benefices and endowment of new ones', he was also energetic and successful in remedying the disgracefully inadequate provision of churches, schools, and clergymen for the rapidly increasing population of London. Soon money was to flood into the Bishop's 'Metropolitan Churches Extension Fund', and several local associations for church extensions were set up, benefiting districts such as Bethnal Green, Islington, St Pancras, Paddington, and Westminster. The Fund was subsumed into the London Diocesan Church Building Society in 1854.

The Bishop thus introduced a new concept, for the idea of building parish-churches (as opposed to proprietary chapels) with private money was new in the diocese. Very soon private landlords were giving land for church-building purposes in developing residential areas, and, in addition, often contributed towards building costs. In the long term, especially in London, private zeal over-provided churches (especially during the 1860s and 1870s), not a few of which are fine works of architecture, but which were surplus to requirements almost as soon as they were erected, which might indicate that Anglican church-building in English cities was backed more by hope, zeal, and the desire to create a visible Church presence than by reasoned analysis.

There was another difficulty. In spite of its energetic activities and undoubted influence on national life, the Evangelical Movement within the Church of England was in a weak position in that it lacked coherent arguments in upholding historical ecclesiastical principles, and, like many of the Nonconformist groups, tended to be over-dependent on charismatic preachers rather than on tradition, on the legitimacy of Apostolic Succession, and on ritual (all things the High Church Tractarians valued), for in the Evangelical tradition the major emphasis was on the Bible and on direct experience.

With the growth of urbanisation, as has been made clear above, the Church of England experienced a decline in its congregations, a disturbing phenomenon of indifference to religion, the mushrooming of Dissenting groups, and the decay of its influence in national and political life. Nevertheless, Anglicanism also experienced a revival within itself, Evangelical in nature, that partly stemmed from outside criticism, and partly grew as an attempt to counteract the charismatic preaching of Nonconformist pastors. The Established Church attempted to demonstrate it was capable of servicing the new England, so the parish, the parson's freehold, private patronage, and the training of ministers all had to come under scrutiny, and, ultimately, had to change. After all, the parochial system was predominantly rural (and had served the countryside well), but it was difficult to translate it to new urban conditions. In short, the Anglican Church was not well-prepared to deal with the changing structure of the nation, so it responded by developing systems of urban parishes in order to retrieve the situation. The parochial system, expanded and adapted for contemporary conditions, was seen by Churchmen as a means of rescuing society from its parlous state, but parochial systems needed churches, clergy-houses, and other buildings, and these cost money. Furthermore, the system of pew-rents might work in well-heeled places like Kensington, but would not be popular in poorer manufacturing districts, so many new churches were obliged to provide free pews, which placed an added burden on over-stretched finances. Obviously, new churches should have as many sittings as possible, but this aim clashed with the established institution of the family pew. In the eighteenth century the high-backed, well-cushioned, and carpeted pew (also called the 'box-pew') was a feature of many churches, and ensured a modicum of comfort for the 'owner' who paid a 'rent' for the privilege of having his or her own pew. But such pews took up a lot of space, and disadvantaged those who could not afford their own pews. At the beginning of the nineteenth century the idea of sitting on plain benches where ever a seat could be found, with no concepts of proprietorship, would have been unthinkable. As Eastlake (1872) put it:

> 'to sit on uncovered wooden benches as congregations do now in half the modern churches of London — to make, in short, no distinction between the rich and poor assembled in common worship — would have been considered something altogether incompatible with the requirements of a genteel congregation. In this dilemma it was obvious that the only expedient by which a certain number of sittings could be obtained without doubling the size and cost of the church was the erection of galleries, and these were freely adopted, without the slightest reference either to ancient precedent or to architectural effect'.

Provincial church-building societies were unable to keep pace, year by year, with increasing populations, and the percentage of persons that could be accommodated in Anglican churches in urban areas was very small. Evangelical Churchmen set up trusts in a number of cases to ensure a succession of devoted and like-minded ministers, thus replacing the patronage of a living with committees. Historically, the right of bestowing Church benefices lay with a variety of groups and individuals, including Oxbridge colleges and private patrons (often aristocrats or at least landed gentry), so the change was a remarkable innovation. The Evangelicals were deeply serious, provided more services, emphasised preaching, insisted that rectors (clergymen

of parishes where the tithes [a rent-charge in commutation of the tenth part of the produce of land and stock allocated for Church purposes] were not impropriate [placed in the hands of laymen]) should live permanently in their rectories, encouraged the development of religious societies, and conscientiously carried out their official duties with zeal and devotion. The demands of long sermons, static congregations, and finance ensured that churches should be large, should have good acoustics to enable The Word to be heard, should have comfortable seating so as not to distract the congregation from The Word, and should have good visibility so that the minister could be seen from all parts of the church. There were also the questions of maintaining standards of comfort in seating for those who were used to it, and of providing adequate heating during inclement weather.

One of the great problems was that incumbents of parishes were grossly over-worked, for everything in parochial life centred on them, including the running of schools, the chairing of meetings, the directing of visiting, the conducting of services, and (even more time-consuming and exhausting) the raising of funds. Unfortunately, the incumbent was left with virtually no time in which to study, or to have much of a social life, with the result that he very frequently had little or no knowledge or appreciation of contemporary life. Evangelicals (much given, on the whole, to abstinence from alcoholic drink) had been keen to condemn worldliness and the study of secular matters, with the result that they relied on denunciation rather than on intelligent analysis of important current issues, and were regarded by many thereby as 'unclubbable'. Critics complained of the commonplace abuse heaped upon scepticism, other branches of Christianity, and non-Christians, and noted that the clergy might be more effective if they could dispute points and win them in fair debate. But the Evangelicals were ill-equipped to do this, for their intellectual bases were no match for the arguments of their enemies (secular and non-secular). Scolding was of little avail against scepticism, and after Charles Robert Darwin's (1809-82) *Origin of Species* appeared in 1859 the scolding became a shriller rant.

CHAPTER III

The Roman Catholic Revival

Pugin's Contrasts *and its Impact; Other Publications by Pugin; Pugin's Buildings;
Other Roman Catholic Churches*

The two great rules for design are these: 1st, that there should be no features about a building which are not necessary for convenience, construction, or propriety; 2nd, that all ornament should consist of enrichment of the essential construction of the building. *The neglect of these two rules is the cause of all the bad architecture of the present time.*
AUGUSTUS WELBY NORTHMORE PUGIN (1812-52): *The True Principles of Pointed or Christian Architecture* (London: Henry G. Bohn, 1853), 1.

Pugin laid the two foundation stones of that strange system which dominates nineteenth-century art criticism and is immortalised in the Seven Lamps of Architecture: *the value of a building depends on the moral worth of its creator; and a building has a moral value independent of, and more important than, its esthetic value.*
KENNETH MACKENZIE CLARK (1908-1983): *The Gothic Revival. An Essay in the History of Taste* (London: John Murray, 1962),149.

Pugin's *Contrasts* and its Impact

Augustus Welby Northmore Pugin (1812-52) converted to Roman Catholicism in *c.* 1834, and in 1836 he published his *Contrasts; or, A Parallel between the Noble Edifices of the Fourteenth and Fifteenth Centuries, and Similar Buildings of the Present Day; Shewing the Present Decay of Taste: Accompanied by Appropriate Text.* A second edition, *Contrasts: or, A Parallel between the Noble Edifices of the Middle Ages, and Corresponding Buildings of the Present Day; Shewing the Present Decay of Taste: Accompanied by appropriate Text*, was published in London by Charles Dolman (1807-63) in 1841. *Contrasts* was a devastating polemic in which Pugin claimed that 'Pointed Architecture' (i.e. Gothic) was produced 'by the Catholic faith', and that it was destroyed in England by the ascendancy of Protestantism. Classical architecture was described as 'Pagan', and was, with Protestantism, regarded as a 'monster'. King Henry VIII (1509-47) was stated to have 'exceeded Nero' in tyranny and cruelty, the Reformation was 'a dreadful scourge', Protestant Reformers were 'Church plunderers and crafty political intriguers', and 'Catholic excellence' was contrasted with 'modern degeneracy'. Mediæval 'Catholic' architecture had a 'wonderful superiority' over the buildings of the Renaissance and Classical Revivals, for in it, and in it alone, 'the faith of Christianity was embodied, and its practices illustrated'. The 'great test' of architectural beauty was 'the fitness of the design to the purpose for which' it was intended, and the 'style of a building should so correspond with its use that the spectator' could at once 'perceive the purpose' for which the building was erected. Buildings of the nineteenth century were weighed in the balance against those of the fourteenth century and found wanting; a 'Catholic town' of 1440 was painfully compared with the same town in 1840 (where everywhere the churches were ruinous or had been destroyed); glorious mediæval altars were contrasted with mean modern ones; St George's Chapel, Windsor, in the Middle Ages, was contrasted with the irredeemably Protestant Chapel Royal at Brighton (with its pulpit as the centre of attraction instead of the altar); a mediæval canopied tomb was compared with a modern work for James Harris, 1st Earl of Malmesbury (1746-1820), by Sir Francis Legatt Chantrey (1781-1841) of 1820; Chichester market-cross was shown with King's Cross police station by Stephen Geary (1797-1854); and the monument to a mediæval bishop was favourably contrasted with that to the 'Right Reverend Father in God, John Clutterbuck, D.D.,' and his two wives (the whole ensemble shown insensitively plonked against real mediæval work defaced with *graffiti*). Even more startling, the drawings lampooned the architecture of William Wilkins (1778-1839), Sir Robert Smirke (1780-1867), Sir John Soane (1753-1837), George Dance Junior (1741-1825), John Nash (1752-1835), William (*c.*1771-1843) and Henry William (1794-1843) Inwood, Charles Cole (*c.*1738-1803), and Henry Rose (d. *c.*1853) — the last for his feeble work (1839-40) at the church of St Saviour and St Mary Overie (today Southwark Cathedral). Now many of these names were, or had been, professionals who had reached the top, and who occupied (or had occupied) positions of distinction: for a young man in his twenties to ridicule them was an astonishing (and brave) thing to do. Pugin, in *Contrasts*, stressed that art is intimately connected with the state of the society that produces it, painted the Middle Ages as offering the only exemplars for the good life, and argued that only when the piety and communal spirit of the mediæval period had been re-established could a true and noble Christian architecture re-arise. Pugin weighted his case with considerations of ethics and morals, and his favoured style in *Contrasts* was that of the fourteenth century (and English fourteenth-century Second Pointed at that). Pugin laid several important foundations for later architectural criticism in *Contrasts*: a value of a building depends on the *moral* worth of its designer; a building has a *moral value* that is more important than any *æsthetic* value; and a building must *express the purpose* for which it was designed. Sir George Gilbert Scott, one of the most prolific and successful of Victorian architects, claimed to have been stimulated and inspired by Pugin's writings, and was from the moment he read them a new man: he became obsessed with the revival of Gothic architecture.

Of course Gothic had enjoyed a certain fashionable notoriety in the eighteenth century, but it began to be more than fashionable when it was given the Royal *Imprimatur* at Carlton House (1807) and Windsor Castle (from 1824). After the Palace of Westminster was destroyed by fire in 1834, the terms of the architectural competition stipulated that the designs for the new Parliament buildings should be either Elizabethan or Gothic in style, reflecting a growing taste for what was seen to be an indigenous 'English' architecture. That competition was won by Charles Barry (1795-1860) in 1836, and the building was commenced in 1840: Pugin was employed to design much of the detail, and so one of London's most important buildings was clothed in Gothic (although the underlying discipline of the design is Classical).

As far as an appreciation of Gothic as a serious style was concerned, the foundations had already been laid by Thomas Rickman (1776-1841), whose *An Attempt to discriminate the Styles of English Architecture from the Conquest to the Reformation* was the first systematic treatise on English Gothic architecture of any worth, and it appeared in numerous editions after its publication in 1817. More information about Gothic architecture and detail was provided in the works of Matthew Holbeche Bloxam (1805-88), whose *The Principles of Gothic Architecture* first appeared in 1829, and came out in several editions after that.

Then John Keble in his *Lectures on Poetry* (1832-41) described Gothic architecture as the most beautiful of all architectural styles, and by far the most in harmony with the mysteries of religion (*Lecture 3*). But Keble, the Tractarians, and the Oxford Movement were outside the Roman Catholic Church, and wanted to defend Anglicanism by recovering its historical links with the pre-Reformation Church, the Caroline High Churchmen, and Sacramentalism. Pugin saw *his* Roman Catholicism in terms of revival of the highest expression of art found in the creations of the Middle Ages, and so desired continuity between the Roman Catholic Church of his day and the English Church of the fourteenth and fifteenth centuries. Thus Pugin's vision was of mediæval English Catholicism, not modern Ultramontanism (the principles and practice of absolute papal supremacy outside Italy, north of the Alps), with its love of Baroque splendour.

Pugin's architecture and design of artefacts were based on study, and such scholarship also involved a knowledge and revival of liturgical practice. While Anglicans were rediscovering the meaning of the Sacraments, Pugin sought to provide settings and artefacts to beautify Catholic worship. Pugin gave Ecclesiology, intimately associated with his love of ritual, symbols, and detail, an important rôle, and one that was hugely significant outside the Roman Catholic Church.

Other Publications by Pugin

Contrasts was an intemperate but powerful polemic, according to which the superiority of 'Catholic' architecture of the fourteenth century was clear. Everything good or noble in architecture was only possible through the beneficent influence of the Roman Catholic Church; destruction and vandalism, irreverence, and loss of sensitive perception were the direct result of the Renaissance and the Reformation; and the degraded state of architecture and artefacts was due to the absence of 'Catholic' feeling among architectural practitioners and the loss of an informed and civilised ecclesiastical patronage. *Contrasts* was followed by *The True Principles of Pointed or Christian Architecture set forth in Two Lectures delivered at St Marie's, Oscott* (1841), *The Present State of Ecclesiastical Architecture in England* (1843), and *An Apology for the Revival of Christian Architecture in England* (1843). In all of these the message was loud and clear: Classical architecture was pagan, earthbound, and no more sophisticated than Stonehenge in the essence of its structural system; whilst Gothic was not a style, but a principle, a moral crusade, and the only mode of building possible for a Christian nation.

In pure architecture, Pugin wrote in *True Principles*, the smallest detail should have a meaning or serve a purpose, and even the construction itself should vary with the material employed, for designs should be adapted to the materials with which they were executed.

Furthermore, the external and internal *appearance* of an edifice should be illustrative of, and in accordance with, the *purpose* for which it is intended. Pugin was vitriolic about cement dressed up to look like ashlar or carved ornament, and he saw Gothic as offering a mode of building where ornament and function would have meaning: it also provided, he felt, a way out of the architectural eclecticism of his day. Private judgement, he wrote in *An Apology*, was running riot, and every architect had a theory of his own, a disguise with which to invest the building he erected. One architect might breathe nothing but the Alhambra and another the Parthenon, while a third would be 'full of lotus cups and pyramids from the banks of the Nile', and a fourth, from Rome, might be 'all dome and basilica'. Yet another might loot the works of Stuart and Revett (*The Antiquities of Athens*, published from 1762) for Greek details applied to lodges, centenary chapels, reading-rooms, and fish-markets, 'with some Doric work and white brick facings'. Styles, he claimed, were *adopted* instead of arrived at by a series of logical steps, whilst ornament and design were *adapted to* edifices rather than *generated by* the structures themselves. He denounced what he called a 'carnival' of architecture, the professors of which appeared to be 'tricked out in the guises of all the centuries and all nations': Turks, Christians, Egyptians, Greeks, Swiss, and Hindoos marched side by side, and mingled together. Worse, some architects, 'not satisfied with perpetrating one character', appeared in 'two or three costumes in the same evening'. Pugin warned against the study of the prints of buildings, and the widespread custom of imitating parts of them: in other words there was a tendency to loot the source-books of Gothic and apply the pieces to a design. Scott, in his *A Plea for the Faithful Restoration of our Ancient Churches* (1850) referred to capricious 'restorers' who were glad to lose an ancient detail as an excuse to introduce a 'favourite morsel' of Gothic from Bloxam or the celebrated *Glossary* by John Henry Parker (1806-84) of 1836 (with many subsequent editions). Pugin seemed to suggest that architectural books of this type in the hands of practitioners were potentially as dangerous as the Bible in the hands of Evangelical Protestants.

To Pugin a revival of mediæval architecture would herald a regeneration of Roman Catholicism. Furthermore, Gothic was more suited to the times than was Classicism: Classical buildings put the elevations first, but in Gothic architecture the elevations were dependent upon, and subservient to, the plan. In addition, Classical architecture was based on pagan exemplars and was imported, whereas Gothic was grown on native soil and was only associated with pre-Reformation Christianity. In *An Apology* he wrote that if the Anglican Church required bell-towers, spires, naves, chancels, screens, fonts, altars, sacred symbols, and ornaments, it was reasonable to ask if the models for these various features were to be found in the Classical temples of Antiquity or in the 'ancient pointed churches of England'. He further argued that the revival of mediæval architecture was based on sound and consistent principles, and was appropriate for religion, government, climate, and the needs of society because that architecture was a 'perfect expression of all we should hold sacred, honourable, and national, and connected with the holiest and dearest associations', from the Monarchy downwards. He stated that England was ideally placed to 'revive ancient excellence and solemnity', for it had 'immense power, vast wealth, and great though often misdirected zeal'. England, while the last to abandon *Christian* architecture, was foremost in 'hailing and aiding its revival', using 'perfect models for imitation', and, in any case, its institutions were essentially those of the Middle Ages. Although he recognised that England was no longer the same England as it had been in the fifteenth century, Pugin and some of the great Roman Catholic families longed to bring the nation back to the ideals of that period, at least in terms of the Universal Religion, and were more sympathetic to English mediæval precedents than to Roman ones.

One of Pugin's key aims was to establish a continuity between the Roman Catholic Church in nineteenth-century England and the great legacy of fourteenth- and fifteenth-century buildings and artefacts that had survived. To him great art and Catholicism were intimately connected, and he sought a revival of *English* Gothic art and architecture, partly to emphasise that continuity. Such a programme required a revival of liturgical scholarship, the father of which (in the Roman Catholic Church) was Daniel Rock (1799-1871), recusant priest and chaplain to the Earl of Shrewsbury, whose *Hierurgia: or the Holy Sacrifice of the Mass* came out in 1833, and contained much that revealed the customs of the early Church and how these had continued. Rock followed this work with his *The Church of our Fathers* (1849-53), which dealt with religious ritual and belief before and after the Norman invasion of 1066, and is a very full account of religious observance of the mediæval period. Rock's descriptions of mediæval ceremonial in churches (which Pugin was keen to revive, with appropriate settings) influenced some Roman Catholics, and fine standards of liturgical practice with beautiful surroundings (as at St Chad's Cathedral, Birmingham) were achieved, as a result, in some places. However, the longing for a revival of English liturgy, English Gothic, and English ceremonial was not shared by all Roman Catholics by any means (as the numbers of Classical church-interiors testify), for there were Ultramontane and non-English (notably Irish) strands of opinion within Roman Catholic society for which Englishness held no attractions. As it happened, the 'majestic chasuble', 'apparelled albs', and 'flowing surplices' began to make appearances in Victorian Anglican circles, and it is beyond dispute that Pugin's influence on High Anglicanism was immense.

Pugin's Buildings

Pugin's work for Barry's Palace of Westminster was in the Third Pointed, or Perpendicular, style which, by the 1840s, began to be regarded as too late, too near the beginnings of the hated Renaissance, and too much associated with the Reformation and the despised Tudor period. Given Pugin's association of the moral tone of society with architecture, Perpendicular would not do. In *True Principles* he opined that 'the moment the *flat* or *four-centred arch* was introduced, the spirit of Christian architecture was on the wane. *Height* or the *vertical principle*, emblematic of the resurrection, is the very essence of Christian architecture'. Scott, in his *Plea for the Faithful Restoration of our Ancient Churches*, took his cue from Pugin, stating that the Perpendicular style should be rejected, for few could 'fail to perceive in it' a want of 'that warmth of religious feeling which is to be found in the works of earlier periods' (a dubious conclusion, as all students of Perpendicular will agree). To Scott, however, the Perpendicular style contained unmistakable signs of corruption and decay. Morality, religion, and architecture were now thoroughly joined in unholy wedlock.

Nevertheless, Pugin's early church buildings, such as St Mary's (or Marie's), Derby (1837-39), **(Plate 1)** and St Alban's, Macclesfield (1838-41), **(Plate 2)**, are both in the Perpendicular style, with western towers (that of St Alban's was never completed), large traceried windows and small chancels, so are not unlike some of the better Commissioners' churches for the Anglicans. St Wilfrid's, Hulme, Manchester, of 1839-42, is First Pointed, or Early English, in style, that is with lancets, which was cheaper than providing large traceried windows. Nevertheless, one would expect pinnacles and other enrichments in First Pointed work, but at St Wilfrid's there are only massiveness and simplicity. He also used First Pointed at Mount St Bernard Abbey in Leicester-

1. *Roman Catholic church of St Mary, Bridge Gate, Derby (1837-39), by Pugin, showing his early use of the English Perpendicular style. It was Pugin's first large parish-church, and one of many financed by Lord Shrewsbury. The 'western' tower, in fact, is situated to the south, indicating that orientation was of little importance in Victorian Roman Catholic churches. St Mary's (sometimes referred to as St Marie's) was similar in design to St Alban's, Macclesfield (Plate 2). (EH. BB67/64 [1966]).*

2. *Interior of the church of St Alban, Chester Road, Macclesfield, Cheshire (1838-41), by A.W.N. Pugin, partly financed by the Earl of Shrewsbury. It is entirely in the English Perpendicular Gothic style, and has extraordinarily slender piers. Both St Mary's, Derby, and St Alban's were designed before Pugin turned to the Second Pointed (Decorated Gothic) style as his exemplar (CC. BB66/4304 [1996).*

shire, founded in 1835 for a community of Cistercian monks by Ambrose Lisle March Phillipps (later de Lisle) (1809-78), a Cambridge man who had been converted to Roman Catholicism in the 1820s, and who admired Continental Roman Catholic art and architecture. Phillipps was introduced into his novel *Coningsby* (1844) by Benjamin Disraeli, thinly disguised as 'Eustace Lyle'. Phillipps was convinced that only monasticism would Christianise places like Manchester, and he worked tirelessly for the reunion of the Roman Catholic and Anglican Churches. For the latter cause he had more support from Tractarians than from the Roman Catholic authorities, and indeed Phillipps believed Anglican Orders were valid and Anglican theology (because pre-Tridentine) was more authentically 'Catholic' than that prevailing in his own Church, a poisonous view to Ultramontanes. Another influential Cambridge convert of the period was Phillipps's friend, Kenelm Henry Digby (1800-80), who came to Roman Catholicism through a study of mediæval antiquities and the scholastic system of theology. Phillipps received help from his friend John, 16th Earl of Shrewsbury, who was to become an important patron of Pugin.

Mount St Bernard was the first abbey to be erected in England since the Middle Ages, and its severe First Pointed style was suited both to the Cistercian Order and to the intractable Charnwood rock with which it is largely constructed (though there are freestone dressings). Pugin's Roman Catholic Cathedral of St Barnabas in Nottingham of 1841-4 was also First Pointed, and the building was financed to a great extent by the Earl of Shrewsbury. At St Chad's Cathedral, Birmingham, of 1839-41 (the first Roman Catholic cathedral to be erected in England since the mediæval period [Plate 3]), Pugin chose brick as his material, and the twin western towers with spires look back to the *Backsteingotik* of fourteenth-century North Germany (especially the Baltic towns): the tracery and many other details were firmly of the fourteenth-century type, and so were Decorated or Second Pointed. This style was favoured by Pugin as it seemed to fall between First Pointed (which was imperfect,

experimental, and not fully developed) and Perpendicular or Third Pointed (which was held to be decadent, was associated with an alleged decline in religious zeal, was the style associated with the first Tudors, and was dangerously near the Reformation and the Break with Rome). Second Pointed Gothic styles were more fully developed, highly sophisticated, and associated in Pugin's mind with the period in England when Roman Catholic observance was at its strongest. There is, however, much evidence which suggests this view is erroneous, and that observance was at its most impressive in the period immediately before the Henrician and Edwardine iconoclasm of the sixteenth century.

George Gilbert Scott, in his *A Plea for the Faithful Restoration of our Ancient Churches*, saw the 'whole range of pointed architecture, whether in its earlier or later forms, in its humbler or more glorious examples, as the one vast treasury of Christian art, wonderfully produced, and as wonderfully preserved for our use', as a chain, every link of which was necessary. He opined (drawing on Pugin) that if a choice must be one fitted for European adoption, then the Geometrical or early Middle Pointed style would be the ideal. First Pointed was not suitable for revival, for it was never 'fully developed' and was 'confessedly imperfect in many essential features', whilst Perpendicular lacked 'religious feeling' and was 'corrupt' and 'decayed'. Scott felt that the 'Lancet' or 'Early English' style was the only variety of First Pointed which could claim perfection, but it excluded mullioned and traceried windows, and therefore did not quite come up to scratch. When 'window-heads were filled with never-ending combinations of flowing tracery — when the rigid stone had been rendered plastic, and taught to bend and entwine itself with all the endless ramifications of vegetable life' — a perfection of elegance had been attained, for not only were windows filled with exquisite tracery, but the tabernacles, pinnacles, screen-work, and every part of the building were decorated with an elegance and richness which nothing could surpass. Yet Scott asked if this style fully satisfied, and suggested that as the Geometrical variety of Middle Pointed

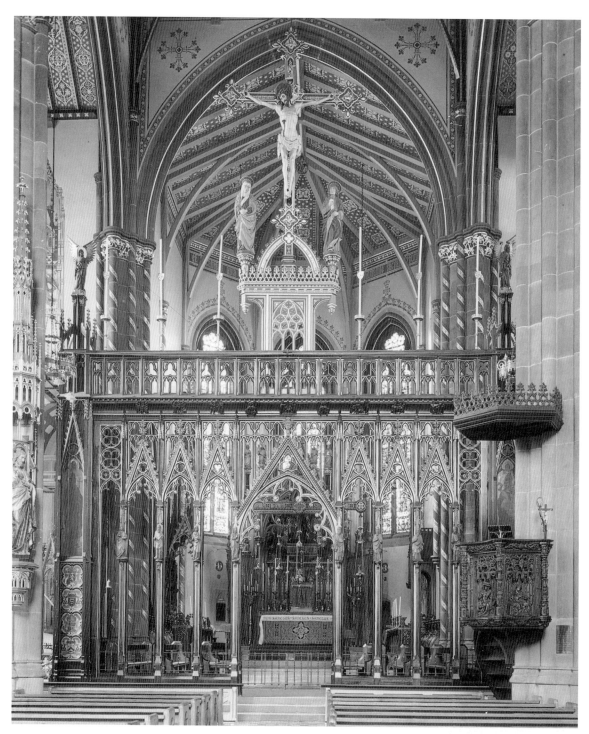

3. *Interior of the Roman Catholic Cathedral of St Chad, Birmingham (1839-41), by A.W.N. Pugin, showing the sumptuous chancel-screen and Rood before mutilation in recent years. The style is Second Pointed* (EH.A42/ 170 [1941]).

either embodied some of the grandeur of the 'Early English' style or some of the elegance of the Flowing or Curvilinear style, so it was probably the logical choice. It was the 'one and only variety of pointed architecture... common to all the most favoured nations of Christendom'. Its great merit, in short, was its *completeness*.

Pugin's most beautiful church, that of St Giles at Cheadle, Staffordshire, however, was firmly in the English Second Pointed style (later than Geometrical Middle Pointed), and was designed in 1840 for the Earl of Shrewsbury. 'Perfect Cheadle' **(Plate 4 and Colour Plate I)** was a revival of a type of English parish-church of the time of Edward I (1272-1307), and it is without

question Pugin's masterpiece, where he was able to lavish his skills without penny-pinching. The interior, glowing with colour, is based on scholarly study of mediæval precedents, and is one of Pugin's finest ecclesiastical works. He was to spend £20,000 of his own money on St Augustine's, Ramsgate (1845-51), where he was both paymaster and architect, and he considered it to be one of his best achievements **(Plate 5)**: it is in the Second Pointed style, and is part of a complex of buildings designed on Pugin's principle that the 'external and internal appearance of an edifice should be illustrative of, and in accordance with, the purpose for which it is designed'.

Apart from his great creations at Cheadle and Ramsgate, Pugin's work is, on the whole, disappointing: in most cases there was a shortage of money, and Pugin's prickly and fanatical personality cannot have made relations with his patrons

4. Exterior of the Roman Catholic church of St Giles, Cheadle, Staffordshire (1841-46), from the south-east, by A.W.N. Pugin. It is entirely in the Second Pointed style of the early fourteenth century, and is a revival of a type of English parish-church, dating from the reign of King Edward I (1272-1307). The spire is one of the most perfect produced during the Gothic Revival, and has two sets of crocketed pinnacles. Over the chancel-arch is a bell-cote, and the chancel is quite distinct (MC. F 260494 [1994]).

5. Interior of the Roman Catholic church of St Augustine, Ramsgate, Kent (1845-51), by A.W.N. Pugin. It is in the Second Pointed style (Decorated Gothic), and was sumptuously fitted out by the architect (EH. B43/1205).

easy. In any case, the Roman Catholic Church in England was a minority Church, with æsthetic and stylistic leanings (if it had any at all) towards Roman exemplars: Classical, Italianate, and Baroque architecture seemed more suited than Gothic, which, in any case, was associated in the minds of many with the Anglican Church. Furthermore, to be told by a recent convert that the Pointed style was the only one fitted for a 'Christian' or 'Catholic' country must have been hard to swallow, while it must also be remembered that many priests were Irish, and Pugin himself noted that there was 'no country in Europe where the externals of religion' presented 'so distressing an aspect' as Ireland: in larger Irish towns there was a 'lavish display of the vilest trash about the altars', and the clergy were all too often 'filled with the most anti-Christian ideas of art'. In short, educated taste was uncommon among the Roman Catholic clergy, and æsthetic awareness was often non-existent. To judge from the destruction of so many fine interiors in Roman Catholic churches in the last forty years or so (St Chad's in Birmingham **[Plate 3]** is a lamentable example of so-called 're-ordering'), this is as true as it was in Pugin's day.

Other Roman Catholic Churches

It should be remembered that Roman Catholicism in England was mainly rural and aristocratic until it was changed profoundly by the arrival of Irish paupers in the slums of Victorian England. Like the Anglicans, the Roman Church had to create a popular urban ministry to cater for multitudes (where before there had been handfuls), and to restore faith to the nominally Roman Catholic Irish poor.

In its missions to the poor the Roman Church copied the self-help of friendly societies, the clubs in public-houses, and the temperance organisations, while certain aristocratic and landed Roman Catholics (imbued, no doubt, with Pugin's visions) dreamed of restoring some mediæval dream-world. However, religious devotions tended to follow French and Italian forms, and were supported by the Ultramontanes, who were deeply loyal to the Papacy and to the person of the Pope. Ministry was sacerdotal, and involved pastoral care of the underprivileged. Before Victoria came to the Throne Roman Catholic Masses at the Bavarian and Sardinian embassy chapels in London would be attended by those who were willing to pay considerable sums to hear the operatically-inspired services, and Vincent Novello (1781-1861) attracted a fashionable audience to hear his virtuosity on the organ at Moorfields Chapel, but such splendours could not be found in the average urban Roman Catholic church.

Early nineteenth-century Roman Catholic churches took their cues from Anglican proprietary chapels, for they had class-exclusiveness (enshrined in the seating arrangements largely dictated by Protestant tradition) combined with the devotional atmosphere of a Dissenters' chapel. Unlike later Roman churches, there were no statues; churches were generally locked; weekday services were rare; altars and decorations were dismal and meagre; and pews and seats were let out for fees. From the beginning of Victoria's reign there was a revulsion against 'Protestant' pew-rents which kept both the Roman Catholic and Anglican poor away from church. Curiously, many Roman Catholic services bore all the hallmarks of Protestant revivalism, and indeed Evangelicals and Ultramontanes shared much, winning souls in the spiritual deserts of teeming English cities. It is a curious fact that many Roman Catholic divines seemed to owe debts to the Protestant Dissenters, and preferred Wesleyan and Whitefieldian observances to those of the Established Church. It must be remembered that all non-Anglicans were Nonconformists, and so Roman Catholics were also regarded as Nonconformists, and that the Roman Catholics felt the refined gentility of the Established Church was no way to reclaim souls: more effective were popular sermons, admonitory batterings to bring the sinful to repentance, and the exploitation of any means to bring the sinner under the sanctifying drip of The Precious Blood.

At the second National Synod of the Roman Catholic Church in 1855 finance was a sore point: door-money, pew-rents, and seat-fees were discussed at length. The Continental system of open churches had its champions, but in England the repugnance felt by persons of refined and genteel feelings when forced to endure the proximity of a large congregation of malodorous poor was a major obstacle to its adoption. Some Roman Catholic churches charged nothing at early Masses, but made a charge when Persons of Quality arrived for the fashionable eleven o'clock Mass: even then the livestock left by the poor would lie in wait for the tender flesh of the well-fed, and would cause much dismay. Some clerics favoured house-collections to entry-fees or

6. Roman Catholic Cathedral of St John, Salford, Manchester (1844-55), by Weightman and Hadfield. This is an example of the archæological eclectic approach, synthesising several elements derived from mediæval buildings: the crossing-tower and spire are based upon the western tower of the church of St Mary Magdalen, Newark, Nottinghamshire (thirteenth and fourteenth centuries); the nave is based upon elements from the church of St Peter, Howden, Yorkshire; and the choir is derived from parts of Selby Abbey, Yorkshire. From Eastlake (JSC [1872]).

seat-rents, and levied taxes according to the ability to pay, allowing free standing-room at Mass, but charges of a penny per seat at Low Mass and tuppence at the High Mass. By the 1860s, devotion to The Blessed Sacrament was on the increase, and Communions on common Sundays were numerous. Services were many, were accessible to the people, and most were free. Along aisles many altars were set up, and devotion to Our Lady became usual. Churches became more lavishly furnished than Protestant Nonconformist chapels, and took on a distinctly Roman Catholic appearance.

When Pugin died, worn out and insane, in 1852, aged only forty, there were a few distinguished Roman Catholic architects who followed his theories and architectural language, but most Roman Catholic churches erected in the 1850s were dull. An exception was the Cathedral of Salford (1844-55) by John Grey Weightman (1801-

7. Exterior of the Roman Catholic church of The Holy Name of Jesus, Manchester (1869-71), by J.A. Hansom. The upper part of the tower was designed by Adrian Gilbert Scott (1882-1963 – grandson of 'Great Scott'), and was completed in 1928 (JSC [1994]).

8. Interior of the Roman Catholic church of The Holy Name of Jesus, Manchester, showing the unusual connection of the transept with the chancel-arch by means of diagonally struck arches. The entire church is rib-vaulted, with the webs constructed of polygonal blocks of terracotta (for lightness), and the dominant style is French Gothic of the thirteenth century. The reredos (1890) is by Joseph Stanislaus Hansom (1845-1931) (EH. BB66/ 2289 [1966]).

72) and Matthew Ellison Hadfield (1812-85): this represents the eclectic and 'archæological' approach to architecture, for the design had a tower and spire based on those of the church of St Mary Magdalen, Newark, Nottinghamshire, a nave modelled on St Peter's, Howden, Yorkshire, and the choir on Selby Abbey **(Plate 6)**. Also eclectic was Joseph Aloysius Hansom (1803-82), whose churches of St Walburga, Preston, Lancashire (1850-54), Holy Name of Jesus, Manchester (1869), St Philip Neri (now the Cathedral-church of Our Lady and St Philip Howard), Arundel, Sussex (1870-73) — the last for the Duke of Norfolk — are of particular distinction. Both the Manchester **(Plates 7 and 8)** and Arundel **(Plates 9 and 10)** churches reflect a mid-nineteenth-century interest in and study of Continental Gothic, in this case French: there are echoes of Chartres, Reims, and Amiens in Manchester, while Bourges and French Gothic of *c*. 1300 predominate at Arundel. Yet (especially at Arundel) the detail tends to be mechanical, whilst the figure-sculpture is sentimental and vapid.

It is not surprising that Roman Catholic architects turned to the Continental (especially French) early Second Pointed style for their

9. Roman Catholic Cathedral-church of Our Lady and St Philip Howard, Arundel, Sussex (1870-73), by J.A. Hansom, from the south-east, showing the revival of French Gothic exemplars of the thirteenth century (EH. BB81/1876 [1876] © His Grace the Duke of Norfolk).

models, for, after all, French churches of around 1300 were tall, impressive, had apsidal chancels, and had no associations with Anglicanism. Pugin's son, Edward Welby Pugin (1834-75), was spectacularly successful in suggesting triumphalism in his buildings, notably the Franciscan church of St Francis, Gorton, Manchester of 1864-72, an essay in the style of the late-thirteenth century: this large and impressive church was built of brick, with very generous and robustly detailed stone dressings, and its west front (with a tall striped bell-turret set over a *Cruxifixus* rising from the middle buttress between two enormous traceried windows) was a showpiece of Continental Gothic Revival. At the close of the twentieth century this stupendous building lay abandoned, its windows smashed, its doors wide open, and rubbish and filth all over the interior (although moves were afoot to rescue it). The younger Pugin's Continental leanings were also demonstrated in the church of the City of Mary Immaculate (also known as All Saints), Barton-upon-Irwell, Lancashire, of 1867-8, with its sumptuous capitals in the nave arcades, and splendidly confident interior.

Another convert, Henry Clutton (1819-93), was the architect of the church of St Francis of Assisi, Notting Hill, London, of 1859-60: this is a tiny building of stock brick relieved by bands of black bricks, and is in a severely simple French-provincial Gothic style based on thirteenth-century examples. It was enlarged by the young John Francis Bentley, who also designed most of the fittings, as well as the exquisite baptistry of 1863 and sumptuous high altar and reredos **(Plates 11 and 12)**. Bentley was responsible in 1870 for the high altar of the Dominican Convent, Portobello Road, Kensington (formerly occupied by nuns of the Third Order of St Francis), the chapel of which was designed by Clutton in 1862 in a robust French Gothic style modelled on exemplars of the thirteenth century. Later, Bentley (who converted to Roman Catholicism in 1862) produced one of the most distinguished late-Victorian Roman Catholic churches, the Holy Rood, Watford, Herts., of 1883-1900, the style of which returned to late Decorated and

10. Interior of the Roman Catholic Cathedral-church of Our Lady and St Philip Howard, Arundel, Sussex, from the west, showing the French-Gothic style of the end of the thirteenth century revived (EH. BB81/1884 [1884]) © His Grace The Duke of Norfolk).

11. High altar in the Roman Catholic church of St Francis of Assisi, Pottery Lane, Notting Hill, Kensington, London (1863), by John Francis Bentley. It is constructed of alabaster, richly inlaid with marble and mosaic. The altar-frontal has short marble colonnettes with capitals, supporting the slab itself (or mensa*): the central panel is painted, while on either side are elements much enriched with inlays. The first super-altar has circular recessed panels separated from each other by inlays of black foliate patterns of proto-Art Nouveau style. The reredos itself is surmounted by a leaf-cornice, and by four panels of eight-pointed star-shapes each containing a painted figure. A corbel carries a Throne above with a* Vesica Piscis *or mandala shape inlaid with mosaics. The Pelican in Piety surmounts the gilded canopy over the Throne. In the centre of the altar is a tabernacle set behind an ædiculated front, with a brass door enriched with enamels and precious coloured stones* (GLPL. 70/11180 HB [1970]).

12. Baptistry of the Roman Catholic church of St Francis of Assisi, Pottery Lane, Notting Hill, Kensington, London, by John Francis Bentley, of 1861, showing the scholarly revival of early French Gothic (GLPL. 70/11179 HB [1970]).

Perpendicular Gothic, and is built of flint with stone dressings in an East Anglian manner. Bentley was to become the architect of the greatest Roman Catholic church in England, Westminster Cathedral. This will be discussed later, for its design draws together many threads that will be outlined below.

As the century progressed, many architects of distinction produced competent designs for the Roman Catholic Church. In 1878 a competition was announced for the design (to be 'Italian Renaissance') of a new church for the London Oratory of St Philip Neri and the church of the Immaculate Heart of Mary at Brompton. The design chosen was by Herbert Augustus Keate Gribble (1847-94): it is an essay in Roman Baroque with a sumptuous interior of the *Gesù* type largely decorated in 1927-32 by Commendatore C.T.G. Formilli **(Plates 13 and 15)**.

13. Exterior of the London Oratory of St Philip Neri and the church of the Immaculate Heart of Mary at Brompton, Kensington, London (designed from 1878), by H.A.K. Gribble. It is a fine essay in Roman Baroque (J. Allan Cash, G.3028).

14. Neo-Classical interior of the Roman Catholic chapel at Prior Park, Bath, of 1844-82, designed by J.J. Scoles and influenced by French eighteenth-century exemplars (RFW. 2452 [R.F. Wills] NMR. A46/6085 [1946])

It should be remembered that there were many Roman Catholics with Ultramontane or Counter Reformation sympathies who did not share Pugin's love of mediæval English Gothic architecture and artefacts, and who felt no desire to restore the English Church of the fourteenth and fifteenth centuries. To such persons the only architectural style in which to build was Classical or Renaissance, with some Baroque flourishes, and, in any case, the associations of Gothic with Anglicanism were too strong to be ignored.

An excellent example of a Roman Catholic place of worship in which no trace of Gothic can be found exists at Prior Park, Bath, Somerset, where a chapel was added next to the west wing of the Palladian mansion. Begun in 1844 to designs by Joseph John Scoles, it was not completed until 1882 **(Plate 14)**. It is a Neo-Classical basilica with the Corinthian Order carrying the entablature from which springs a coffered barrel-vault, and the east end is apsidal with a hemi-dome carried over the entablature which is supported on engaged paired columns. The refined architectural style is overwhelmingly French, of the eighteenth century, and is far-removed from Puginesque mediævalism.

The Jesuit church of St Wilfred, Preston, Lancashire, was remodelled in 1878-8, and the exterior was re-cased in a North Italian Renaissance style in the 1890s. The stunning Italian-inspired interior has a barrel-vaulted ceiling, the entablature is carried on Corinthian columns with shafts of pink granite, and the apsidal sanctuary has a hemi-dome with hexagonal and lozenge-shaped coffers. Marble, alabaster, mosaics, and gilding enhance the opulence. Designed by Father Ignatius Scoles, S.J. (1834-96), and Samuel Joseph Nicholl (1826-1905), St Wilfred's is a superb monument to Ultramontane church architecture inspired by Italian precedents **(Plate 16)**.

Roman Baroque, however, was an unfamiliar style in England, and it seems to have been selected by the Oratorians because of the Roman connections of the Order. Nevertheless, Gothic remained the favoured style for the majority of churches throughout the Victorian period: among distinguished designs in that style for the Roman Catholics are the churches of St John the Baptist, Norwich, by George Gilbert Scott, Junior (1839-97), and his brother, John Oldrid Scott (1841-1913), of 1884-1910 (a splendid and noble essay in the First Pointed Lancet style of Early English Gothic **[Plates 17 and 18]**, for, influenced by the work of

15. Interior of the London Oratory of St Philip Neri and the church of the Immaculate Heart of Mary at Brompton, Kensington, London, showing the rich Baroque style of the architecture, with massive piers separating the chapels on either side of the nave, a plan derived from Il Gesù *in Rome. Decorations were largely by Commendatore C.T.G. Formilli* (EH. BB49/155 [1948]).

16. Interior, looking towards the altar, of the Roman Catholic church of St Wilfred, Preston, Lancashire, of 1878-80, designed by the Rev. Ignatius Scoles and S.J. Nicholl. An exceptionally rich interior, heavily influenced by Italian exemplars (EH. BB66/2684 [1966]).

17. Exterior of the church of St John the Baptist (now the Roman Catholic Cathedral), Norwich (1884-1910), by G.G. Scott Junior and J.O. Scott, from the north-east. It is, as Pevsner says, an 'amazing church', built with funds supplied by the Duke of Norfolk. The style is predominantly First Pointed, or Early English Gothic, with lancets much in evidence (EH. BB52/247 [1951]).

John Loughborough Pearson [1817-97], taste had moved away from early Middle Pointed to First Pointed and even to more 'primitive' early Burgundian Gothic of the late-twelfth or early-thirteenth centuries); the Jesuit church of the Immaculate Conception, Farm Street, London, by Joseph John Scoles, of 1844-49 (in careful late Decorated Gothic); and St James, Spanish Place, Westminster, by Edward Goldie (1856-1921), of 1885-1918 (a very scholarly and serious interior, vaulted throughout, in a mixture of early French and English Gothic styles, which has some

remnants of decorations by John Francis Bentley dating from 1891).

But it was Pugin who gave Ecclesiology, intimately associated with his love of ritual, symbols, and detail, such an important rôle. Something of the quality of his work and output could be discerned in the exhibition devoted to Pugin held in the Victoria & Albert Museum in London in 1994, and once more his designs and personality were placed before the public. However, there was an aspect of the exhibition and its accompanying publication that was

18. Interior of the church of St John the Baptist (now the Roman Catholic Cathedral), Norwich: the nave with its vaulting and massive piers, showing the powerful thirteenth-century style adopted by the Scotts. All in all, this is a highly scholarly work, based on sound understanding of historical styles (EH. BB52/746 [1951]).

uncomfortably tainted by Hegelian-Pevsnerian interpretations of Pugin's significance and influence. For instance, Kenneth Clark, in *The Gothic Revival*, with truth observed that almost all the best work of the Revival was done after the death of Sir George Gilbert Scott (1878), so it is perhaps very strange that certain great architects (e.g. Bentley, Bodley, Garner, Pearson, George Gilbert Scott Junior, and Sedding), who really inherited Pugin's mantle and carried forward his lessons, have been given short shrift by Pevsnerians and other historical determinists, who have falsely claimed some International and other Modernists to have been Pugin's heirs. Such patent nonsense is still fed to susceptible minds in schools of architecture and art history, and is doubly deplorable for the damage it causes.

Pugin could be a designer of genius, and his influence was immense. Much of his *œuvre* is exquisite, delicate, and rich, but the man's importance does not lie solely in his skills as a designer. Pugin was a proselytiser, and an effective proselytiser at that: he argued that to revive the Gothic style, it was necessary to revive the old forms of worship, and that meant the Roman Catholic Revival.

The single-mindedness and phenomenal energies of Pugin were largely responsible for the triumph of Gothic as a style used for church architecture from the beginning of Queen Victoria's reign, while Pugin's own designs, notably those for the church of St Giles, Cheadle, Staffordshire, were of a quality to attract admiration and emulation. However, Pugin's influence was of far greater importance among architects designing for the Anglican Church. It is to the Anglican Revival that we now turn.

CHAPTER IV

The Anglican Revival

*The Revival of the Anglican Liturgy; The Impact of Ecclesiology; The Church-Building Age;
The Gothic Revival in the 1840s; The* Rundbogenstil

*We have not originated a new style, but are called upon to re-awaken one which has for centuries lain
dormant; and it is absurd to argue that, because those who originated it did not scruple, during its progress, at
destroying specimens of the earlier varieties, to make way for what they thought better, we are equally free to
destroy their works to make way for our own.*
GEORGE GILBERT SCOTT (1811-78): *A Plea for the Faithful Restoration of our Ancient Churches*
(London: John Henry Parker, 1850), 25-26.

The Revival of the Anglican Liturgy

During the course of the nineteenth century the Church of England enjoyed a ceremonial revival that was remarkable for its beauty, its scholarship, its impact, and its integrity. Its influence was immense, and it led to the creation of a great number of very fine works of architecture as well as to the making of countless artefacts of considerable quality, such as altar-frontals, reredoses, vestments, chalices, candlesticks, lecterns, and all manner of church furnishings. The regeneration of Anglican ceremonial worship was one of the most extraordinary, civilised, and scholarly phenomena ever to occur in England. It gained momentum thanks to the efforts of many individuals and texts, but its true progenitor was John Rouse Bloxam, Lloyd's student, learned Ecclesiologist, and meticulous scholar. He was for a time (1837-40) Newman's curate at Littlemore, had known Rock, and was a patron of Pugin, with whom he carried on an interesting correspondence, for Bloxam was Pugin's chief link with the Oxford Movement). He became friendly with Ambrose Lisle March Phillipps de Lisle, with whom he corresponded on a possible reunion of the Anglican and Roman Catholic Churches (a scheme with which Phillipps de Lisle was in sympathy), and remained on good terms with Newman until the latter's death. He collected much material on customs, liturgies, and

rites, abstracting this from many sources (printed and otherwise), and published this privately as *The Book of Fragments* (1842).

Subsequently, Bloxam's efforts were continued and expanded, and a vast antiquarian collection of material was made under the ægis of the Cambridge Camden Society which described and recorded the survival of pre-Reformation ornaments, artefacts, and customs; the practices of the Caroline Church; and details of parish and cathedral ceremonies that owed their origins to earlier (even pre-Tridentine) times. Interestingly, the collection, published as *Hierurgia Anglicana: Documents and Extracts Illustrative of the Ritual of the Church of England after the Reformation* (1848), also contained Puritan criticisms of ceremonies and practices, so it gave a very broad picture of Anglican liturgical customs from the sixteenth century, and was scholarly as well as intended to have practical application. In addition, it claimed lawful authority for ceremonial and decorations, and so became a catalyst for what was to become known as Ritualism. It provided the basis for the restoration of daily prayer, regular Communion, archaeologically and liturgically correct Eucharistic vestments, appropriately decorated altars (with candles), the revival of Church music (including ancient forms), seemly celebration of ecclesiastical Feasts and Festivals, and much else that was required (apparently to the astonishment of many) by the ecclesiastical statutes. Not surprisingly, Bloxam was called the 'Grandfather of the Ritualists', although it was on account of the *Hierurgia Anglicana* that he ceased collecting similar material himself.

Bloxam's brother, Matthew Holbeche Bloxam, was also an immensely significant figure in ecclesiological and liturgiological circles: influenced by his friend, the architect Thomas Rickman, he brought out the first edition of *The Principles of Gothic Ecclesiastical Architecture*, published in Leicester in 1829, a remarkable and scholarly achievement for a young man then in his twenties. As the *Dictionary of National Biography* observed, it was an important book, and 'justly entitled its young author to rank among the authorities of' the Gothic Revival. It should be remembered that Bloxam's tome was several years *ahead* of Pugin's more celebrated publications, and *twenty years earlier* than those of the influential John Henry Parker. Bloxam's *Principles* came out in new editions in Leicester in 1836 and 1838, and in 1841, 1843, 1844, 1845, 1846, and 1849 the fourth, fifth, sixth, seventh, eighth, and ninth editions were printed at Oxford University Press. A tenth edition of 501 pages was published at Rugby in 1859, and a German edition of the seventh edition came out in Leipzig in 1847. Prompted by 'Great' Scott, Bloxam was prevailed upon to revise and expand the work, and the eleventh edition, in three volumes, was published by George Bell & Sons in London in 1882, with a total of 1049 pages, including additional material on vestments and church arrangements. Apart from this and other books, he published nearly two hundred scholarly essays on antiquarian and ecclesiological matters, including several on sepulchral monuments. However, Bloxam's great *Principles*, illustrated with numerous admirable woodcuts by Thomas Orlando Sheldon Jewitt (1799-1869 — who, with his brother, Llewellynn Frederick William Jewitt [1816-86], prepared numerous fine illustrations for Parker including the celebrated *Glossary of Terms used in Grecian, Roman, Italian, and Gothic Architecture* [1836, with subsequent editions]), must stand as one of the earliest (and most scholarly) influential texts of the whole

ecclesiological movement and Gothic Revival.

It is odd that the Bloxam brothers have not been given the credit they deserve by later writers, although Eastlake gave M. H. Bloxam a cursory nod in his *A History of the Gothic Revival* (1872): only The Revd. Anthony Symondson, S.J., seems to have recognised the importance of J. R. Bloxam (as an influence on ceremonial revival) in recent years, but M. H. Bloxam was unquestionably of great significance in the history of ecclesiology, and his impact on the Gothic Revival should be better recognised.

The Impact of Ecclesiology

Although Pugin's polemical writings had been aimed at the revival of a Roman Catholic mediæval England, they struck all sorts of responsive chords among Anglicans (many of whom had already been intellectually, emotionally, and æsthetically prepared), and, as Scott admitted, Pugin was the decisive influence on many Anglican Gothic Revivalists. 'The thunder of Pugin's writings' awakened Scott from his 'slumbers', and, although Scott did not know Pugin, the latter was, in Scott's imagination, a 'guardian angel'.

Mention has been made above of the University Societies at Oxford and Cambridge which led to the study of church architecture in the 1830s and 1840s. If the Evangelicals had been the most significant group behind shifts in national consciousness in the first half of the nineteenth century, the High Church, Tractarian, or Puseyite party within the Church of England assumed an important rôle in the second, and certainly from the time of the appearance of *The Ecclesiologist*. Anglican churches had been shamefully neglected since the depredations of the Henrician, Edwardine, Elizabethan, and Commonwealth periods: the Ecclesiologists demanded why it was that private houses were kept clean and comfortable when the House of God often had broken or blocked windows, damp walls, rotting roofs, and ancient decorative features hidden or mutilated. They also explained in their publications the arrangements and purposes of the fabric of mediæval churches to a largely ignorant, surprised, and often suspicious

Protestant nation. Suggestions were made for the restoration and furnishing of naves and chancels, and extremely cautious moves towards rubrical reform were mooted. From the very beginning the Oxford Society cautioned against over-zealous works that might 'restore' historic buildings within inches of their lives. Scott noted that 'an old church is so common and so familiar an object that we are often in danger of forgetting its value, and it is only by cultivating a correct appreciation of what our churches *really are* that we shall obtain a true and earnest feeling for their conservation'. In spite of these warnings many insensitive schemes virtually scraped away genuine fabric that was in any way damaged, decayed, or inconvenient, and left mediæval buildings looking like dull and mechanical copies of old work (some were not even copies, but guesses approximating to what the architect thought might have been appropriate, which often was nothing of the kind).

However, there is no doubting that the architectural Societies of Oxford and Cambridge were immensely successful in promoting the cause of Gothic art and architecture. As Eastlake put it, 'graduates who left their college rooms for curates' quarters in remote parishes', or who 'settled down as doctors and attorneys in many a country town, carried with them a pleasant recollection' of field-days and explorations, study-visits to churches, meetings, lectures, papers, and lively discussions about mediæval architecture. The converts went forth as missionaries, with all the zeal of youth, to rescue England from its spiritual and architectural torpor. Pugin wanted to revive Gothic architecture by reviving Roman Catholicism, but the Ecclesiologists wished to revive the Anglican Church by resurrecting the Gothic style.

However, the nation was partly indifferent to these aims, and partly anti-clerical, while Dissent and Roman Catholicism were gaining ground: as noted above, the Great Reform enactment of 1832 transferred power from a class which generally supported the Anglican Church to classes in which Dissent was predominant, so Anglicans knew their influence in national affairs was being reduced, and was likely to further

diminish. Another problem was the Evangelical party, to which symbolism, ceremony, sacred imagery, and decoration were unacceptable, but for which Sabbatarianism, simplicity, severity, and sermonising were more important than 'idolatrous gewgaws' and 'superstitious' practices. Chancels, with their Popish Rood-screens, sedilia, piscinæ, aumbries, and credence-tables, were regarded almost as survivals from the Dark Ages. Altars were a 'scandal and a stumbling-block' to right-minded Protestants, and even Crosses were never displayed in rigidly Evangelical surroundings because of their Papist associations. As for Easter Sepulchres and other suspect 'Popish' features, the chances were that the average Evangelical had no idea what they were, what they were for, or why they were there. The Evangelicals, in short, saw the Ecclesiologists and the Gothic Revival as a threat to Protestantism, and indeed to the needs of society, arguing that two or three plain utilitarian brick preaching-boxes with plaster ceilings could be erected for the price of one stone church with groined vaulted ceiling (or elaborate timber trussed roof), chancel fitted out with crypto-Papist paraphernalia, stained-glass windows with images, and all the rest of it. An ideal Evangelical church-building was freed from any 'semblance of religious superstition', and innocent of those suspect 'artistic attractions' which could be dangerous delusions ensnaring the unwary and leading them to Rome: it was, in essence, cheap and utilitarian, without any appeal to æsthetic sensibilities.

Against such views the Ecclesiologists, Tractarians, and High Church party could marshal many serious charges: the Evangelicals had permitted building fabric to fall into decay; church-services had become slovenly; children were permitted to grow up uninformed as to the nature and significance of the English Liturgy and the Sacraments; Baptism was a mere naming-ceremony frequently performed in the house of the parents instead of in a church; Confirmation was often dispensed with; the observance of Saints' Days was confined to the denizens of the Cathedral Close; many undergraduates only learned about Lent and Advent when at

University; and the long sermons were a signal for general somnolence.

A transformation of Anglican services from conventional and scarcely revered meetings into a picturesque rite, with a corresponding revival of rubrical usage, sacred music, art, and architecture, was a remarkable achievement, and there is no doubt that the High Church party won a great deal in the space of only a generation. Parochial clergy with Tractarian High Church leanings brought Christianity, literacy, and morality to the poorer quarters of London and many other towns and cities: the parochial buildings and splendid churches of the Victorian Gothic Revival must have seemed like oases of civilisation and hope, as citadels of faith and Anglicanism within the urban built fabric. Charles Kingsley (1819-75), in *Alton Locke, Tailor and Poet* (1850), described a new Anglican church being built in a poor quarter of a town:

> ... month after month I had watched it growing; I had seen one window after another filled with tracery, one buttress after another finished off with its carved pinnacle; then I had watched the skeleton of the roof gradually clothed in tiling; and then the glazing of the windows .... Were they going to finish that handsome tower? No; it was left with its wooden cap, I supposed, for further funds. But the nave, and the deep chancel behind it, were all finished, and surmounted by a cross; and beautiful enough the little sanctuary looked, in the virgin purity of its spotless freestone...

> And then there was a grand procession of surplices and lawn sleeves;... the bell rang to morning and evening prayers — for there were daily services there, and Saints' day services, and Lent services, and three services on a Sunday, and six or seven on Good Friday and Easter Day. The little musical bell above the chancel-arch seemed always ringing;... And then a Gothic school-house rose at the churchyard end,... and women came daily for alms;... it was a pleasant sight, as every new church is to the healthy-minded man,... — a fresh centre of civilization, mercy, comfort for weary hearts, relief from frost and hunger; a fresh centre of

> instruction, humanizing, disciplining, ... to hundreds of little savage spirits; altogether a pleasant sight...

Now tracery, buttresses with carved pinnacles, tiled roofs, and glazing were only one aspect, but the *deep chancel*, *Cross* over it, *many* services, and *Sancte*-bell above the *chancel-arch* were another, and unthinkable in Protestant-Evangelical terms. Gothic church-architecture had roots in the rich panoply of mediæval religion, far removed from Sabbatarianism of the Dissenting or Protestant variety, Evangelical ideals, or the tradition of sermonising to packed static congregations. The Gothic Revival was a reminder of the Christian Revival, and, although at first associated with the Tractarians and with the Roman Catholics (via Pugin's arguments), began to be adopted by the Evangelicals and Dissenters (often with ludicrous results, for the style had no historical connections with Evangelical or Dissenting practice).

However, such a profound change had an immense impact on the building trades as well as on architecture. Demand was created for encaustic tiles, stained-glass windows, elaborate metal work, quality church-furnishings, vestments, and anything connected with a full and scholarly revival of mediæval forms of worship and architecture. Architects, artists, and craftsmen had to learn Gothic, with its details, mouldings and styles, whilst the construction industries were turned upside-down. Architectural design, freed from the tyrannies of symmetry demanded by Classicism, could blossom anew in the climate of the Gothic Revival, for architects could experiment with asymmetrical compositions, with façades pierced with openings only where they were needed, and with the breaking-up of larger masses to provide cunningly detailed buildings with a prominent vertical emphasis. Pugin's 'True Picturesque', derived from logical planning and disposition of volumes where needed, began to be employed on a nationwide basis.

The Ecclesiologists embraced Pugin's ideas about architecture, editing them for Anglican use, and soon Second Pointed Anglican churches, complete with screens, sedilia, and all the marvellous riches of Decorated Gothic were being built by High Churchmen. There was another point to all this: the Gothic Revival was a visible expression of the revival of Sacramentalism, and an affirmation of the continuity of the Catholic tradition within the Church of England. But Second Pointed was not only the approved liturgical and functional style for the Ecclesiologists: it was often brutally imposed upon real mediæval churches so that they lost their Perpendicular and Early English fabric to an invasion of Victorian Middle and Second Pointed. Scott was to argue eloquently against that sort of thing, even though his office was guilty of it (as in the insensitive rebuilding [in a mechanical First Pointed manner] of the north aisle of the extraordinary mediæval church of St Mary de Castro, Leicester).

Now the period of greatest influence of the Ecclesiologists also coincided with an astonishing amount of church-building by the Anglicans: by 1873 about a third of all parish-churches had been restored, while between the accession of William IV in 1830 and the death of the Prince Consort in 1861 about 1,500 new churches had been built in England. From around 1840 to the end of the century about 100 churches were built each year in England, and almost every existing church was restored (with varying degrees of sensitivity and success). There was another side to the coin, however, and that was the tyranny exercised by the Ecclesiologists in the reviews and criticisms of new churches or restorations. *The Ecclesiologist* could make or break the reputation of an architect: it had a party-line which had to be adhered to in matters of style; the provision of certain elements was closely watched; and the 'correctness' of the architecture was carefully (even pedantically) monitored. Indeed, *The Ecclesiologist* must not be underestimated as an architectural journal of immense power and influence. When English Second Pointed Gothic was *de rigueur*, the Ecclesiologists encouraged the copying of bits of real mediæval buildings on the grounds that architects had to learn the alphabet, grammar, and syntax of Gothic before they could even begin to attempt to create original compositions. To this end the Ecclesiologists selected buildings, parts of buildings, and details which they regarded as worthy of emulation, and made them familiar in publications. But this was regarded only as a beginning.

The Church-Building Age

'That we live in a Church-building age is... manifest', observed the Reverend William Pepperell in his series of papers (published as *The Church Index* in 1872) dealing with the churches of Kensington. 'Of the fifty-three Churches and Chapels in Kensington, fifteen have been erected and opened within the last five years; sixteen others within ten years; and in all within the past twenty years there have been no less than forty-three erections... Whatever the verdict of posterity may be upon these buildings from an artistic point of view, it will not hesitate to accord the high merit of distinguished energy and liberality. As to Architecture, some few of these erections embody and will hand down to future times examples of the improved taste of our day'.

As has been observed earlier, churches were deemed necessary to raise or set the tone of an urban neighbourhood, and, in the case of a populous city like London, small ecclesiastical parishes were created. In places such as the parish of Kensington, which experienced a phenomenal amount of building in the Victorian period, the earliest church accommodation to be provided (in addition to the existing parish-church of St Mary Abbots — soon to be rebuilt by George Gilbert Scott in 1869-79) was a proprietary chapel, erected, without any charge to the parish, by private individuals as a commercial enterprise. However, *The Christian Observer*, the main publication of the Evangelical party, went so far as to condemn the proprietary chapels without reservation, mostly because of their commercial associations. Some church-building followed, supported by the Government under the post-Waterloo *Acts*, and the Kensington Vestry obtained grants, facilitating the erection of the 'Commissioners' churches' of St Barnabas, Addison Road (in the late-Perpendicular style of Gothic — erected 1826-29 to designs by Lewis Vulliamy [1791-1871]), and Holy Trinity, Brompton (in the baldest First Pointed Lancet style [but subsequently altered] — also erected 1826-29, this time to designs by Thomas Leverton Donaldson [1795-1885]). Now the way in which the 'Commissioners' churches' were realised resembled the provision of public housing later: the Government provided grants on certain conditions; the Vestries raised the balance (often by borrowing); and pew-rents were set to support and maintain the churches. As a benefit, the presence of the new churches would help to bring respectability to the immediate areas around them, and provide a reassuring visible presence of the Established Church.

The Bishop of London, C. J. Blomfield, campaigned for funding from private sources for church-building, especially in the East End of London, and stated it was the duty of landowners and property-owners in London either to build churches or to contribute towards their costs. Furthermore, he created the pattern of small ecclesiastical districts, each of 'manageable size', and each with its church, schools, and charities. Thus the large parish of St Mary Abbots, Kensington, was subdivided, and the vicar from 1845, John Sinclair (1797-1875), followed Blomfield's policies in creating new ecclesiastical districts within the parish, and, in turn, these districts were further subdivided, each new division requiring its own church. After his death, it was said of Sinclair that under his régime the 'Old Court Suburb parish' of Kensington became more like 'an episcopal see'. As the new churches were created, they acquired parochial rights and duties, and each new district was subdivided as soon as it was necessary to do so. By these means, any Anglican could promote a church, and a vicar could be appointed, but it was the responsibility of the bishop and the Ecclesiastical Commissioners to determine the boundaries of the new district and deal with difficulties, the main one of which was that the incumbent of the larger area from which the new district was to be carved out would lose not only part of his 'territory', but income from pew-rents and other emoluments. This could cause distress, even hardship, and, often, animosity.

In the case of Kensington, new Anglican churches built under Sinclair's ægis consisted of two basic types: there were the estate churches erected or promoted by landowners to make their speculative housing developments more attractive to leaseholders (a good church was deemed not only to give some kind of heart to an area, but to improve tone and provide a convenient place of worship within walking distance [an important factor when, in many conventional households, church-going was obligatory, even for servants]), and the 'private' churches promoted by clergymen in order to foster a type of Churchmanship, be it 'High', 'Low', or 'Broad'. Generally, estate churches tended to be of the Low Church type, built to accommodate as many people in the new district as possible, and were therefore unritualistic, often with galleries, and with small chancels. Private churches tended to be more High Church, promoted by clergymen and their supporters in order to foster Ritualism and Tractarianism. In Kensington there were animosities between the High Church Tractarian and Low Church Evangelical parties, but the national and diocesan funding (which was so important in poorer parts of London) was relatively insignificant because the parish on the whole was wealthy. Some estate churches were erected by landowners or developers, who paid the entire cost, but more usually the landowner presented the sites for church-building or sold them for much less than market value, leaving vicar-designates and church-building committees to raise the money for the fabric itself. In some cases temporary prefabricated churches (often of iron) were erected while funds were being raised and plans drawn up, and once their usefulness had passed, the temporary structures were sold to other districts or parishes. Private ventures usually had to find the money to pay for the site as well as the building. Once churches had been built the High Church establishments relied on donations (alms), and Low Church ones on pew-rents and donations.

Now this over-provision of churches (as well as the rivalries of High and Low Churchmen) was a recipe for future disaster: there was an assumption that Anglican clergymen would always come from the higher, well-heeled echelons of society, and would therefore have substantial (or sufficient) private incomes; and it was also hoped, optimistically, that Kensington residents would always be prosperous, disposed to attend church, and able to put plenty of cash in the collection-plates. In almost all cases, however, the churches were under-endowed, and by the end of the century it became clear that some districts were too small to support their churches in the future. In later years it was generally true that most vicars no longer had comfortable private incomes; multiple occupation of houses originally intended for family occupation, and the exodus of families from Kensington, led to dramatic declines in church-attendance, although celebrated centres of Anglo-Catholicism such as St Cuthbert, Philbeach Gardens, continued to flourish because they drew their congregations from a very wide area rather than from parish or district alone.

Estate churches in Kensington varied from the brick-and-stone St James, Norlands, to the southern churches of St Jude, Courtfield Gardens, St Luke, Redcliffe Square, St Mary, The Boltons, St Paul, Onslow Square, St Peter, Cranley Gardens, and St Stephen, Gloucester Road, all of which were faced in stone, usually Kentish rag, which contrasted with the stucco-and-brick dwellings. Such churches embodied the intention to provide accommodation for the inhabitants of well-to-do, London suburban parishes: they attempted to satisfy contemporary notions concerning the clear demarcation of nave, aisles, and chancel with the demands for comfortable seating which had evolved in Evangelical worship involving long sedentary periods during sermons. In addition, as many sittings as could be managed were intended to gain the best benefit from pew-rentals, so in churches such as Bassett Keeling's extraordinary (Pevsner called it 'atrocious', but the 1991 edition of *London 3: North West* toned this down to 'quirky') St George's, Campden Hill, galleries provided many more seats.

In the case of the parish-church of St Mary Abbots, Kensington, the old church (completed in 1704) was declared unsafe in 1866, but it is likely that the desire of Archdeacon Sinclair to build a new church 'on a scale proportioned to the opulence and importance' of a great metropolitan parish had more to do with the decision to demolish and provide a new structure in the Gothic Revival style. Such a desire for importance, show, and status enshrined in a building was common throughout the country, and was intimately connected with the ambitions of Churchmen to match their rhetoric with architectural grandeur. St Mary's church was faced with ragstone with Bath stone dressings, unlike St Cuthbert's, Philbeach Gardens, Kensington, where the red-brick facings were in stark contrast to the Classically-inspired houses that were erected in the crescent-shaped street, but in this case the choice of brick allowed more expenditure on the internal fixtures, whilst the material was regarded as more 'truthful' by High Church Tractarian architects (influenced, no doubt, by Butterfield's All Saints, Margaret Street). Similar examples can be found among the Tractarian churches in other parts of London.

Kensington also boasted some spectacular Roman Catholic churches. Brompton Oratory was a major centre for conversion and authority, although the building itself was a poor thing until it was replaced by the great Baroque church that stands there today **(Plates 13 and 15)**. In fact, the Oratory is the visible expression of that Ultramontane tendency in the Roman Catholic Church in England, and its erection was largely supported by rich Roman Catholic laymen (including the family of the Duke of Norfolk). Also in Kensington was the sometime Pro-Cathedral of Our Lady of Victories (1867-69), designed by George Goldie in a robust French Gothic style, but its finance was raised largely by borrowing, and the debt was not paid off until 1901. The enchanting little church of St Francis of Assisi, Pottery Lane **(Plates 11 and 12)**, was built at the expense of Father Henry Augustus Rawes (1826-85), an Oblate of St Charles Borromeo, and there were, on occasion, wealthy priests who could finance their own churches. Grander enterprises, however, relied on the support of rich laymen or the generosity of the pious.

Nonconformists (never very influential in places like Kensington) often came to grief when enthusiastic pastors imagined they would attract larger congregations than they actually achieved, and there was much financial over-extension. Nonconformists generally, throughout the country, remained faithful to Classicism until they became infected with the Gothic bug in the 1850s.

The Gothic Revival in the 1840s

At first (until *c.* 1845) the Revival from the 1820s was largely dominated by the Perpendicular style, although there were many essays in First Pointed or Early English Gothic. The church of Holy Trinity, Bishop's Bridge Road (or Gloucester Terrace), Paddington, of 1844-6 (demolished 1984), by Thomas Cundy II (1790-1867) and Thomas Cundy III (1820-95) was typical of the type of Anglican church with a small chancel, insubstantial piers, galleries, and Perpendicular tracery that the Ecclesiologists detested **(Plate 19)**. Pugin himself noted in his *Apology* that galleries were 'contrary to the intentions of the Anglican Church. They are of comparatively modern origin'. *The Ecclesiologist* went further and called Holy Trinity 'a heap of misapplied ornament; battlements, finials, gurgoyles guiltless of gutters, ... in tasteless confusion'.

As has been made clear, it began to be regarded as essential, when developing new residential areas, to provide a church convenient for the inhabitants. The church of St James, Norlands, in Northern Kensington, was such an example, and was erected (to designs by Lewis Vulliamy in 1844-5) of white Suffolk bricks with minimal stone dressings in a thin, unconvincing First Pointed Lancet style, with Geometrical tracery in the tower above the door. The interior piers and trusses are impossibly spindly, but there were galleries in 1850 which would have made the interior less fragile-looking. St James's church was very much Gothic 'on the cheap' (it cost £4,941, towards which the Church Building Commissioners made a grant of £500), and was uncomfortably like the Inwoods' church of St Mary, Eversholt Street, London (1824-7), in style — a starved, bare, and papery piece of stock-brick Gothic lampooned by Pugin in *Contrasts*.

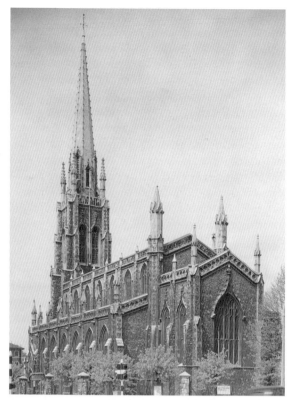

19. *Exterior of the church of The Holy Trinity, Gloucester Terrace, Paddington, London (1844-46), by Thomas Cundy II and III. A typical Anglican church of the period, with small chancel, Perpendicular-style tracery, and stone facings somewhat incongruous in the sooty London atmosphere* (EH. AA71/2651 [1964].

Now such architecture did not meet with the approval of the Ecclesiologists. George Gilbert Scott and his partner (from 1835 to 1846), William Bonython Moffatt (1812-87), however, produced an important church, St Giles's, Camberwell Church Street, South London, designed in 1841 and consecrated in 1844, with a big chancel (separated from the nave by a tower with a tall spire), Geometrical (Middle Pointed) tracery, and an exterior that was tough and sturdy: *The Ecclesiologist* pronounced it as 'one of the finest' churches of 'modern days'. The building must be regarded as more successful than the church of St John the Evangelist, Ladbroke Grove, London (1844-45), by John Hargrave Stevens (d.1875) and George Alexander (d. 1884), who

20. Interior of the church of St Paul, West Street, Brighton, Sussex (1846), by R. C. Carpenter. The screen (with loft and Rood) was added some twenty years later by Bodley, and the painting above the chancel-arch was by Bodley's pupil, Robert Anning Bell (1863-1933) (EH. B44/2892 [1944]).

planned a conventional English First Pointed cruciform building with a crossing-tower and spire based on that of the parish-church at Witney in Oxfordshire. St John's is representative of a somewhat timid early-Victorian Gothic Revival essay that depended on copies of bits and pieces culled from real mediæval buildings, but in which those bits and pieces were composed without *élan*, verve, or any startling leaps of imagination. *The Builder* and other journals were favourable in their criticisms of what is rather a dull building (*The Ecclesiologist* hoped the architects would do better in the future), but Scott's St Giles's was of more interest because its construction showed an advance in operative skills, and it was firmly early Second Pointed, which was *the* approved style for the next decade or so. The church of St Mark, Swindon, Wiltshire (1843-45), was erected as the parish-church of New Swindon (and as the railway church) by the Great Western Railway Company at a cost of £5,000 to designs by Scott and Moffatt: here the style is firmly Second Pointed, with a fine west window that incorporates elaborate and scholarly Curvilinear tracery.

Although Scott's work attracted some favourable attention, Ecclesiologists began to move towards the idea of building exemplars rather than to rely on criticism alone to obtain improvements in design. One of the first attempts to provide a church erected under the supervision of learned Ecclesiologists was Christ Church, Kilndown, Kent, begun in 1839 to designs by Anthony Salvin (1799-1881), but transformed inside between 1840 and 1845 by Alexander James Beresford Hope (1820-87), who created a proper chancel with altar by Salvin, and Rood-screen and stalls by Richard Cromwell Carpenter (1812-55). *The Ecclesiologist* in 1845 praised the chancel as a *whole* of colour not to be seen in any other English church, and Kilndown can be regarded as the first Camdenian Ecclesiologically-approved chancel in England. Soon the Ecclesiologists began to draw up lists of approved architects (e.g. William Butterfield, who had designed the chandeliers, tapers, and lectern for Kilndown) they considered capable of creating churches in accordance with rules and principles they perceived as being akin to an exact science.

Carpenter obtained the commission to build St Paul's, West Street, Brighton, Sussex, in 1846, which was Puginesque, and in the Second Pointed style **(Plate 20)**. Another, even more important, church by Carpenter was St Mary Magdalene, Munster Square, London, of 1849-52, also in the Second Pointed style, and built of Kentish ragstone, a material which was ill-suited to London, and it has to be admitted it has not worn well. The interior, however, with its high timber roof, distinct chancel, and furnishings, was a model of Tractarian principles (*The Ecclesiologist* enthusiastically called it 'the most artistically correct new church yet consecrated in London'). St Mary's was built under the ægis of Edward Stuart (1820-77), who had read for his first degree at Oxford, where he had been profoundly influenced by Pusey and others. Stuart proved to be an effective incumbent, educating the poor and their children, and bringing Christianity, literacy, and decency to a deprived area of London. St Mary's became a model of considerable importance for architects in the period 1870-1900, as will be seen. Carpenter was also responsible for the designs of the College of St Nicholas at Lancing

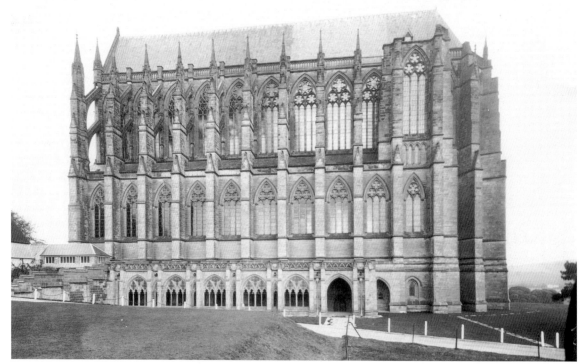

21. The stupendous chapel at Lancing, Sussex (begun 1868, but designed earlier), a powerful essay in the Geometrical or early Second Pointed style of Gothic, much influenced by French exemplars. The design was by Richard Herbert Carpenter (1841-93) and William Slater (1819-72). The cloisters (1912-20) were realised by Temple Moore, based on designs by Slater, and the west front of the chapel was completed by S. Dykes Bower in the 1970s (EH. CC46/446 [c.1944-5]).

in Sussex, but the spectacular Geometrical Gothic chapel, begun in 1868 **(Plate 21)**, was designed by Richard Herbert Carpenter (1841-93) and William Slater (1819-72), but not completed until the 1970s to designs by Stephen Ernest Dykes Bower (1903-94). This tremendous building, with its canted east end, is predominantly in the style of French Gothic of the thirteenth century with fifteenth-century proportions: it is vast, and very high, with few rivals.

One of the contributors to Kilndown church, as noted above, was William Butterfield, with whom Henry Woodyer (1816-96) had worked in 1844. Woodyer created his first masterpiece, Holy Innocents, Highnam, Gloucestershire (1849-51), in a robust and elaborate Second Pointed style, shortly after he left Butterfield's office **(Plate 22)**. His patron was the wealthy Thomas Gambier Parry (1816-88) — who was responsible for the

spectacular frescoes (1850-71), and the church is regarded as having one of the most important early examples of painted internal polychrony in an Anglican church, rivalling Pugin's work at Cheadle, and indeed it can in some respects be regarded as a fulfilment of the Puginesque ideal **(Colour Plate II)**.

Benjamin Ferrey (1810-80) received the *Imprimatur* of Ecclesiological opinion with his church of St Stephen, Rochester Row, Westminster, of 1846-50, a competent essay in Second Pointed Gothic Revival, erected and endowed at the expense of Angela Georgina Burdett-Coutts (1814-1906) in memory of her father, Sir Francis Burdett (1770-1844). Contemporary illustrations **(Plate 23)** of this building show a crisp precision, a hardness, and a sharpness that anticipate later interiors by Butterfield and George Edmund Street. The latter architect rose to demands in *The*

22. Exterior of the church of the Holy Innocents, Highnam, Gloucestershire (1849-51), by Henry Woodyer. It is in the Second Pointed style, and Pevsner described the whole ensemble as 'immensely impressive' (MC. B290494 [1994]).

Ecclesiologist for a greater simplicity in the design of rural churches, and produced the robust and charming First Pointed St Mary's, at Par, in Cornwall of 1847, where plainness, clarity, and toughness are well to the fore. Street was also to argue that a town church should have high, smooth walls of coloured bands, with panels; windows would be set high and would be large to admit as much light as possible without inviting vandalism; towers were to be set back from the line of the street; and a piling together of motifs, like those of a Continental town church, was to be sought. *The Ecclesiologist* published appreciations of Italian Gothic architecture as early as 1846, and in 1848 Benjamin Webb (1819-85), Secretary of The Cambridge Camden Society, and later of The Ecclesiological Society, published his *Sketches of Continental Ecclesiology* in which he praised the brick construction

of Italian churches: the emphasis of the Gothic Revival was moving away from English exemplars to the Continent.

Ecclesiologists, however, were starting to abandon archæological correctness and copying in favour of a search for a modern style suitable for the grimy atmosphere of the Victorian urban milieu, with its thousands of coal-burning domestic fires, steam-engines, and polluting industries. Town churches, like those designed by Thomas Cundy II and R.C. Carpenter in the 1840s, were usually of stone, such as Kentish rag, which is essentially a country material (though even there it looks lifeless and dull), and did not look well in, or stand up to, London. By the end of the 1840s it was opined that new forms and materials suitable for the urban environment were essential for any new developments, and, in any case, the published illustrations of buildings such as the interior of Ferrey's St Stephen's **(Plate 23)** gave an impression of hard, sharp details and impervious surfaces that prompted what was to happen later. Italian and Continental models seemed to offer certain ways forward, because they were adapted to tight urban sites, and because, in the case of Italian exemplars, the colour of the buildings' interiors was derived from the stones and other materials used to face the walls (structural polychromy), rather than applied using paint (as Pugin had done in his interiors).

The *Rundbogenstil*

Parallel with Gothic Revival churches there arose a revival of interest in the round-arched styles, varying from Norman or Romanesque Revival to a more eclectic *Rundbogenstil* (round-arched style) in which Italian, Lombardic, and Germanic motifs could be found. George Ernest Hamilton's (*fl.* 1831-49) *Designs for Rural Churches* of 1836 contained some thin efforts in Gothic which would not have earned much favour (to understate the case) among the Ecclesiologists, but the book did contain some designs for churches in the Romanesque style, which reflected a growing interest in the round-arched styles in general. Such an interest originated in Germany, and it embraced the Early Christian, Byzantine,

23. *Interior of the church of St Stephen, Rochester Row, Westminster, London (1846-50), a competent essay in the Second Pointed style of the Gothic Revival by Benjamin Ferrey (1810-80). The illustration shows the crisp hardness and precision of the architecture that could never be mistaken for mediæval work, and indeed the drawing anticipates later interiors. From* Eastlake (JSC [1872]).

I. Interior of the Roman Catholic church of St Giles, Cheadle, Staffordshire (1841-46), by A.W.N. Pugin. The style is Second Pointed (Decorated) throughout, and the sumptuous enrichments are carried out wherever they could be applied. The lower chancel is divided from the nave by a chancel-arch, and is further demarcated by the exquisite screen, with coving, parapet, and Rood (MC. D260494 [1994]).

II. *Interior of the church of the Holy Innocents, Highnam, Gloucestershire (1849-51), by Henry Woodyer, with what is regarded as one of the most important examples of painted internal polychromy in an Anglican church, rivalling Pugin's work at Cheadle, and in many respects can be seen as a fulfilment of the Puginesque ideal. The style is Second Pointed, and the spectacular wall-paintings were carried out by Thomas Gambier Parry* (MC. A290494 [1994]).

III. Chancel of the church of All Saints, Margaret Street, London (1849-59), by William Butterfield, showing the vaulted ceiling recalling the church of St Francis in Assisi, and the very rich treatment of the reredos, the lower part of which (usually hidden behind a curtain) shows Butterfield's characteristic use of richly coloured tiles (MC. F100590 [1990]).

IV. Interior of the church of All Saints, Margaret Street, London, by Butterfield, looking north across the chancel, and showing the polychrome decorations. The robust Middle Pointed tracery, fine ironwork, glowing colour, and high-level windows (necessary because of the confined urban site) should be noted (MC. G140590 [1990]).

V. Interior of the church of All Saints, All Saints Avenue, Boyne Hill, Maidenhead, Berkshire (1854-7), by G.E. Street. The style is Geometrical Middle Pointed, with structural polychromy of brick with stone dressings (including marble): the architectural treatment derived from Street's studies in Italy and Germany, especially in the chancel, where the walls are clad in bands of blue-black and white brick, buff and red tiles, and slabs of veined marbles and alabaster. Marble inlays and sculptures were by Thomas Earp, ironwork was by James Leaver, and glass by John Hardman. The Ecclesiologist *declared it was 'seldom more pleased' with any design than this* (MC. C080801 [2001]).

VI. Church of St Leonard, Beauchamp Almshouses, Newland, Worcestershire, designed by P.C. Hardwick in an early French Gothic style, and consecrated in 1864. The chancel, with piscina and sedilia, is exceptionally rich, and the entire ensemble is a fine example of Victorian polychrome ecclesiastical decoration carried out by the firm of Clayton & Bell, following a scheme devised by James Skinner (1818-81), first vicar of Newland, warden of the Beauchamp Community, and protégé of Dr. Pusey. Over the chancel-arch is the Last Judgement, with Christ in Majesty flanked by the Archangels Gabriel and Michael, with the Twelve Apostles throned. The east wall depicts the Resurrection and the Ascension, the reredos was carved by Boulton of Cheltenham (with colouring added in 1928), and the window is by John Hardman (MC. B110901 [2001]).

VII. Chancel of the church of St Mary, Studley Royal, West Riding of Yorkshire (1871-78). Burges's inventive genius is displayed. Wall dados are lined with alabaster, there is double-tracery to the windows, and the walls are decorated with carved and painted ornament. Sculpture was by Thomas Nicholls, stained glass was made by Saunders & Co., and the designers of the details were Frederick Weekes (1833-93) and Horatio Walter Lonsdale (1843-1919), all under Burges's direction. The chancel ceiling is decorated with Apostles, Prophets, and Martyrs in procession, and the gilded vault over the altar radiates glorious light (MC. F280901 [2001]).

VIII. Interior of the church of Christ the Consoler, Newby Hall, Skelton-on-Ure, West Riding of Yorkshire (1871-6), in a mixture of Continental First and Middle Pointed styles, designed by William Burges. On the left is the pulpit and the elaborate gallery for the organ. Above the chancel-arch is the sculptured Ascension by Thomas Nicholls. Nave, clearstorey, and aisles are enlivened with shafts of black Irish marble, and the glowing chancel has a low vault carried on short shafts of red, green, and black marbles. The low screen is of marble enlivened with porphyry, mosaics, and alabaster; the reredos is carved, with the Prophets in white alabaster; and the glorious east window tracery is in two distinct planes. The whole is a composition of jewel-like richness (MC. 828 0901 [2001]).

24. Liturgical apsidal east end and campanile *of the church of Sts Mary and Nicholas, Wilton, Wiltshire (1840-46), by T.H. Wyatt and D. Brandon. It is an essay in the* Rundbogenstil *with a pronounced Italianate flavour* (MC. C140901 [2001]).

and Romanesque round-arched styles of Italy: the German word *Rundbogenstil* is applied to all these 'round-arched' styles, many of which can be traced to a German enthusiasm for Italy, and the *Rundbogenstil* is related to Germanic precedents (notably in the works of Karl Friedrich Schinkel [1781-1841], Leo von Klenze [1784-1864], Ludwig Persius [1803-45], and Friedrich von Gärtner [1792-1847]), to the new interest in Italian non-Classical architecture found in the writings of Webb, Street, and others, and to the impact of the Italianate designs of Barry and his contemporaries.

A convincing exercise in the Italian basilican manner of the *Rundbogenstil*, with a tall *campanile*

attached to it by means of a miniature gallery with richly ornamented colonnettes, is the church of Sts Mary and Nicholas, Wilton, Wiltshire, of 1840-46 **(Plates 24 and 25)**, by Thomas Henry Wyatt and his partner David Brandon: this important (if startling) church was built for the Russian-born Catherine, Countess of Pembroke, and her son, the Rt Hon Sidney Herbert (1810-61), Secretary-at-War from 1852 under Lord Aberdeen during the Crimean campaigns, and later 1st Baron Herbert of Lea (1810-61 — an admirer and collector of mediæval Italian art). It was recognised as a building of quality in numerous journals, and even in the influential *Allgemeine Bauzeitung* of Vienna. It is pre-

25. Interior of the church of Sts Mary and Nicholas, Wilton, Wiltshire, showing the sumptuous apse (MC. A140901 [2001]).

26. Christ Church, Christchurch Road, Streatham Hill, London (1840-42), a basilica with campanile *in the* Rundbogenstil, *from the south-west. J.W. Wild, architect* (GB.EH. AA73/1492 [1964]).

dominantly Italian Romanesque in style, with the clear form of a basilica (that is, with clearstoreyed nave, lean-to aisles, and three apses at the east end, the basilican form clearly expressed at the west end). Sts Mary and Nicholas contains black columns from the Temple of Venus at Porto Venere (*c*. 2 BC) in the chancel-aisles, and several examples of Italian Romanesque Cosmati-work (fine inlaid twisted colonnettes) from the thirteenth-century Shrine of Capoccio that used to stand in the church of Santa Maria Maggiore in Rome. Many of the fittings and much of the stained glass are of considerable antiquity too, but there is insufficient space here in which to catalogue all the riches in this remarkable and beautiful church. The contemporary Christ Church, Streatham, London, of 1840-42, with its fine brick exterior and impressive *campanile*, by James William Wild (1814-92), is a clear re-working of the Early Christian Italian basilican type but influenced by German precedents: nevertheless, it is

stylistically eclectic, and contains Byzantine, Italianate, Egyptianising, Romanesque, Lombardic, Saracenic, Venetian, and other allusions. It is certainly among the most original and remarkable of all early-Victorian churches. Its polychrome interior has recently been renovated. **(Plates 26 and 27)**.

Henry Roberts (1803-76) designed the dull Romanesque church of St Mary at Elvetham Hall, Hampshire, in 1840-41, but the church of St Mary at Wreay, Cumberland, consecrated in 1842, is anything but dull: it is an extraordinary mixture of French and Italian elements with a liberal dose of Rhineland Romanesque, and has a strange and wonderful apse. The church was designed by the gifted Sara Losh (1785-1853) **(Plate 28)**, who was also responsible for the cross and primitivist mausoleum in the churchyard. Also in the round-arched style can be mentioned All Saints', Ennismore Gardens, London (1848-49), by Lewis Vulliamy — a pretty essay in Lombardic Romanesque; St John the Evangelist, Kensal Green (1844), by Henry Edward Kendall (1805-85) — a somewhat gritty Neo-Romanesque edifice of stock brick and flint, detested by Pevsner, who thought it 'atrocious', but it is not a bad building at all; and the very strange, even ungainly St Mildred's, Whippingham, Isle of Wight (1854-62), by Albert Jenkins Humbert

27. The newly renovated interior of Christ Church, Streatham Hill, London, showing the Byzantinesque detail of the basilican arrangement, and apsidal chancel based on Early Christian precedents, with fragments of surviving decorations by Owen Jones (1809-74), who also decorated the capitals (Martin Charles A160402 [2002]).

(1822-77) and Prince Albert — with Romanesque nave and transepts, Italian Romanesque Royal Pew, and First Pointed tower and chancel.

However, the Gothic Revival occupied at least the moral high ground, and the *Rundbogenstil* did not have the association with Christianity and morality the Goths had appropriated for their own cause, largely because of Pugin. Later in the century there were to be several distinguished buildings designed using *Rundbogenstil* variations: they will be illustrated and described later, for reasons that will become apparent.

28. Interior of the church of St Mary, Wreay, Cumberland (commenced 1842); an extraordinary Rundbogenstil *basilican church by Sarah Losh (1785-1853), daughter of John Losh (of an old Cumberland family), owner of the Walker Iron Works, Newcastle upon Tyne* (JSC [1988]).

CHAPTER V

The Search for the Ideal

Ruskin; The Anglican Crisis; All Saints Church, Margaret Street

It had long been a project of the Cambridge Camden Society to found a model church, which should realise in its design and internal arrangements a beau ideal of architectural beauty, and fulfil at the same time the requirements of orthodox ritual. Some years after the Society was transferred to London, an opportunity presented itself for the execution of this scheme.
CHARLES LOCKE EASTLAKE (1836-1906): *A History of the Gothic Revival*
(London: Longmans, Green, & Co., 1872), 251.

Ruskin

George Gilbert Scott recognised the influences of Pugin and of John Ruskin on English architecture. Both men, however, were bigots: Pugin was obsessionally anti-Protestant as only a convert can be; Ruskin was insanely anti-Papist; each equated architecture with moral worth; and both argued polemically, leaving out anything inconvenient to the promotion of their causes. In his *The Stones of Venice* (1851-53) Ruskin made an extraordinary attempt to dissociate Gothic architecture from Ritualism and 'Popery', and trumpeted against the attractions of Roman Catholicism. Of 'all the fatuities' he wrote, 'the basest' was being 'lured into the Romanist Church by the glitter of it, like larks into a trap by broken glass; to be blown into a change of religion by the whine of an organ-pipe; stitched into a new creed by gold threads on priests' petticoats; jangled into a change of conscience by the chimes of a belfry'. He went on to denounce the Roman Catholic Church for forsaking Gothic and turning to Renaissance architecture: 'Gothic was good for worship... it could frame a temple for the prayer of nations', but Renaissance architecture 'was full of insult to the poor'; the 'proud princes and lords rejoiced in it'; it 'would not roof itself with thatch or shingle and black oak beams'; 'it would not wall itself with rough stone or brick'; 'it would not pierce itself with small windows where they were

needed'; and it 'was good for man's worship'. 'Romanism', he went on, 'instead of being a promoter of the arts, has never shown itself capable of a single great conception since the separation of Protestantism from its side'. Now one of the effects of this sort of stuff was to remove prejudices against Gothic among Evangelical Anglicans and Nonconformists alike: Ruskin's polemical writings identified Romanism with Renaissance and (worse) Baroque architecture, and painted Gothic as fit to 'frame a temple for the prayer of nations, or shrink into the poor man's winding stair'. Ruskin's burning zeal for a Christian social order placed over the Gothic Revival a mantle of romantic democracy, and commended mediæval architecture to the artisan (who was more likely than not to be a Nonconformist).

Ruskin's name is associated with 'Ruskinian Gothic', a term connected with structural polychromy (colour in the materials used in a building, rather than applied to surfaces), naturalistic sculpture, and Italian Gothic. In his *Seven Lamps of Architecture* (1849) he demonstrated his concerns for ornament, surface, qualities of light, and colour, in all of which he detected human emotions, joys, and skills of the creative craftsman. He celebrated Continental Gothic, contrasting it with what he thought was the mean-spirited architecture of mediæval England,

and went as far as to say much English Gothic work was thin, wasted, and insubstantial, even in thirteenth-century examples. To him, Italian Gothic, colour, and pattern were infinitely superior, and his writings helped to contribute to a climate in which rich textures, strong modelling, and violent colouring were introduced to the English Gothic Revival in the mid-century. Now colour in Italian architecture often consisted of inlaid marbles set in smooth surfaces, and helps to explain much about the development of Victorian 'structural polychromy', and indeed about the pronounced Italian influences that were to enter Gothic Revival buildings from the 1850s, not least because of the *Rundbogenstil* movement that had developed in Germany.

Ruskin also advocated the use of colour in various courses of differently coloured stones, which he claimed was analogous to geological beds, and he argued against interrupting the purity of this horizontal-layered effect by means of vertical divisions such as shafts, colonnettes, or buttresses. However, Victorian experiments involving, for example, bands of limestone and contrasting bands of sandstone in wall-construction, to emulate the effects of, say, different colours of marble in Italian work, ended in disaster, for mixing limestones and sandstones brings about early and spectacular failure of the stone, with the result that buildings such as 'Great' Scott's enormous church of All Souls, Haley Hill, Halifax, Yorkshire, have visibly eroded.

It seems extraordinary that a visitor to Venice could virtually ignore the glories of Renaissance architecture there, but this is what Ruskin did, as he concentrated on mediæval work. Even Classical elements, such as triglyphs, were declared by Ruskin to be ugly because they were not based on any natural organic form, whilst he denounced geometrical fret ornaments because the type was only found in crystals in bismuth (a reddish-white brittle metal, with a low melting-point, sometimes occurring as a mineral in crystals). He then declared of Venetian billet-decoration that 'nothing could be ever invented fitter for its purpose', but to detect natural forms

in billet-mouldings and unnatural ones in geometrical fret indicates an outrageous bias at best, and odd thought-processes at worst. In short, Ruskin's claims that ornaments deriving from plants and carved by morally superior artisans were better than the hated Classical ornament simply will not stand up to serious examination, while his double standards in denouncing Greek triglyphs yet praising Venetian billets as 'fit for their purpose' are glaringly obvious. How he got away with that sort of thing defies analysis, but architectural theories are not reckoned by their content: they are judged by their influence (much of it baleful). Nevertheless, Ruskin and Venetian Gothic became inextricably linked, and his name was involved as the begetter of a type of polychrome Victorian Gothic loosely based on eclectic motifs that originated in Italy. Ruskin was the *populiser* of a tendency that was already present in Ecclesiological circles in the 1840s, and which had been encouraged by Benjamin Webb, by *The Ecclesiologist*, and by G.E. Street.

The last architect argued for massiveness, powerful contours, depth of recesses, freedom in distributing openings in a façade (concentrating windows in some areas, and leaving other parts of walls blank), and the use of structural colour. He also seemed to favour a rugged toughness, even in matters such as tracery, and in this and in other respects his approach is similar to that of Ruskin, although the pseudo-morality and humbug about 'organic' ornament, mercifully, are absent. Street argued for the development of Gothic, and for borrowing from the mediæval buildings of many European countries. What is more, he supported Pugin's concepts of the 'true Picturesque' (where the elevations, forms, and silhouettes of buildings grew naturally from the plans), but he purged the arguments of symbolism, moralising, and irrational polemics. Street was to publish his *Brick and Marble in the Middle Ages: Notes of a Tour in the North of Italy* in 1855, in which his arguments were encapsulated. The combination of the popular writings of Ruskin, the advocacy by The Ecclesiologists of brick and polychromy, and the widely-travelled and scholarly Street's suggestions of casting the net ever wider for sources of Gothic Revival architecture was irresistible: so-called 'High Victorian' Gothic architecture was born, and dominated the Revival until the 1870s. However 'High Victorian' is not a label that is entirely satisfactory (it poses a question as to what is 'Low Victorian'), so dates, or 'mid-Victorian' will be used to describe it instead: Gothic Revival of the 1850s and 1860s is perhaps an even better way of describing it, but 'mid-Victorian' will have to do.

The Anglican Crisis

The Ecclesiological Society's campaign to restore the beauty of liturgical practice in appropriate settings, aided by such works as *Hierurgia Anglicana*, was greatly helped by numerous clerics who began to rise to positions of eminence within the Anglican Church. William Maskell (*c*.1814-90), Oxford-educated High Churchman and mediævalist, contributed to Anglican liturgical studies with his important *The Ancient Liturgy of the Church of England, according to the uses of Sarum, York, Hereford, and Bangor, and the Roman Liturgy arranged in parallel columns, with Preface and Notes*, which came out in 1844, followed by *Monumenta ritualia ecclesiæ Anglicanæ; or, Occasional offices of the Church of England according to the ancient use of Salisbury* (1846-7). Maskell's works gave impetus to the revival of Anglican ceremonial based on mediæval precedents, but, perhaps even more importantly, helped the evolution of what became known as *Ritualism*, in which the Eucharist was to be placed once again at the centre of Anglican worship.

Thus Ritualism was not an empty ceremony, with fancy theatrical goings-on for reasons only of show. As the history of Anglicanism demonstrates, most Ritualist clergymen worked in poor working-class parishes, and per-ceived ritual as a means by which ignorant congregations could be taught. Ranting about Sacramental Doctrine was regarded as counter-productive: what was needed was the beauty of ceremonial, properly done, in order to *show* the proletariat what was the essence. Reverence, beauty, mystery, and devotion could inspire respect (earnest nagging had the opposite effect), and there is no doubt that poor parishes derived

great benefit from Ritualist clergymen who not only taught, but set examples, and, by acts of charity and educating the young, brought civilisation to parts of poor urban areas where otherwise life would have been grim in the extreme. There is also some evidence that such clergymen found the ground where they toiled not unreceptive to their brand of Churchmanship, for some Catholic feeling seems to have survived in certain areas, notably in relation to hatred of Utilitarianism, the Poor Laws, and the burial of the dead.

Some Ritualists based their arguments for ceremonial partly on the Ornaments Rubric of the *Book of Common Prayer*: this had been placed at the beginning of the Order for Morning and Evening Prayer in 1549, was confirmed by Parliament in 1604, and retained in the 1662 *Prayer Book*. It declared that chancels should remain as they had been, and that ornaments of the church 'and of the ministers... at all times of their ministration' should be retained and used as they were authorised by Parliament in the second year of the reign of King Edward VI. Others, however, felt that the Rubric was out of date, and could not really provide a sound basis for Ritualism in the nineteenth century. Better arguments had to be called upon, and scholarly investigations led to innovation.

Then *The Directorium Anglicanum; being a manual of Directions for the Right Celebration of the Holy Communion, for the saying of Matins and Evensong, and for the Performance of other Rites and Ceremonies of the Church according to the Ancient Uses of the Church of England. With Plan of Chancel and Illustrations*, edited by John Purchas (1823-72), came out in 1858. Purporting to use the Orna-ments Rubric as its source, it remained a key work for Anglican ceremonial until around 1914, but, as Father Symondson has pointed out, it owed far more to the *Pontificale Romanum* (1664 edition) and to the *Ceremonio della Basilica Vaticana* by Giuseppe Baldeschi (1791-1849), in the translation (1839) by John Duncan Hilarius Dale (*fl*. 1835-50), than it did to Anglican custom, legality, or his-tory. Thus its arguments depended largely on Roman Catholicism of the *post-Reformation period*, although this was obscured, yet Purchas's tome helped to promote a strand of Ritualism within the Church of England that drew its inspiration from Western (Northern) European Roman Catholicism. Some clergymen, perhaps uncomfortably aware of the shaky claims in much of Purchas's work, tended to endeavour to promote ideas of continuity of worship with the *pre-Reformation pre-Tridentine Church*, the Caroline Church, and the Church of England *from* the Reformation. They also tended to stick to authorised approved forms of worship, introducing Catholic elements where they thought they were appropriate. However, no matter from which stream it derived, Ritualism had a considerable effect on the design of late-Victorian churches, as will be seen.

The Ecclesiological Society became a national body with Beresford Hope as its President in 1845, a year of crisis for the Church of England. As has been outlined above, Newman, alienated by Evangelical reaction to *Tract XC*, feeling very deeply the devastating attack on his arguments by Roman Catholic divines, and horrified by Evangelical collusion with Prussia to establish an Anglican Bishopric in Jerusalem (an event that rocked both the Church and international relations), had gone over to Rome in that year.

Under Frederick Oakeley, a proprietary chapel in London's Margaret Street had become a centre for Tractarian worship, and Oakeley was supported in his endeavours by Beresford Hope. The *Tract XC* ructions and the controversy over the Jerusalem affair led Oakeley to follow Newman to Rome, and the Evangelicals were confirmed in their worst fears: Ecclesiology and Ritualism led to Rome, crypto-Papist mischief lurked in every Gothic niche, and heresy peeped from behind every *Ecclesiologist*-approved clustered pier. More was to come: in 1847 George Cornelius Gorham (1787-1857) was presented to the Living of Brampford Speke, near Exeter, but the Bishop (Henry Phillpotts [1778-1869] — whose liturgical opinions had been influenced by his chaplain [from 1847], William Maskell) objected to Gorham's strongly Calvinistic views, and refused to institute him. Gorham took his case to the ecclesiastical Court of Arches, but in 1849 that Court judged in favour of the Bishop, so

Gorham appealed to the Judicial Committee of the Privy Council, which reversed the judgement, ruling in favour of Gorham, in 1850, who was duly instituted into the vicarage in 1851, despite all other and subsequent attempts by Phillpotts to prevent it. Thus the State (once again) was seen to have power to over-rule the authority of the Church in matters of doctrine, and many more Tractarian-minded clergy went over to Rome, while some Anglican Evangelicals also left the Church to become Dissenters.

A Church in crisis requires drastic solutions. William Upton Richards (1811-73), who succeeded Oakeley in 1847, was a member of The Ecclesiological Society, and determined to build a more appropriate setting for Tractarian-inspired devotions as an act of faith. This coincided with the evolution of an idea within The Ecclesiological Society to build a model, exemplary church, for, as the architectural criticisms in *The Ecclesiologist* demonstrated, many new churches were found wanting, and the Society (like contemporary philanthropic housing-societies, such as the Society for Improving the Condition of the Labouring Classes) decided that the provision of an exemplar was the way forward, because architect-bashing in the Press was all very well, but did not invariably improve matters in respect of church-design.

Significantly, the Ecclesiologists narrowed the possibilities of choice in such a venture. Gothic, in the flood of creative invention, it was held, reached its apogee in the Second Pointed work of the early fourteenth century, so that was the style plumped-for, because it united the best elements of Gothic, and was the common architectural language of the most cultivated nations of Europe (this was also Pugin's belief). The theory of the Ecclesiologists was that, once architects had fully studied and absorbed the Second Pointed style, and had become adept at using it in their designs, a newer and finer Gothic would emerge, appropriate to the nineteenth century, and quite unlike the hated and 'decadent' English Perpendicular. Of course the 'decadent' argument about Perpendicular was strongly influenced by Pugin, who associated the style with the Reformation, with the Break with

Rome, with the start of the Renaissance period, and with a decline in religious observance. However, we know that late-Gothic English mediæval churches often demonstrate that the country was anything but irreligious, and indeed that early sixteenth-century devotion to the churches and to religious observances was impressive, so the Puginian-Ecclesiologist arguments are false, and cannot be sustained by fact. Besides, the unbiased student of English mediæval architecture must conclude that English Perpendicular Gothic, unlike anything else in Europe, was not 'decadent' at all, and indeed was probably the greatest, most original, and most beautiful architectural style to emanate from England at any time: a study of fan-vaults and Devon chancel-screens should be enough to prove the point.

Ecclesiologists wanted to put church-design and -building on sound bases. The trouble with the 'archæological' or 'copy-book' approach to design in the tentative early phases of the Victorian Gothic Revival was that architectural works were far too often timid re-hashes of bits of 'approved' buildings, lacking vitality or invention (and not always felicitously put together). Another problem was that stone (especially the ubiquitous Kentish ragstone) was often used in the heavily polluted cities (notably London), so many new churches (even including R.C. Carpenter's church of St Mary Magdalene, Munster Square, London, of 1849-52) looked like scrambled pieces of church architecture from rural England placed in contexts where they weathered badly and looked inappropriate. As has been mentioned above, however, Ferrey's church of St Stephen, Rochester Row (although it had a Bargate ragstone exterior), had a Second Pointed interior approved of by *The Ecclesiologist*: contemporary illustrations (e.g. **Plate 23**) show a hard, sharp interior, like a machine-made artefact, that bore little resemblance to a real mediæval church. An appropriate image for a modern church had been found, and it should be remembered that the power of a picture in architectural circles counts for far more than words.

In the 1840s, the Tractarians, determined to convert a sometimes hostile or even indifferent urban proletariat to a high-minded Anglicanism for the good of Society as a whole, and perceiving that the image of a rural church was not suitable for this purpose, decided to encourage the building of fortresses of faith, strong and tough — 'urban minsters' — with high, hard-surfaced walls, coloured bands of stone and brick, big windows and high clearstoreys out of the reach of vandals and above the surrounding buildings, towers set back from the street (but with clearly defined stages), and large chancels. This concept derives from the precedent of the slum-mission, mingled with ideas culled from the writings of Ruskin, Street, and Pugin, and was to present grand and awe-inspiring services, processions, and dignified ritual to attract the urban poor. Indeed, as alluded to above, there is evidence that the urban proletariat, while indifferent to (and contemptuous of) Evangelical Christianity, still possessed some latent feelings

29. Exterior of the church of St Peter, Kirkgate, Leeds, Yorkshire (1839-41), by R. D. Chantrell. It is a scholarly mixture of Perpendicular (Third Pointed) and Decorated (Second Pointed) styles (EH. AA76/757 [1880]).

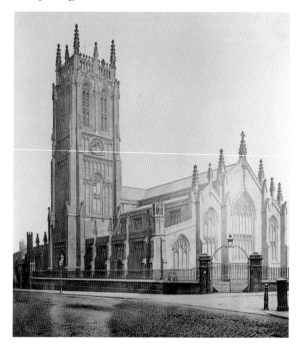

30. Interior of the church of St Peter, Kirkgate, Leeds, showing the chancel and the galleries. The reredos was added by Street in 1872 (EH. AA85/157 [1880]).

and instincts that could be traced back to the popular religion of pre-Reformation England.

A potent model for the notion of an urban minster, bringing religion, education, and civility to the poor, could be found in the work of Walter Farquhar Hook (1798-1875), Vicar of Leeds from 1837 until 1859. Hook was a High Churchman, who introduced Tractarian principles into his parish with considerable success, but was bitterly opposed in his efforts there by Low Church Evangelicals. His was the guiding spirit behind the rebuilding of the parish-church of St Peter, Kirkgate, Leeds (1839-41): the building was a serious, learned mixture of Decorated (Second Pointed) and Perpendicular styles of Gothic **(Plates 29 and 30)**, and was

erected to designs by Robert Dennis Chantrell (1793-1872). Beresford Hope envisaged for London some great urban minster, with schools, mechanics' institute, clergy-house, and church, which, like the example described in Kingsley's *Alton Locke*, would be an edifying sight for urban Man.

Meanwhile, a figure highly influential in matters of taste lived beside the highest in the land. In the 1840s Albert Francis Charles Augustus Emmanuel, Prince Consort (1819-61), taking as his cue the work of the German 'Nazarenes' (the ideals of which were introduced to English art by William Dyce [1806-64]), and advised by Professor Ludwig Grüner (1801-82) of Dresden, did much to promote the use of colour in architecture, spurred on by his appreciation of Italian art and architecture, and especially of the Italian-influenced *Rundbogenstil* imported from Germany: colour was to be used by arranging naturally coloured materials in carefully contrived layers and patterns, and by reviving Italian techniques of fresco-painting.

So the climate had been established for transforming Richards's Margaret Street chapel. Gradually, various threads drew together: the chapel was to be rebuilt on Tractarian lines; the Ecclesiologists wanted to create an exemplary urban minster; and there was a general High Church desire to express confidence in the future of Anglicanism after all the defections to, and challenges from, Rome.

All Saints Church, Margaret Street

William Butterfield had made himself known in Ecclesiological circles as early as 1842, and by 1843 was superintending the design of ecclesiastical furnishings: very shortly he was established as an arbiter of taste regarding church-fittings, from plate to pulpits. Publication of his work began with *Instrumenta Ecclesiastica* in 1844 (the year in which he was elected a member of The Camden Society, as it was then) and continued until 1847. Through Beresford Hope he was appointed architect for the rebuilding of St Augustine's College in Canterbury, and by 1849 had designed the Tractarian College at Millport, Greater Cumbrae (the Cathedral of the Isles) for George Frederick Boyle (1825-90), later (1869) 6th Earl of Glasgow. In that year he was chosen as architect for the model church of The Ecclesiological Society, for which Beresford Hope not only provided funds, but many ideas.

Several priests were to live communally on the site to keep up the daily requirements of Tractarian observance, whilst the musical tradition already established in the chapel was to be maintained, and given an appropriate setting. Thus a clergy-house and a choir-school were to share the cramped, almost square site with the church itself. In 1849 the area in which All Saints was to be built consisted of dingy houses and shops: the urban minster would provide Tractarian services and a ministry, and

moveable seats instead of pews were to be provided, thus destroying the undesirable social divisions of rented pews that had done something to alienate the urban working classes.

All Saints, designed and built 1849-59, was one of the first major Victorian buildings in which constructional colour was used, and it marks the beginning of a powerful, robust phase of the Gothic Revival. It is an experiment in encrustation with a skin of brick and tile, rather than full, deep, true structural polychromy, but it provided an admirable exemplar of permanent colour in the facing materials, and flags the start

31. Exterior of the church of All Saints, Margaret Street, Westminster, London (1849-59), by William Butterfield, showing the decorative brickwork, the tower and broach-spire rising from the site, and the clergy-house and school on either side of the entrance court. Here was an urban citadel of faith (MC. A090979 [1979]).

of Butterfield's polychrome style. Mindful of the incongruous and shabby appearance of ragstone in the urban setting, Butterfield chose red brick with bands, voussoirs, and diaper-work of black brick, with Bath stone dressings, for the exterior. Lead and slate were used for the broach-spire and the roof. The permanent colour may also have had a religious as well as a practical reason for its adoption: in 1830-33 Charles Lyell (1799-1875) had published his *Principles of Geology* which severely dented belief in the literal meaning of *Genesis*, so the layering effect of the polychrome may have been partly a re-assertion of the divine elements in English clays and rocks as a *riposte* to Lyell's work (a notion not entirely innocent of Ruskin's not altogether wholesome influence).

Butterfield placed the church on the northern part of the site, with the choir-school, masters' rooms, and library in the south-west corner, and the clergy-house in the south-east, both buildings joined to the church and providing a frame to the small court that is approached through an arched gateway from the street. This court, set over the common basement, is almost claustrophobic, and the effect of verticality (enhanced by the deliberately over-sized buttress and pinnacle on the south face of the aisle beside the gabled porch to the church) is stupendous. High, banded, and diapered walls, the steeply-pitched roofs, the tough tracery of the church windows, the chunky sash-window frames of the school and house, and the soaring banded broach-spire enter the language of the Sublime **(Plate 31)**. Here is no feeble *pot-pourri* timidly garnered from mediæval rural churches, but a powerful, vital, tough urban design, brilliantly conceived for its position. The tightness of the site dictated a solution where the ingenious planning was also dependent upon a free type of fenestration: here was Pugin's 'True Picturesque' of his Bishop's Palace at Birmingham of 1839-41 developed to new heights of inventive virtuosity. Here was a modern church to satisfy the demands of the revived Anglican ritual as well as the aims of architectural excellence: it was a true citadel of faith, much influenced by Continental Gothic precedents.

Yet what styles can be found at All Saints?

Certainly there is Middle Pointed work in the tracery of the church-windows, the belfry-stage of the tower, and the tall, pinnacled buttress (cunningly placed to draw the eye to the entrance which is approached diagonally across the court), but diaper-patterns in brickwork were associated with Perpendicular or Tudor work, and the tower and the spire would not be out of place in Lübeck or other cities in Northern Germany. The chancel roof, rising higher than that of the nave, is also German in origin. At the west end there are even echoes of Monza Cathedral. So there are English, Italian, and *Backsteingotik* precedents in the composition as well, but the design as a whole was startlingly new: Butterfield created a *perception* of the past and invented a new and vital synthesis of styles, mixing them with great originality. George L. Hersey (in his *High Victorian Gothic*) has likened the arrival of All Saints in the context of the muted tones of early-Victorian London to that of a 'Congo chieftain' appearing in a performance of *Les Sylphides*, and there is nothing from which to dissent in his comparison.

If the massing, colour, composition, and detail of the exterior are arresting, the interior is even more so. The difficult site freed Butterfield to illuminate the church by means of high clearstorey windows to the three-bay nave and the chancel: the only other windows were the high five-light window; the smaller three-light windows illuminating the baptistry, the west, and east of the north aisle; and the traceried windows in the south aisle. The Tractarian arrangement is apparent: the deep, wide, high chancel with raised floor creates a visual climax at the east end, emphasising the importance of the altar **(Colour Plate III)**. Although the square-ended chancel is of the English type, the stepped arrangement up to the gradine is German, while the vaulted ceiling recalls the church of San Francesco in Assisi. English brick mediæval churches are rare, so some of Butterfield's structural polychromy derives from Germany, but the interiors owe more to Italy (the circular motifs of the nave arcades are suggested by Venetian prototypes), so he achieved a stylistic mix in which southern and northern European Gothic precedents played their parts. Controlled polychrome patterns of strict geometrical shapes are created using granite, marbles, bricks (glazed and unglazed), tiles, and stone dressings with coloured mastic inlay. The piers of the nave-arcades have shafts of polished red Peterhead granite set on black-marble bases, and with vigorously-carved alabaster capitals; the moulded arches are developed Second Pointed; and the spandrels are decorated with rich patterns of coloured bricks, tiles, and other materials.

From the very moment when its patterned walls first rose, All Saints (as Paul Thompson has noted) has been recognised as a building of exceptional originality and significance. Street said of it that of all the new churches it was 'the most beautiful, vigorous, thoughtful, and original', and Henry Heathcote Statham (1839-1924) identified it in 1912 as 'the one Gothic revival church which is still as interesting... as when it was built' **(Colour Plate IV)**. The British Almanac declared the interior of All Saints to be 'beyond question.. the most gorgeous... in the kingdom'. Colour and æsthetic effects (some critics detected therein the 'Pagan art-harlot' with painted 'bold cheek') were contrived to arise from 'construction' rather than from 'superaddition', and thus differ from Pugin's work at St Giles's, Cheadle, where the decorations are painted on plaster, although some of the motifs are not unlike each other. Whilst Webb and Ruskin probably were catalysts towards the decision to apply theories of polychromy to practical use, the actual source for the essential elements of the patterns on the internal walls was very likely Specimens of the Geometrical Mosaics of the Middle Ages of 1849 by Matthew Digby Wyatt (1820-77). William Dyce himself painted the reredos and chancel, considered by Beresford Hope to be 'no whit inferior to the vault of St. Jacques at Liège, or Sta. Anastasia at Verona'.

However, All Saints was to spawn its imitators, notably the 'Rogue Goths' (see the next Chapter), who showed off too much for some tastes, and were so given to restless 'Go' that they were censured by their peers. 'Great' Scott was none to happy with some of these developments,

for in his Personal and Professional Recollections (1879) he complained of 'no end to the oddities... Ruskinism, such as would make Ruskin's very hair stand on end; Butterfieldism, gone mad with its endless stripings of red and black bricks; architecture so French that a Frenchman would not know it, out-Heroding Herod himself;... "original" varieties founded upon... ignorance...; violent strainings after a something very strange, and great successes in producing something very weak; attempts at beauty resulting in ugliness, and attempts at ugliness attended with unhoped-for success. All these have given a wild absurdity to much of the architecture of the last seven or eight years' (i.e. c.1864-72).

However, all that lay in the future, but there can be no question of Butterfield's impact with his great church. Contemporary opinion found nothing effeminate or luxurious in All Saints: on the contrary, it was full of virility, and an admirable contrast to Pugin's 'weak patternings'. To The Ecclesiologist All Saints had affinities with Pre-Raphaelite paintings, and the startling use of colour was seen to parallel the exploitation of certain violent tones in the work of John Everett Millais (1829-96). The overall effect, however, was austere, manly, and even Sublime. Some critics saw the complex as an endeavour to 'shake off the trammels of antiquarian precedent, which had long fettered the progress of the Revival', but others perceived the 'speckled and spotted' patterns as having connotations with nursery toys, and even as having undertones of cruelty, abrasiveness, coarseness, and sensationalism. One or two have suggested Butterfield was colour-blind. Much has been written about his alleged hatred of beauty, his deliberate cultivation of the 'ugly', his 'holy zebra' or 'stripey bacon' style of Gothic, his use of the 'discordant', his 'ruthless-ness', and his 'assaults' on the senses. Much of this, including speculations that Butterfield was uneducated, untravelled, and puritanical, is nonsense, as is the suggestion that his work was, somehow, sadomasochistic. His All Saints is a brilliant piece of three-dimensional design, with assured and complex massing on a difficult site; it demonstrates the practical use of materials (which have worn well) appropriate for the

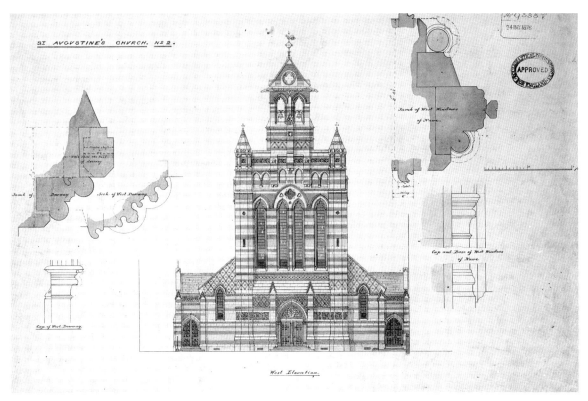

32. *Butterfield's drawing of the west front of St Augustine's, Queen's Gate, Kensington, London (1870-77), as approved by the Ecclesiastical Commissioners for England. It has the stripey structural polychromy so characteristic of Butterfield's work, and there is a double bell-cote over the composition* (V & A. D.59-1908).

sooty atmosphere of a Victorian city; the interior decorations were, to a large extent, permanent, and are extremely rich and colourful; it was the exemplary Ecclesiological building; and its inventive architecture was based on a rich historical set of precedents, yet it could not be confused with a mediæval church or damned as a mere copy of an *Echt*-Gothic structure. Indeed, All Saints was an intensely modern building when it was conceived, especially for its planning, fenestration, exposed brickwork, and remarkable polychrome decorations. Sensible materials, used with imagination, an ingenious plan, and a scholarly yet inventive approach to design, based on a sound understanding of precedents from many countries and periods, combine in one of the Victorian period's greatest works of architecture. Its influence was to be considerable, as Thomas James was to note in his 'On the Use of Brick

in Ecclesiastical Architecture' in *The Ecclesiologist* of 1861, and G.E. Street was to recognise. The building showed that the Gothic Revival could be freed from the slavish copying of precedents. Its influence spurred designers on to new things even before it was completed: All Saints' was the Tractarian begetter of hosts of polychrome churches, and the finest memorial to the Oxford Movement, glowing, noble, and assured.

Butterfield was a prolific architect, who was rarely dull in his designs. Space precludes a full list of his buildings, but important ecclesiastical buildings by him include Balliol College chapel, Oxford (1854-57); St Matthias, Stoke Newington, London (1849-53) — Butterfield's first completed London church, which demonstrates his control of structural massing and composition; St Alban's, Holborn, London (1859-62 — destroyed) — which had 'originality not only in the form but

33. Chapel of Rugby School, Warwickshire (1870-72), by Butterfield: the structural polychromy is spectacular, the massing is assured, and the style is mostly Second Pointed (except for the Perpendicular window in the apse) (JSC [1988]).

in the relative proportion of parts', as Eastlake put it — and in which much structural polychromy, diaper-work, and other stridently colourful effects were employed; All Saints, St Alban's Road, Babbacombe, Devon (1865-74) — 'one of Butterfield's most important churches, and especially in its interiors extremely characteristic of this most wilful of' High Church architects, as Pevsner noted; Keble College chapel, Oxford (1867-83) — an astounding *tour-de-force* of strident angularity, chequered, lozenge, and stripey polychromy, and massive, vertical, thrusting, over-sized buttresses, the whole described by Goodhart-Rendel as 'possibly one of the three or four buildings in Oxford of most architectural importance', which is high praise indeed; St Augustine's, Queen's Gate, Kensington, London (1870-77) — a tall, violently polychrome build-ing, with double bell-cote at the west end, reminiscent of a mixture of North German and French Gothic **(Plate 32)**; and the chapel of Rugby School, Warwickshire (1870-72) — one of Butterfield's most assured compositions (the climax of which is the massive tower with octagonal belfry-stage and huge gargoyles), which Pevsner described as 'amazingly resourceful' with 'pronounced' polychromy **(Plate 33)**. Indeed, at Keble College and at Rugby School the polychromy is spectacular, and the scale is tremendous, overwhelming, Sublime. Butterfield continued to use vivid, harsh polychromy after the 1860s, when it was going out of favour with the younger generation of architects. And it has to be said that All Saints, Margaret Street, was already slightly old-fashioned when it was completed, for the Revival had moved on, and different emphases evolved.

CHAPTER VI

Mid-Victorian Church Architecture

Viollet-le-Duc; Some Works by George Edmund Street; Other Mid-Victorian Churches;
Rogue Goths; William Burges and John Loughborough Pearson

In 1850 and 1860... the list of English architects who devoted themselves more specially to the building and
restoration of churches was largely increased. Messrs. E. Christian, J. Clarke,
S.S. Teulon, and J.H. Hakewill, were among those who followed, with more or less tendency to individual
peculiarities, in the footsteps of Mr Scott; while a certain number of younger men, including Messrs G.E.
Street, H. Woodyer, W. White, and G.F. Bodley, showed an early inclination to strike out in a new line for
themselves.
CHARLES LOCKE EASTLAKE (1836-1906): *A History of the Gothic Revival*
(London: Longmans, Green, & Co., 1872), 289.

Viollet-le-Duc

Eugène-Emmanuel Viollet-le-Duc (1814-79) became a convinced Goth in the 1830s, and in 1854 the first volume of his important *Dictionnaire Raisonné de l'Architecture Française du XVe au XVIe Siècle* (1854-68) was published, from which date the French architect became an important arbiter of the Gothic Revival, and in particular championed the architecture of mediæval France, as well as the importance of structure, purpose, dynamics, techniques, and the visible expression of these. His rationalist beliefs were enshrined in his *Entretiens sur l'Architecture* (1863-72), and it is clear that the illustrations in his works had a profound influence on English architects: it has long been the case that architects copy from pictures, images, and design-motifs, without necessarily reading the explanatory matter, and it was through Viollet-le-Duc's fine illustrations that a taste for French Gothic (and especially early French Gothic) began to supersede previous liking for early Middle Pointed and a current interest in polychrome Italian Gothic. William Burges (1827-81) admitted the importance of Viollet-le-Duc, and said 'we all crib from Viollet-le-Duc...., although probably not one buyer in ten ever reads the text'.

Some Works by George Edmund Street

As early as 1852 George Edmund Street was promoting his 'True Principles of Pointed Architecture', and arguing for development, drawing on a wider geographical area than that favoured by Pugin. In his *Brick and Marble in the Middle Ages* (1855), Street argued for rationalisation, and drew attention to a wide range of Continental precedents. Reaction to the strong polychrome and æsthetic of 'Ruskinian Gothic' set in with the 1860s, and the models for a purer, more real, robust, primitive, and essential Gothic began to be identified as early French buildings. The monochrome, tough, even rough early French Gothic seemed to offer architects a new ideal. Stern French exemplars, such as those of Laon Cathedral, or the massive early-Gothic churches of Burgundy, seemed more vigorous, less effete, than the luxuriant Second Pointed so beloved by the Ecclesiologists. Tough French First Pointed (with its massiveness, grandeur of scale, and complete lack of frivolous frippery) was seen as more appropriate to the needs of designers of urban citadels of faith in the towns of the 1860s, for it was bold, broad, strong, stern, masculine, and uncompromisingly robust. The so-called 'muscular' phase of the Gothic Revival had arrived.

There is little doubt that one of the most distinguished architects of the Gothic Revival was G. E. Street, an inventive designer whose work was rarely dull, and sometimes rose to greatness. One of his happiest compositions, an early village church of stone, is St Mary the Virgin, Wheatley, Oxfordshire, designed in 1855 in the English First Pointed style, with varied groups of lancets, sparing use of plate trac-

34. Church of St Mary the Virgin, Wheatley, Oxfordshire (1855-68), by G.E. Street. It is in the English First Pointed style, has no clearstorey, and its nave, chancel and aisles are separately roofed and gabled. The powerful belfry-steeple consists of an octagonal spire set on four steeply-pitched gabled elements each containing openings of elementary plate tracery. There are four steeply-pitched gabled lucarnes on the oblique planes of the spire. Beautifully detailed and confidently composed, the design owes something to Street's earlier church of St Mary the Virgin, Par, Cornwall (1846-8), also an exercise in bold juxtaposition of solid geometrical forms (GB. 125/69. EH. BB86/7031 [1969]).

ery, and powerful steeple-belfry, completed in 1868 **(Plate 34)**.

Butterfield was to continue with his startling use of structural colour (his 'streaky-bacon' style) throughout his career (although many of his interiors, alas! have been tamed by means of plentiful applications of white paint), but in Street's works of the 1850s and 1860s a massiveness combined with deceptive simplicity can be found, and from the mid-1850s Street used bold constructional polychromy, notably in his churches of All Saints, Boyne Hill, Maidenhead, Berkshire (1854-5) **(Colour Plate V)**, St James-the-Less, Westminster (1859-61) **(Plate 36)**, Sts Philip and James, North Oxford (1860-66) **(Plate 35)**, St George, Oakengates, Shropshire (1861-3) **(Plate**

35. Exterior of the church of Sts Philip and James, North Oxford (1860-66), by G.E. Street. It is an essay in thirteenth-century First Pointed Gothic, with a pronounced Burgundian influence. Note the French-inspired apse, with plate-tracery, and the massive crossing-tower with broach-spire and huge lucarnes. From Eastlake (JSC [1872]).

36. *Interior of the church of St James-the-Less, Westminster (1859-61), by G.E. Street, showing the polychrome brickwork, apsidal chancel, and massive piers. The rasping, harsh effects of the edges of the arcades should be noted* (EH. BB88/4066 [1967]).

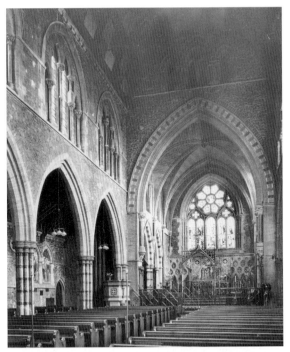

37.   Interior of the church of St George, Oakengates, Shropshire, by G.E. Street, of 1861-3, one of his most accomplished early works. Note the inventive plate-tracery, the robust arcades (with structural polychromy), and tunnel-vaulted chancel with closely-set chamfered transverse arches (GB. 161/69. EH. AA80/195 [1969]).

38.   Interior of the church of St John the Evangelist, Montpellier Road, Torquay, Devon (1861-85), by Street, showing the nave with clustered piers, stone-vaulted chancel, and east window with Geometrical tracery. The church was completed by A.E. Street, and contains much fine glass by Morris & Co and Clayton & Bell (EH. B43/1434 [1943]).

37), and St John the Evangelist, Torquay, Devon (1861-85) **(Plate 38)**.

At Boyne Hill, Street's polychrome master-piece forms the nucleus of a remarkable group of parochial buildings comprising a Picturesque composition of 1854-65, and reflects his studies in Germany and Italy. The superb interior of the church glows with rich structural colour **(Colour Plate V)**, and the roof is painted. Glass by John Hardman (1812-67), marble inlay and sculpture by Thomas Earp (1828-98), and ironwork by James Leaver complete the exotic ensemble. Both St James-the-Less and Sts Philip and James have Continental-inspired apsidal chancels, and have a massiveness, solidity, and toughness not present in Butterfield's designs. For instance, Street's monolithic circular piers are quite unlike the clustered shafts in All Saints', Margaret Street,

and he favoured the earlier, primitive plate-tracery to the more developed bar-tracery so beloved by Pugin and Scott. The Westminster church has a powerful polychrome brick interior, with the notched brick of the arches suggesting a rasping, almost ferocious, saw-like power **(Plate 36)**, but at Oxford the influence of thirteenth-century First Pointed Burgundian prototypes is pronounced, notably in the belfry-stage of the powerful tower, in the massive, over-sized lucarnes on the broach-spire, in the plate-tracery of the apsidal chancel, and in the severe lancets **(Plate 35)**. Both churches have huge, vigorously-carved capitals to the piers. At St John's, Montpellier Road, Torquay, the chancel has a square end, a large Geometrical-traceried east window, and a pronounced First Pointed flavour (not least in the plate-tracery of the clearstorey) in the rest of its parts. The tower of St John's is unusual, with its saddleback roof and wheel-tracery in the gables, but the chief interest of the church is in its dramatic situation high above the harbour, and in the uncommonly rich furnishings (including a reredos by Earp; ironwork by Street himself; candlesticks, font-cover, and lectern by Street's son, Arthur Edmund [1855-1938]; and stained glass by Morris & Co. and Clayton & Bell). Here Street eschewed his massive primitive monolithic piers, and used clustered shafts of polished Devon marble, with bands of differently-coloured marble. The chancel is stone-vaulted. Much less massive in treatment (although the church is large), but with pronounced vertical

39. Exterior of the handsome church of St Mary Magdalene, Rowington Close, Paddington, London (1867-73), by Street. The style is First Pointed, and the church was the first centre for High Anglicanism in Paddington, having been built for the Rev Dr Richard Temple West (d.1893), who had been a curate at All Saints, Margaret Street. Note the structural polychromy of the belfry-stage of the tower (EH. BB56/ 2256 [1874]).

elements, was Street's design for the church of St Mary Magdalene, Paddington, London (1867-73): the style is First Pointed, the chancel is poly-gonal, and the stone spire rises directly from a polygonal striped belfry-stage over the tower **(Plates 39 and 40)**. In all these churches Street displayed his mastery of form, his sureness of touch in placing elements together, and his apparently effortless drawing on scholarship for his themes.

Other Mid-Victorian Churches

The 1860s were rarely dull when it came to church-design, and colour was certainly well to the fore. An unexpectedly rich interior can be found in the church of St Leonard, part of the Beauchamp Almshouses, at Newland, Worcester-shire (1862-64), by Philip Charles Hardwick (1822-

40. Interior of the church of St Mary Magdalene, Rowington Close, Paddington, London, showing the sumptuous treatment, the polygonal chancel, and the Crucifixion reredos by Thomas Earp. On the left is a narrow passage-aisle (GB. B116/67. EH. BB77/2747 [1967]).

92): paired marble columns in the early French Gothic style, the beautifully decorated walls, and the splendidly opulent sedilia are particularly enjoyable **(Colour Plate VI)**.

William White, who worked in George Gilbert Scott's office as a young man, employed flint, brick, and stone on his small church at Smannell in Hampshire (1856), which also has tracery set flush with the outside plane of the walls, and tumbled brickwork on the porch. White's essays in large churches began with his unfinished All Saints, Notting Hill (begun 1852, consecrated 1861), but his masterpiece is unquestionably St Michael's, Lyndhurst, Hampshire (1858-70). The latter is a big red- and yellow-brick First Pointed structure, with odd tracery and strange cross-gables **(Plate 41)**: the interior, of yellow, white, and two colours of red brick, exploits the rasping notched bricks already encountered in Street's St James-the-Less, Westminster, but White's piers have dark shafts around them, with elaborate capitals and shaft-rings carved by G.W. Seale. The main trusses of the roof are decorated with life-size angels. St Michael's is of particular interest not only because of its startling, large, bright, and coloured interior, but because of its furnishings; these include the reredos (1864) by Frederic, Lord Leighton (1830-96); the stained-glass (1862-63) by William Morris (1834-96) in the east and south transept south windows and by Sir Edward Coley Burne-Jones (1833-98) in the east window; and a monument in the north wall of the chancel by Street. White's St Saviour's, Aberdeen Park, London (1865), was another example of his rich treatment, especially in the fine brick interior embellished with stencilled patterns **(Plate 42)**.

However, the Lyndhurst church (which led

41. Exterior of the church of St Michael, Lyndhurst, Hampshire (1858-70), by William White. Note the First and Middle Pointed styles of the details, but the strange cross-gables add a wilful note. The building is constructed of red brick with dressings. From Eastlake *(JSC [1872]).*

42. Interior of the church of St Saviour, Aberdeen Park, London (1865), by William White. An example of polychrome Gothic using brick construction, much influenced by the work of William Butterfield. The church was largely financed by F.T. Mackreth of Canonbury Park, but it was no longer used for worship in 2002 (EH. AA77/6248 [1966]).

43. Interior of the church of St Peter, Vauxhall, London (1863-65), by J.L. Pearson, showing the nave with plate-tracery in the clearstorey, the vaulting, and the apsidal chancel with Burgundian deep-set lancets. The style is early French First Pointed (EH. BB77/6815 [1965]).

The Ecclesiologist to regret the 'affectation of originality') lacks the insistence on robustness, muscularity, and primitive Gothic that were to become features of the more advanced mid-Victorian work: St Michael's also cannot be upheld as an entirely successful composition (for its elements are somewhat discordant), but it is of enormous interest because of its individuality and rich furnishings.

Ecclesiologists then took the idea of the 'town church' or 'citadel of faith' pioneered in Butterfield's All Saints, Margaret Street, a stage further, and by the 1860s were arguing that missionary activity and a Church presence in poor parts of the towns should become priorities. Beresford Hope, in his influential *The English*

Cathedral of the Nineteenth Century (1861), proposed huge buildings with tall naves illuminated by clearstoreys, to stand in the urban matrix. One of the first of such 'town churches' was St Peter's, Vauxhall, London (1863-65), designed by John Loughborough Pearson (1817-97) in 1860: Eastlake felt this was a fine example of Pearson's 'originality in design', and 'one of the most successful instances of modern ecclesiastical architecture in London'. St Peter's is essentially a tall clearstoreyed brick nave continuing into an apsidal chancel, the whole with a ribbed ceiling-vault, and with lean-to aisles separated from the nave by means of robust stone piers. The style employed by Pearson was very early French First Pointed **(Plate 43)**.

Yet perhaps we have to turn to a remodelling to see the High Victorian style at its most developed. This is the Albert Memorial Chapel, created in Henry III's chapel attached to St George's Chapel, Windsor, Berkshire. The mediæval fabric was worked over, and the interior remodelled by Baron Henri-Joseph-François Triquet(t)i (1804-74); around the walls below the windows is a band of panels of etched marble by Jules-Constant Destréez, while on the centre-line of the chapel are three monuments to Prince Albert (by Triquet(t)i), the sumptuous *Art-Nouveau* monument to Prince Albert Victor Christian Edward, Duke of Clarence and Avondale, and Earl of Athlone (1864-92), of 1898 by (Sir) Alfred Gilbert (1854-1934), and the simpler memorial to Leopold George Duncan Albert, Duke of Albany, Earl of Clarence, and Baron Arklow (1853-84), by Sir Joseph Edgar Boehm (1834-90) **(Plate 45)**. In this amazingly rich interior (with vault decorated with Salviati mosaic), Continental influences from France, and especially from Germany, are very strong, and it was Continental Gothic which dominated most of the 1860s.

Curiously, however, Benjamin Ferrey's church of St Michael, Chetwynd, Shropshire (1865-67), harks back to English exemplars, and although it is of red sandstone, it has a tower and spire modelled on the limestone churches of Rutland, whilst the rest of the features are early Second Pointed, so it is a curiously old-fashioned design for its date **(Plate 44)**. Oddly backward-looking, too, was George Gilbert Scott's church of St Mary Abbots, Kensington, London (1869-75), a large, solid essay, impeccably detailed, in the Early English style, and built of Kentish ragstone with Bath stone dressings. One of its best features is the arcaded covered way with stone vault and early Middle Pointed tracery, added in 1889-93 to designs by John Oldrid Scott. Yet the elder Scott's church of St Michael, Leafield, Oxfordshire (consecrated 1860, but not completed until 1874), is a muscular interpretation of the early thirteenth-century style with lancets, quat-refoils, and a mighty crossing-tower and spire.

Very different is Scott's mighty church of All Souls, Haley Hill, Halifax, Yorkshire (1855-59),

44. *Church of St Michael, Chetwynd, Shropshire, by Ferrey, of 1865-67. The tower with broach-spire is based on precedents from Rutland, and the style is Early English or First Pointed in general; while some of the larger windows have Geometrical tracery (Middle Pointed), many other windows are lancets. From* Eastlake (JSC [1872]).

which Scott himself thought his best work, built for Colonel Edward Akroyd: it is a mixture of First and Second Pointed, with piers and capitals of the early French Gothic or Canterbury type, and the tower and spire are unquestionably fine, based solidly on an understanding of historical exemplars, but, as indicated above, the choice of contrasting stones to achieve structural polychromy has resulted in spectacular and wide-spread failure of the materials **(Plates 46 and 47)**. The building is contemporary with Square Congregationalist church, Halifax **(Plate 111)**, and may be seen as an Anglican response to an ambitious Nonconformist statement. (It is a sad reflection on our times that the Anglican church was, in 1994, in the hands of a Preservation Trust,

45. Interior of the Albert Memorial chapel, St George's Chapel, Windsor, Berkshire, as remodelled by de Triquet(t)i, with panels around the walls by Destréez, Art-Nouveau *monument of the Duke of Clarence and Avondale by Gilbert (1898), and Second Pointed cenotaph of Prince Albert (foreground) by de Triquet(t)i* (Reproduced by permission of the Dean and Canons of Windsor).

46. (left) All Souls' church, Haley Hill, Boothtown (Akroydon), Halifax, Yorkshire (1855-59), by (Sir) George Gilbert Scott, and thought by him to be his best work. Nevertheless, the church is now cared for by a Preservation Trust. The exterior (seen from the south-west) shows the clearstoreyed nave with lean-to aisles, handsome tower and spire, and transept. Masonry has not weathered well, thanks to Scott's injudicious mix of sandstone and limestone, a perilous experiment in structural polychromy which resulted in chemical reactions. Tracery is of the Geometrical type, that is Middle Pointed, and the rest of the openings are First Pointed (EH. AA77/53078 [1968]).

47. Interior of All Souls, Haley Hill, Halifax, by Scott, and very typical of the work of this prolific Goth. Nave-piers and capitals are of a French early Gothic type, and resemble those in Canterbury Cathedral. The Geometrical Middle Pointed tracery is clearly visible, and the style is a synthesis of First and Second Pointed Gothic Revival (EH. BB78/5718 [1978]).

48. Church of St Columba, Kingsland Road, Haggerston, London (1865-74), by James Brooks: it is a citadel of faith, with plate-tracery, and has a fortress-like character. It is an example of how the Gothic Revival turned to primitive First Pointed French exemplars. From Eastlake (JSC [1872]).

49. Church of St Chad, Shoreditch, London (1867-9), by James Brooks. Built (like St Columba's, Haggerston) under the ægis of the Shoreditch and Haggerston Church Extension Fund, it and the adjoining clergy-houses were in an early French Gothic style, of brick, with plate-tracery (GB. EH. AA77/2976 [1964]).

while the Congregationalist building was demolished [except for the steeple]). Another impressive Scott church is St George's, Doncaster, Yorkshire (1854-58), a large late-Geometrical or early-Decorated essay with a tower in the Perpendicular style.

It was Eastlake, in his great work on the Gothic Revival, who first saw in the work of the 1860s a 'muscular' type of architecture: clustered piers gave way to huge oversized cylinders with robustly-carved massive capitals; models tended to be more archaic, such as early Burgundian Gothic of the thirteenth century; and vivid polychromy gradually fell from grace. Among the most successful 'muscular' 'town-churches' were those by James Brooks erected of brick in the East End and other parts of London: these include the great complex of St Columba, Kingsland Road, Haggerston (1865-74) **(Plate 48)**, and St Chad's, Shoreditch (begun 1867) **(Plate 49)**, both of which had plate-traceried windows puncturing plain unbuttressed walls, and both of which were firmly French thirteenth-century Gothic in style. At St Columba's (Brooks's undoubted master-piece, but declared redundant in 1975), the site included the massive citadel-like church, clergy-house, mission-house, and school **(Plate 48)**. Brooks was also to design the stone church of St Andrew, Plaistow, Essex (1867) **(Plate 50)**, and the brick churches of the Ascension, Lavender Hill, London (1876), and of the Transfiguration, Lewisham (begun 1880) **(Plate 51)**. Brooks employed wide, high naves; tiny, almost vestigial aisles; lofty clearstoreys; wide, short lancets of the Burgundian type; plate-tracery; apsidal east ends (but not invariably); and French Gothic of the thirteenth century in his work. At Holy Innocents, Hammersmith (1887-91), Brooks still drew on early French Gothic for his inspiration, but (taking his cue from Street and Bodley) he employed a wide nave with narrow passage-aisles driven through powerful external buttresses. Again, he used brick with stone dressings **(Plate 52)**. With the sophisticated designs of James Brooks the Gothic Revival firmly entered the category of the Sublime.

In some ways Brooks's church of St John the

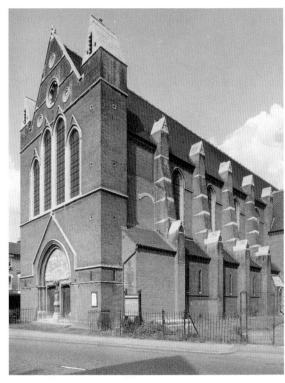

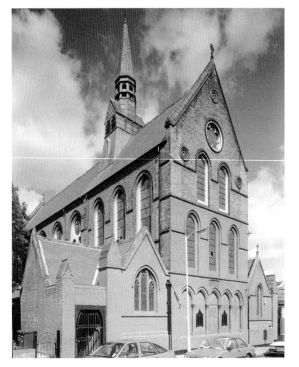

50. (top left) Church of St Andrew, Plaistow, Essex (1867-70), by James Brooks: it is a tough essay in French First Pointed Gothic Revival. Note the apsidal east end with deeply-set lancets, the continuous arcade of the clearstorey (with some blind arches), and the simple yet massive dignity of the timber roof-structure. From Eastlake (JSC [1872]).

51. (bottom left) Church of the Transfiguration, Algernon Road, Lewisham, London (begun 1881), by James Brooks: it is an example of his vast urban citadels in the First Pointed style, with plate-tracery. Sadly, the building has been subdivided inside (MC. B090901 [2001]).

52. (top right) Church of the Holy Innocents, Padderswick Road, Hammersmith (1887-92), from the south-west, by James Brooks: the aisles are driven through openings in the massive buttresses (GB. 223/ 65. EH. AA80/4776 [1965]).

53. *Interior of the church of St John the Baptist, Holland Park, Kensington, London (1872-1911), by James Brooks. It is entirely vaulted, and is a sophisticated mixture of Burgundian Gothic and English Cistercian elements of the thirteenth century* (GLPL. 70/12040 [1970]).

54. *Church of St Margaret, Leiston, Suffolk (1853), by E.B. Lamb, and described by Pevsner as 'undauntedly and frantically original'* (EH. AA78/6362 [1966]).

Baptist, Holland Park, London (1872-1911), is his most impressive **(Plate 53)**: it is entirely vaulted, and has an apsidal chancel and Lady Chapel. Here, however, he mixed Burgundian Gothic with English Cistercian prototypes of the thirteenth century, but it is a pity the church acquired its dismal, feeble, and incoherent west front to designs by John Standen Adkins (born 1859) of 1909-11, for this detracts from the nobility of the exterior.

Rogue Goths

Harry Stuart Goodhart-Rendel (1887-1959) defined 'Rogue Goths' as those who did not meet with the approval of the Ecclesiological Establishment, and whose works were not marked by scholarship, serenity, or tact. Among the more celebrated (if that is the word) 'Rogues'

were Enoch Bassett Keeling (1837-86), Edward Buckton Lamb (1806-69), Samuel Sanders Teulon (1812-73), and George Truefitt (1824-1902) — all four of whom were practitioners — and Thomas Harris (1830-1900) — whose *Victorian Architecture* (1860) and *Examples of the Architecture of the Victorian Age* (1862) earned him some opprobrium. Keeling and Lamb both designed for the Evangelical persuasion, and it shows: both attracted the displeasure of the Ecclesiologists; both gloried in repetitive notchings and chamferings; both expressed their roof-structures in an outlandish, restless way; and both seemed to want to jar the beholder with saw-toothed arrises on every side, threaten with scissor-shaped trusses, and shout loudly with barbaric, harsh polychromy. Lamb's St Margaret's, Leiston, Suffolk (1853) **(Plate 54)**, was described by

Pevsner as 'undauntedly and frantically original', with a roof of 'antics of carpentry' leaping out from low walls, and 'gargantuan' *Flamboyant* tracery. Antics of carpentry recur in the same architect's St Mary Magdalene, Canning Road, Addiscombe, Croydon, Surrey (1868-70), a church described by Pevsner as having a 'nightmarish interior, a debauch of High Victorian inventiveness comparable only to Lamb's other churches' of Christ Church, West Hartlepool (1850-54), and St Martin, Gospel Oak, Hampstead (1862-65). Lamb's churches have a 'purposefully composed cacophony', and deserve study, 'chiefly as a reminder of how far some Victorian church architects were from a mechanical imitation' of the mediæval past. Pevsner saw the work of Lamb and other Rogues as the 'ruthless individualism' necessary as a 'counterpart of Pearson's noble

correctness', but it is doubtful if this comment holds water: contemporaries, who were better architects than the 'Rogues', saw them as self-advertisers, given to commercialism, and, above all, addicted to 'Go'. Mention should be made here of another church in which the roof structure played an overpowering part in the design: this was St Clement's, Treadgold Street,

56. Church of St George, Campden Hill, London (1864-5), by E. Bassett Keeling, showing the slender cast-iron piers, gallery, polychrome notched brickwork, and rather frantic roof-structure. The piers were later cased in concrete, the galleries removed, and the apse demolished. From The Building News *(30 September 1864) (JSC [1864]).*

55. Church of St Clement, Treadgold Street, The Potteries, Kensington, London (1867), by J.P. St Aubyn. The ingenious roof-construction partly supported on cast-iron columns is particularly interesting, but the polychrome interior has been painted out (GLPL. 70.10.HB 12037 [1970]).

The Potteries, Kensington, London (1867), erected through the efforts of the Reverend Arthur Dalgarno Robinson to designs by James Piers St Aubyn (1815-95). This ingenious roof is carried partly on corbels built into the walls, and partly on slender cast-iron columns **(Plate 55)**.

Bassett Keeling suffered vitriolic criticism in the pages of *The Ecclesiologist* and elsewhere. Whilst he claimed his churches were in the style of 'Continental Gothic, freely treated', others said they were 'atrocious' specimens 'of coxcombry', and examples of 'acrobatic Gothic'. Like Lamb, Keeling exploited carpentry in his roofs and gallery-fronts, but he also employed a degree of spikiness and rasping sharpness undreamed-of by White or Street, and his polychrome treatment was violent in the extreme. His most extra-dinary churches were in London: St George's, Aubrey Walk, Campden Hill (1864-5 — altered and damaged almost beyond recognition) **(Plate 56)**, St Mark's, Notting Hill (1862-3 — destroyed), and St Paul's, Anerley Road, Norwood (1864-6 — destroyed). St Mark's had arcades of spindly cast-iron piers and spiky arches of red, black, and white brick voussoirs, the arrises of which were notched, like those of the scissor-trusses carrying the roof; St George's had violent, harsh polychromy, scissor-trusses, and much notching, with arcades carried on cast-iron clustered shafts; and St Paul's had a glorious interior enriched by painted stencilled patterns over the whole of the wall-surfaces. In all three churches galleries were provided for (but in St Paul's never built), carried on cast-iron piers, none of which would have been approved of by The Ecclesiologists, who sought severity, unmoulded planes, and a more primitive, early-Gothic style based on Continental precedent. Zulu war-shields rather than Burgundian Gothic were suggested by Keeling's sharply-pointed arches, and it has to be said that for the 1860s his work was beginning to look out of date. Eastlake doubtless had Keeling in mind when he referred to 'those younger architects who for a while mistook licence for freedom in design and conceived that the conditions of Gothic art were not thoroughly fulfilled unless half an elevation differed from the other and every edge in masonry or woodwork

were notched or chamfered'. From the 1860s, clustered piers (especially thin cast-iron piers) were eschewed in favour of huge cylinders, while polychrome surfaces became quieter, and a restless, violent jaggedness was superseded by something more austere, archaic, and tough as the Revival moved through the 1860s and '70s. By the 1860s Keeling's galleries were very old-fashioned (and unsuited to Tractarian worship), while his external treatment using Bath, Red Mansfield, and Kentish Rag (unsuitable for the London climate) showed early and spectacular distress.

Lamb, Keeling, Truefitt, Harris, and even Teulon employed an originality, a bold eclecticism, and a showmanship more suited to commercial-ism that did not go down well among the arbiters of taste. Even so, Teulon's church of St Stephen, Rosslyn Hill, Hampstead (1868-71), an example of French Gothic, freely treated **(Plate 57)**, with its walls of fine, hard brick (ranging in colour from pale grey to Indian red) and stone

57. Interior of the church of St Stephen, Rosslyn Hill, Hampstead, London (1868-71), by S.S. Teulon, showing the polychrome interior, tough roof-construction, and massive west window (EH. AA75/ 813 [1965]).

58. Interior of the church of St Mary, St Mary's Road, Ealing, London (1866-74), by S.S. Teulon. The notched polychrome-brick horseshoe arches create an exotic Oriental effect, while the extraordinary structure of cast-iron piers carrying the powerful and original roof shows a Victorian 'Rogue Goth' at his most inventive. Unfortunately the original polychrome decorations were obliterated in the 1950s (AFK. G.26589 [1989]).

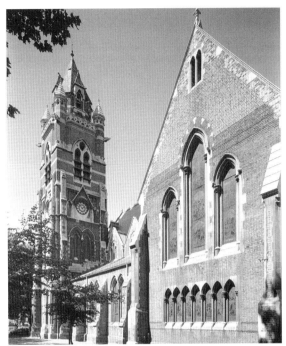

59. Exterior of the church of St Mark, Sandringham Road, Dalston, London (1862-76), from the south-east. Church by Cheston, tower by Blackburne, and the whole in a wildly restless Rogue Gothic style, drawing heavily on Northern French and Flemish exemplars (MC. A300701 [2001]).

dressings, attracted favourable notice, even from Eastlake, and there is no doubting the extraordinary inventiveness of his work at St Mary's, St Mary's Road, Ealing, London (1866-74): the tower, in the words of Pevsner, is 'eccentrically elephantine', but the interior, with its notched-brick horseshoe arches, 'iron stovepipe columns supporting the pierced wooden gallery, and the riot of punched-out tracery spandrels', effectively disguises the fact that St Mary's is basically a Georgian preaching-box by James Horne (d. 1756) of 1735-40, transformed beyond all recognition by one of the more successful Rogue Goths. Regrettably, the riot of polychrome decorations was obliterated by Goodhart-Rendel with a feeble blue-and-cream paint-out of 1955 **(Plate 58)**.

No such approval from Eastlake came to

Chester Cheston (flourished 1833-88) for one of the wildest pieces of Rogue Gothic ever conceived **(Plate 59)**. The enormous church of St Mark, Dalston, London, was designed in 1862, and work began in 1864, but consecration did not occur until 1870, after which Edward Lushington Blackburne (1803-88) added the violently busy tower (that owes much to French Gothic Revival churches of the previous decade or two). Inside the church (a vast auditorium), piers are slender, of cast iron, and carry high pointed arches of polychrome notched brick. The style is vaguely First Pointed Continental Gothic (with a strong dose of stripey Zulu colouring), with lots of lancets and a large wheel-window at the west. Where the transepts join the nave there are stained-glass windows *in the roof*, an unprecedented piece of eccentricity without parallels. The entire *ensemble* has to be seen to be believed **(Plate 60)**.

There can be no arguing with the fact that the more extreme works of 'Rogues' such as Lamb, Keeling, Teulon, and Blackburne were rather restless, and indeed tiring. Furthermore, those 'Rogues' had close connections with the Evangelical Low Church wings, and even with Protestant Nonconformity (Keeling's father was Isaac Keeling [1789-1869], Methodist minister, and at one time President of the Methodist Conference). Keeling's work of the 1860s received a ferocious critical battering in the architectural press, so that by the end of the decade he had taken such strictures to heart, and his work became less frantic (e.g. at Sts Andrew and Philip, Golborne

Road, North Kensington [1869-70 — demolished in the 1950s]).

To men of the up-and-coming generation of architects, the 'Rogues' were addicted to harshness, brutality, studied ugliness, systematic exaggeration, profusion of coarse carving, distortion of detail, notchings, zig-zags, and were too loud by half. In short, they were guilty of 'Go', a term that meant the 'rage' the 'height of fashion', 'in a restless state', 'in constant motion', 'slightly drunk' (Keeling actually died of drink, aged 49), and, in the context of buildings, an 'architectural rant'. John Thomas Micklethwaite (1843-1906) contributed several articles to an

60. Interior of the church of St Mark, Dalston, London, showing the thin piers, notched-brick arches, and barbaric, rasping polychrome effects. Note the stained glass in the roof of the transept (MC. C300701 [2001]).

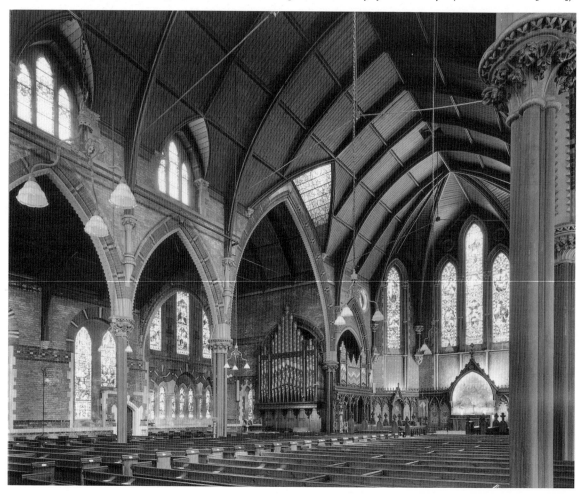

ephemeral journal called *The Sacristy* in 1870, but they were republished in his important book, *Modern Parish Churches* (1874): in his writings Micklethwaite denounced 'Go', over-pedantic antiquarianism, and vulgar commercialism as the enemies of good architecture. To Micklethwaite, 'Go' affected originality, but had none; the clichés employed by architects of the 'Rogue' variety were in fact overdone stale tricks, used again and again; and 'acrobatic Gothic' was shallow, indicative of excess and gross vulgarity. Ugliness and showing off were not signs of originality, taste, or strength.

However, even more important, Micklethwaite turned against his own master, George Gilbert Scott, whose pupil he had become in 1862, and, with others of his generation, repudiated almost the whole mid-Victorian Gothic architec-

61. Church of St Mary, Studley Royal, Lindrick, Yorkshire (1870-78), by William Burges. View from the south-east. Burges's 'muscular' treatment of First and Early Second Pointed (of the Geometrical type), heavily influenced by Continental exemplars, is clearly expressed (EH. AA77/5719 [1968]).

tural output as having led nowhere and been an aberration. Advocating a return to rational ecclesiastical design, the study of liturgical requirements to determine the plan and volume of a church, the need to evolve a type of architectural solution for the future, the abandonment of ecclesiological antiquarianism (and dreamy mediævalism), and, most significantly, a return to principles of design established by Pugin and R. C. Carpenter, he pointed the way forward to the evolution of late-Victorian church architecture.

William Burges and John Loughborough Pearson

Nevertheless, despite Micklethwaite's strictures of 'Go' and advocacy of a way forward, drawing on the early Gothic of Pugin and Carpenter, and rejecting much of the work of the 1850s and 1860s, there were some talented architects who drew heavily on Continental prototypes yet created

62. Interior of Christ Church, Appleton-le-Moors, North Riding of Yorkshire, of 1862-5, by J.L. Pearson. The style is predominantly early French First Pointed (GB. 388/66. EH. BB86/7071 [1966]).

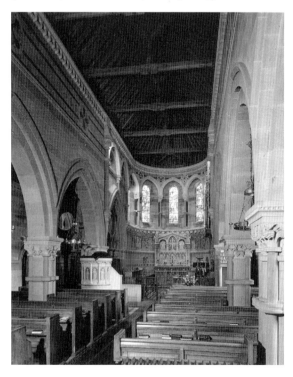

new works of great beauty and integrity. Two of the most important, arguably, were William Burges and John Loughborough Pearson.

Cheston's vivid polychromy and spiky, thin architecture were out of date in style when St Mark's, Dalston, was consecrated in 1870, and, as we have seen, Keeling's work had become altogether more calm by then. 'Go' was definitely becoming unfashionable. William Burges, however, was one of the most successful synthesisers of the early First and Middle Pointed styles, notably in his two spectacular churches of St Mary, Studley Royal (1870-78) **(Plate 61 and Colour Plate VII)**, and Christ the Consoler, Skelton-on-Ure (1870-76) **(Colour Plate VIII)**, both in Yorkshire, and both could hardly differ more from the work of the 'Rogues'. In these designs Burges employed powerful geometrical shapes, decoration flowing over with symbolism, strong heraldic colours, and tough, even threatening, sculpture. Burges's biographer, Professor J. Mordaunt Crook, has said of Burges that he 'combined an unerring sense of mass with an insatiable relish for ornament. Above all, he understood scale. He could make small things look large, and large things look enormous. Even among his own generation of "muscular" Goths — Street, Teulon and Butterfield for instance — he stands out as a master of architectural shock-tactics.' Both churches are First Pointed (with Middle Pointed elements), but it is much tougher early Gothic than was ever seen in the Middle Ages. Eastlake perceived that Burges was painstaking and scholarly, devoted to the study of architectural precedents, notably early French Gothic, but that he was also capable of giving full attention to figure-drawing and to decorative sculpture. Pevsner described St Mary's at Studley Royal as the 'ecclesiastical masterpiece' of William Burges, an opinion with which one can concur. The building was financed by Henriette Anne Theodosia (*née* Vyner), Marchioness of Ripon, and Ripon Cathedral is quoted in some of the tracery. Pevsner celebrated the interior of the church as a 'Victorian shrine', in which Early English quotations are found (the circular piers with Purbeck shafts are based on the piers of Salisbury Cathedral) together with imaginatively treated el-

ements juxtaposed with tremendous confidence. At Skelton, Christ the Consoler was built by Lady Mary Vyner as a memorial to her son, Frederick Grantham Vyner, who was murdered in 1870 by Greek bandits: the church is very opulent, and the entire ensemble (like St Mary's, Studley Royal) has glass designed by Frederick Weekes (1833-93) and made by Saunders & Co. of London. Pevsner myopically described the interior as 'full of determined originality', 'even if of a somewhat elephantine calibre', but Goodhart-Rendel more sensitively observed of the church that it was one of the most 'remarkable' of the nineteenth century, and, to him, 'one of the most beautiful'. The visitor to the church faces a positive bombardment of decoration and sculptures: some of the details seem almost alive.

It would be very difficult to fault Burges for his sureness of touch, unerring judgement of powerful detail, and overwhelming effects in his buildings. At Studley Royal and Skelton, two commissions carried out for rich patrons, members of the same family, is what Professor Crook has called 'The High Victorian Dream', perfectly realised by an architect of genius who used his historical precedents with scholarship and originality. Both churches are exquisite shrine-like buildings, almost unbearably beautiful, by a master who understood scale,

63. Church of St Mary, Freeland, Oxfordshire (1869-71), by J.L. Pearson, showing the north-eastern tower, apsidal chancel (with lancets), and plate-tracery in the nave. The style is early French First Pointed (EH. 595/70 [c.1870]).

64. Interior of St Mary's church, Freeland, Oxfordshire, showing the plate-tracery and the sumptuous, vaulted chancel (EH. 918/68 [1968]).

contrast, and the importance of colour and detail.

Some of the most distinguished churches of the 1860s and 1870s were designed by Pearson, including Christ Church, Appleton-le-Moors, Yorkshire (1862-5), with its plain walling, unchamfered arches, toughly detailed roof, and apsidal chancel. Pearson's inspiration came from the Continent, especially the vigorously carved capitals of the nave arcade **(Plate 62)**. Pearson was also responsible for the handsome but tiny church of St Mary, Freeland, Oxfordshire (1869-71), with nave, apsidal chancel, and north-eastern tower with saddleback roof **(Plate 63)**. Nave windows have plate-tracery, and the apse is pierced with lancets. Pearson's use of apses is always masterly, and St Mary's is a superb example of his skill in handling an architecture based on French early

thirteenth-century precedents. As Pevsner has pointed out, the interior **(Plate 64)** demonstrates 'the Ecclesiologists' theories of the "beauty of holiness"', with its aisleless nave, sumptuous chancel, and decorations by Clayton & Bell. The chancel is roofed with a rib-vault of pinkish-grey stone carried on a red wall-shafts, and there are beautiful thirteenth-century style paintings on the walls.

Pearson carried out extensive works at the church of St Michael, Garton-on-the-Wolds, East Riding of Yorkshire, for Sir Tatton Sykes (1772-1863 — 4th Baronet) in 1856-7. He rebuilt the chancel in a Romanesque style incorporating some original features, and the chancel-arch is his too. However, Street was brought in by the 5th Baronet in 1872, and under Street the amazing

65. St Augustine's, Kilburn Park Road, Paddington, London (1870-77), by J.L. Pearson. The tower and spire derive from the Abbaye-aux-Hommes *at Caen, Normandy (MC.A280494 [1994]).*

*66. Chapel of St Michael in the church of St Augustine, Kilburn Park Road, Paddington, London, decorated by Clayton & Bell. It is a sumptuous example of Victorian Gothic Revival (*EH. BB622/489 [1896]).

scheme of interior decoration was carried out, with wall-paintings by Clayton & Bell (1873-6), who also did the stained-glass windows. These astonishing and beautiful paintings were restored in 1986-91 by Donald Smith and Wolfgang Gärtner under the ægis of the Pevsner Memorial Trust. Pearson was once more engaged in 1878 to complete the decorative work. The ceilings of the nave, chancel, and tower are also painted in strong patterns, all by Clayton & Bell. Pearson designed the paving of the nave and chancel (the latter laid in various coloured marbles in the style of the Cosmati, but it has not worn well), and Temple Lushington Moore (1856-1920) redesigned the seating in the nave in 1899. So remarkable is the interior of this church that a monograph on the wall-paintings by the late Jill

Allibone was published by the Pevsner Memorial Trust in 1991 (Plate 67).

Pearson's great church of St Augustine, Kilburn, London (1870-98 — erected under the ægis of an Anglo-Irish Anglo-Catholic clergyman, R. C. Kirkpatrick, for a largely middle-class congregation), was also inspired by early French Gothic churches, this time of Normandy (Plate 65), where the model for part of the exterior was the *Abbaye-aux-Hommes* (St-Étienne), Caen, but the interior, with its very deep internal wall-piers (invisible from the outside) and narrow passage-aisles (a scheme wholly unlike English mediæval exemplars) was derived from two important French prototypes — the Cathedral of Albi (1282-1512) and the church of the Cordeliers, Toulouse (mid-fourteenth century). Frederick Moore Simpson (1855-1928), in an important paper on 'Architectural Developments During Victoria's Reign' published in *The Architectural Review* (1897), observed that the church of the Cordeliers

67. *Interior of the church of St Michael, Garton-on-the-Wolds, East Riding of Yorkshire, showing the chancel-arch with triple opening in the gable above, all by Pearson, and the remarkable scheme of decoration by Clayton & Bell, initiated by Street from 1873. The oak screen is by Street (1875), made by Rattee & Kett. The paintings around the chancel-arch show the Tree of Jesse with the Virgin and Child at the apex: below are the Four Doctors of the Western Church* (MC. A27090 [2001]).

plan (one not unlike that of King's College Chapel, Cambridge) was one 'eminently fitted for English church worship'. He noted that it made an enormous impact on the planning of churches in the last three decades of Victoria's reign. This is significant, because Albi has been perceived as *the* exemplar for English architects, but other churches were at least as important as models.

Nearly all Pearson's windows are tall lancets, although there are sometimes a few examples of elementary plate-tracery and he often employed elaborate rose- or wheel-windows **(Plate 65)**. Many of his churches gain authority and *gravitas* from having stone or brick vaults, and St Augustine's is no exception. Brick, too, is the material used inside and out, with stone dressings and First Pointed details. The chancel is defined by a screen, but otherwise the interior forms an unbroken space, ten bays long, entirely covered by vaulting. Arcades support a gallery extending round the church and crossing the transepts, and the architectural effect is mysterious, grand, noble, and even Sublime **(Colour Plate IX)**. Off the southern transept is the chapel of St Michael, with an apsidal sanctuary and gilded ribs above a somewhat prickly Gothic reredos **(Plate 66)**.

Pearson's slightly later church of St Michael, Poplar Walk, Croydon, Surrey (designed 1876 and built 1880-83), has one of his finest interiors, lit by lancets and lights in plate-tracery, and brick-vaulted throughout. The style is French First Pointed. He was to quote French Gothic again at Truro Cathedral, Cornwall (1879-1910), a fine and scholarly building in which French and English First Pointed are convincingly synthesised. In composition **(Plate 68)**, there are echoes of Lincoln Cathedral (also suggested by the tower over the crossing, the two western towers, and the two sets of transepts).

The Lincoln connection was no whim on Pearson's part. When the See of Truro was revived in 1876, the bishop appointed was Edward White Benson (1829-96), who had been Chancellor at Lincoln from 1872, and Pearson himself had been involved in restoration work at Lincoln from 1875. At Truro the central and western towers and spires **(Plate 68)** have similarities to the steeple

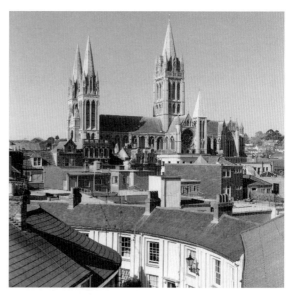

68. *Truro Cathedral, Cornwall (1880-1910), by J.L. Pearson. Note the resemblance of the central and western towers to the great composition of St Augustine's, Kilburn Park Road, Paddington, London, so their source is St-Étienne, Caen. Otherwise the building is entirely First Pointed Early English, strongly influenced by Lincoln Cathedral* (AFK. G.14448 [1976]).

of St Augustine, Kilburn, so their source is St-Étienne, Caen, with a dash of Coutances Cathedral, but the rest of the ensemble is mostly Early English (e.g. Whitby Abbey), though with many French quotations (e.g. Caen and Bayeux), not least the sexpartite vault over the nave. The circular baptistry is one of the richest, most successful, and scholarly elements of the whole design.

Pearson employed First Pointed at the church of Sts Agnes and Pancras, Ullet Road, Sefton Park, Liverpool (1882-5), designed with western transepts that became a narthex. Described by Pevsner as 'the noblest Victorian church in Liverpool', it was built at the expense of Douglas Horsfall, a wealthy local stockbroker: materials were hard red brick with sandstone dressings outside, and ashlar Bath stone for the interior. To the south of the chancel is a chapel with a reredos by G. F. Bodley, and it is to the work of Bodley and his contemporaries that we now turn.

CHAPTER VII

Some Anglican Churches of the Last Decades of Queen Victoria's Reign

Introduction: the Liturgical Background; The Revival of English Late-Gothic Styles; All Saints, Cambridge, and Bodley's Later Work; Anglo-Catholicism

Nearly all the best work of the [Gothic] Revival was done after the death of Gilbert Scott.
KENNETH MACKENZIE CLARK (1908-83): *The Gothic Revival. An Essay in the History of Taste*
(London: John Murray, 1962), 219.

The church of St John, in Tue Brook, a suburb of Liverpool, is an admirable model [of works in which respect for the English tradition is conspicuous], recently completed from the design of Mr G.F. Bodley, whose earlier work, St Michael's, at Brighton, was one of the first to attract attention by its quaint and original character, but who in this instance has returned to that type of Middle Pointed art which reached its highest grace towards the middle of the fourteenth century.
CHARLES LOCKE EASTLAKE (1836-1906): *A History of the Gothic Revival*
(London: Longmans, Green, & Co., 1872), 369.

Introduction: the Liturgical Background

Eastlake (1872) was able to single out Sir Arthur William Blomfield (1829-99), Brooks, Basil Champneys (1842-1935), Edward William Godwin (1833-86), George Gilbert Scott Junior, and John Pollard Seddon (1827-1906) as talented, rising stars in the Gothic Revival firmament after the generation of Goths alluded to earlier.

One of the great problems of dealing with the work of English Gothic Revivalists from around 1878 (when 'Great' Scott died) is the vast accretion of prejudice and misunderstanding that obscures both facts and honesty. Today, it is largely true that the Late Goths still tend to be dismissed as limp copyists, leading the movement to decline. However, as the experiments with Continental Gothic and structural polychromy began to pall, and taste moved away from the massiveness, rhetoric, and Sublime over-emphasis of 'muscular Gothic' (eschewing 'Go' altogether, as ungentlemanly, and only for charlatans), a new delicacy began to become apparent in the work of several gifted and scholarly Goths. Thus the late-Victorian Gothic Revival was the result of a reaction to (and even

a revulsion of feeling from) the work of the 'Rogues', the questionable vulgarity of 'Go', and North Italian and French influences, all of which were perceived as leading nowhere. A return to Pugin and Carpenter was seen by several pupils of 'Great' Scott as a means of purifying the Revival and making a fresh start.

It should be remembered that in the first decades of the twentieth century, buildings such as Keble College, Oxford, by Butterfield, were ridiculed as 'Victorian monstrosities' (most people thought Keble was by Ruskin), and the works of Street and others were not taken seriously. This was undoubtedly partly because commentators of the late-Victorian period had turned away from mid-Victorian taste (some polychrome interiors were painted out in the early years of the twentieth century and afterwards), and it was not until Harry Stuart Goodhart-Rendel and others (including William Richard Lethaby [1857-1931]) began to defend the architects active in the 1850s and 1860s that the reputations of men like Butterfield and Street began to be rehabilitated. However, much damage was done to the later Goths by Pevsner, who called the mid-Victorians 'High Victorians', and credited them with originality, seeing them as 'pioneers' of design, and therefore, by some strange mental alchemy, as being forerunners of Modernism. Thereafter, the works of many late Goths have been treated dismissively, as 'mere' historicists, and not given the attention they deserve.

Yet there were many, until Pevsner raised tough mid-Victorian work to his pantheon of approved architecture, who saw the late-Victorian Gothic Revival as a fulfilment of early promise, and the logical artistic pinnacle of the work of Pugin, Carpenter, and other early Goths. As Kenneth Clark wrote (1928), nearly 'all the best work' of the Gothic Revival 'was done after the death of [Sir] Gilbert Scott'.

It is not just the writings of Pevsner that raise difficulties today. Most of the late Goths were steeped in religion, religious buildings, liturgical requirements, and so on, and were real scholars: many of them were Anglo-Catholics. In the early twenty-first century very few commentators or critics have any religious faith, and are most certainly ignorant of the requirements of ritual. Yet at the end of the nineteenth and beginning of the twentieth century *The Architectural Review*, one of the most progressive architectural journals of the day (founded in 1896), was not only edited (1896-1901) by an Anglo-Catholic Churchman (Henry Wilson [1864-1934], who had worked in the offices of John Belcher [1841-1913], John Oldrid Scott, and John Dando Sedding [1838-91— who took Wilson into partnership]), but had several committed Churchmen on the Editorial Board. Among items published in the earliest volume's of *The Architectural Review* were papers on Bentley, Bodley, Brooks, Butterfield, Pugin, Pearson, George Gilbert Scott Junior, and Alexander 'Greek' Thomson (1817-75), which suggests considerable open-mindedness, as Thomson was never a Goth, and indeed detested Gothic. Significantly, Wilson saw art, architecture, and religion as being closely allied, and admired Roman Catholicism for its very visible integration with the daily life and art of Western European towns and cities. It became widely recognised that it was R. C. Carpenter who had

introduced Pugin's architectural style and ideals into the Anglican Church with his church of St Mary Magdalene, Munster Square, London, a building that owed much to the old Austin Friars church in London (destroyed). Ecclesiologists such as Beresford Hope saw broad churches without triforia or clearstoreys (such as St Mary Magdalene) as ideal for town churches, but the presence of nave arcades was still a problem, because the piers tended to obscure the altar from certain positions in the aisles. What became clear was that churches in which the space was chopped up began to be regarded as unsuitable for 'Modern Gothic', the protagonists of which (Bodley, Thomas Garner [1839-1906], Thomas Graham Jackson [1835-1924], Micklethwaite, Scott the Younger, and Sedding) were all Churchmen, and, with the exception of Sedding (a pupil of Street), were all pupils of 'Great' Scott (and all reacted against the architecture of their masters). Bodley was the eldest of these, and already established: the others were very much the up and coming men. Bodley had worshipped at St Paul's, Brighton, then attended Butterfield's All Saints, Margaret Street, and the same architect's St Alban's, Holborn. Garner and Scott also worshipped at St Alban's, Holborn, and Micklethwaite attended St Mary Magdalene, Munster Square. In addition, as Father Symondson has pointed out, Street was church-warden at All Saints, and Sedding held the same office at St Alban's, Holborn. Thus all these architects (their ages in 1870 ranged from 27 [Micklethwaite] to 43 [Bodley], but the rest were in their early- to mid-thirties) were Churchmen, all attending Anglican churches where Anglo-Catholic Ritualism was being practised. It is probably significant that the liturgies practised at St Alban's, Holborn, and All Saints, Margaret Street, were, in 1870, considerably influenced by Roman Catholicism, while the English strand was evident at St Mary Magdalene, Munster Square. The Roman tendencies were therefore associated with Butterfield's architecture, and the English with Carpenter: to Micklethwaite and others, therefore, the Carpenter/Pugin model was the more desirable one to emulate. Micklethwaite was the critic who appealed for rationalism in church design, and his admiration of Pugin and Carpenter influenced future developments. Large, open volumes, accommodating artisans and mechanics, labourers and the poor, and the 'people at large', were essential to emphasise the equality of all before the Eucharist, and the main reason for church-building should be to bring Christianity to all, and especially the urban poor, who would, thereby, be redeemed.

It would appear that the mid-Victorian poly-chrome experiment was, by 1870, besmirched with its associations: these were Roguery and 'Go'; antiquarianism, especially that drawing on Continental exemplars; Ecclesiological stylistic dictatorship; and, on the one side, Low Church associations, yet, on the other, modern Roman Catholic influences. Micklethwaite returned to Puginian arguments concerning architectural logic and rationalism; to a consideration of the liturgy as the starting-point for church-design; and the need to build for posterity, where beauty and function (rather than style) would determine the form and character of a building.

The Revival of English Late Gothic Styles
Pearson's church of St Augustine, Kilburn, has been mentioned above. The Albi arrangement of wall-piers with openings driven through them is also found at the beautiful church, also named after St Augustine, at Pendlebury, South Lanca-shire (1871-74), designed by Bodley & Garner, the first of a series of outstandingly fine churches by this partnership, and one that was to be profoundly influential. The change of style from Bodley's earlier works is startling, for instead of the tough lancets and simple geometry of the wheel-window, the architects reverted to delicate tracery of the fourteenth-century type, and there were other aspects that deserve note.

Bodley's career spanned virtually the entire Victorian period. In the 1840s he worked in George Gilbert Scott's office at the same time as Street and White, but reacted against the style of 'Great' Scott after 1850, and turned for his precedents to the work of Butterfield, Street, and White, as well as drawing on texts by Ruskin. Much of his early designs therefore share certain characteristics with mid-Victorian work, and in the late 1850s he was as 'muscular' a Goth as any. In 1858, the year John Purchas's *Directorium* was published, Bodley was commissioned by John Beanlands, curate of St Paul's, Brighton (by R. C. Carpenter, as previously noted), to design the new church of St Michael and All Angels, Brighton (1858-61) — later gloriously extended from 1865 to designs by Burges and John Starling Chapple (*fl.* 1859-99). Although St Michael's is 'muscular', the stained-glass windows contain a considerable proportion of white glass, and the colouring was influenced by late-mediæval English and Flemish glass, pointing to a new direction for English Gothic Revival away from French and Italian Gothic exemplars. The stained glass was by Morris, Marshall, Faulkner, & Co., the first significant ecclesiastical commission for this firm.

Morris, Marshall, Faulkner, & Co., founded in 1861, also carried out works at Bodley's earlier 'muscular' church of All Saints, Selsley, Gloucestershire (1858-62), and was also involved in works at Bodley's mature work at the church of St Martin-on-the-Hill, Albion Road, Scarborough, Yorkshire (1861-3), a large and powerful essay in the thirteenth-century style, with a vast, high interior, and an unceiled wagon-roof. There is a large rose-window in the west wall of the nave. Of St Martin's, *The Ecclesiologist* said that the style was 'severe Early Pointed, the tower and spire in particular showing evident marks of extremely early French style', but inside the building Bodley limited his use of structural polychromy and applied his first large-scale design of painted decoration, harking back to Pugin and mediæval examples, although it was confined to the chancel and east wall of the nave, and was completed in 1864. St Martin's is particularly interesting for its lovely pre-Raphaelite interior to which Dante Gabriel Rossetti (1828-82), Ford Madox Brown (1821-93), William Morris, and others contributed. Bodley designed the Rood-screen and reredos, and some of the stained-glass is by Morris.

Now all these connections are interesting with respect to Bodley's change of direction. Clearly the influence of Morris and his firm was significant, but so was that of Purchas and his book. Purchas became a curate at St Paul's, Brighton, in 1861, when St Michael and All Angels, Brighton, was consecrated, and he and Bodley were acquainted. It is clear that the plan of the sanctuary of St Michael's was modelled on Purchas's work: indeed, Bodley's later designs for sanctuaries, with their large reredoses and high gradins, owed virtually everything to Purchas's scholarship, the second edition (1866) of which, edited by Frederick George Lee (1832-1902), contained illustrations by Edmund Sedding (1836-68), brother of John Dando Sedding. Both brothers had worked in Street's office, and both were deeply sympathetic to Anglican Ritualism. They worshipped in the church of St Mary, Crown Street, Soho, where John Charles Chambers (1817-74) had been appointed perpetual curate in 1856, and Richard Frederick Littledale (1833-90 — an associate of J. M. Neale, one of the founders of the Cambridge Camden Society) joined him in 1861. As Father Symondson has pointed out, St Mary's was a 'river of ritualistic activity into which many tributaries flowed': the Seddings lodged with Chambers while they worked in Street's office; Littledale introduced Edmund Sedding to Purchas; and Purchas introduced young Sedding to Lee. Thus Lee's version of Purchas's *Directorium* acquired Sedding's illustrations, pronounced 'full of Catholic feeling' and 'correct taste' in 'Christian art', but which owed perhaps more to nineteenth-century Continental Roman Catholic design in Northern Europe than to pre-Reformation English models.

So Roman Catholic liturgical practices and design became important parts of Victorian Anglicanism. John Dando Sedding's ecclesiastical leanings were Ritualistic Anglo-Catholic, and he, in turn, influenced most of his pupils to follow suit. Father Symondson has made clear that Edmund Sedding's association with the *Directorium* connected Neale through Littledale with the 'progressive architectural movements of the late nineteenth century', and Neale was a patron of both Street and Bodley.

All Saints, Cambridge, and Bodley's Later Work
With All Saints, Jesus Lane, Cambridge (1862-71), Bodley decisively broke with the mid-Victorian

Continental Gothic style. The church consists of a nave with one aisle and a thin chancel, and the interior was decorated with stencilled patterns by William Morris **(Plate 69)**. Stained-glass windows were also by Morris's firm, and include designs by Edward Coley Burne-Jones, Ford Madox Brown, and Morris himself (1865-6). Now All Saints is unquestionably English- and Pugin-inspired work in the style of the late-thirteenth and early-fourteenth centuries, and makes a return to the 'homely and sweet' native styles, as *The Ecclesiologist* put it, so it was recognised at the time as an important work.

It is very curious that several commentators have claimed Bodley's change of style at All Saints was forced on him by certain conservative dons at the University of Cambridge, given that he was already moving in that direction. However, *The Ecclesiologist* saw things differently: it noted, 'with some satisfaction', that Mr Bodley '…had…restricted himself to pure English forms. The time for a reaction from exclusively French or Italian types' had arrived. A cursory trawl through the architectural and ecclesiological press of the time shows that opinion was already moving away from mid-Victorian 'muscularity' towards English exemplars: 'conservative dons' had little to do with this.

It was with the church of St John the Baptist, West Derby Road, Tue Brook, Liverpool (1868-71), however, that Bodley's acceptance of fourteenth-century English exemplars became complete, and the resultant masterpiece makes this glowingly apparent **(Colour Plate X)**. Eastlake noted that at Tue Brook Bodley had revived the leading elements of the style 'carefully and ably', and had introduced very beautiful colour 'which pervades the whole building from its primary construction to the last touch of embellishment'. Indeed, not 'all the scientific treatises on polychromy could have supplied a better scheme', wrote Eastlake, who felt that in 'this truly remarkable work the genuine grace of Mediæval art seems at length to have been reached', high praise indeed. The church was erected at their sole cost by the Reverend and Mrs J. C. Reade, and Eastlake felt that 'for correctness of design, refined workmanship, and artistic decoration' the building could

69. Church of All Saints, Jesus Lane, Cambridge (1863-69), by Bodley. Interior from the west, showing Bodley's tendency to revert to the style of Pugin's work of the 1840s. The screen and Rood were not part of the original design, and the painted decorations were carried out over four decades, derived from late mediæval examples from East Anglia (EH. BB80/2703 [1980]).

'take foremost rank among examples of the Revival', a comment that may wholeheartedly be endorsed. In so many ways St John's displays Bodley's scholarship, exquisite taste, and sense of rightness in ecclesiastical art, for he designed and supervised virtually everything. The chancel-arch acquired a mural by C. E. Kempe, and there is some decent glass by Morris & Co. Altogether, the interior of St John's is a wonderful, lovely ensemble, and in the 1990s still looked marvellous (having been beautifully restored in the 1970s by Stephen Dykes Bower), although parts of the roof had suffered from wet-rot, and, after repairs, awaited re-colouring. St John's is one of the half-dozen or so first-rate Anglican church-interiors in which colour and architecture blend into a satisfying whole.

Bodley went into partnership with Thomas Garner in 1869, and Garner had 'pronounced English sympathies'. At their church of St Augustine, Pendlebury, mentioned above, they drew on the severe style of Albi, but formed internal openings through the wall-piers to create narrow passage-aisles to give the congregation access to their seats in the nave. Apart from Albi Cathedral (which is the exemplar that is usually quoted), the church of the Cordeliers, Toulouse, is sometimes mentioned, but it is far more likely that Bodley & Garner took as their starting-point the well-known Dominican church, Gent, in Belgium, a plan and perspective of which had been published in *The Building News* (30 July 1869), and which reappeared in *Church Design for*

Congregations: its Development and Possibilities (1870) by James Cubitt (1836-1912), an important publication that has not had the attention from modern commentators that it deserves. The arrangement of a huge unbroken interior space (without a chancel-arch), permitting a clear view of the altar, was nothing short of revolutionary: the wide, spacious nave; narrow passage-aisles; monumentality; and uncluttered, unified volume, covered with a coloured timber wagon-vault (instead of stone vaulting) over the whole of the nave (including the choir and sanctuary) pointed

70. Church of St Augustine, Pendlebury, Greater Manchester (1870-74), by Bodley & Garner, from the west, showing the wall-piers (pierced by arches to form aisle-passages, and carrying transverse vaults to stiffen the walls) – a scheme that derives partly from the mediæval Cathedral of Albi, partly from the church of the Cordeliers, Toulouse (both in France), and (mostly) from the church of the Dominicans, Gent (Belgium). The rich decorations of the chancel are typical of Bodley's return to late-mediæval styles (EH. BB69/ 2245 [1871]).

to the future. This daring mixture of tough, early French Gothic and very delicate English fourteenth- and fifteenth-century detail was a taste of things to come. The east window is vast, and has flowing Curvilinear tracery of the fourteenth-century type, but with certain features reminiscent of fifteenth-century work. In addition, the Rood-screen and reredos look to a late-Gothic and Flemish ancestry **(Plate 70)**.

Now the Pendlebury church demonstrated how a large congregation could be accommodated, yet provided with unobstructed views of the high altar. Bodley had experimented with designs to accomplish something similar at his

71. Church of the Holy Angels, Hoar Cross, Staffordshire (1872-76), by Bodley & Garner, showing the crossing-tower derived from the tower of the church of St Mary, Ilminster, Somerset, the design of which is, in turn, derived from the crossing-tower of Wells Cathedral. The style is entirely Second Pointed (or Decorated), although the tower is just beginning to turn to Perpendicular themes (MC. A260494 [1994]).

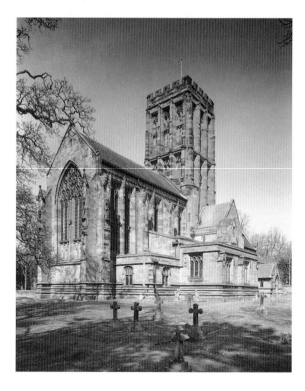

72. Church of St Mary the Virgin, Clumber Park, Nottinghamshire (1886-89), by Bodley & Garner, from the south-east. The spire is modelled on the mediæval parish-church of St Patrick, Patrington, Yorkshire, and the great east window has tracery of the flowing late Decorated or late Second Pointed style (EH. AA77/ 5679 [1967]).

73. Interior of St Mary's, Clumber Park, Nottinghamshire, from the east. It is one of Bodley & Garner's eclectic master-works. The unaisled nave has blind arcading along its walls, and a wall-passage above, while the chancel is almost the same length as the nave. The screen and stalls were carved by the Reverend Ernest Geldart (EH.AA77/5693 [1967]).

church of St Salvador, Dundee (1865-8), where he was probably influenced by the plan of Gerona Cathedral, in Spain (which also has wall-piers or internal buttresses). At Pendlebury, Bodley & Garner went a lot further than Pearson did at Kilburn in Anglicising the Albi (or, more obviously, Gent) type and ensuring visibility. Pendlebury marks the beginnings of the 'modern' Victorian church, covered inside with painted decorations. It was the first of a series of outstandingly fine churches by the Bodley/ Garner partnership (which lasted until 1897), and one that was to be profoundly influential.

Like many of the finest churches of the Gothic Revival, Pendlebury was built at the expense of a wealthy individual: in this case the benefactor was Edward Stanley Heywood (1829-1914). One of Bodley & Garner's most enchanting creations was the church of the Holy Angels, Hoar Cross, Staffordshire (1872-1900), where scholarship, refinement, and sumptuous detail were combined in the one estate church for a small congregation. Conceived as a memorial to Hugo Francis Meynell Ingram (d. 1871), of Hoar Cross and Temple Newsam, it was paid for by his widow. Holy Angels was consecrated in 1876, but was later lengthened by a bay, acquired a Lady Chapel and another chapel north of the 'chantry-chapel', and a narthex was added in 1906 to designs by Cecil Greenwood Hare (1875-1932), who took over Bodley's practice after the latter died **(Plate 71 and Colour Plate XI)**.

74. Vaulted chapel to the south of the chancel at St Mary's church, Clumber Park, Nottinghamshire, by Bodley & Garner (EH. AA77/5688 [1967]).

Pendlebury and Hoar Cross are examples of very different approaches to church design: the former is large, is essentially one big space with powerful wall-piers carrying the nave-arcade, has no transepts, and the chancel is not emphasised either inside or out; the latter has a nave (without clearstorey), lean-to aisles, transepts (with tall crenellated panelled tower in the Perpendicular style over the crossing), chancel taller than the nave, and the chapels mentioned above. Apart from the tower (which is based on that of the church of St Mary, Ilminster, Somerset, the design of which is, in turn, derived from the crossing-tower of Wells Cathedral), the style is entirely Second Pointed (or Decorated), with side-windows mostly square-headed with hood-moulds, and larger windows with intricate tracery (the east window has six lights with elaborate Geometrical tracery above, the north transept has Intersecting tracery, and the south transept has Reticulated tracery). Like Pugin's

churches, Holy Angels is compartmented inside. The aisleless clearstoreyed chancel has a ceiling of tierceron vaults, but the transepts and nave have timber wagon-roofs: this chancel is breathtakingly beautiful, with lavish enrichments, statuary under canopies, and much ogee work, with crockets, resembling the celebrated Percy tomb in Beverley Minster, Yorkshire. Bodley's designs for the reredoses, screens, font-cover, and flooring are exquisite: particularly enjoyable is the Meynell monument between the chancel and the 'chantry-chapel', while the stained-glass, by Burlison & Grylls, goes well with the refined architectural language of this marvellous church. Now Pendlebury emphasised structure, but Hoar Cross was an exercise to show how exquisitely delicate and lovely late English Decorated and Perpendicular Gothic could be.

Another beautiful (and stunningly well-sited) Bodley & Garner church (though apparently designed by Bodley alone) is that of St Mary the Virgin at Clumber Park, Nottinghamshire (1886-89), erected for Henry Pelham Archibald Douglas, 7th Duke of Newcastle-under-Lyme (1864-1928 — a nephew of Beresford Hope): it is an extremely refined eclectic work, with a spire modelled on that of the uncommonly fine mediæval church of St Patrick at Patrington, Yorkshire **(Plates 72-74)**. Cruciform on plan, it consists of an aisleless nave, a chancel with a chapel to the south and sacristies to the north, short transepts, and a central tower with octagonal spire. It is vaulted, and was Bodley's own favourite design. Now Clumber church stands, separated from the lake by a stretch of greensward, and backed by fine mature trees. One has to try to imagine it as intended, as a church in the park of a great house (demolished in the 1930s): today, it stands as a poignant memorial to the 7th Duke and to his Anglo-Catholicism.

Another church in the Sublime æsthetic category is the unforgettable St Bartholemew, Ann Street, Brighton (1872-74), perhaps the only English Gothic Revival church of the period that can rival Brooks's vast East End and South London masterpieces. St Bartholemew's was designed by Edmund Evan Scott, for the celebrated Anglo-Catholic

Father Arthur Wagner (1825-1902). When the latter's father, H. M. Wagner (1793-1870), became Vicar of Brighton in 1824 there were only the mediæval parish church of St Nicholas and a couple of proprietary chapels to minister to the Anglicans of the town: when he died there were seventeen churches and five chapels-of-ease, but only one parish. The elder Wagner built St Paul's (by Carpenter) for his son before the latter was ordained.

Arthur Wagner imbibed his Ecclesiology at Cambridge in the 1840s, and from the very start of his career was a convinced Ritualist, and brought an impressively robust Anglo-Catholicism to Brighton. Being fabulously rich, he was able to build churches on a grand scale, and his life was devoted to ministering to the poor and to building churches for the care of the souls of all (but especially of the poor). Although Wagner got some of the best architects of the day (Bodley,

75. Exterior of the mighty church of St Bartholomew, Ann Street, Brighton, Sussex (1872-74), by E.E. Scott. The huge front has a canopied statue set on the wall high over the west door, and above are four small lancets and a huge circular window. The side elevation is articulated at high level by buttresses (the external expression of the wall-piers), between which are lancets (AFK. G.17012 [1978]).

Burges, Richard Herbert Carpenter, and Pearson) to design buildings for him, he went to a local man, E. E. Scott (seemingly unrelated to the famous dynasty of 'Great' Scott, but probably connected with Frederick William Hyde [*fl.* 1875-82], another local man, in a professional capacity for a brief period [1875-76]), whose great church outshone all Wagner's other creations: St Bartholemew's is of plain brick, with lancets and a huge circular window **(Plate 75)**; its nave is higher than that of Westminster Abbey or Amiens Cathedral; it is almost completely devoid of any ornaments, so is very severe; and its architecture is tougher and bolder than that of Butterfield or Street. Articulation of the nave walls is by wall-piers forming three-sided recesses, and so the essence of the form is from the same sources as those of St Augustine's, Pendlebury (i.e. Albi, the Cordeliers at Toulouse, and the church of the Dominicans, Gent). The originally unfinished east end was embellished in the Arts-and-Crafts manner to designs by Henry Wilson (who, as noted above, had worked with Belcher, J. O. Scott, and J. D. Sedding) **(Plate 76)**.Father Wagner's churches were visible expressions of his Ritualism, and were often defaced with Protestant *graffiti*. As he moved (with many of his contemporaries) towards Anglo-Catholicism, he came under the scrutiny of the guardians of Evangelical Protestantism, and was summoned to the Jerusalem Chamber to stand before the Judicial Committee of the Privy Council to explain himself. His curates were openly denounced as Papists, and, on his own patch, he was also beaten up by thugs.

As these matters should be appreciated if ecclesiastical architecture is to be understood, it is as well, at this point, to explain, briefly, what is meant by Anglo-Catholicism.

Anglo-Catholicism
Anglo-Catholicism is Catholicism of the Anglican type, or according to the traditions and scholarship of the English Church. In England, it was claimed that the Anglican Church, even as Reformed, was the national branch of the Catholic Church in its historical sense: the Tractarians held that the English Church was 'a

76. St Bartholomew's church, Ann Street, Brighton, Sussex (1872-74), by E.E. Scott, showing the internal wall-piers that form arched recesses, suggestive of nave arcades. Above is a vestigial triforium of three slit lancets to each bay, and above that are the tall clearstorey windows. The powerful east end by Henry Wilson terminates the vista in a composition of Sublime power (EH. C44/177 [1943]).

branch of the Church Catholic', and this was emphasised by the great deference paid by the Church of England (as part of the Catholic Church) to tradition. Thus the revival of rituals and liturgies was part of that deference to tradition.

So the term 'Anglo-Catholicism' came into use in the 1830s. It should be emphasised that scholarship and historical continuity lay behind much of the revival both of Anglicanism and Gothic: in the early years of Victoria's reign the main efforts were expended on the recovery of the meaning and precious nature of the Sacraments, because the Sacraments were no longer widely understood (even, it seems, by some clergymen). During the 1840s and 1850s, apart from the well-publicised secessions to the

Roman Catholic Church, the main controversies in the Church of England were those connected with Baptism and the Eucharist. As far as architecture was concerned, both Sacraments were important, and brought about architectural responses, but of the two the Eucharist was by far the more significant in the evolution of Anglican worship and the design of churches and their altars.

In the 1850s, George Anthony Denison (1805-96 — who had been up at Oxford when the Tractarians began their activities), archdeacon of Taunton, defined his doctrinal position on the Eucharist in three sermons preached in Wells Cathedral in 1853 and 1854. In these, he explicitly affirmed the Real Presence of the Elements, and the consequent adorability of the Sacrament (though not of the sensible species). This doctrine defines the actual and objective presence of the Body and Blood of Christ in the Eucharistic Sacrament. Thus Denison upheld the Sacrament as a true symbol (a symbol being what it represents), whilst the Protestant / Calvinistic / Evangelical persuasions denied the reality, claiming that the Body and Blood were present only in an allegorical sense (an allegory representing what it, in itself, is not).

The Evangelical Alliance instituted a prosecution, and Denison's views were declared contrary to the Articles of Religion by John Bird Sumner (1780-1862), Archbishop of Canterbury. Previously, in relation to the Gorham case, Sumner (chosen by the Whig premier as Archbishop) had concurred with the judgement of the Privy Council whereby it was determined that a clergyman of the Church of England 'need not believe in baptismal regeneration'. After this, Bishop Phillpotts of Exeter had accused the Archbishop of promoting heresy in the Church, and the Anglo-Catholic party within the Anglican Church lost several clergy to Rome. Although in Denison's case he was sentenced to deprivation, he appealed to the Court of Arches, which resulted in a reversal on a technical point in 1857, and an appeal against this decision was dismissed by the Judicial Committee of the Privy Council (1858) without any determination of the substantive question, all of which (as in the Gorham case) merely served to illustrate the uncertainty of the law, and the Anglican Church's position *vis-à-vis* the State was seen by High Churchmen as anomalous.

To Anglo-Catholics the Eucharistic Controversy was absurd, because, it was argued, the doctrine of the Real Presence could be defended by reference to the Catechism in the *Book of Common Prayer*, the early Church, and the writings of Anglican divines from Latimer's time. Keble and Pusey (among others) had defended the doctrine too.

Another clergyman, this time the Bishop of Brechin, Alexander Penrose Forbes (1817-75 — also much influenced by the Oxford Movement when up at that University in the 1840s), got into trouble in 1857 when, at a meeting of the diocesan synod, he delivered his primary charge, which took the form of a manifesto on the Eucharist in which he defended the doctrine of the Real Presence. Uproar ensued, and at an episcopal synod it was proposed that a declaration on the doctrine should be issued on the authority of the College of Bishops: the motion was lost, but a declaration of similar import was issued by the Bishops of Edinburgh, Argyll, and Glasgow, intended to injure Forbes. Keble intervened and published various ripostes, but Forbes was formally tried in 1860, admonished, and censured.

These were only two cases. The High Church, Tractarian, or Ritualist parties within the Anglican Church had always attracted displeasure in certain quarters. Some of the practices introduced by High Church clergy again came before the Judicial Committee of the Privy Council in the case of Westerton *v.* Liddell (1857), when 'Ritualistic' services at St Paul's, Knightsbridge, came under attack from those who disapproved of what came increasingly to be regarded as crypto-Popery leading to 'perfumed Rome' itself. However, the result of this case (which included a declaration that liturgical candles were 'contrary to law' except for the purpose of 'giving necessary light') was not regarded as entirely discouraging to the Ritualists (among whom the figure of Father Wagner of Brighton was conspicuous at the centre of the

floraison), and over the next two decades there was a widespread increase in ritual usages, such as vestments, altar-lights, and incense.

In 1860 the English Church Union was formed to uphold High Church principles and to assist clergy who attracted the disfavour of the Low Church Protestant Evangelical parties. However, the latter responded by forming the Church Association in 1865 with the express purpose of prosecuting Ritualists and preventing the increase in Ritualistic practices. Matters came to such a pass that a Royal Commission was appointed in 1867, which recommended that parishioners aggrieved by Ritualism should be granted help to stop such practices, and indeed between 1867 and 1871 the Judicial Committee of the Privy Council was openly hostile to the Ritualists.

To give another example, Arthur Heriot Mackonochie (1825-87), of St Alban's, Holborn, was systematically persecuted for his Ritualism, and from 1867 until his premature death was harried through the ecclesiastical courts in a vicious series of campaigns by the Church Association. Mackonochie was suspended for three years, and supported during that time by the English Church Union, which also paid his not inconsiderable costs.

John Purchas, the distinguished ecclesiologist, when perpetual curate (from 1866) of St James's Chapel, Brighton, was prosecuted in 1871 for his Ritualistic practices, including the so-called 'Six Points' (facing eastwards during celebration of the Eucharist; using the mixed chalice; employing unleavened bread; placing lights on the altar; wearing linen vestments; and burning incense). The Judicial Committee of the Privy Council (predictably) ruled against Purchas, and specifically forbade the use of vestments and the eastward position, a judgement that High Churchmen pronounced as 'tyranny'.

Official and public hostility was perceived by High Churchmen to be persecution, and, as a result, Ritualism became widespread, for there is nothing like persecution to intensify religious devotions: many clergymen believed that Ritualistic practices were incumbent upon them (yet those practices were condemned as illegal by mechanisms set up outside the Church and by some shades of opinion within the Church), and held that the approved rubrics of the Church were sloppily disregarded or neglected by many Low Church Evangelicals.

The Ritualists' position was not helped when Archibald Campbell Tait was enthroned as Archbishop of Canterbury in 1869. It will be recalled that Tait had contested the claims made by Newman in *Tract XC*, and opposed interpretations of the Articles of the Church of England in any sense favourable to 'Romanist' beliefs and practices which those Articles had been framed expressly to condemn: he argued that the *Tract* was grossly distorted in its reasoning. Tait became Archbishop of London in 1856, and in 1859 he withdrew the licence of Alfred Poole, curate of the church of St Barnabas, Pimlico, London, on the grounds that Poole's practice of Confession was inconsistent with that recognised by the *Book of Common Prayer*. In 1859 Tait also had to contend with the uproar occasioned by the riots at the church of St George-in-the-East, Wapping, occasioned by the introduction of Ritualistic innovations by the High Church incumbent, Charles Fuge Lowder (1820-80), on whose head fell the wrath of a blaspheming anti-Papist mob, and, later, of the Church Association. Tait's tenure of the Throne of St Augustine therefore began during violent controversy, and just as Disestablishment of the Anglican Church of Ireland became a reality, so it was not an easy time for any Archbishop. In 1874, the *Public Worship Regulation Act* (37 & 38 Vict. c. 85) attempted to bring to an end several years of disputes.

Nevertheless, in 1878-81, four Ritualistic Anglican clergymen were imprisoned for disobeying the orders of Courts against the jurisdiction of which they protested. The result of all this was that illegal usages within the Church became widespread, and in due course the Bishop of Lincoln (Edward King [1829-1910 — consecrated Bishop in 1885]) had proceedings in respect of illegal ritual instituted against him in 1889, and was cited before his metropolitan, the Archbishop of Canterbury (by then Edward White Benson [Primate from 1882]), to answer charges of sundry ritual offences committed in 1887 during the administration of Holy Communion in the Diocese of Lincoln. These 'offences' included using lighted candles on the 'Holy Table' when these were not needed for light, mixing water with wine in the chalice during the Service and consecrating the 'mixed cup', facing the 'Holy Table' while celebrating, causing the *Agnus Dei* to be sung after the prayer of Consecration, and making the Sign of the Cross in the air, among other heinous crimes. The Archbishop heard the case, and in the end pronounced (1890) no admonition on or condemnation of the Bishop although the Sign of the Cross and the mixing in the chalice during the Service were proscribed. The Church Association, outraged by this result, appealed to the Judicial Committee of the Privy Council, but in 1892 the appeal was dismissed and the Archbishop's judgement upheld. The 'Lincoln Judgement' aided the progress of the Ritualistic and Doctrinal Movements within the Anglican Church that had evolved from the Oxford Movement and Tractarianism, and which had become known as Anglo-Catholicism. Furthermore, the publication of the influential *Lux Mundi* (Light of the World) encouraged the progress of soundly-based intellectual criticism of Biblical topics, and strengthened the vitality of the Anglo-Catholic Movement.

Yet matters were by no means plain sailing. Anglo-Catholicism attracted strong and violent opposition, notably from the Protestant Truth Society, founded in 1890 by John Kensit (1853-1902), the militant agitator: he organised a band of itinerant preachers called 'Wycliffites' who raided Ritualistic churches throughout the country, interrupted services, and even attempted to secure the election to Parliament of men devoted to the destruction of Ritualism. Needless to say, Brighton was a happy hunting-ground for such activities, and Father Wagner attracted the loathing of the Society's activists: Brighton churches were daubed with slogans, and damage was done to furniture and fittings. Architecture and design gave visible expression to Ritualistic tendencies, and indeed were essential to the development of the Anglo-Catholic Movement: the elaborate and beautiful reredoses, sedilia, piscinæ, Rood-screens, and chapels with statuary and altars were demanded by Anglo-Catholicism, and designers such as Bodley rose to the occasion. That something as lovely as the interior of Clumber church, with its Rood-screen, priest's- and choir-stalls carved by the Reverend Ernest Geldart (1848-1929), stained glass all by Kempe (Bodley's first pupil), and statue of Our Lady by another pupil of Bodley, the young John Ninian Comper (1864-1960), should arouse hatred and destructive impulses is sobering and of great concern, for such a beautiful ensemble should, in a just world, attract only admiration and profoundly moving responses. Here was an architectural and artistic creation designed to bring the beholder to his or her knees, and at Clumber Bodley and his team served the ardent Anglo-Catholic Duke of Newcastle very well.

Protestant bigots were gleeful and High Churchmen were appalled by certain events in the 1890s. Leo XIII (Pope 1878-1903) began to speak of 'separated brethren', and in his letter *Ad Anglos* (1895) revealed his especial concern for the conversion of England. Prompted by certain enlightened and forward-looking French clergy who proposed that Anglican Orders should be recognised as valid by the Roman Catholic Church, the Pope appointed a Commission to examine the subject in 1895, but that Commission (loaded as it was with very conservative Italian clerics) reported adversely, and in the Bull *Apostolicæ Curæ* of 13 September 1896 Leo XIII pronounced that Ordinations performed by the Anglican Rite were utterly invalid and altogether null. This provoked further anti-Roman Catholic controversy, and assisted the extreme Protestant parties in their attacks on Anglo-Catholicism and on Ritualism generally. It also led to Garner's conversion to Roman Catholicism, which seems to have been one of the reasons why his partnership with Bodley ended in 1898. In 1899 the Archbishops of Canterbury and York condemned the use of incense and lights in processions, and most of the diocesan bishops accepted this condemnation. Furthermore, in 1900 Reservation of the Blessed Sacrament in Anglican churches was condemned, but although several bishops tried to secure obedience within their dioceses, the condemnation was not enforced effectively on a national basis. So lax did matters become that a Royal Commission on ecclesiastical discipline was appointed in 1904 which reported in 1906 that many practices were 'clearly inconsistent with and subversive of the teaching of the Church of England'. Nevertheless, Anglo-Catholicism survived, continuing the best traditions of the Oxford and Tractarian Movements, building on and developing modern Biblical scholarship, while also involving artistic endeavours and tradition in worship within the Church.

CHAPTER VIII

The Late-Victorian Church
in Several Manifestations

Architectural Consequences: Introduction; St Agnes, Kennington; Roman Catholic Developments; Anglican Liturgiology; The Arts-and-Crafts Influence; Stylistic Changes; Other Late-Gothic Churches

Bodley fills an important position in the history of English ecclesiastical architecture. If Pugin, Scott, and Street were the pioneers whose work went hand in hand with the Oxford movement in its early days, Bodley is their counterpart in the last quarter of the nineteenth century.
PAUL WATERHOUSE (1861-1924): Entry on Bodley in *The Dictionary of National Biography Supplement* (January 1901-December 1911) (Oxford: Oxford University Press, 1920), 189.

Where the Chancel can be of considerable length, then there is no doubt that a high Rood Screen is the greatest possible ornament to the interior, but I think it requires very considerable depth behind it to give it its true value. It is curious, however, the prejudice one frequently meets against a Screen.
TEMPLE LUSHINGTON MOORE (1856-1920): *Architectural Association Journal*, **xxii** (1907), 36.

Architectural Consequences: Introduction

The result of the various cases alluded to above was that Anglo-Catholic clergy continued to defend their positions in their sermons, and the persecution encouraged the advance of Ritualism, especially as a means of expressing the Eucharistic doctrine as a grave and dignified ceremony in Anglican churches. It was even more significant, in that what had been the Oxford Movement and Tractarianism in the 1830s and 1840s evolved into a vigorous Anglo-Catholicism, and from around the end of the 1860s Anglican ecclesiastical architecture was greatly stimulated by Catholic principles similar to those that had fired Pugin. So powerful was the Anglo-Catholic response to persecution that very soon a type of plan for churches was evolved, and craftsmen were encouraged in the production of ornaments, furnishings, artefacts, and everything required for Anglo-Catholic ceremonial. The close involvement of leading architects with the theological and liturgical issues of the time ensured the type of the late-Victorian church: all were Anglo-Catholics, all believed that the twentieth-

century Anglican Church would be Anglo-Catholic; and all were men of great talent and learning.

St Agnes, Kennington

The design principles embodied in Albi and Gerona Cathedrals and in the church of the Dominicans, Gent, gloriously realised at St Augustine's, Pendlebury, suited the needs of Anglo-Catholicism, and the exemplar for the late-Victorian church had arrived. George Gilbert Scott Junior for a time shared a drawing-office with Bodley and Garner in Church Row, Hampstead, and it was Scott who introduced J. D. Sedding to the others. Many of the points made in later years in papers given by Bodley, Scott, and Sedding are identical, and it is probable these derived from discussions held during the time spent at Church Row. It was Scott who created the next most influential Anglican church building with his church, school, and vicarage of St Agnes, Kennington, London (1874-91 — destroyed). The designs for this were published in 1875, and aroused a storm of disapproval, for the style was

77. Interior of the church of St Agnes, Kennington Park, London (1874-91 – destroyed), by George Gilbert Scott Junior. One of the most influential church-designs of the late nineteenth century, it combined late Perpendicular Gothic with certain Continental features, notably the Flügelaltar. *The beautiful Rood-screen (completed under the direction of Temple Moore) was used liturgically* (GB. Copy Negative 1964 of a photograph taken c.1890. EH. AA75/2102 [1964]).

strongly influenced by the late fourteenth- and early fifteenth-century English Perpendicular that for so long had been anathematised from the time of Pugin onwards for supposed decadence. Critics found the low pitches of the gables, the square-headed windows, unorthodox buttresses, and plan hard to take. This plan included tiny transepts that did not project beyond the walls of the aisles, chapels at the ends of each aisle, and a sanctuary raised so that the altar was at eye-level. Gradually, however, the sensitive refinement of Scott's work gained its admirers. C. E. Kempe carried out most of the furnishings and painted decorations as well as the stained-glass windows: furniture included the parclose screens enclosing the chapels; the carved, painted, and gilded triptych, or *Flügelaltar* (designed by Scott and Temple Moore), based on the fifteenth-century German exemplar at Oberwesel, and set well in front of the east window leaving a passage behind it; and the Rood-screen and loft constructed to be used liturgically **(Plate 77)**.

Pearson's church of St Augustine, Kilburn, had been founded as a result of attempts to suppress Ritualism in the parish: St Agnes was also founded as an Anglo-Catholic church by a faction that had been obliged to break with the parish in order to establish its own place of worship. Its founder was a mediævalist, and St Agnes's soon became famous for its pre-Reformation English ceremonials based on the old Sarum Rite: plainsong, well-designed embroidered vestments, processions with banners, and singing from the Rood-loft would have gladdened all Anglo-Catholic hearts and provoked Evangelicals to outraged distraction. The curates of St Agnes's were also mediævalists, and in due course carried their ideals to other parishes: in short, St Agnes's was a catalyst in very many ways for the evolution of ecclesiastical and liturgical design for decades to come. Nevertheless, its architecture, the beauty of its rituals, and its mediævalism were extremely suspect in certain quarters: such suspicions were exacerbated (and were said to be justified) when its architect, Scott, became a Roman Catholic in 1880.

However, Scott made a great contribution to liturgiology as well as to the design of churches. In 1881 he brought out an interesting volume entitled *An Essay on the History of English Church Architecture prior to the Separation of England from the Roman Obedience* in which he set English ecclesiastical architecture within an historic context, relating it back to early Roman basilicas. The *Essay* contained illustrations of early altars (over which were baldachins) and of the churches. In the text Scott argued that liturgical use must therefore influence (and even dictate) plans and internal volumes of churches (something that should have been obvious, but clearly was not as widely understood as it should have been).

Roman Catholic Developments

This was not the only influential text. Roman Catholic intellectuals also busied themselves with studies of liturgy and how it affected congregations in terms of seating, movement within a church-building, and much else. They were also concerned to study the practicalities of

early-Christian, mediæval, and (particularly interestingly) recusant worship. Many, like their Anglican counterparts, were mediævalists, steeped in the study of ancient liturgical texts, and many revered Pugin and his works.

One of the most influential of these Roman Catholic ecclesiologists (or liturgiologists) was Edmund Bishop (1846-1917), who was an expert on the development of church archi-tecture and styles, and who, in 1881, gave an important paper on the baldachin (or *baldacchino*), which he insisted was a necessary part of any Christian altar. When Frederick Arthur Walters (1849-1931) designed the Jesuit church of the Sacred Heart, Edge Hill, Wimbledon (1886-1901), he provided a *baldacchino* over the high altar, and the build-ing acquired furnishings and stained glass by members of the Guild of St Gregory and St Luke (of which Walters was a member), a body founded to promote the study of Christian antiquities and to disseminate the principles of Christian art. However, the plan of the church ensured that views of the altar from the aisles were obscured by the nave-arcades.

Leonard Aloysius Scott Stokes (1858-1925), also a member of the Guild, and a former pupil of Street and Bodley, created a Roman Catholic equivalent of St Augustine, Pendlebury, at the church of St Clare, Arundel Avenue, Sefton Park, Liverpool (1888-90), though there is more than a touch of Pearson's St Augustine's, Kilburn, there too, but the handling of Gothic, though dependent to a certain extent on the *Wandpfeiler* (wall-pier) arrangement of the Dominican church in Gent for its general arrangement, is actually very original, and the triforium-gallery also pierces the wall-piers as well as the aisle-passage. Stokes's wide nave enables the congregation to have good views of the altar.

John Francis Bentley was another member of the Guild, and Bishop's influence on Westminster Cathedral is clear. Not only is the building **(Plates 78 and 79)** a development of the wall-pier system of Albi and Gent (Byzantinised), but there is a splendid *baldacchino* over the high altar that was entirely due to Bishop's badgering of a reluctant Bentley. A careful

78. Exterior of the Roman Catholic Cathedral of Westminster (designed from 1894), from the liturgical south-west, by John Francis Bentley. It features Diocletian or Thermal windows in the clearstorey, and is in the Byzantine Revival style (EH. CC73/ 1952 [c.1910]).

79. Interior of the Roman Catholic Cathedral of Westminster from the east, with the high altar and its baldacchino in the foreground (AFK. W.602 [1955]).

study of Bentley's brilliant designs for the Cathedral will show that, despite its details, it owes much to the ideals of the later Gothic Revival, especially in terms of space, visibility, and liturgical research.

Bentley worked on his designs for Westminster Cathedral from 1894, a vast brick pile with stone dressings in the Byzantine style **(Plates 78 and 79)**. Cardinal Henry Edward Manning (1808-92 — who had converted from Anglicanism in 1851) had proposed a building based on the Constantinian Basilica of San Pietro in Rome (destroyed when the present Basilica was erected in the sixteenth century), but Cardinal Herbert Alfred Vaughan (1832-1903 — Manning's successor) insisted on something Italian or Byzantine, so Bentley combined a basilican form with constructional systems and stylistic elements derived from Byzantine, Early Christian, and Romanesque exemplars he had studied in Rome,

Pisa, Milan, Ravenna, and other places. Such a stylistic choice was prompted by a growing interest in Byzantine forms at the time, but it also seems that the Church Hierarchy was anxious to create a distinctive building which would emphasise the historical and Roman connections (remembering that the Hierarchy had only been restored in the 1850s), which would be a dignified and suitable Cathedral — impressive, modern, yet joined to the great traditions from the time of St Peter the Apostle, and which could not be confused with the Anglican Abbey down the road. It should also be remembered that Gothic and Gothic Revival (despite Pugin) were primarily associated with the Church of England, so there were good reasons why the new Roman Catholic Cathedral should be distinctive and different.

Bentley's scheme draws on many precedents. First there is the vast nave covered with pendentived domes, and the high passage-aisles running through gigantic wall-piers supporting transverse barrel-vaults ending in

Diocletian windows; those aisles have chapels beyond them. Essentially this develops the Albi system, with Pearsonian overtones, but there is also a Baroque second element taken from the plan of the mother-church of the Society of Jesus in Rome, *Il Gesù* (begun 1568), by Jacopo Barozzi da Vignola (1507-73) and Giacomo della Porta (*c.*1533-1602): like *Il Gesù*, Westminster Cathedral has wall-piers through which are passages; side-chapels; transepts that barely project beyond the outer walls of the side-chapels; a dome over the crossing; barrel-vaults about the easternmost dome; and an apsidal east end. The third precedent is the desire for spatial clarity that grew from the Gothic Revival, and Bentley's Cathedral incorporates many of the planning and structural systems that had been discussed and experimented with at length by ecclesiologists, liturgiologists, and Goths: Westminster Cathedral could be Gothicised and still have the same plan. Finally, Bishop's influence is clear when the great *baldacchino* is considered, although Bishop, as a Puginian, could hardly approve of Bentley's stylistic solutions.

Anglican Liturgiology

In 1879 John Wickham Legg (1843-1921) founded the St Paul's Ecclesiological Society (which might be regarded as having similar aims to those of the Roman Catholic Guild of St Gregory and St Luke) in order to further studies in liturgiology, ecclesiology, and allied subjects. Legg was also the founder of the Henry Bradshaw Society, a body which printed rare liturgical texts: for the Society Legg himself edited the *Westminster Missal* (1891-97), and for the Clarendon Press the *Sarum Missal* (1916). However, Legg also provided a vast amount of scholarly evidence to show that from 1660 to 1833 traditional Anglican Church doctrines and practices prevailed far more commonly than the Oxford Movement had led people to believe. Extremely critical of a growing tendency among Anglo-Catholics of introducing then current liturgical practices, without proper historical inquiry, from France or Belgium, he was also suspicious (as well he might be) of liberal theology and change for the sake of change.

Indeed in 1909 and 1911 he published learned and rather ferocious pamphlets opposing any revisions of the *Prayer Book*, claiming that the then generation lacked both the knowledge and the taste to do so with any success. What Legg would have said about recent developments must remain a subject for bemused speculation, but there can be no doubt he would have disapproved, and done so with vigour.

Legg's work for the Henry Bradshaw Society was recognised as having no parallels in other countries, and even Roman Catholic commentators (e.g. Henry Thurston, S. J., in the Introduction to the 1937 edition of *The Mass* by Adrian Fortescue [1874-1923]) acknowledged that liturgical studies and research into the origins of the Mass owed much to Anglican scholarship. Legg came to the conclusion that, like Pugin, modern liturgiologists and architects should take their inspiration from the Middle Ages, and remember that the *Prayer Book* directed that chancels should remain 'as in times past'. He declared that mediæval liberty of practice was preferable to the attempts of the Roman Catholic 'Congregation of Rites to establish all over the world the iron uniformity which is the aspiration in most things of the nineteenth century', something Roman Catholic architects themselves found very restricting. He also opined that all that was 'Roman' was 'not ancient', and, remembering the High Churchmen of old, that not every pre-Oxford Movement clergyman was a Puritan.

It is interesting that Legg found Bodley's work most unsatisfactory for basing his altars too closely on Purchas's publication and on contemporary Continental models that were erroneously imagined to be derived from mediæval precedents. Indeed, he regarded Bodley's designs as having taken much from designs evolved during the Counter Reformation, dressed up in German *Spätgotik* garb. The problem with buildings like St Augustine's, Pendlebury, for Legg, and those who thought like him, was that it was rather like a large room 'with an altar at one end', and not sufficiently rooted in English liturgical history to be entirely satisfactory. Perhaps more to Legg's taste were the exemplars of the Austin Friars church and the Puginian/Carpenterian themes derived from the church of St Mary Magdalene, Munster Square: these were also influences on Micklethwaite when he designed St Paul's, Augustus Road, Wimbledon Park, London (1888-96), in partnership (1876-92) with Somers Clarke (1841-1926). There, the tall and handsome nave-arcades support a wagon-roof (there is no clearstorey), and stylistically the building is a satisfying mixture of Second Pointed and Perpendicular. The church was glazed and furnished by Kempe, who also provided the beautiful Perpendicular Rood-screen **(Plate 80)**.

Bodley, however, carried out numerous commissions to design furnishings and fittings in Anglican churches, and was much sought-after. For example, he added the lovely Rood-screen and narthex to Carpenter's church of St Paul, Brighton (which became famous for its Ritualist services under the cherubic Father Wagner). He also designed a sumptuous reredos for the church of St Barnabas, Pimlico, London, which his pupil, John Ninian Comper, saw in 1892, and did not think it had the 'old Gothic ring

about it, nor … the grave and real character' of a Tractarian church. Towards the end of his life, Bodley designed (1899) the handsome reredos for St Mary de Castro, Leicester, with plenty of vine-scroll or trail ornament, originally intended to have a red background, but realised in green.

So, in a remarkably short time, the wheel had moved full circle, and the Gothic Revival had returned to the period beloved by Pugin — English Second Pointed — but carried out with far greater *bravura* and confidence than had been apparent in the work of the 1840s. English churches were being built and fitted out with wonderfully crafted artefacts, the like of which had not been seen since the 1520s, and, gradually, it was to the late-mediæval period that architects increasingly turned for their inspiration. Bodley's late style was followed by numerous architects, including Edward Graham Paley (1823-95) and his partner Hubert James

81. Exterior from the south-west of the church of St George, Buxton Road, Stockport, Cheshire (1893-97), by H.J. Austin & E.G. Paley. It is an essay in a refined and coherent Perpendicular (Third Pointed) style, and was built at the expense of the brewer, George Fearn. The spire, with its thin flying buttresses, is loosely derived from that of the parish-church at Louth, Lincolnshire (EH. BL 14811A [1900]).

80. Interior of the church of St Paul, Augustus Road, Wimbledon Park (1888-96), by J.T. Micklethwaite and Somers Clarke. Furnished and glazed by Kempe, this interior comes close to realising the ideal of an authentic mediævalising architectural setting for soundly-based Anglican liturgy (GB. EH.AA78/373 [1960]).

Austin (1841-1915), whose noble church of St George, Buxton Road, Stockport, Cheshire (1893-97), is a late and ripe example: Pevsner described this splendid church as a 'masterpiece of the latest historicism, designed just before the most original younger English architects began to turn away from the strict Gothic Revival', but the style was Perpendicular (Third Pointed), and a powerful, assured, spectacular Perpendicular at that **(Plates 81 and 82)**. It was not a cheap church, and was paid for by George Fearn, a local brewer, whose munificence helped to create the grandest church in Stockport and for miles around. The panelled effects of external wall-surfaces were an innovation, and the design is soundly based on precedent, used with verve and

imagination: St George's is one of the most satisfying of all large churches erected in the Victorian period, and must be recognised as among the most successful architectural ensembles of the time. Indeed, Pevsner brackets St George's, Stockport, with Bodley's own late church of St Mary, Eccleston, Cheshire (1894-99), as the 'most majestic of the representations of Victorian historicism'.

St Mary's **(Plates 83 and 84)** did not owe its existence to a brewer, but to Hugh Lupus Grosvenor, 1st Duke of Westminster (1825-99), whose monument (designed by Bodley, with effigy carved by Léon-Joseph Chavalliaud and designed by Farmer & Brindley) occupies a position between the chancel and the south

82.   Interior of the church of St George, Stockport, Cheshire, from the west, showing the panel-like effect of the upper part of the nave wall-surfaces. This is an example of the imaginative and sensitive interpretation of Perpendicular Gothic which was a feature of the Gothic Revival during the last years of Queen Victoria's reign (EH. BL 14814A [1900]).

83. South elevation of the church of St Mary, Eccleston, Cheshire (1894-99), by Bodley, and reckoned to be one of his finest churches. It is in a starkly rectangular type of Gothic, but with Second Pointed tracery. Originally there was a miniature spire over the tower (EH. AA77/6529 [1969]).

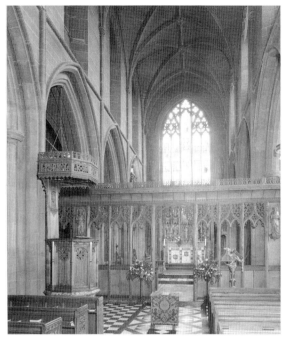

84. Interior of the church of St Mary, Eccleston, Cheshire, by Bodley, from the west. It is entirely of ashlar, is rib-vaulted throughout with transverse, diagonal, and ridge-ribs, and there is no structural change marking the chancel (which was a feature of many late mediæval Perpendicular churches in England, especially in East Anglia, where the chancel was simply screened off, although there was usually a greater richness in the treatment of the timber chancel-roof inside). Nave-piers are eclectic, with elements drawn from a range of First, Second, and Third Pointed features. Bodley's use of ornament is confined to the roof-bosses and furnishings, including the fine reredos (by Farmer & Brindley) and the screen (EH. AA77/6517 [1969]).

chapel. The Bodley church is largely Second Pointed, although the furnishings (by Watts & Co.) show a delicious blend of the 'refined and inventive ornament' based on fourteenth- and fifteenth- century exemplars for which Bodley is celebrated. Pevsner admired the interior, where the architect's 'sensitive Gothic, redolent of scholarly and patrician Anglicanism', can be seen to advantage, especially the impressive red-sandstone ribbed vaulting. Pevsner also noted the grouping of mouldings and shafts on the arcade-piers as neither strictly Decorated nor strictly Perpendicular. The reredoses (carried out by Farmer & Brindley) are particularly beautiful, and the screens which define the chancel are good examples of Bodley's work, although the screens are uncoloured, which is a pity in such a large space entirely enclosed in sandstone, and there is an argument that some scholarly applications of colour and gilding would improve the ensemble. Stained glass throughout was by Burlison & Grylls. None of the architectural splendour would have been possible without the Tractarians, the Anglo-Catholic Movement, and, ultimately, Pugin: and it was money, too, which helped, for there is no doubt that the finest Victorian churches were privately funded by wealthy patrons.

The Arts-and-Crafts Influence

A return to the intricacy and finely-crafted work that took as its inspiration English late-Gothic art coincided with the rise of the Arts-and-Crafts Movement, an English social and æsthetic phenomenon that grew from a dissatisfaction with the quality of design in mechanically manufactured artefacts, especially after the Great Exhibition of 1851. It had its origins in an admiration for traditional art and craftsmanship, and in a romantic longing to recapture the supposed ideal of the mediæval Craft Guilds: these notions can be traced to the theories of Jean-Jacques Rousseau (1712-78 — who advocated the teaching of manual skills to everybody), to the writings of Pugin, and to the polemics of Ruskin. The key figure of the Movement was William Morris, who first built his own house and then designed the furnishings for it, then founded the firm of Morris, Marshall, & Faulkner in 1861, which produced wallpapers, the ornamental parts of stained-glass windows, printed patterns, furniture, and much else. Thus the firm re-created hand-crafted industry in a machine age. The Movement influenced young architects and designers, crusaded to make towns beautiful, sought to reform Society so that ugliness would be abolished, and argued for the preservation and protection of old buildings. The philosophy of doing the minimum to conserve buildings without altering their character was developed, largely as a reaction against certain drastic 'restorations' of churches carried out by certain Victorian architects who favoured virtual rebuilds in a revival of mediæval styles (or *pot-pourris* of bits of mediæval churches cribbed from Bloxam or Parker) rather than a sensitive conservation of old fabric. In fact the Movement and its adherents, especially William Morris, were responsible for the founding of The Society for the Protection of Ancient Buildings (SPAB — affectionately known as 'Anti-Scrape'). However, the Arts-and-Crafts Movement, which grew out of the Gothic Revival, also influenced that Revival, notably in its last phase.

Stylistic Changes
In the 1880s, then, questions about planning, liturgical requirements, visibility, and so on were in the air, and we have seen how the Roman Catholic Guild of St Gregory and St Luke brought its influence to bear at Walters's church in Wimbledon. There are two Anglican churches in London where the Arts-and-Crafts influences may be seen to their best advantage.

The first is St Cuthbert's, Philbeach Gardens, Earl's Court, London (1884-87), by Hugh Roumieu Gough (1843-1904), a vast and lofty brick structure with lean-to aisles, the whole modelled on Transitional and Cistercian mediæval types (the immediate model being Tintern Abbey), with a Frenchified *flèche* on the roof, the dominant architectural language being First Pointed. From 1887 until 1914, however, Gough's great barn-like cavernous interior was lavishly beautified with fittings and furnishings, so that the church became a monument to Anglo-Catholic taste as well as to the Arts-and-Crafts Movement **(Plate 85)**. Among the designers involved in this sumptuous work were W. Bainbridge Reynolds, the Reverend Ernest Geldart, J. Harold Gibbons, and Gilbert Boulton. St Cuthbert's was built under the ægis of the Reverend Henry Westall, who made the church the most flourishing High Church foundation in Kensington, with the result that on Good Friday, 1898, it was raided by John Kensit and his cronies, who proceeded to disrupt the Service of the Adoration of the Cross (a once-popular mediæval practice revived at St Cuthbert's). Kensit was duly depicted on one of the misericords in the chancel complete with the ears of an ass. The beautification of St Cuthbert's was carried out by craftsmen (many of them amateurs) who were organised into Craft Guilds to work under professionals: the stone diaper-work around the walls was made by the Guild of St Peter; the chancel-stalls were created by the Guild of St Joseph; and the handsome vestments were designed and worked by the Guild of St Margaret. All the Guild-members were 'united to emulate in piety and generosity'.

Thus at St Cuthbert's certain tendencies, imported from Belgium (Brugge in particular) by W.H.J. Weale (the founder of the Guild of St Gregory and St Luke, who had been closely involved in the Guild of Sts Thomas and Luke in Flanders) were developed. Although Father Symondson has drawn attention to the importance of the Guild of St Gregory and St Luke in the 1880s in Roman Catholic circles, the Flemish connection has been often overlooked, yet Weale was active in Brugge from the mid-1860s, and the Dominican church in Gent was illustrated by Cubitt as early as 1869, that is just before the important churches of St Augustine, Kilburn, and St Augustine, Pendlebury, were built. Thus,

85. *Interior of the church of St Cuthbert, Philbeach Gardens, Kensington, London, from the west, showing the nave arcades that owe much to Cistercian types of the First Pointed variety. Piers are of polished Torquay marble. Beautification of the church (1887-1914) converted the bare interior into a monument of Anglo-Catholic Taste. Gough designed the Rood-loft (1893), but the reredos (1899-1900), in a Spanish mediæval style, was by the Reverend Ernest Geldart (1848-1929). Decorations of surfaces were carried out by specially-created Guilds of newly-trained craftsmen working in the Arts-and-Crafts spirit* (EH. AA78/6916 [1965]).

although Albi is always quoted as the model for Pearson's and Bodley & Garner's great works, the church of the Dominicans, Gent, is actually far closer to Pendlebury than is Albi.

The second London church where Arts-and-Crafts influences can be studied with benefit is Holy Trinity, Sloane Street, Chelsea (1888-90), designed by John Dando Sedding, who had studied with Street, and who was intimately connected with the Arts-and-Crafts Movement. Sedding was a passionate Anglo-Catholic, and perceived religious art and architecture as being at the core of European culture. Moreover, he saw art, and especially ecclesiastical art, as essential to the civilising and redemption of the urban masses. Aware of the problems of ugly, polluted, hideous, miserable conditions in the worst parts of urbanised England, he demanded that the priest and artist should bring beauty that would be seen by the poor man without envy or despair. Religion and Art influence each other, Sedding declared. Devoted to the Incarnation, from which the Sacraments flowed, Sedding argued that the altar must be the centre of Christian worship, for there God, operating through and in matter, made the Incarnation real and living in the Eucharistic Sacrament. Fired with zeal to bring living churches to the people, and to create beautifully crafted art for the people, Sedding saw Christ in art and architecture: if He were not, then art and architecture would be meaningless.

With his church of The Holy Trinity (**Plates 86 and 87**), Sedding achieved his ambition to create a church fully decorated and furnished by contemporary artists. He took as his starting-point the English Perpendicular Gothic style as it had been left at the end of fifteenth and beginning of the sixteenth century. Taking up certain 'threads of the Gothic tradition' (as he put it), he wove 'them into the weft of modern' needs and theories. The style of Holy Trinity therefore returned to a very late Perpendicular Gothic of the St George's Chapel, Windsor, type (although all the tracery was Second Pointed), but in the furnishings and fittings Gothic, Renaissance, and Arts-and-Crafts themes were mixed with spicings of Byzantine and *Art Nouveau* elements adding flavour to an already rich brew. Of course, the church was well-funded, and the patron was a wealthy aristocrat, George Henry, 5th Earl Cadogan (1840-1915). Thus the interior of Holy Trinity is a wonderful repository of examples of design dating from the 1890s to the 1914-18 war. Sedding's work was carried on after his death by his pupil and successor, Henry Wilson, whose work at the church of St Bartholemew, Brighton, has already been mentioned. Holy Trinity contains fine work by Morris & Co., Burne-Jones, William Reynolds-Stephens (1862-1943), and many others. Reynolds-Stephens later designed the beautiful *Art Nouveau* fittings (including the screen and font) in the tiny church of St Mary the Virgin, Great Warley, Essex (consecrated 1904) the architect for which was Charles Harrison Townsend (1851-1928) (**Colour Plate XII**).

86. Exterior of the church of The Holy Trinity, Sloane Street, Chelsea, London (1888-90), by J.D. Sedding. The style has returned to that of late Perpendicular of the St George's chapel, Windsor, Berkshire, type, although window-tracery was in a sumptuous Second Pointed style of Curvilinear form. The striped structural polychromy is a survival of an earlier fashion pioneered in the works of Butterfield and Street. From a photo-litho by Sprague & Co. (EH. BB88/1866 [1888]).

87. Interior of the church of The Holy Trinity, Sloane Street, Chelsea, London, with (inset) a plan of the building, by J.D. Sedding. Note the transverse arches linking the piers of the nave to the aisle walls and the vaults spanning from those transverse arches. This is an excellent example of what is known as Free Gothic, or Arts-and-Crafts Gothic, and the building also incorporates certain Renaissance features, and touches of Byzantine and Art-Nouveau themes as well (EH. BB88/1865 [c.1888]).

Marvellous though these things are, Holy Trinity, apart from being very freely treated Gothic, is important because of its planning. The very large, high, clearstoreyed nave of four bays is continued in one further bay containing the choir (raised on a higher level and reached by a broad flight of steps), and the high altar (which was to have had an elaborate triptych as its reredos **[Plate 87]**) dominates the vista from the nave and is set in a further shorter bay with its own celure. The chancel is separated from the nave by low screens (or *cancelli*). To the north is a three-bay aisle ceiled with barrel-vaults running transversely, and containing an altar at the east end. This is, in fact, the Lady Chapel, with a remarkable altar raised within its sanctuary: in style the altar owes much to Early Christian

models, but over it is a Classical *baldacchino*, and the ensemble suggests Reservation of the Blessed Sacrament (retaining a portion of the Eucharistic elements after the celebration of that Sacrament). The south aisle is little more than a passage.

Now Holy Trinity has very little that is mediæval about it, despite the nods to late Perpendicular and Second Pointed tracery: Sedding's design enables the high altar to be visible from all parts of the nave, and the church is clearly a response to its architect's belief that the ceremonial of the Roman Catholic Church would sooner or later be adopted by Anglicans.

It is clear that Holy Trinity was conceived with its large, wide, high nave and the positioning of the high altar to facilitate a visual bond between the participants in the congregation and the Eucharistic Sacrament. In other words it was designed with the Mass in mind, and Sedding must have been influenced by Bishop and other Roman Catholic liturgiologists in arriving at the final form of this remarkable church.

Sedding was also responsible for the design of the church of Our Holy Redeemer, Exmouth Market, Clerkenwell, London (1887-95), an Italianate Early Renaissance Revival building, quite different in character from Holy Trinity, Sloane Street. It has a starkly simple west front crowned by a vast Tuscan pediment (with mutules resembling those of the church of St Paul, Covent Garden [1631-2], by Inigo Jones [1573-1652]) over a striped façade (punctured by a circular window) that rises above a plain brick wall in which is set a semi-circular-headed door. Crammed uncomfortably close to this powerful elevation is Henry Wilson's later *campanile*, an essay in the Early Christian Italian Romanesque style, that would not look out of place in Rome or Ravenna, except for the rather fussy fenestration in the lower stages **(Plate 88)**. Inside, the church has groin-vaults carried on an entablature supported by massive Corinthian columns (the capitals of which were carved by W. Pomeroy), giving a splendid Italian Renaissance impression that reminded Walter Horatio Pater (1839-94) of the Renaissance churches in Venice, and of Sir Christopher Wren's (1632-1723) London churches, as they might have looked when fresh and clean.

Our Holy Redeemer was intended to serve as a new parish-church for a poor district, and Sedding chose the Renaissance style as a means of exposing the congregation to art and to the altar and the Eucharistic Sacrament. To this end the sanctuary was raised and the altar placed within an enclosure and protected by a handsome *ciborium* enhancing the Italianate effect. There was no intervening choir or screen (the choir and organ were sited in a gallery to the west). This arrangement was achieved by adopting the scheme of a cross within a square which Wren had used in several City churches in the seventeenth century, so even the basic geometry harks back to the Renaissance and to Carolean models, and the Classical allusions also connect the building with Roman Catholic exemplars. From its beginnings the liturgies used in Our Holy Redeemer owed much to Rome, and, like its architecture, eschewed mediævalising ecclesiology.

A second church by Sedding and Wilson may be recalled here: St Peter's, Mount Park Road, Ealing (1889-93), resembles Holy Trinity in many respects, and demonstrates how the curvaceous forms of late Gothic could still be drawn upon and used with virtuosity and originality.

Mention has been made above of round-arched styles used in the 1840s and later, of which the most interesting examples of the earlier period were at Wilton, Wreay, and Streatham. The English versions of the *Rundbogenstil* were influenced by the works of Leo von Klenze especially, notably the *Allerheiligenhofkirche* (1827-37), and by Friedrich von Gärtner's *Ludwigskirche* (1829-40), both in Munich. The *Rundbogenstil* (by that time reinforced by Persius's beautiful *Friedenskirche* [1845-48] and Schinkel's Court Gardener's house [1829-31], both in Potsdam) re-emerged in the Italian-Romanesque basilica of St Barnabas, Cardigan Street, Jericho, Oxford (1869-87), designed by (Sir) Arthur William Blomfield, a pupil of P.C. Hardwick: the building, erected at the expense of the Anglo-Catholic Thomas Combe (who was an early patron of the Pre-Raphaelites), is rendered, with brick bands and other features, and the handsome *campanile* and noble *baldacchino* are in the *trecento* Italian-Gothic style. At the east

88. West front of the church of Our Holy Redeemer, Exmouth Market, Clerkenwell, London (1887-88), by J.D. Sedding. It is an Italianate Early Renaissance Revival building, with a vast Tuscan pediment crowning the composition. The campanile *is by Henry Wilson, and mixes Early Christian and Italian-Romanesque styles (EH. BB77/6818).*

end of the basilica is a large apse crowned with a hemi-dome embellished with the *Pantocrator* reminiscent of Sicilian Romanesque churches. At this point, the Romanesque style veers more strongly towards an Early Christian basilican style, a flavour reinforced by the various fittings (including the low *cancelli*) reminiscent of those in the basilica of San Clemente in Rome **(Colour Plate XIII)**.

The *Rundbogenstil* can also be found in the gritty Rhineland-Romanesque church of St Michael and All Angels, Ladbroke Grove, Kensington, London (1870-71), by James (1823-98) and James Stanning Edmeston (d. 1887): the church is faced with brick and terra-cotta, Red

IX. *Interior of the church of St Augustine, Kilburn Park Road, Paddington, London (1870-77), by J.L. Pearson. It is a remarkable synthesis of Gothic features from many European churches: the internal buttress arrangement is based on the Cathedral at Albi and the church of the Cordeliers, Toulouse, in France; the galleried section is derived from the hall-church of St Barbara at Kutná Hora (Kuttenberg), east of Prague; and the bridges over the transepts owe their origins to those in St Mark's in Venice. Motifs based on the rose-window of Byland Abbey, Yorkshire, the west end of Peterborough Cathedral, and the piers of the transeptal arrangement of the chapel of the Nine Altars at Fountains Abbey, Yorkshire, are all integrated within this scholarly and subtle design. The style is First Pointed throughout. Paintings (some of which were designed by Pearson himself) up to gallery level and featuring Biblical scenes are by Clayton & Bell (also responsible for the stained-glass windows), and the stone screen was added in 1890 to designs by Samuel Joseph Nicholl (1826-1905). The church is vaulted throughout, and carved decorations were executed by Thomas Nicholls* (MC. A190394 [1994]).

X. Church of St John the Baptist, West Derby Road, Tue Brook, Liverpool (1868-70), by George Frederick Bodley, beautifully restored by Stephen Dykes Bower. Interior from the west, showing the change of style from mid- to late-Victorian Gothic Revival. The east window has tracery of the Decorated Second Pointed type, and the exquisite screen emulates late-mediæval precedent. Clearstorey windows are sited over the spandrels rather than over the arches of the nave-arcade. Clearstorey walls are decorated with glowingly coloured stencilled patterns, and the wall-painting is by Charles Eamer Kempe (1837-1907). This is one of the finest Anglican church-interiors of the Gothic Revival (MC. D180901 [2001]).

XI.   Chancel of the church of the Holy Angels, Hoar Cross, Staffordshire (1872-76), by Bodley & Garner, showing the exquisite Rood-screen and the canopy (based on the Percy tomb in Beverley) over the Meynell Ingram tomb. This lovely church shows the work of Bodley & Garner at its best (MC. B260494 [1994]).

XII. *Interior of the church of St Mary the Virgin, Great Warley, Essex (consecrated 1904), by Charles Harrison Townsend, with exquisite* Art Nouveau *screen and other fittings by William Reynolds-Stephens. The apse windows were designed by George Heywood Maunoir Sumner (1853-1940), who made other contributions to this lovely ensemble* (MC. D011088 [1988]).

XIII. Interior of the fine basilican church of St Barnabas, Cardigan Street, Jericho, Oxford (1869-87), designed by A.W. Blomfield, and built at the expense of Thomas Combe (1797-1872 – Director of the Clarendon Press) for Anglo-Catholic worship. The north aisle was added to Blomfield's designs in 1888-9, the pulpit (designed by Blomfield) was made by Heaton, Butler, & Bayne, and the decorations of the east end are also by Blomfield, of 1893. Stylistically, the church is Italian Romanesque, with a touch of Early Christian, but the pier-capitals are French First Pointed, and the baldachin is Trecento *Italian Gothic. Decorations on the north wall of the nave consists of brilliant tiles in the spandrels and rows of Martyrs between the clearstorey windows (derived, no doubt, from exemplars in Ravenna): they appear to have been by Powell & Sons* (MC. A260701 [2001]).

XIV. Interior of the church of St Mary Magdalene, East Moors, North Riding of Yorkshire (1881-82), a charming work of Temple Moore, based on early designs of 1876 by G.G. Scott Junior. The south aisle is of two bays, separated from the nave by a pier carrying a beam, rather than the more usual arcade (MC. A280901 [2001]).

XV. Interior of the church of St Cyprian, Clarence Gate, London (1901-3), by John Ninian Comper, showing the 'last development of a purely English Parish Church', in which Perpendicular precedents are clear. All fittings were designed by Comper, including the Rood-screen (completed 1924), the font and font-cover (1930-2) – in which Comper drew on Classical as well as Gothic themes), and the celure over the high altar (1948). The entire design is based upon principles popularised in Dearmer's Parson's Handbook *(MC. A210901) [2001]).*

XVI. Interior of the Lady Chapel (1906-10) of the Cathedral-church of Christ in Liverpool in Honour of His Resurrection, designed by Giles Gilbert Scott, with Flügelaltar *by Scott and Bodley, made by G.W. Wilson. The Second Pointed style owes much to Continental precedent* (MC. E180901 [2001]).

Mansfield, and Forest of Dean stone dressings, and has an apsidal sanctuary, a baptistry, and a south chapel. The Edmestons were the son and grandson respectively of James Edmeston (1791-1867), architect and hymn-writer: his pupils included 'Great' Scott, Scott's partner, Moffat, and James Edmeston Junior. His many hymns included 'Lead us, Heavenly Father, lead us'.

Another Rhenish Romanesque example is All Souls, Harlesden, London (1875-76), by Edward John Tarver (1841-91). However, the *Rundbogenstil* was more often used for Nonconformist churches or chapels after the 1840s, for Gothic had been appropriated as *the* style by the Anglican Church and (to a large extent) by the Roman Catholics, although, as has been outlined above, the Roman Catholic Church was less wedded to Gothic than were the Anglicans, and even chose the Byzantine version of the *Rundbogenstil* for its great Cathedral of Westminster.

Between 1874 and 1903 John Pollard Seddon remodelled a brick preaching-box of 1843. This is

the church of St Catherine, Hoarwithy, Herefordshire, and Seddon chose an Italian Romanesque style for the exterior (complete with a handsome cloister-walk that runs along the south side of the church). He added an apse and two half-apses to the east end of the original building to form a trefoil on plan, and the interior of this is Byzantino-Romanesque, with four monolithic shafts of grey Devonshire marble carrying the structure overhead. The eastern apse has a *Pantocrator* in mosaic in the Byzantine style, and the ambo is in Cosmatiesque work. This sumptuous interior was decorated by G. E. Fox, the stalls (1883) and prayer-desk (1884) were carved by Harry Hems of Exeter, and the glass was made by S. Belham & Co. to designs by Seddon, his pupil H.A. Kennedy (*fl.* 1885-1920), and H.G. Murray. Seddon's intervention was at the behest and expense of the vicar, William Poole, and his five east windows were designed in 1904 to Poole's memory **(Plates 89-90)**.

89. Exterior of the church of St Catherine, Hoarwithy, Herefordshire (1874-1903), from the south, by J.P. Seddon, showing the Italianate campanile and Romanesque loggia (GB.808/70.EH.AA81/1446 [1971]).

90. Interior of the church of St Catherine, Hoarwithy, Herefordshire by J.P. Seddon, showing the Byzantine style of the architecture and the apsidal east end (GB.960/69.EH.AA/014719 [1969]).

An undersung and extremely interesting building is the church of St Sophia (or The Wisdom of God), Lower Kingswood, Surrey (1890-2), an essay in a Free-Byzantine style designed by Sidney Howard Barnsley for Dr Edwin Freshfield and Sir Cosmo Bonsor. It is of red brick with stone dressings, has herringbone brick friezes, and consists of a two-bay nave (with narrow aisle-passages) and chancel in one volume, with an apse. Barnsley was responsible for the decorations on the timber wagon-roof. Within the church are nine genuine Byzantine capitals: the two large capitals in the north and south nave-arcades are from the church of St John at Ephesus (fourth century); from the same church is the sixth-century capital on the south end of the west wall at the top; the two of *c.*400 on the west wall above the door are from the church of St John Studion at Constantinople; those at the east end of the nave are from the Bogdan Serail

91. Church of The Wisdom of God, Lower Kingswood, Surrey (1890-92), otherwise known as St Sophia, designed by S.H. Barnsley, a fine example of Byzantine-influenced Arts-and-Crafts work. The mosaics were by Powell of Whitefriars (1903) (GB. 682/70 EH. AA80/174 [1970]).

(north) and from a site near the Blachernæ Palace (south), both at Constantinople; and the two capitals on the west wall at the north end are also from the Blachernæ Palace. There is also an eleventh-century piece of a frieze on the west wall at the north end, originally in the church of the *Pantocrator* in Constantinopole. The furnishings of the church (also designed by Barnsley) are delightful Arts-and-Crafts pieces, some of which are inlaid with mother-of-pearl, the style of which is reminiscent of the work of Ernest Gimson (1864-1919), which is not surprising, since Barnsley and his brother Ernest (1863-1926) were to work with Gimson making furniture from the 1890s. Furthermore, Sidney Barnsley, William Richard Lethaby, and Robert Weir Schultz (1860-1951) all worked in Norman Shaw's office, and in 1889 Schultz and Sidney Barnsley visited Greece together, later producing *The Monastery of St Luke of Stiris in Phocis* (1901), which is an important document of the Byzantine Revival. So St Sophia's, Lower Kingswood, is one of the most important examplars of that Revival, designed immediately after Barnsley's return from Greece **(Plate 91)**.

As has been indicated, in the last decade of Queen Victoria's reign various architects connected with the Arts-and-Crafts Movement developed Free-Gothic styles, or experimented with variants of the *Rundbogenstil*, and especially with those variants having a Byzantinesque flavour. An interesting essay in the Italian Romanesque style is St Aidan's, Roundhay Road, Leeds (1891-94), by Robert James Johnson (1832-92), a pupil of Scott. The inspiration was clearly the churches of Ravenna, and the church contains important mosaics by Sir Frank William Brangwyn (1867-1956), who served his apprenticeship with William Morris. Arthur Beresford Pite (1861-1934), Professor of Architecture at the Royal College of Art (1900-23), designed the parish-hall and Christ Church, Brixton Road, Lambeth, London (1898-1903) — a free mixture of the *Rundbogenstil*, in which Byzantine, Mannerist, and Palladian motifs were synthesised in one composition. Pite introduced a large central space into the planning of the church, and

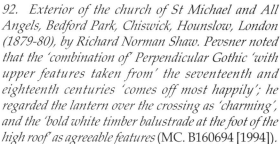

92. *Exterior of the church of St Michael and All Angels, Bedford Park, Chiswick, Hounslow, London (1879-80), by Richard Norman Shaw. Pevsner noted that the 'combination of' Perpendicular Gothic 'with upper features taken from' the seventeenth and eighteenth centuries 'comes off most happily'; he regarded the lantern over the crossing as 'charming', and the 'bold white timber balustrade at the foot of the high roof' as agreeable features (MC. B160694 [1994]).*

93. *Church of St Michael and All Angels, Bedford Park, Chiswick, Hounslow, London (1879-80), by Richard Norman Shaw. Pevsner described this church as 'Shaw at his best, inexhaustible in his inventiveness'. The pulpit is in seventeenth-century style, of 1894, and the whole ensemble is a triumphant marriage of late Gothic Revival with Arts-and-Crafts detail (MC. A160694a [1994]).*

the design was probably influenced by Bentley's Westminster Cathedral.

Pite's work dates from the end of the nineteenth and beginning of the twentieth century, but earlier in Victoria's reign there were some stylistic oddities, even for Anglican buildings. St Peter's, Kensington Park Road, London (1855-57), by Thomas Allom (1804-72) was one of the very few Anglican Victorian churches to be built in the Classical style. It has an engaged Corinthian temple-front (with pediment) flanked by quadrants at the corners, and with a square tower surmounted by an octagonal lantern. The interior consists of a nave and aisles with Corinthian columns carrying an entablature over which was a clearstorey of lunettes. These columns also support the galleries, and the

apsidal chancel was created by Edmeston and Barry later in 1879. Now the choice of the Classical idiom for St Peter's was no doubt dictated by the fact that this was an estate church, built in a speculative housing development on a tight site, flanked by tall terrace-houses all of which had Italianate detailing. The west front of St Peter's provided a terminating feature in Kensington Park Road when viewed from Stanley Gardens, and was a handsome centrepiece in the terrace of houses in Kensington Park Road itself.

The Arts-and-Crafts Movement is also associated with the Domestic Revival, or Old English style, involving Picturesque compositions using elements from vernacular architecture such as tall chimneys, gables, tile-hanging, mullioned and transomed windows, timber-

94. Church of St Chad, Hopwas, near Lichfield, Staffordshire (1881), by John Douglas. South elevation showing the curiously domestic appearance to which the brick- and timber-framed construction contribute (EH. AA83/854 © Staffordshire County Council [1969]).

95. Church of All Saints, Richard's Castle, Batchcott, Shropshire (1890-93), by Richard Norman Shaw, from the south, showing the massive south-western tower based on mediæval Shropshire exemplars. Tracery is of the Reticulated Second Pointed type, with ball-flower decoration derived from mediæval originals in Ludlow, Leominster, and elsewhere in the vicinity (EG. BB77/3545 [1977]).

framed elements, and leaded lights. Certain aspects of these essentially domestic mediæval themes were occasionally used in ecclesiastical architecture: Richard Norman Shaw (1831-1912) used a free eclectic mix (including a Perpendicular lower part with certain upper features derived from the seventeenth and eighteenth centuries) at the church of St Michael and All Angels, Bedford Park, London (1879-82) **(Plates 92 and 93)**, but at Hopwas, Staffordshire, John Douglas (1830-1911) used brick and timber-framed gables and upper-works at his remarkable church of St Chad (1881), which at first glance looks like a piece of domestic architecture **(Plate 94)**. Both these churches reflect their architects' interest in the design of dwellings, and their use of elements taken from vernacular buildings (a phase we refer to as the Domestic Revival).

Shaw's All Saints church at Batchcott (Richard's Castle), Shropshire (1890-93), is very different, being faced with small rock-faced stones, and having Reticulated tracery set within straight-headed windows, although the western nave-window is Perpendicular, and the western aisle-window has Decorated features with ball-flower ornament derived from that at the church of St Laurence, Ludlow, or from the profuse ball-flower decorations at the Priory church of Sts Peter and Paul, Leominster, Herefordshire (both early

fourteenth-century in date). So the basic architectural language at All Saints is Decorated Gothic (or Second Pointed): the massive crenellated tower stands aside from the south aisle (as is the case with several mediæval churches in the area), but the interior of the body of the church is unfinished and disconcertingly bare, save for the reredos **(Plates 95 and 96)**. Shaw's jumbling together of archæologically-based motifs has been seen by some observers to be jocular, but another explanation is that he wished to give the building the suggestion of having been extended and altered over many centuries, just as were real mediæval churches.

Even earlier, just before Shaw's Bedford Park church, Philip Speakman Webb (1831-1915) — who had worked for Street and who had joined Morris, Marshall, Faulkner & Co. in 1861 (and so had imbibed both the Gothic Revival and an Arts-and-Crafts outlook) — built his only church, St Martin's, Brampton, Cumberland (1874-78), for the Howard family, Earls of Carlisle. Webb mixed his styles, freely, in an attempt to distance himself from historicism or archæology: the inventive interior has transverse tunnel-vaults over the north aisle, a timber lean-to roof with dormers over the south aisle, and the nave ceiling is flat apart from a fan-like coving. Like Shaw's Bedford Park

96. Interior of All Saints' church, Richard's Castle, Shropshire, by Shaw, showing the spacious nave-arcade and the winged reredos (EH. BB77/3549 [1977]).

church, the wooden parts originally were painted pale green. Stained-glass windows were by Morris and Burne-Jones, displaying occasional precursors of *Art-Nouveau* forms **(Plate 97)**.

Edward Schroeder Prior (1852-1932), the distinguished Arts-and-Crafts architect, designed the church of St Andrew, Monkwearmouth, Sunderland (1906-7), reckoned to be one of the best churches of the Arts-and-Crafts Movement. His earlier Victorian church of Holy Trinity, Bothenhampton, Dorset (1884-89), is closer to First Pointed, and is simple and economical, with three transverse stone arches over the aisleless nave, motifs that recur at Roker. Bothenhampton has an altar-front of gesso by William Richard Lethaby which was shown at the 1889 Arts-and-Crafts Exhibition.

The Roker church was supervised during its construction by A. Randall Wells (1877-1942), who also acted as Clerk of Works at Lethaby's church of All Saints, Brockhampton, Herefordshire (1901-2), one of the most perfect syntheses of Gothic forms and details (freely interpreted) with Arts-and-Crafts ideas. An Anglican church, All Saints was funded by Alice Foster as a memorial to her parents, and was built by direct labour: it incorporates concrete vaults and thatched roofs, and the architectural language was remarkably fresh and new, redolent with references, but avoiding direct quotations. Even the tracery,

though Gothic in spirit, owed little to archæology, but everything to Lethaby's theories of merging lancets with the rose-window as the origins of tracery. No student of the Arts-and-Crafts Movement, of Victorian churches, and of the influence of the Vernacular Revival on design should miss this charming building.

Other Late Gothic Churches
Most late-Victorian Anglican churches were in some sort of Free-Gothic style (often drawing on Perpendicular themes). Very many churches were built at that time, for the Church of England was very much alive and well, and was actually attracting more and more worshippers, not unconnected with the beauty and dignity of the liturgy. Many of the planning and liturgical issues discussed above led to a type of church in which the Eucharist played a far more important rôle than was the case when Queen Victoria ascended the Throne.

One of Scott's pupils, Temple Lushington Moore, produced memorable compositions based loosely on mediæval precedents (such as St Columba's, Cannon Street, and St Cuthbert's, Newport Road, both in Middlesbrough, Yorkshire, and both powerful, ruthless, fortress-like buildings) at the beginning of the twentieth century. Moore had worked on the church of St Agnes, Kennington, while with Scott, and imbibed many of Scott's liturgical and architectural concerns. Moore's own churches deserve to be better appreciated. Among his finest works are the completion of Scott's church of St Mary Magdalene, East Moors, North Riding of Yorkshire (1881-82 — a delightful building **[Plate 98]** consisting of a nave and chancel without any division [but covered by a pretty painted wagon-roof] and a south aisle of two bays [again with a painted roof, this time lean-to **(Colour Plate XIV)**]); All Saints, Peterborough (1886-94 — a Gothic building in which Second Pointed and Perpendicular are judiciously mingled); St Peter's, Barnsley, West Riding of Yorkshire (1885-1911 — with a very wide nave and passage-aisles, again influenced by the church of the Dominicans, Gent); St Botolph's, Carlton-in-Cleveland, North Riding of Yorkshire (1895-97 —

97. *Interior of the church of St Martin, Brampton, Cumberland (1874-78), by Philip Webb. The north aisle has a ceiling treated as transverse tunnel-vaults, while the south aisle has a timber lean-to roof with tie-beams and dormers, and the nave-ceiling is flat except for the fan-like coving. Pevsner said of Webb that he 'was a man inventive in the extreme, sometimes to the verge of what we would now call the gimmicky, a man of character and imagination and one who in order to free himself from the fetters of historicism fiercely mixed his styles'. The five-light east window, like the rest of the glass in the church, was designed by William Morris and Edward Burne-Jones, made 1878-80 (*MC. L270989 [1989]).

with low, square-headed aisle and clearstorey windows **[Plate 99]** , and Moore's favourite device of elongated piers merging into the arches of the nave-arcades without capitals **[Plate 100]** — the young Giles Gilbert Scott [1880-1960], son of George Gilbert Scott Junior, worked on this building when articled to Temple Moore); and St Mary's, Sledmere, East Riding of Yorkshire (1893-98 — reckoned by Pevsner, with predictable bias, to be 'patently dull', but by Goodhart-Rendel [with more perspicacity] to be 'one of the loveliest churches in England' **[Plate 101]**).

Moore carried out a great many works in Yorkshire in the course of his career, much of it near Helmsley, largely through connections established by Scott the Younger. One of his patrons was William Ernest Duncome (1829-1915), 1st Earl of Feversham (who put up most of the money for the church at East Moors), and another was Charles Norris Gray, vicar of Helmsley from 1870 (who, with Feversham's help, provided outlying hamlets with new or improved places of worship). Another important patron was Sir Tatton Sykes (1826-1913 — 5th

98. *(Above) Exterior of the church of St Mary Magdalene, East Moors, North Riding of Yorkshire (1881-82), designed by George Gilbert Scott Junior and completed by Temple Moore. The lean-to south aisle is shown, with the crocketed bell-spirelet at the west end* (MC. B280901 [2001]).

99. *(Below) Exterior of the church of St Botolph, Carlton-in-Cleveland, North Riding of Yorkshire (1895-7), by Temple Moore, showing the square-headed clearstorey windows* (MC. E280901 [2001]).

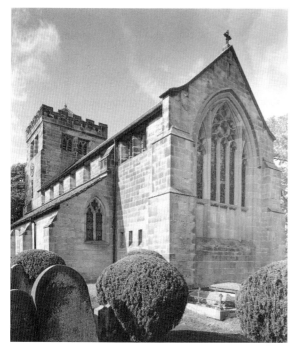

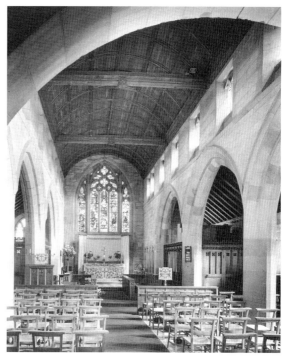

100. *Interior looking east of the church of St Botolph, Carlton-in-Cleveland, North Riding of Yorkshire, showing Temple Moore's favourite device of the piers merging into the arches of the nave-arcades without capitals* (MC. C280901).

Baronet), who was Moore's client for St Mary's, Sledmere.

Apart from his distinguished buildings, Moore designed some exquisite church furnishings and carried out sensitive restoration-work. One of his happiest creations is the lovely Roodscreen (decorated by Bodley) in the church of St Swithin, near Bideford, Devon. His sumptuous turn-of-the-century high altar (with riddell-posts, vignette frame to the reredos, elegant brattishing, and Watts fabrics for hangings) in his church of St Mark, Mansfield, Nottinghamshire (1894-7 — another example of the passage-aisled arrangement with wall-piers and no clearstorey), most regrettably, has been altered and spoiled. Moore also carried out some fine works almost up to his death, but the dates carry them too far beyond the scope of this book.

William Douglas Caröe (1857-1938), who studied with Pearson in the early 1880s, produced a

101. *Interior of the church of St Mary, Sledmere, East Riding of Yorkshire (1893-98), by Temple Moore. The screen, loft, and Rood were carved by John Thompson & Co., and there is no chancel-arch* (MC. C270901) [2001]).

fine Free-Gothic design for the church of St David, Exeter (1897-1900): it has a wide tunnel-vaulted nave, with each bay expressed by transverse arches, and the tall, narrow aisles are passages through the internal buttresses from which spring vaults. Caröe's great church of St Barnabas, Walthamstow (begun 1902, dedicated in 1903), forms a happy group with its church-hall and vicarage set in a delightful garden. Mr Service has referred to the 'endless felicities' of Caröe's designs for the church, and there should be no dissent from that description: it is a noble work.

(Sir) Charles Archibald Nicholson (1867-1949) and his partner from 1895, Hubert Christian Corlette (1869-1956) — who worked for a while with John Belcher, — designed the church of St Matthew, Old Mill Road, Chelston, Torquay (1895-1904), an example of Arts-and-Crafts-influenced Gothic, with a fine and unusual font and font-cover by Gerald Moira, the figure-groups being by F. Lynn Jenkins. The same architects were responsible for St Alban's, St John's Road, Westcliffe-on-Sea, Southend-on-Sea, Essex (1898-1908), an interesting church built of flint, rubble, and red-brick dressings, in a Free-Gothic style, with pretty furnishings inside (including a Rood-screen and fine reredos).

Towards the end of the nineteenth century, Bodley's pupil, John Ninian Comper, experimented further with English Perpendicular, and, in his work, came closest to fulfilling the ideas of liturgiologists such as Legg. Comper's style, therefore, was a very far cry from structural polychromy, primitive Burgundian Gothic, or muscular over-emphasis. In Comper's hands the Gothic Revival became delicate and jewel-like, and he created many beautiful things. He designed the charming Lady Chapel in Scott's church of St Matthew, Great Peter Street (1849-51), of 1892, in a sumptuous, very late, English Perpendicular Gothic style. Among other small-scale works of Comper may be mentioned the exquisite chapel of St Sepulchre **(Plate 102)** in the south aisle of Street's great church of St Mary Magdalene, Paddington (1895): the contrast with the work of the 1860s and 1870s could not be more successfully demonstrated, especially when Comper's work is viewed in the context of Street's

102. Chapel of St Sepulchre in the crypt of the church of St Mary Magdalene, Rowington Close, Paddington, London (1895), by J.N. Comper. It is the latter's first important work, a 'lovingly created world of painstakingly accurate' Perpendicular detail, as Pevsner described it. This chapel is in complete stylistic contrast when compared with the earlier architecture of St Mary Magdalene's itself (see Plates 39 and 40) (EH. 118/66 [1966]).

massive inverted and normal arches in the crypt. Exquisite also is Comper's lovely Lady Chapel of c.1900 in the church of St Barnabas, Pimlico (1847-50), by Thomas Cundy II.

Comper's work, however, was not 'pure' Perpendicular, for he drew heavily on late-mediæval precedents from northern Europe, and especially from manuscript sources and the ecclesiastical art and artefacts of Flanders. It is very curious that so many commentators when dealing with the Gothic Revival have tended to gloss over the Flemish connection. It should be remembered that Belgium was not difficult to reach in the nineteenth century, that its towns are close together, and that its size means that very many buildings can be visited in quite a short time. Belgian exemplars undoubtedly influenced the planning of late-Victorian churches, and in the hands of masters such as Comper, details from Flanders also played a significant part.

In 1893 Comper gave a paper, *Practical Considerations on the Gothic or English Altar and Certain Dependent Ornaments* which impressed Micklethwaite, Legg, and others. The most important models for Comper were the great churches of East Anglia, in which chancels were within the same vast volume as the nave, only demarcated by means of screens and (sometimes) by a celure. Legg sought solutions to the problem of designing chancels and churches that would be historically and aesthetically valid, that would respect the ideals of the Oxford Movement, and that would be acceptable within the constraints of the Anglican rubrics relating to order and ornament.

At the Roman Catholic Downside Abbey, Somerset, Comper designed a lovely altar for the Lady Chapel in 1896 (it was replaced in 1913), and also carried out decorations there: his work was a fulfilment of Pugin's mediævalising ideals. From 1901 to 1905 Garner designed and built the wonderful Perpendicular chancel at Downside, and there, at the Abbey, is one of the finest results of liturgiological and ecclesiological scholarship in England, as rich and inventive as any work of the late Middle Ages, and, what is more, clearly architecture of religious conviction.

Then, in 1899, appeared the *Parson's Handbook*, by Percy Dearmer (1867-1936), which went into many subsequent editions, and was enormously influential. Dearmer had been curate at St Anne's church, South Lambeth Road, London (where he had introduced Morris designs for the altar, under the direction of Selwyn Image [1849-1930] in 1891), and became vicar of St Mary's, Primrose Hill Road, London, in 1901, where he put many of the principles enshrined in his book into practice. St Mary's (begun 1871) was designed by the little-known Michael Prendergast Manning (*fl.* 1851-1902) in a tough, no-nonsense style of Middle Pointed in red brick with stone dressings, but Dearmer whitewashed the interior and set up an 'English' altar. For many years high altars had been set raised and approached by many steps, with candle-sticks set on shelves: Dearmer, taking his ideas from people such as Legg and Comper, showed there was no authority for this arrangement, and that Engish mediæval altars were set low, had very little on them apart from a couple of candle-sticks, and had the ends enclosed by curtains. Dearmer reinforced the view that much that passed as authentic mediæval ceremonial was based on Roman Catholic Counter-Reformation practice (some of it often of quite recent date), and that true English ceremonial was simple, dignified, and beautiful.

Dearmer's work had a huge impact. Far too many churches were whitened (including many where structural and other polychrome decorations were ruined or obscured), and during the 1920s and 1930s 'English' altars with riddell-posts and curtains became almost *de rigueur*. Although his *Parson's Handbook*, in the words of the *Dictionary of National Biography*, 'was an attempt to recall the Church to the native English tradition in matters of liturgy and ceremonial', and Dearmer 'saw that art is not mere decoration but an essential and integral expression of the worship offered to God in religion', he has been criticised for watering down the fervency of the Anglo-Catholicism of men like Legg and Comper, trivialising their principles, and encouraging a certain commercialism.

It was Comper, however, who created two of the greatest masterpieces of Anglican church design. The church of St Cyprian, Glentworth Street, Clarence Gate, London (1901-3), was his first complete church (though it was designed at the time [1888-1908] Comper was in partnership with William Bucknall [1851-1944]), and the building was inspired by the stately church of St Mary, Attleborough, Norfolk. Although strictly speaking it is not Victorian, it represents the culmination of late-Victorian tendencies in Anglican church design, and for many years was regarded by many as the most satisfactory church from a liturgical point of view. Like St Mary's, Attleborough, it had a prodigious screen running across the nave and aisles, and the white-painted walls set off Comper's lavish gilded and painted furnishings (many of which were gradually added over the next two decades) **(Colour Plate XV)**. Comper himself described St Cyprian's as following the 'fully developed type of the English parish-church' in which the high altar is made 'public to the whole body of worshippers' without violating 'the earlier tradition … which veiled the altar from view'. The high altar was designed to be in the new progressive English mode of the period: Comper wrote that, by 'the richness of its coverings, no less than by its size and austere isolation, it expresses its supreme and august importance… It is the emphasis of the… altar which is of real consequence; and the reredos and curtains around it and the canopy over it are solely for the purpose of giving dignity' to it.

As Comper pointed out, this was the 'ideal of the English parish-church before and after the introduction of the Book of Common Prayer', and it was 'for the realisation of this ideal that the new church of St Cyprian' had been prepared. Its design neither sought nor avoided originality, and its aim was not to reproduce any period of the past, but only to fulfil the needs of the time, 'and to do so in the last manner of English architecture which for us in England is the most beautiful manner of all'. In his *Further Thoughts on the English Altar: or Practical Considerations on the Planning of a Modern Church* (1933), Comper described St Cyprian's as a 'lantern', with the altar as 'the flame within it'.

In Comper's later masterpiece, St Mary's, Wellingborough, Northamptonshire (1904-31), precedents were again used, but the palette was greater, pulling together threads from late-Perpendicular fan-vaulting (with pendants for the nave ceiling), Renaissance details (for the screen and font-surround), and other allusions. As Father Symondson has sagely observed, in St Mary's 'Anglo-Catholic aspiration, the fruit of liturgiology, the incarnational principle of theology, the indebtedness of the Christian tradition to history, and the primacy of beauty in the service of God' can all be found in St Mary's, where the 'accretive legacy' of European church architecture may be studied with benefit. Of this church, Comper said that only 'to its contemporaries does [it] owe nothing'.

Of all his generation, perhaps only Comper retained a strong intellectual and practical connection with the liturgical problems of church-building. His greatest strengths were in synthesis, and in the design of detail (his restoration of the Rood-screen in the church of Sts Peter and Paul, Eye, Suffolk, is felicitous). Moore, however, arguably, was the better architect, and his work was refreshingly free from stylistic or theoretical inhibitions. In terms of planning for liturgical purposes, though, his work did little to advance beyond ideas propounded by G. G. Scott Junior.

One of the last and grandest works of the Gothic Revival is the Cathedral-Church of Christ in Liverpool in Honour of His Resurrection, designed by (Sir) Giles Gilbert Scott, grandson of 'Great Scott' and son of George Gilbert Scott Junior (who, it will be recalled, had become a Roman Catholic in 1880). There had been attempts to find a design in 1885, when an architectural competition was held, but another competition was announced in 1902 which was won in 1903 by Scott, a pupil of Temple Moore, and assistant to Thomas Garner. The problem with Scott was his youth and his brand of religion, so Bodley was called in to oversee the design and to add solid Anglican respectability. Now although this great building was designed and erected after the Victorian period had ended, it is included because it is the climax of one of the most creative periods in English architectural history, and because it is essentially a nineteenth-century building.

The assessors for the competition were Bodley and Norman Shaw, and they chose five designs out of 103 entries. The five were young Scott, Paley & Austin of Lancaster, C. A. Nicholson, Malcolm Stark (born *c*.1854), and the former chief assistant to Bodley & Garner, Walter John Tapper (1861-1935 — no mean ecclesiastical architect himself).

Scott's winning design had twin towers, and differed in very many ways from the building as executed. Scott set up on his own in 1903, but had to work closely with Bodley at first. Work on site began in 1904, and the collaboration between Scott and Bodley is most obvious in the Lady Chapel (1906-10), an exquisite jewel-like building, with a stone-vaulted ceiling, the precedents for which were clearly Continental. The *Flügelaltar* in the Lady Chapel (designed by Bodley and Scott, and executed by G. W. Wilson) adds to the Continental flavour, overwhelmingly German, and very, very beautiful **(Colour Plate XVI)**.

In 1910 Scott (by then freed from Bodley's influence) abandoned the twin towers and created a central tower. The interior of the Cathedral proper was completely freed from Bodleyanisms, and Scott designed two transepts flanking the tower and the vast arched portals to the north and south which add complexity to the impressive internal volumes. The nave has a floor-level much lower than that of the chancel, with its vast Spanish *retablo* (designed by Scott and made by Walter Gilbert and L.Weingartner) terminating the vista at the east. Around the chancel are lower aisles, little more than wide passages, connecting with another passage behind the high altar. The nave is wide, with vestigial aisles, and the central volumes of the building are breathtaking. Thus, the ideals of visibility by removing the barriers of nave-arcades were carried to a logical conclusion. The western parts of the Cathedral were completed under Frederick Thomas (1898-1984), who became a partner in Scott's firm in 1953, and senior partner on Scott's death in 1960. He continued to be associated with the Cathedral until 1980, but most of the design-drawings were the work of Roger Pinkney (1900-90).

Arthur Stanley George Butler (1888-1965), in his entry in the *Dictionary of National Biography* (1971) on Scott, wrote that when looking 'at the whole exterior sixty years later one is struck by the dependence on mass rather than intricacy, and on well-proportioned stone surfaces, deftly pierced by windows betraying no more than a Gothic ancestry'. When Scott died, he had been connected with the Cathedral for fifty-eight years, compared with Sir Christopher Wren's thirty-four-year association with St Paul's Cathedral in London. Pevsner sourly opined that 'Scott, though younger than Wren, was more tired towards the end, and the style of his building has

worn worse than Wren's'. This is a serious misjudgment, for Liverpool Anglican Cathedral contains one of the most impressive interior spaces ever conceived: there the Gothic Revival was never more Sublime.

However, the story of Gothic did not end with Scott, Comper, or Temple Moore. It continued with the work of Stephen Dykes Bower, who was influenced (among others) by Frederick Charles Eden (1884-1944), a pupil of Bodley. Dykes Bower, in the 1960s and 1970s, designed and carried out the Gothic enlargement of the church of St James, Bury St Edmunds, Suffolk, visibly confirming its recent status as a Cathedral. It is important to realise that this was achieved when hardly 'anything comparable was being done', and when architectural opinion gave 'no encouragement to stylistic appropriateness' or good manners in design, but only to what was, in Dykes Bower's words, 'spuriously represented' as 'modern' or 'contemporary'. At Bury St Edmunds (or St Edmundsbury) Dykes Bower demonstrated his belief that 'more permanent satisfaction and interest would derive' from architecture demonstrating 'that new work should look, not different, but natural and harmonious; that gave opportunity for the exercise of skills and craftsmanship not extinct but only neglected and under-used'.

'Building for our own time' is a dismal phrase that is nearly always a clarion call demanding the tenth-rate and the ugly. Dykes Bower often talked of 'beauty' in architecture, a word *never* used by Modernists and Relativists: he was a brave man, and accomplished much in a climate in which indifference, hostility, and wilful misunderstanding of everything he stood for made his task much more difficult than it need have been. The Commissars of cultural totalitarianism and philistine bullying did not help one of the great exponents of the late Gothic Revival.

In the beginning of the twenty-first century the Gothic Design Practice is carrying out a noble Gothic design for the crossing-tower at Bury, creating an appropriate work to crown Dykes Bower's masterpiece. It is a fitting note on which to end this Chapter.

CHAPTER IX

Non-Anglican Buildings for Religious Observance

Introduction; Nonconformists and their Architecture; The Buildings

The Protestant House of Prayer reveals a very different temperament and a very different world from the
church of mediæval Catholicism. Not even the most sympathetic lover of Gothic can deny that the majority of
mediæval churches were singularly ill-adapted to preaching and congregational worship,
with their echoing vaults and long-drawn aisles.
ANDREW ALASTAIR LANDALE DRUMMOND (1902-66): *The Church Architecture of Protestantism.*
An Historical and Constructive Study (Edinburgh: T. & T. Clark, 1934), 19.

Introduction

In the last quarter of the nineteenth century the round-arched, Romanesque, Early-Christian, or Byzantine styles began to be exploited as the range of historical precedents available to designers widened once more. The 'moral' arguments in favour of Gothic were starting to wear thin, and, in any case, the Gothic Revival had become *the* style of the High Church, Anglo-Catholic, Tractarian tradition in the Anglican Church, so it was natural Nonconformists, Evangelicals, and Roman Catholics would endeavour to cast their stylistic nets over wider seas than mere Gothic waters. Nevertheless, it is surprising how many groups (even Nonconformists) sought to ape the Anglicans, probably because Pugin had done his work well, and partly because of the social position enjoyed by the Established Church. Architectural style seems to have associations with caste and class: Gothic, from around 1840 until the end of the century, was certainly respectable, and in any case, Ruskin had successfully identified the Renaissance and Baroque styles with Popery, while setting Gothic up as a style suited to his notions of romantic democracy and dissociated from Ritualism and Papistical practices. As has been indicated above, Ruskin effectively removed prejudices against the Gothic styles among Evangelical Anglicans and Nonconformists by connecting those styles with the Good and Moral life, and by arguing that Gothic had been abandoned by 'glittering', 'perfumed', idolatrous Romanists.

Sometimes, Gothic of a deliberately foreign type was used for specific reasons. One of the oddest of oddities of the late-Victorian period is the Roman Catholic church and mausoleum of the Emperor Napoléon III (1808-73), the Empress Eugénie (1826-1920), and Napoléon-Eugène-Louis-Jean-Joseph, Prince Impérial (1856-1879), at Farnborough, Hampshire (1887-8), designed by Hippolyte-Alexandre-Gabriel-Walter Destailleur (1822-93) in the French *Flamboyant* style of late Gothic, with an incongruous dome on top of it **(Plate 103)**. The mausoleum is in the grounds of St Michael's Abbey, which has a centrepiece capped by a tall *flèche* also designed by Destailleur, and Romanesque and First Pointed elements derived from the buildings of the former Benedictine Abbey at Solesmes (Sarthe) in France. Here was an example of French Gothic being used for a purpose, to connect the Bonaparte dynasty with France by means of a stylistic allusion, and to show that a part of France was enshrined in Hampshire.

With regard to the Byzantine style, Bentley's great Cathedral at Westminster has already been described, but, much earlier, Liverpool acquired its large Greek Orthodox church in Berkley Street, Toxteth, Liverpool (1865-70), designed by Henry Sumners (flourished 1861-78): the latter church is of brick with stone dressings, and has high Byzantine cupolas **(Plate 104)**. Later, John Oldrid Scott exploited the Byzantine style with his scholarly, handsome, and impressive Greek Orthodox Cathedral of Western Europe, St

103. Mausoleum of the Emperor Napoléon III, the Empress Eugénie, and the Prince Impérial of France at Farnborough, Hampshire (1887-88), by H.-A.-G.-W. Destailleur. It is in the French Flamboyant *style of late Gothic, and has an incongruous dome on top* (MC. Q010801 [2001]).

104. *Exterior of the Greek Orthodox church, Berkley Street, Toxteth, Liverpool (1865-70), by Sumners. It is in a Byzantine Revival style, with big cupolas (JSC [1994]).*

105. *Greek Orthodox Cathedral of Western Europe, St Sophia, Moscow Road, Bayswater, London (1877), by J.O. Scott. It is a revival of the Byzantine style (GLPL. 75/5/12760).*

106. *Exterior of the synagogue at Prince's Road, Toxteth, Liverpool (1874-82), by Audsley. It has Romanesque and Gothic elements, but the entrance-arch has Moresque lobed features, and the wheel-window is entirely North European Gothic in style (JSC [1994]).*

Sophia, Moscow Road, Bayswater, London (1877) **(Plate 105)**, clearly alluding to traditional Greek Orthodox buildings based on ancient Byzantine prototypes of the Eastern Roman Empire. Not far from this Cathedral is the spectacularly showy New West End Synagogue, St Petersburgh Place, Bayswater, London (1877-79), by Audsley and Joseph, the design of which is closely based on that of the Prince's Road, Toxteth, Liverpool, Synagogue **(Plate 106)** by George Ashdowne Audsley (1838-1925) of 1874-82 (illustrated in *The Illustrated London News* of 1882). Both buildings mix Gothic, Byzantine, and Moresque themes: at Toxteth, for example, the materials are common bricks, with red-brick and terra-cotta dressings, while the portal is stylistically Gothic, in the early-thirteenth-century manner, but set within a Moresque lobed arch, and the wheel-window is entirely North European Gothic. Inside, the Ark of the Torah scrolls is formed to resemble a Byzantine church, with five cupolas. Thus, as far as synagogues were concerned, they tended to be designed in ways that avoided an appearance resembling buildings of Christian denominations, except for the use of selected morsels here and

there within some overall exotic confection. Indeed, Byzantinesque styles, craftily mingled with Moresque elements, seem to have been favoured for synagogues, and there are one or two Egyptianising examples, Egypto-Classical essays, and other eclectic buildings for Jewish observances. Clearly, architects of synagogues looked back to the ancient synagogues of mediæval Spain (hence the Moresque themes), in some instances, but also drew on Byzantine, Egyptian (there is a good example of an Egyptian Revival synagogue in Canterbury, Kent), and Classical elements in others. Interiors were often very rich, with the foci on the Ark of the Torah Rolls and on the reading-platforms. Sometimes the style of synagogue architecture could be described as Oriental Gothic, or even as Orientalising Byzantine-Gothic. Thus synagogues did not always escape entirely from the Gothic Revival, and the resulting buildings are often curious, whilst Classical and round-arched elements were also employed in the architecture of synagogues, often promiscuously mixed with other styles in inventive and imaginative ways.

One of the most dignified, beautiful, and extraordinary of exotic Victorian places of worship is the delightful Shah Jehan mosque, Oriental Road, Woking, Surrey (1889), designed by William Isaac Chambers (flourished in the 1870s and 1880s) for Dr Gottlieb Leitner, who founded a centre for Oriental Studies in Woking. The building is precisely orientated towards Mecca, has a fine onion-dome crowning the composition (the internal dome is carried on squinches), and has a pretty frontispiece that could have strayed from Brighton Pavilion. Indeed, the Picturesque Orientalism went down like a lead balloon with the Editor of *The Building News*, who was unduly sniffy about the mosque, wishing it had been erected in Jericho or in some other place 'never to have troubled us'. Here again was a deliberate use of an architectural style to signify that the building was not a church, not a chapel, not a synagogue, but a mosque, very Indian in style, rather than Arabic, but it is also interesting because it is a late-nineteenth-century throwback to a style of Regency *exotica* to be found in places such as Sezincote or Brighton, and

therefore not likely to be taken seriously by architectural critics so indoctrinated with the effusions of Pugin and Ruskin.

Nonconformists and their Architecture
At this point a few outline notes on the various denominations to be found among Non-conformists (a term defined above) will not be out of place, and an attempt will be made here to mention the most important groups. Methodists, for example, only became known as Non-conformists in the nineteenth century: originally (in the Protestant sense), a Methodist was a member of a religious society, established at Oxford in 1729 by John (1703-91) and Charles (1707-88) Wesley, with the object of promoting piety and morality, but the term subsequently became associated with an adherent of those evangelistic religious bodies that originated directly or indirectly from the work of the Wesleys and of George Whitefield (1714-70), the leader of the Calvinistic branch of Methodism. Wesleyans, as Methodists were known, originally saw themselves as part of the Anglican Church, but quickly became an independent sect, as their 'Enthusiasm' did not go down well among the rational, decorous Churchmen of Georgian times. The Whitefield-led groups tended to be more severely Calvinistic, and the Wesleyans themselves evolved seceding groups which became known as Primitive Methodists (almost completely a working-class denomination with numbers of small and unpretentious chapels), the United Methodist Free Church, and others accepting in the main the Arminian theology of Wesley (so-called after James Arminius [1560-1609] who denied the Calvinistic doctrine of absolute predestination and irresistible Grace). Methodist chapels will often have the words WESLEYAN CHAPEL and a date or a plaque on the entrance-front.

Another significant group of Nonconformists was the Unitarian persuasion, which affirmed the unipersonality of the Godhead (as opposed to the more orthodox Trinitarian view), and ascribed Divinity to God the Father only. Unitarianism grew out of a protest by Theophilus Lindsey (1723-1808), Vicar of Catterick, against the imposition of Anglican orthodoxies as Tests of belief in general. Unitarians believed that each congregation should have independent authority, that God was Unity, and that there should be freedom for (and tolerance of) the differences in religious beliefs. A Unitarian was essentially a liberal, tolerant monotheist, and, although Unitarians were not numerous, they were significant in municipal and political terms, and erected some important buildings that reflected their influence and power. In fact, Nonconformists generally had considerable strength in the provincial manufacturing towns, and certainly wielded clout in municipal affairs in places such as Birmingham, Bradford, Leeds, Leicester, Manchester, Newcastle, Oldham, Salford, Sheffield, and Wolverhampton: in Liverpool, Churchmen and Dissenters were openly hostile to each other, and this reflected the growing influence and success of Nonconformists in business and commerce. So powerful were the Unitarians in Leicester (and produced so many mayors) that the Unitarian chapel was known as the 'mares' nest'. In Birmingham, a spectacular example of Geometrical Gothic, adapted to Nonconformist use, was the Church of the Messiah, a Unitarian centre built in 1862 (to designs by John Jones Bateman [1817-1903]) on arches over the Birmingham Canal: its sheer size indicated the importance of Unitarianism in Birmingham under the leadership of the powerful Chamberlain and Nettlefold families. It was demolished in 1978.

An important Dissenting sect was that of the Baptists, who held that Baptism ought to be administered only to believers, and by immersion (and so required the unusual feature of an immersion-font in their chapels): this group was also called the Anabaptists, and its members were often successful in the world of commerce. Also significant were the Congregationalists, who took their name from the substitution of 'Congregation' for 'Church' by the sixteenth-century English Reformers: in the Congregationalist system the whole local body of worshippers was distinguished from 'The Church', or company of communicants, and each congregation was independent in the management of its own affairs. Congregationalists were also called Independents, so 'Independent Chapel' was a self-governing Nonconformist group. Congregationalists or Independents also carried considerable influence in municipal and political life, and were particularly strong in places such as Bradford, Halifax, and London.

The Presbyterians were governed by Presbyters or Presbyteries in which no higher order than that of Presbyter or Elder was recognised: each congregation was governed by its Session (which consisted of the Minister and the other Elders), the Sessions were subordinate to the Presbytery, the Presbyteries were subject to the Synod, and the Synod could be over-ruled by the General Assembly of the Presbyterian Church.

Quakers, or members of the Society of Friends, founded by George Fox (1624-91) in 1648-50, had Meeting-Houses with no architectural pretensions whatsoever, and indeed Quaker buildings often adopted a modest domestic air. The Friends, however, had considerable influence, economically and politically, and seven of Birmingham's nineteenth-century mayors were Quakers.

One sect of Nonconformists managed to produce several distinguished works of architecture. Edward Irving (1792-1834) arrived in London from Scotland in 1822. 'Byron scarely leapt into fame with more suddenness than did Irving', and the preacher's 'oratory was pronounced worthy of his melodious and resonant voice, noble presence, commanding stature, and handsome features ... marred only by a slight obliquity of vision'. He seems to have been the preaching equivalent of the pictorial Biblical visions of Francis Danby (1793-1861) and John Martin (1789-1854), and soon became enmeshed in the study of unfulfilled prophecy. His eloquence transformed his small and poor congregation into a large and rich one, and he was able to move to a new church in Regent Square, regarded as one of the handsomest in London. A congregation of a thousand flocked thither Sunday after Sunday to hear him preach for three hours at a time. In 1828, he became convinced of the imminence of the Second Advent, and in 1830 the first instance of a woman speaking in 'unknown tongues' occurred. Soon these outbursts became habitual, and the Regent Square church witnessed several public outbreaks of unintelligible gibberish in which Irving rejoiced, observing that the 'bridal jewels of the church' had been recovered. Irving was removed from the pulpit at Regent Square in 1832, and broke with Presbyterianism. His flock followed him, and so was founded the 'Holy Catholic Apostolic Church', otherwise known as the 'Irvingites'. In 1833 he was deprived of the status of clergyman by the presbytery of Annan and accused of heresy.

However, the Church survived for a time, claiming Irving's relationship to it was rather like that of John the Baptist to the early Christian Church, thus he was the forerunner and prophet of the coming dispensation. The services adopted (1842) were based on the Anglican, Roman Catholic, and Greek Orthodox liturgies, with Presbyterian echoes, and 'lights, incense, vestments, holy water, chrism, and other adjuncts of worship were in constant use'. Ceremonial was best seen in the impressive First Pointed church in Gordon Square, Bloomsbury, London (1850-54), designed by John Raphael Brandon (1817-77 — who later committed suicide). Known as Christ the King, Gordon Square, the building is now (2002) the University of London Anglican Chaplaincy. Eastlake described it as one of the 'largest and most imposing churches in England', and its style is a scholarly evocation of the 1230s-1240s **(Plate 107)**.

The Irvingites put up some distinguished churches. Pearson designed their church at Maida Avenue, Paddington (1891-3), and William McIntosh Brooks (1800-49) designed (in association with William Wilkins) the Perpendicular Gothic church at Albury, Surrey (c.1837-39). Unfortunately, Irving's own publications hardly live up to the architecture, and perusal of them is unrewarding, other than to arouse wonder that such stuff attracted any following at all. It would seem, as the *Dictionary of National Biography* observed, that Irving's 'extravagant assumptions in the pulpit served to provide frivolous society in London with a new

107. Interior of the former Catholic Apostolic (Irvingite) church, Gordon Square, London, now the Anglican church of Christ the King, part of the University of London Anglican Chaplaincy. It is a scholarly re-creation of First Pointed (Early English) Gothic of c.1230-50 by Raphael Brandon, and is cathedralesque in its scale (Photograph by J.M. Lickfold. EH. BB64/1063 [1941]).

sensation', and that his vast opinion of himself (Thomas Carlyle [1795-1881], the sage of Ecclefechan, called it 'inflation') 'made him a ready prey to flatterers and fanatics'. Dr Thomas Chalmers (1780-1847), who was assisted by Irving in the parish of St John, Glasgow, from 1819 to 1822, opined that his harangues were 'woeful', and that 'his prophecies and the excessive length and weariness of his services' might 'unship him altogether'. Like many charismatic preachers, Irving was intellectually weak, and aspects of his behaviour and utterances suggest he was deficient in judgement and common sense. His 'voluminous writings', observed Richard Garnett (1835-1906), were 'a string of sonorous commonplaces, empty of useful suggestion and original thought', although the 'poverty of matter' was in part 'redeemed by the dignity of the manner'. However, Irving's 'exalted pitch' soon became 'exceedingly tiresome', and this problem seems to have been endemic among preachers, as any student of the dusty 'Theology and Religion' shelves in antiquarian bookshops can attest.

There were other Dissenting chapels run by small sects, or even by individual preachers, which might have had names such as Enon or Elim Chapel, Bethesda, or even gloried in the nomenclature of 'Tabernacle' in order to emphasise the temporary nature of such humble buildings (as opposed to the grander, more permanent churches of Anglicans, Roman Catholics, and some Nonconformists), and to make a connection with the Old Testament and the idea of the Chosen People.

The Buildings

The main Nonconformist groups have been outlined above, and the essentials of Nonconformist church architecture have been sketched. Nonconformist churches were built in great numbers in the Victorian period, and indeed there were many more of them than Anglican churches erected in that time: however, they have not attracted the attention they deserve (until recently) for many reasons, not least because they were seldom by the 'big names' among Victorian architects, and because, like many Evangelical Anglican churches, they often lacked architectural distinction: thus they did not enjoy the *Imprimatur* of that arbiter of Taste, *The Ecclesiologist*, in matters of church architecture.

108. Interior of Dukinfield Unitarian chapel, Chapel Street, Dukinfield, Cheshire (1840-45), by R. Tattersall, showing the thin quatrefoil piers (with cast-iron cores) and galleries, and arrangement of organ, central pulpit, Communion-table, and boards with Lord's Prayer and first Commandment (the latter stressing the One-ness of God). This arrangement is quite unlike the chancel of a Roman Catholic or Anglican church (EH. BB76/6230).

At the start of the Victorian period, Nonconformist chapels tended to be simple preaching-boxes, with the plan-type alluded to above (that is, a rectangular room with seats facing a pulpit sited at the end opposite the entrance-doors, a gallery [and therefore with fenestration consisting of two superimposed windows around the building to illuminate the volumes above and below the gallery], some sort of vestibule arrangement and stairs to the gallery, and usually a Classically-inspired entrance-front to the whole ensemble), so architectural enrichment or show was reserved for the entrance- or street-frontage.

An early enthusiasm for Gothic was not shared by Nonconformists, who abhorred a style so intimately connected with pre-Reformation England (until Ruskin identified Renaissance and Baroque styles as more immediately Romanist).

109. Unitarian chapel, Stockport Road, Gee Cross, Cheshire (1848), by Bowman & Crowther of Manchester. It looks to all intents and purposes from the outside like an Anglican church, and is in the Middle and Second Pointed styles (JSC [1994]).

Yet, as has been made clear above, Nonconformists had been discriminated against until the reforms of 1828 and 1829, and they shared the discrimination with Roman Catholics. Gothic and Nonconformism are uneasy bedfellows, and it has to be recognised that Georgian chapels are frequently more harmonious compositions than their often hamfisted Victorian Gothic successors. Our idea of Victorian churches embraces the strident polychromy of Butterfield, the muscularity of Street and Brooks, the scholarly delicacies of Bodley, and the nobility of Pearson, while the rasping, rattling barbarities of Keeling and Cheston can intrigue. Yet Nonconformist architecture is perhaps nearer the spirit of 'Roguery', and that is probably partly why it has sometimes failed to be taken seriously.

Yet as Gothic Revival churches became more common, and as its novel and fashionable status grew, the antipathy towards Gothic as a style for Nonconformist churches began to wane. Charles Barry designed Upper Brook Street chapel in Manchester (said to be the first Gothic Nonconformist chapel in England) in the First Pointed style, erected 1837-39, and the same style was used in the Dukinfield Unitarian chapel, Cheshire (1840-45), designed by Richard Tattersall (1802-44) **(Plate 108)**, although the great west window is Geometrical. Dukinfield marked the beginning of a series of distinguished Unitarian chapels, including the impressive Gee Cross, Stockport Road, Hyde, Cheshire, of 1848, which to all intents and purposes looks like an Anglican parish-church from the outside **(Plate 109)**: Gee Cross eschews the central pulpit of Dukinfield, has a chancel complete with Communion-table (although the font is also in the chancel), and is in Second Pointed style (even with a broach-spire), and clearly was influenced by the views of the Ecclesiologists and by buildings for the Anglican Church. The architects were Henry Bowman (1814-81) and Joseph Stretch Crowther (1832-93) of Manchester, who were very up-to-date and progressive in their architectural ideas. The same architects were responsible for the Mill Hill Unitarian chapel, Park Row, City Square, Leeds, Yorkshire (1848), in which the Second Pointed style is mixed with

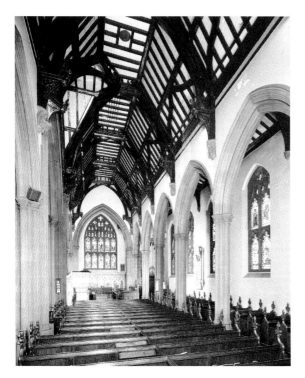

110. Interior of Mill Hill Unitarian chapel, Park Row, City Square, Leeds, Yorkshire (1848), by Bowman & Crowther. It was much influenced by the design of Leeds parish-church (see Plates 29 & 30), and mixes Second Pointed and Perpendicular elements (EH. BB66/1773).

Perpendicular windows **(Plate 110)** in an extraordinarily impressive design much influenced by Leeds parish-church (1839-41): indeed, the building does not really look like a Nonconformist church at all.

All of which brings us to an interesting point: Nonconformists, in spite of their history, often found themselves opposing or rivalling Anglicans in daily life: socially and economically they increased their influence, and played an enormous part in Victorian political affairs (notably in local, municipal government). Such a rising profile required architectural expressions, so the modest late-Georgian or Classical pedimented chapel (although built in numbers well into Queen Victoria's reign) was often replaced by a much grander edifice that aped the fashionable Gothic of the Anglicans from the 1850s (a good example of this was the impressive

111. Square Congregationalist church tower and spire (based on the steeple of Pugin's church of St Giles, Cheadle, Staffordshire) at Halifax, Yorkshire (1855-57), by J. James. It is in the Second Pointed style, but the building itself is no more. To the left is the simple Georgian chapel of 1772 which it superseded: this latter building is typical of traditional Nonconformist chapel-architecture before Dissenters succumbed to fashionable Gothic Revival (JSC [1994]).

Square Congregationalist church, Halifax, Yorkshire, of 1855-57, by Joseph James [1828-75]: it was a fine essay in the Second Pointed style of Gothic, and was partially funded by Sir Francis Crossley [1817-72], the carpet-manufacturer and philanthropist. By the 1990s, however, James's Gothic church had been demolished, leaving only the ambitious tower and spire (the latter derived from Pugin's church of St Giles at Cheadle, Staffordshire), standing, yet, ironically, the simple chapel of 1772, which it replaced, survived **(Plate 111)**. It should be noted that not only was a style being aped, but that the term 'church' was substituted for 'chapel': architectural ambitions and a rising social profile went together.

From the 1850s, indeed, Nonconformists sometimes succeeded in adapting Gothic to their

112. *The noble Classical Congregationalist church at Saltaire, Yorkshire (1858-59), by Lockwood & Mawson, from the east. On the left is the mausoleum of Sir Titus Salt, founder of Saltaire (GB. 634/74. EH. BB86/7041 [1974]).*

own needs, but, more often, the use of the style, and an attempt to achieve a Gothic solution to what was essentially the creation of a preaching-box, produced less than satisfactory results, for the large, static congregations of Nonconformist services and the central position of the pulpit were at odds with a type of mediæval church architecture that evolved because of pre-Reformation liturgy and practice. Later, from the 1870s, Nonconformity began to develop more experimental architecture which reflected the centralised type of plan: Waterhouse's Congregationalist chapels at Lyndhurst Road, Hampstead, and at Duke Street, Mayfair (both in London and both of the 1880s), are good examples of this new freedom (see below).

Henry Francis Lockwood (1811-78), then in partnership with Thomas Allom, designed the extraordinary Great Thornton Street Independ-

ent chapel, Hull, Yorkshire, of 1843 which was firmly Classical, with a fine octastyle Corinthian portico and wings on either side, but it, alas, has been demolished. Lockwood, with his partners Richard (1834-1904) and William Mawson (1828-89), designed the distinguished Classical Congregationalist church at Saltaire, Yorkshire, built in 1858-59 for the industrialist and philanthropist Sir Titus Salt (1803-76): it has an impressive semicircular Corinthian portico above which is a circular belfry with engaged Corinthian columns, and attached to the north side is the mausoleum of Salt **(Plate 112)**, prominent Congregationalist, sometime Mayor of Bradford, and local M.P. Classical too was the Particular Baptist chapel in Belvoir Street, Leicester, of 1845, by Joseph Aloysius Hansom — an architect remembered today as the inventor of the Patent Safety Cab (known as the Hansom Cab) and as the founder of *The Builder* in 1842. This chapel, known as the 'Pork Pie', has a large centralised elliptical space embellished with engaged Roman Doric columns, two circular staircases featuring paraphrases of the Corinthian palm-capitals from the Tower of the Winds in Athens, and a clearstorey with primitive unfluted Greek Doric columns. It was part of an education centre in 2001.

John Tarring (1806-75) seems to have worked solely for the Congregationalists, producing uninspired designs that looked rather like Commissioners' churches. Indeed, from the middle of the century, various denominations seem to have employed architects of their own persuasion (a curious exception was the choice of the Roman Catholic Hansom by the Baptists of Leicester), but this did not always result in architecture of distinction. The batterings many buildings received in the pages of *The Ecclesiologist* and *The Builder* tended to make congregations in search of designers turn to specialist and more distinguished professionals. Furthermore, some denominations tried to evolve some sort of party-line in matters of design, and the Wesleyan architect-clergyman, Frederick James Jobson (1812-81), brought out his important book, *Chapel and School Architecture* (1850), in which he insisted chapels were not theatres, concert-halls, or ware-

houses, and should not look like these building-types. Like the Commissioners, Jobson favoured Gothic, not only because it suggested the 'House of God', but because it was reasonably economical: however, he insisted upon good sight-lines and clear acoustics, and that the processional way down the centre of the nave (essential in Anglican churches) should never be used, because it was necessary for seating the congregation. Thus a Nonconformist arrangement of pews was nearly always a large section of seats in the middle of the space with access-passages on either side.

As has been indicated above, Joseph James was one of the better architects producing designs for the Nonconformists in the middle of the century. Mention has been made of his fine Second Pointed Congregationalist church in Halifax, but only two years earlier he had produced a similar and equally scholarly

114. Brookfield Unitarian church, Hyde Road, Gorton, Manchester (1869-71), a high-quality essay in the Middle Pointed style designed by Thomas Worthington. The influence of Ecclesiology is clear (JSC [1994]).

113. Interior of Todmorden Unitarian church, Yorkshire, showing the Anglican influence. Piers are marble cylinders and the entire ensemble is very grand (EH. BB75/5117 - print kindly provided by the Historic Chapels Trust).

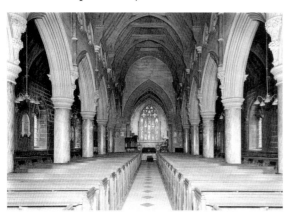

Middle Pointed church for Barnsley, Yorkshire. The Halifax church, as has been noted, had a tall steeple clearly influenced by (of all places!) Pugin's at Cheadle, while the huge traceried window and the main gable of the façade were quotations from the east end of Selby Abbey. Other competent Gothic essays, all with swash-buckling spires, were the Unitarian church, Fielden Square, Todmorden (1869), a Second Pointed ensemble **(Plate 113)**, which would easily pass for the parish-church, by John Gibson (1817-92); and Brookfield Unitarian church, Hyde Road, Gorton, Manchester (1869-71), a Middle Pointed essay of high quality **(Plate 114)**, with a superb Tractarian-inspired interior (though adapted for Unitarian worship), de-signed by Thomas Worthington (1826-1909). The Todmorden church, set high among trees above the town, was built as a memorial to John Fielden (1784-1849), cotton-manufacturer and philanthropist, by his sons, Samuel, John, and Joshua: it has a fine interior, much influenced by the Tractarian revival of Gothic. Monton Unitarian church, Monton Green, Eccles, Lancashire, of 1875, is another relatively scholarly Nonconformist church by Worthington that looks like an Anglican establishment. Thomas and his son, later Sir Percy Scott

115. Exterior of the Unitarian church at Ullet Road, Sefton Park, Liverpool, by Thomas and (Sir) Percy Worthington, of 1896-1902. It bears certain resemblances to Worthington's work at Manchester College, Oxford (MC. G180901 [2001]).

Worthington (1864-1939), were responsible for the Ullet Road Unitarian church, Sefton Park, Liverpool (1896-1902), one of the most ambitious Unitarian churches in England, with Second Pointed features, but with much Arts-and-Crafts detail in the cloister, library, vestry, and hall. The entire ensemble is built of hard, red brick, with red-sandstone dressings. Stained-glass was by Morris & Co., the beaten-copper doors were by Richard Rathbone, and the frescoes in the library and vestry were by Gerald Moira (*c.*1867-1959). Light-fittings were designed in the *Art-Nouveau* style **(Plates 115 and 116)**.

From around 1865, however, there was a gradual retreat from Gothic by Nonconformists in general, although architects such as Worthington continued to handle the style with considerable *élan*, and to adapt it for Non-conformist use. For the Unitarians, however, many churches were erected that looked

116. Interior of the Unitarian church at Ullet Road, Sefton Park, Liverpool, by Thomas and (Sir) Percy Scott Worthington, of 1896-1902. It is in the Second Pointed style, robustly and freely treated (EH. BB67/7542).

117. *Congregationalist church, 311, Upper Street, Islington, London (1888), from the south-west. A remarkable design by A.A. Bonella and H.J. Paull, showing how the influence of Domestic Revival architecture by Norman Shaw and others was being absorbed at that time* (CC. BB91/18421 [1990]).

indistinguishable (at least on the outside) from respectably Ecclesiologist-inspired Anglican parish-churches. As has been indicated above, not all Nonconformists turned to Gothic with ease, because the very form of a mediæval church was unsuitable for their purposes. Especially interesting is the use of the *Rundbogenstil*, an early example of which is the Central Baptist chapel, Bloomsbury Street, London, of 1845-48, by John Gibson: it has a broad front of white brick with thin stripes, two towers, and a large wheel-window. Some Nonconformists also began to develop an interest in plan-forms freed from Gothic restrictions, and more centralised plans with arms containing galleries began to appear, harking back to earlier arrangements of the eighteenth century. In 1870 Cubitt's *Church Design for Congregations* appeared, which discussed such matters. Cubitt was also to publish *Wren's Work*

and its Lessons (1884), and the *Popular Handbook of Nonconformist Church Building* (1892): he himself designed the Union Chapel, Compton Terrace, Islington (1876), with its octagonal interior and arms; and the Welsh Presbyterian church, Charing Cross Road, London (1888).

Many Nonconformist churches began to require other structures attached to them: these consisted of meeting-rooms, living accommodation for caretakers, church halls, and Sunday schools. The latter provided important educational facilities in the decades before the Established Church began to involve itself in expanding educational efforts at the beginning of the Victorian period. After the passing of important enactments concerning education, the Sunday schools assumed a new significance for the teaching of religion, so buildings to house schools were erected attached to places of

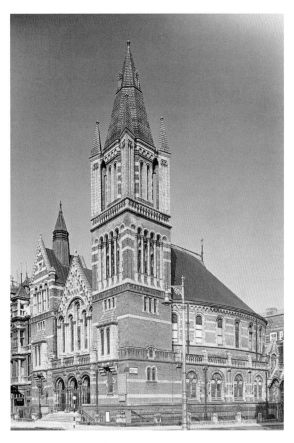

118. King's Weigh-House Congregationalist church, Duke Street, Mayfair, London (1889-91), by Alfred Waterhouse. It is built of brick and terracotta, and is an essay in the Rundbogenstil *(AFK. H.4949 [1949]).*

worship. Tight urban sites required ingenious planning solutions, and so some remarkable architectural compositions, incorporating many functions as well as a church, can be found among Nonconformist establishments. Among these, the Congregational church and schools, Highbury Quadrant, London, of 1880-82, by (Sir) John Sulman (1849-1934) — a massive pile-up of Gothic motifs (demolished) — and the Islington Congregational chapel, Upper Street, Islington, London, of 1888, by Alfred Augustus Bonella (fl. 1881-1908) and Henry John Paull (d. 1888) — a handsome building obviously influenced by the work of R. Norman Shaw — may be mentioned **(Plate 117)**.

The *Rundbogenstil* returned with a vengeance in this later phase of Nonconformist church-building, notably at the King's Weigh-House Congregationalist church on Duke Street, Mayfair, London (1889-91) by Alfred Waterhouse (1830-1905) **(Plate 118)**: this is a hard *Rundbogenstil* essay built of brick and much biscuit-coloured terracotta. Waterhouse was also responsible for the Congregationalist church, Lyndhurst Road, Hampstead, London (1883-84), which is essentially an irregular hexagon with attachments, while the Mayfair building is an elliptical arrangement set on a rectangular base. Brick and terracotta also feature in Hampstead, but this time the colour is darker, with purple brick and majolica dressings. Another hard terracotta *Rundbogenstil* example is the Talbot Tabernacle in Northern Kensington (1887) by William Gilbee Habershon (1818-91) and J.F. Fawckner (1828-98).

As the century neared its end there was a renewal of the idea of the City Mission, or evangelising the urban masses. Many Nonconformist chapels, or churches, or complexes of buildings were erected in an overblown and showy manner that recalled the distortions of architectural detail in contemporary theatres and music-halls. Materials such as terracotta and faïence were used in abundance, and the designs of such buildings seem to have been conceived to look as 'un-churchy' as possible, with the intention of attracting, rather than repelling, possible converts. A spectacular example of a showy Wesleyan establishment in London was erected to designs by Jonas James Bradshaw (d. 1912) and John Bradshaw Gass (1855-1939), both Lancastrians, and both Nonconformists: the building was the Leysian Mission, City Road, Finsbury, London, designed right at the end of Queen Victoria's reign, and completed in 1903. Pevsner (1952) called the front 'exceedingly sumptuous', the 'front of a broad office building: plenty of terra-cotta, a central dome, and scrolly Arts and Crafts ornament': it would be superfluous to comment further, and that extraordinary building is a suitable termination to this brief survey.

Epilogue

*An architect may lay down a most perfect and judicious system of restoration, but it can seldom
be perfectly carried out in spirit, if even in the letter, without the constant co-operation of the clergyman.
The practical workman detests restoration, and will always destroy and renew rather than preserve
and restore, so that an antagonistic influence ought always to be at hand.*
GEORGE GILBERT SCOTT (1811-78): *A Plea for the Faithful Restoration of our Ancient Churches*
(London: John Henry Parker, 1850), 33.

No study (however brief) of Victorian churches can afford to omit a mention of the importance of church restoration, for such work is likely to have taken as much of the energies of the architects and builders of the period as did new structures. Interestingly, some of the biggest offices involved in designing new churches were also those which carried out most restoration work.

Now restoration has often aroused passions, and there is no doubt that many 'restorations' of mediæval fabric were pretty drastic, and obliterated much genuinely old work in favour of mechanical and unsatisfactory new detail. Scott wrote sensitively about the problems of restoration in his *Plea for the Faithful Restoration of our Ancient Churches*, yet, as has been noted above, he could be among the worst offenders: his north nave-arcade, aisle, and clearstorey of the extraordinarily interesting church of St Mary de Castro in Leicester is one of the most insensitively crass of all his efforts in the field, whilst William Butterfield (not a name one would immediately associate with restoration, as his architecture is so uncompromisingly hard and modern) could be sensitive and unobtrusive, as in the marvellous restoration-work at the great church of St Mary, Ottery St Mary, Devon, under the ægis of the Coleridge family (there is a beautiful polychrome font by Butterfield of 1850 in the church), although he, too, could be over-zealous, as in the church of St Mary, Ashwell, Rutland (where he carried out a full Ecclesiological 'restoration' for William Henry, 7th Viscount Downe [1812-57] in 1851). At Ashwell, it has to be said, the character of the church is now more Victorian than mediæval, and Butterfield 'restored' the building within an inch of its life.

However, it has to be realised that, at the beginning of the Victorian era, many churches were in a poor state of repair, and to our eyes often would have looked distressingly bare and plain. Fittings and furnishings were very frequently of dates much later than the end of the Middle Ages: they included tall panelled Georgian 'box-pews', 'three-decker' pulpits, Jacobean or Caroline Communion-rails, and a plethora of funerary monuments. Not unusually, mediæval features, such as piscinæ, sedilia, and altars, were hidden behind plaster, buried, or had been destroyed. Mediæval stained-glass windows were rare, and skills in restoring or re-creating them had to be learned from scratch. Those Victorian architects, reared on Ecclesiology, and cognisant with mediæval architecture, felt duty-bound not only to preserve mediæval churches, but to restore them, with all their furnishings and fittings. Box-pews, Commandment-boards, pulpits, and much else were ruthlessly swept out, and new work in the Gothic style put in. Often, Victorian architects sought a feeling of completeness, of homogeneity, in their restoration-work, so a church and its fittings, begun, say, in the Norman period, and added to over the next seven hundred years, might be reborn in the Second Pointed style, and much genuine Romanesque, First, Middle, and Second Pointed, Perpendicular, Elizabethan, Jacobean, Caroline, Carolean, Restoration, and Georgian work destroyed in the process. It was in response to such drastic 'restorations' that William Morris was to found 'Anti-Scrape' or S.P.A.B. (the Society for the Protection of Ancient Buildings), for real mediæval buildings seldom had that appearance of completeness, as they were added to over a long period, and acquired many examples of different styles in the process. Architects had a regrettable tendency to assess what was the dominant style of a building, and then to make the whole *ensemble* a Victorian version of that style: if no style were clearly dominant, than an arbitrary decision would be made, and one style would be imposed willy-nilly. At the splendid mediæval Cathedral of St Chad, Lichfield, Staffordshire, most of the work we see today is by 'Great' and J. O. Scott, of 1857 onwards, including mouldings, capitals, statues, and window-tracery (only the windows of the apse appear to be genuinely mediæval).

Now Ruskin, in *The Seven Lamps*, had denounced radical, conjectural, and drastic 'restoration', and said that such work could never be restoration at all. When Scott proposed his draconian overhaul of Tewkesbury Abbey in the 1870s, opinion was strongly opposed, and this was the catalyst for the formation of S.P.A.B. Largely through the growing influence of the Arts-and-Crafts Movement, untidiness, elements from different periods and in different styles all jumbled together, and diversity began to be appreciated, and a gentler approach to older buildings began to be adopted, which we would now term 'Conservation', involving the retention of as much old fabric as possible. It is sobering to consider that a unique Anglo-Saxon arcade in the church of St Wystan, Repton, Derbyshire, was destroyed, apparently in 1854, so the S.P.A.B. approach was adopted not before time.

In a brief study such as this there is insufficient space to discuss the designers of furnishings and fittings, but no haunter of churches can fail to be impressed by much of the Victorian work. In the field of stained glass alone there are many fine examples in which sensitive design, scholarship, and excellent colouring go together: the best work was by Morris & Co., Kempe, Clayton & Bell, Burlison & Grylls, and other contemporaries. In metalwork, Francis Skidmore of Coventry provided some lovely objects, including the superb screen in Lichfield Cathedral (1859-63), designed by Scott, which is as fine an example of mid-Victorian work as can be found anywhere. Yet in virtually every aspect of furnishing and fittings, Victorian design and workmanship can arouse our admiration, although it has to be said that much fails to rise to the occasion, and the poor-quality work is truly awful. At their best, Scott, Street, Pearson, and Butterfield could be very good, while Bodley & Garner rarely put a foot wrong, and Burges could, and can, astonish us with his inventiveness. History has not been kind to the 'Rogue Goths': it is impossible to see a Bassett Keeling interior in all its rasping, thumping, polychrome glory now, since the church of St Paul, Anerley Road, Norwood, was demolished in the 1970s; Teulon's work has often been badly treated; but Lamb can still be enjoyed, if that is the correct word.

The most skilled Victorian architects could produce buildings that, by any standards, are wonderful creations, great works of architecture, and repositories for superbly designed and crafted fittings and furnishings. Pearson's St Augustine's, Kilburn, and his Truro Cathedral are unquestionably great buildings, while Bodley's Hoar Cross must be one of the loveliest churches in England, and in Staffordshire, too, Pugin's 'perfect Cheadle' could move the hardest of hearts. St Cuthbert's, Philbeach Gardens, Earl's Court, London, is a treasure-house of marvellous things, and ought to be better known.

It has to be remembered that the riches of Victorian ecclesiastical architecture were created in less than seventy years, that the Gothic styles had to be learned, that craftsmen had to adapt to the demands made by Ecclesiologist-inspired designers, and that materials (such as encaustic tiles) were specially produced for church work. Victorian churches are among England's finest buildings, and contain some of England's best design, craftsmanship, and originality of detail. There can be no question at all that such a legacy is of the greatest importance to our country's heritage.

Select Glossary

Developement [sic] … *cannot be expected from that most numerous class of architects, who veil their own ignorance of existing styles by an affected contempt for those who look to what* has been *as in any degree a stepping-stone to what* shall be. *These persons aim at avoiding servility through the medium of ignorance, and run down as mere copyists those who have taken the pains to attain a knowledge of the only styles which we can, as Christians or as Englishmen, call our own ….*
GEORGE GILBERT SCOTT (1811-78): *A Plea for the Faithful Restoration of our Ancient Churches*
(London: John Henry Parker, 1850), 112-113.

This is intended for the guidance of readers, and has no pretensions of comprehensiveness. The present writer's A Dictionary of Architecture *(2000) and* Classical Architecture *(2001) will help to augment the material here. Some of the entries are reproduced or derived from work previously published and © Oxford University Press 1999: this material is reprinted from* A Dictionary of Architecture *by James Stevens Curl (1999) by permission of Oxford University Press, to which body the author is indebted.*

abacus (*pl.* **abaci**). Flat-topped plate at the top of a *capital*, supporting an *entablature* or an *arch*.

Absolution. Remission or forgiveness of sins declared by ecclesiastical authority.

abutment. 1. Solid structure, e.g. a *pier*, which receives the thrust of an *arch* or *vault*. **2.** Point at which a roof-structure rests on a wall.

Advent. The Coming of the Saviour, i.e. the season preceding the *Nativity* of Christ, now including the four preceding Sundays before *Christmas*.

ædicule, ædicula (*pl.* **ædicules, ædiculæ**). Architectural frame around an opening consisting of two *columns* or *pilasters* supporting an *entablature*, with or without a *pediment*.

Æsthetic Movement. Late-nineteenth-century artistic reaction against mid-Victorian design, divorced from Puginian and Ruskinian 'moral' arguments, involving art for art's sake, and the cult of the *Beautiful*. It was influenced by the arts of Japan and China, and was closely connected with the *Arts-and-Crafts* Movement, *Art Nouveau*, and the *Queen Anne* Revival.

Agnus Dei. Representation of a lamb with a halo, and supporting a banner or the Cross, or both. An emblem of Christ.

aisle. Part of a church on either side of the *nave*, *choir*, and *chancel*, separated from those elements by *arcades* or *colonnades* carrying the *clearstorey*. Aisles are usually lower than naves, except in *hall-churches*.

alabaster. Massive, fine-grained, partly translucent type of gypsum (calcium sulphate), coloured white, yellow, red, and brown, called *bastard alabaster*, often employed for decorative sculpture. It is very common in Victorian churches, and is found in *reredoses*, *panels*, *pulpits*, and in monumental or funerary sculpture.

allegory. Description of a subject under the guise of some other subject of aptly suggestive resemblance. It therefore represents something it itself is not. *See* **attribute**, **symbol**.

altar. Elevated table consecrated for celebration of the *Eucharist*, usually of stone (though after the *Reformation* they were replaced with wooden *Communion-* or *Holy-tables*) found at the east end of a church and in side-chapels. The principal altar is called the *high altar*, and is situated at the east end of the *chancel*. The *sides* (*horns*) of altars are termed *Epistle* (south) and *Gospel* (north). An *altar-frontal* is the detachable finish or cover for the front of an altar, facing the nave: it is also called *antependium*, *altar-front*, or *altar-facing*. An *altar-rail* defines the *sacrarium* from the rest of the chancel. An *altar-screen* or *altar-wall* behind an altar separates the *sacrarium* from the *ambulatory* or *chapels* to the east, and is often of richly-carved work. An *altar-slab* or *altar-stone* is the slab (*mensa*) forming the top of an altar, often carved with five crosses indicating the *Five Wounds of Christ*, and, in *Roman Catholic* churches, having a *Relic* inlaid in the centre. An *altar-tomb* is a monumental tomb-chest or *high tomb* resembling an altar (but never used as such), sometimes supporting recumbent *effigies* or *memorial brasses* on top, and always has solid sides. It is sometimes embellished with *weepers* in niches around its sides. Altar-tombs are sometimes protected by ornate canopies.

ambo (*pl.* **ambones**). Raised *lectern* or *pulpit* in the *nave*, set before the steps of the *chancel*, and used for the readings of the Epistle and the Gospel.

ambulatory. 1. *Aisle* linking the chancel-aisles behind the *high altar*: it can be canted, semicircular, or straight on plan, with *chapels* to the east and the *sanctuary* to the west. **2.** Any place in which to process, walk, or promenade, such as in a *cloister*.

Anabaptist. Member of a German Protestant sect (1521) that held infant *Baptism* was invalid, and that Baptism should be of adults only: it also held 'wild opinions' about levelling and property, a sort of *Protestant* communism.

angle-buttress. *See* **buttress**.

Anglican. 1. Of the Reformed *Church of England* and other churches in communion therewith (e.g. the *Church of Ireland*). The Anglican Church claims to be part of the *Holy Catholic and Apostolic Church*, approves of *Catholic* dogma and ritual, but repudiates certain tenets of the *Roman Catholic Church* as corruptions, and claims independence of the Roman Papacy. The *Established Church* in England (and in Ireland until 1871), it acknowledges the Sovereign as Supreme Governor, with the Archbishop of Canterbury as its senior Churchman (*primate*).

Anglicanism falls into three main groups: *High Church* (which gives a high place to the authority and claims of the *episcopate* and the *priesthood*, to the saving *Grace* of the Holy *Sacraments*, and to those points of doctrine, discipline, and ritual by which Anglicanism is distinguished from *Protestant Nonconformity* [*see* **Dissenters**] and Continental *Calvinism*. In its most ritualistic Catholic observances it is sometimes known as *Anglo-Catholic, Ritualist,* or even *Smells-and-Bells*); *Broad Church* or *Middle-of-the-Road* (which avoids incense, many ritualistic trappings, images, *Stations of the Cross*, etc.); and *Low Church* (which has a more *Protestant* character, shies away from anything suggesting *Catholicism* [even the Cross, and certainly vestments, images, and candles], and is sometimes called *Evangelical*, because it often tends to emphasise Salvation by the Atoning Death of Christ according to the Gospels, denying that either Good Works or the Sacraments have any saving efficacy). **2.** Adherent of the Reformed Church of England or the Established Church.

angle-shaft. Decorative *colonnette* set in right-angled recesses, such as window- or door-openings.

Anglo-Catholicism. Catholicism of *Anglican* type, according to English views: it is the doctrine or perception of the Anglican Church as part of the *Catholic Church*, and emphasises *Ritualism* and the continuity of *High Church* principles with the *pre-Reformation, pre-Tridentine* Church *in* England (though in fact it absorbed much post-Tridentine and even nineteenth-century aspects of *Roman Catholicism*).

annulet. 1. Any horizontal *shaft-ring, band,* or *fillet* encircling a *colonnette* or *column*, especially that repeated under the *echinus* of a *Greek Doric* capital. **2.** Vertical fillet between column-flutes in *Classical* architecture.

Annunciation. Intimation of the *Incarnation*, made by the Angel Gabriel to the Blessed Virgin Mary.

anta (*pl.* **antæ**). Square or rectangular *pier* formed by the thickening of the end of a wall, e.g. in Greek temples, where the side-walls terminate. They are a species of *pilaster* in *Classical* architecture. Where *porticoes* are formed by carrying the side-walls out beyond the front wall, and placing *columns* in line between the antæ, the columns, portico, and temple are described as *in antis. Antæ* do not have *entasis*, and their capitals and bases need not correspond with those of the *Order* proper.

antepagmentum (*pl.* **antepagmenta**). **1.** *Anta* or *pilaster.* **2.** Face of a *jamb* of an aperture, or a moulded architrave around an opening, the top horizontal part of which, across the lintel, is called the *supercilium* or *antepagmentum superius.*

antependium. *Altar-frontal*, or detachable decorated covering for the front part of an altar, facing the *nave.*

anthemion (*pl.* **anthemia**). Honeysuckle ornament, usually found alternating with the *palmette*, in *Classical* architecture.

Antiquity. Period of the *Classical* civilisations of the Græco-Roman world.

Anti-Scrape. *See* **Scrape.**

apophyge. Outward concave curve connecting the *shaft* of a Classical column to the *fillet* over the base and under the *astragal* beneath the *capital.*

apse (*pl.* **apses**). Recess, generally semicircular or polygonal on plan, often half-domed or vaulted, projecting from an external wall, the interior forming a large, deep volume. It is often a feature terminating the *nave* of a *basilica*, and contains the high *altar*. Apsidal chapels are often found at the east ends of *transepts* and *chancel-aisles.*

arabesque. Decorative *scroll-work* and other ornament loosely derived from branches, leaves, tendrils, and vegetation, fancifully and symmetrically intertwined. Arabesques (or *Moresques*) do not contain human or animal figures, and are distinct from *Grotesques.*

arcade. Series of arches on the same plane (i.e. continuous) supported by *piers, colonnettes, columns,* or *pilasters,* either free-standing, or attached to a wall to form a decorative pattern: in the latter case it is called a *blind arcade.* A *nave-arcade* divides a *nave* from an *aisle.* Where blind arcades have overlapping arches, they are referred to as *interlacing* or *intersecting.*

archbishop. Chief *bishop*, the highest dignitary of an *episcopal* Church, superintending the *bishops* of his *province.* A *metropolitan.*

architrave. 1. Essentially a formalised *beam* or *lintel*, it is the lowest of the three main divisions of a *Classical entablature* that rests on the *abaci.* **2.** The lintel, jambs, and mouldings surrounding a window, door, panel, or niche, often corresponding in detail to an entablature architrave.

archivolt. Mouldings forming an ornamental concentric ring around a *Classical* or *Romanesque* arch.

arcuated. Structure employing arches, rather than *columns* and *lintels* (i.e. a *columnar* and *trabeated* structure).

Arminianism. Doctrine embraced by several *Protestant* sects, notably the *Methodists*, which opposed the *Calvinistic* view of absolute predestination and irresistible *Grace.* It is named after James Arminius (1560-1609)

arris. Sharp crease-like edge formed when two surfaces join, e.g. between the *flutes* of a *Greek Doric Order.*

Art Nouveau. Style that evolved from the late *Gothic Revival*, characterised by flowing, swaying, sinuous, vegetal tendril-like lines, and flourished *c*.1888 to *c*.1914.

Arts-and-Crafts. Late nineteenth-century English social and æsthetic movement which had its origins in an admiration for traditional art, craftsmanship, and *vernacular* architecture. It was more of an attitude than a style, but it produced much that was greatly admired and that was influential on the Continent and in America.

Ascension. Ascent of Jesus Christ to Heaven on the fortieth day after His Resurrection.

Assumption. Reception of the Blessed Virgin Mary into Heaven, Her Body preserved from corruption.

astragal. Small convex moulding with a semicircular profile, especially the *ring* separating the *shaft* from the *capital* of most *Classical* columns (except Greek *Doric*).

atrium (*pl.* **atria**). Open court, surrounded by a roofed arcaded or colonnaded walk, laid out before the west end of an Early Christian, Byzantine, or mediæval church (e.g. Sant' Ambrogio, Milan [*c*.1140]). It was the prototype of the *cloister.*

attribute. Object recognised as appropriate to, and symbolic of, any office or person, i.e. suggesting a characteristic quality. Most *Saints* have attributes, often associated with their *Martyrdom* (e.g. St Bartholomew and the knife with which he was flayed, and St Lawrence and the gridiron on which he was roasted).

Augsburg Confession. Protestant statement of belief drawn up by Melanchthon (the græcised name of Philip Schwartzerd [1497-1560], Professor of Greek at the University of Wittenberg), based on Luther's articles, and presented to the Emperor Charles V at the Diet of Augsburg in 1530. It specifically condemned Roman Catholic 'abuses': withholding the Cup during Communion, compulsory celibacy among the clergy, considering that the Mass was a sacrifice, compulsory Confession, festivals, and fasts, monastic vows, and secular authority exercised by bishops. It also clarified the main doctrines held by Lutherans: the Creeds of the Catholic Church; support for the doctrines of St Augustine against those of the Pelagians (who denied Original Sin) and Donatists (who held that their own party was the only true church and that Baptisms and Ordinations carried out by others were invalid); affirmation of justification by faith and the exclusive mediatorship of Christ; opposition to *Anabaptism* on the meaning and administration of the *Sacraments*; and the organisation of the Church, the Ministry, and Christian Rites.

aumbry. Recess in a church wall in which sacred vessels are kept, usually near an altar.

aureole. *Halo* or *Glory* surrounding the figure of Christ, the Virgin, or a Saint. If almond-shaped, it is formed of two interlocking segmental arcs, the whole figure called a *mandala* or a *vesica piscis*. A circular halo surrounding a head only is called a *nimbus*.

Backsteingotik. Simplified mediæval *Gothic* architecture constructed of brick, of the type found in Northern Germany or Poland.

baldacchino. Permanent canopy, especially over an altar, usually carried on columns. It does not have a domed top or a cupola at its apex, unlike a *ciborium*. Also known as *baldachin*.

ball-flower. Characteristic ornament of the *Second Pointed* (*Decorated*) style of *Gothic* (fourteenth century), resembling a small ball, just visible, enclosed within a ball partly cut open, with a trefoil or quatrefoil opening, normally placed at regular intervals in a continuous hollow moulding.

baluster. Upright support in a *balustrade*: it may be a square, circular, turned, or ornamented bar or rod; it can be a *colonnette* or a miniature column; or it can be the bellied, bulbed type of *columella* found in Classical detail.

balustrum. *Altar-rail* or *chancel-screen*.

band. Flat raised horizontal strip running across a façade or projecting slightly from the wall-plane, also called a *band* or *string-course*. A *band of a shaft* consists of a series of *shaft-rings* encircling colonnettes in *Gothic* architecture at the junctions of monolithic lengths, often tying the shafts to the pier behind. This is characteristic of the *Early English* or *First Pointed* period.

banded. Interrupted by plain blocks, as in a *banded column* or *rusticated column*.

Baptism. Immersion of a person in water or application of water by pouring or sprinkling as a religious rite, symbolising moral and spiritual purification, and signifying initiation into the Christian Church. It is a *Sacrament* carried out in churches at a *font*.

Baptist. Member of a *Protestant* religious body that holds *Baptism* should be administered by total immersion only to believers, at first called *Anabaptists*.

baptistry. Building or part of a church containing the font used for the *Sacrament* of *Baptism*.

bar. Moulded stone forming the structure of *bar-tracery* (as opposed to *plate-tracery*).

bar-tracery. *Gothic* window-tracery, in which the *lights* are defined by *bars* of moulded freestone.

barley-sugar column. *Classical* column or colonnette, twisted like a stick of barley-sugar, also known as a *Solomonic* or *twisted* column, often associated with *reredoses*, *Communion-rails*, *funerary monuments*, etc.

Baroque. Florid form of seventeenth- and eighteenth-century *Classical* architecture, characterised by exuberance, movement, convex and concave flowing curves in plan, elevation, and section, illusionist effects, and cunningly contrived and complex spatial inter-relationships.

barrel. Barrel-vault is a continuous elongated arch forming a curved ceiling or roof like half a cylinder.

basilica (*pl.* **basilicas**). Building-type with a clearstoreyed *nave*, two or more lower lean-to *aisles* on each side of the nave, and an *apse* at the end of the nave. The *basilican form* is that often used in church plans.

basket capital. *Byzantine* and *Romanesque capital* carved with interwoven strips resembling a basket-weave.

battlement. *Parapet* with higher and lower alternate parts. The indentations between the higher parts (known as *cops*, *kneelers*, or *merlons*) are the *carnels*, *crenelles*, *embrasures*, *loops*, or *wheelers*. A *crenellated* or *embattled* wall is one with battlements. Miniature decorative battlements occur in the *transoms* of late-*Gothic tracery*, on pier-capitals of the *Third Pointed (Perpendicular Gothic)* period, *Tudor* chimney-pots, and elsewhere.

bay. Regular *structural* subdivision of a church (i.e. a compartment or division in the architectural arrangement), defined along its long axis by *buttresses*, *piers*, *columns*, or *pilasters*, and by the main *vaults* or *trusses* of a roof (although in many churches, especially mediæval ones, the trusses are arranged with little regard for the structural rhythms of the masonry). Windows are usually inserted into the *curtain-wall* of each bay.

bead-and-reel. *Astragal* carved in semblance of a continuous row of bead-like and spool- or reel-like elements.

beak-head. *Romanesque* carving in the form of a series of animal-, bird-, or humanoid-heads with long pointed beaks (or tongues) curving round a lower *roll-moulding*, as in a church doorway. Heads with stumpier cone-like beaks are *cats'-heads*.

Beautiful. One of three æsthetic categories of the eighteenth century, with the *Picturesque* and the *Sublime*. It was associated with that which inspires love, and with smoothness, lack of angularity, and brightness of colour. Understanding of the Beautiful should be accompanied by pleasure, the 'emotion of Taste'.

belfry. 1. Bell-tower, generally attached to a church. **2.** *Stage* of a tower in which bells are hung.

bell. Shape of a *capital*, such as an *Egyptian* bell or the basic form of a *Corinthian* or *Composite* capital. Typical *First Pointed Gothic* bell-capitals resemble inverted bells.

bell-cote *or* **bell-gable**. Small *gable*, usually set over the west wall of a church or over the east wall of the *nave*, immediately above the *chancel-arch*, containing a bell or bells suspended within arched openings. If set over the chancel-arch, a bell-cote is called a *Sancte-cote*, as it carries the *Sanctus* bell.

bench-end. Terminal timber facing of a church-pew, frequently decorated with *poppy-heads*, *blind tracery*, and the like.

Benedictine. Monastic Order based on the rules of St Benedict (480-543). The Rule was regularised in the ninth century. The exemplary plan for the monastery of St Gall, Switzerland (*c*.820), is similar to the layout of many subsequent establishments.

billet. One of a series of short chamfered, cylindrical, prismatic, rectangular, segmental, or cubic projecting members in, or forming, a decorative continuous moulding, its axis parallel to the direction of the series, with sometimes two or more rows of this ornament placed one above the other, and with the billets of one row alternating with those of the other. It is characteristic of *Romanesque* work.

bishop. In the Eastern, Western, Anglican, and other Churches, a clergyman consecrated for the spiritual government and direction of a *diocese*, ranking beneath an *archbishop* and above the *priests* or *presbyters*.

blind. Blank, i.e. with no openings, or sealed up. A *blind arcade* is a row of arches *engaged* or attached to a wall, and *blind tracery* is therefore a pattern on a wall, as though the *lights* had been filled in (but actually only intended as decoration).

boss. Enriched convex block at the junction of *vault-ribs*.

brass. Engraved metal plate, let into a slab of stone or set on top of an altar-tomb. In mediæval times, it was an alloy of copper and tin, called *latten*, and examples abound with incised figures and inscriptions, often with an infill of black resin, enamels, and mastic. The monumental or memorial 'brass' was revived in the nineteenth century *Gothic Revival*, using true brass (an alloy of copper and zinc).

brattishing. 1. Any ornamental parapet, e.g. a *battlement*. **2.** Decorative *Gothic cress* on top of a *cornice, parapet, screen*, etc., generally of openwork consisting of stylised foliate and floral enrichment, often the *Tudor flower*.

broach. *See* **spire**.

bundle-pier. *Gothic pier* resembling a tight bundle of *colonnettes* in which the latter are not actually detached, but are created by the undulating plan-form. *Compare* **clustered pier**.

buttress. *Pier*-like projection of brick, masonry, etc., built either into a wall needing extra stability, or standing isolated, to counter the outward thrust of an *arch, vault*, or other elements. Types of buttress include:

angle: one of a pair of buttresses at the corner of a building set at an angle of 90° to each other and to the walls to which they are attached;

arch: a *flying buttress;*

clasping: massive buttress, square on plan, at the corner of a building, usually of the *First Pointed* period;

Decorated: *Second Pointed* buttress;

diagonal: set at the corner of a building at an angle of 135° to the walls, usually associated with *Second Pointed* work;

Early English: see *First Pointed*;

First Pointed: thirteenth-century type, often of great depth, frequently chamfered and staged, each *stage* being defined by *off-sets*, and the whole structure surmounted by steep triangular *gablets*;

flying: an arched structure extending from the upper part of a wall to a massive *pier* in order to convey to the ground the outward thrust of (usually) the stone *vault*;

lateral: attached to the corner of a structure, seemingly a continuation of one of the walls;

Perpendicular or *Third Pointed*: late-*Gothic* type with elaborately panelled faces, and often with crocketed *finials* of great elegance;

pier: detached external pier by which an arch or vault is prevented from spreading, as in the *chapter-house* of Lincoln Cathedral, where *flying buttresses* are used. Pier-buttresses are usually constructed with a heavy superstructure rising higher than the springing of the flying-buttress arch;

Romanesque: eleventh- or twelfth-century type, really a wide *lesene* of little projection, defining *bays*;

Second Pointed or *Decorated*: fourteenth-century type constructed in *stages*, frequently elaborately enriched (e.g. with canopied *niches* for statuary), and surmounted by crocketed *gables, finials*, and even crocketed *spirelets*;

set-back: like an *angle-buttress*, but not placed immediately at the corner, so the *quoin* of the building is exposed.

Byzantine. Architectural style that developed in the Eastern Roman Empire from the fourth century, and continued where the *Orthodox Church* was dominant long after the fall of Constantinople in 1453.

cable. Convex moulding (*called* **rudenture**) set in the *flutes* of *Classical column*- or *pilaster*-shafts, between the *fillets* but not projecting beyond their faces, and seldom carried up higher than a third of the height of the shaft.

cable-moulding. *Rope-moulding* carved to look like a rope with twisted strands, found in Antiquity, but mostly associated with *Romanesque* work, especially around arches.

Calvinism. Doctrines of the Protestant Reformer John Calvin (1509-64), including particular (i.e. divine) election, predestination (particular redemption [i.e. divine redemption of some, but by no means all, of the human race]), the incapacity for true faith and repentance of natural Man (i.e. moral inability in a fallen state), efficacious or irresistible *Grace*, and final perseverance (continuance of the Saints in a State of Grace until the final State

of Glory). It was largely opposed by *Arminianism*.

came. Cast, extruded, or milled lead rods with a section like an H, also called *lattice*, used in leaded lights (e.g. stained-glass windows) to frame and secure the panes of glass.

campanile (*pl.* **campanili**). Italian bell-tower, usually freestanding. Therefore any bell-tower in an *Italianate* or *Early Christian* style.

cancellus (*pl.* **cancelli**). **1.** Latticed *screen* , especially one (*cancello*) dividing the *sacrarium* or *presbyterium* (hence *chancel*). **2.** In the plural, *balustrades* or railings defining the *choir*, usually attached to *ambones* (*see ambo*).

Candlemas. Feast of the Purification of the Blessed Virgin Mary (2 February), celebrated with a great display of candles.

canopy. 1. Ornamental hood surmounting an *altar, font, niche, pulpit* (where it is called a *tester*), *stall, statue, tabernacle, throne, tomb*, etc., supported on *brackets, colonnettes*, etc., or suspended. **2.** *Canopy of honour, ceele, ceilure, celure, cellure*, or *seele* is a richly coloured and gilded panelled ceiling over an *altar, chancel, chantry-chapel, mortuary-chapel*, etc. **3.** A *town canopy* is a structure resembling an arcaded gabled opening, often with elaborate *pinnacles, finials*, etc., set over a niche or protecting a statue. It often occurs 90° from the usual vertical position on tomb-chests over the heads of effigies, and is also shown in incised slabs and funerary *brasses*. **4.** A canopy over an altar is usually called a *baldacchino* or *ciborium*.

capital. *Chapiter*, head, or topmost element of a *colonnette, column, pilaster, pier*, etc., defined by distinct architectural treatment, and often ornamented.

Cardinal. 1. One of the ecclesiastical princes constituting the Pope's council, or Sacred College, and to whom the right of electing the Pope has been restricted since 1173. **2.** A *Virtue*: the *Theological Virtues* are Faith, Hope, and Charity; and the *Natural Virtues* are Justice, Prudence, Temperance, and Fortitude. **3.** Point of the compass (i.e. north, south, east, west).

Carolean. Of the period of King Charles II (1660-85).

Caroline. Of the period of King Charles I (1625-49).

Carolingian. Style of architecture associated with the reign of Emperor Charlemagne (800-14), but generally accepted as dating from the late seventh century to the early tenth.

carrel, carel, carrol. 1. Aisle divided into *chapels*, or the screens dividing it, or the divisions. **2.** Small enclosure in a *cloister* or library for study. **3.** Light in a *Gothic* window defined by the *tracery*. **4.** Pane of glass secured by *cames* in a leaded light.

castellated. With *battlements*.

cathedra. 1. Chair or seat of a *bishop* in his church. **2.** Episcopal *see*.

cathedral. Church containing the *cathedra*, therefore the principal church of a *diocese* or *see*. The *Cathedral Style* was a phase (*c*.1810-*c*.1840) of the *Gothic Revival* in which mediæval motifs were used in an unscholarly way before the advent of *Ecclesiology*.

Catherine-wheel window. Circular *Gothic marigold*- or *wheel*-window, resembling a wheel, the radiating *colonnettes* suggesting spokes.

Catholic. 1. General, or universal, so the whole body of believers, as distinguished from an individual congregation or sect. **2.** *Ritualist* or *Sacramentarian* aspects of worship associated with *Anglican High Church* or *Tractarian* churches.

Catholic Apostolic Church. Church (also called *Holy Catholic Apostolic*) founded in England around 1835 (also called *Irvingites*), having an elaborate ritual and a complicated hierarchy. It emphasised prophecy, modern miracles, and an imminent Second Coming.

Catholic Church. The whole, universal, Christian Church. In England, it was claimed that the Church, even as Reformed, was the national branch of the Catholic Church. Thus the *unreformed* Western Church was termed the *Roman Catholic Church*.

cat's head. *See* **beak-head.**

cavetto (*pl.* **cavetti**). Concave *chamfer, gorge, hollow, throat,* or *trochilus* moulding, the section of which is a quarter-round, often used on *cornices.*

celure, ceilure, cellure. 1. Part of the roof of a church, panelled, decorated, and coloured, immediately above the *altar* or *Rood,* also called *canopy of honour, ceele,* or *seele.* **2.** The richly decorated ceiling over an altar, *chancel, chantry-chapel, mortuary-chapel,* etc.

cenotaph. Empty tomb, or funerary monument to someone whose body is elsewhere.

chancel. Liturgical eastern part of a church, used by those officiating in the services, and often defined by a *cancellus* (from which the term is derived) or screen. It contains the *sanctuary* and the *altar,* and often embraces the *choir,* especially in larger churches where the chancel is part of the main body of the building east of the *crossing.*

chancel-aisle. Aisle parallel to a *chancel,* often continuing behind the high altar as an *ambulatory,* connecting with the chancel-aisle on the other side.

chancel-arch. Arch at the liturgical east of the *nave,* often carrying a gabled wall above, separating the nave from the *chancel.* It is often splendidly decorated, and beneath it may be found a screen (with or without a *Rood*). Above the roof (usually higher or lower than that of the nave), the gable was sometimes crowned with a *bell-* or *Sancte-cote.*

chancel-screen. *Screen* separating the *chancel* from the body of the church. A large stone chancel-screen is a *pulpitum.* Many English chancel-screens survive, with *brattishing* on top of elaborately carved, coloured, traceried, and vaulted woodwork: they have galleries (*lofts*) which are approached by narrow stairs (many of which have also survived the screens themselves) in the masonry of the church, and often supported *Roods,* so can also be referred to as *Rood-screens.*

chantry-chapel. Chapel or separate part of a church established for the daily or frequent saying of Masses on behalf of the soul of the founder or founders of the *chantry* or *endowment.* Chantry-chapels were usually enclosed by screens (with or without a *canopy*), and were frequently erected over the burial-place of the founder, so incorporated an altar, reredos, tomb-chest, and effigy, as in the mediæval examples in Tewkesbury Abbey and Winchester Cathedral.

chapel. 1. Building for Christian worship, not a *parish-church* or *cathedral,* often without certain privileges normally those of a parish-church. **2.** Room or building for prayer and worship in or attached to a castle, college, etc. **3.** *Oratory* in a burial-aisle, *mausoleum, mortuary-chapel,* or elsewhere, with an *altar* where Masses might be offered for the dead (i.e. a *chantry-chapel*), often containing funerary monuments. **4.** Screened compartment in a large church, usually in *aisles,* to the east of *transepts,* or to the east of the high altar, with its own altar, separately dedicated, and often of great magnificence (e.g. Lady Chapels as at Ely Cathedral or Westminster Abbey). **5.** Place of worship subordinate to the parish-church, erected for the convenience of parishioners (*chapel-of-ease*), when the parish was very large and distances great, or where populations increased. **6.** Place of Christian worship other than buildings of the *Established Church* in England, so usually applied to *Nonconformist* establishments.

chapter-house. Building for assemblies, business, meeting, maintenance of discipline, etc., associated with cathedral, collegiate, and monastic churches, often situated on the east side of the *cloisters,* but sometimes on the north side of the church with access through a *vestibule* or *trisantia.* In larger establishments (e.g. Lincoln Cathedral) chapter-houses were polygonal on plan, with stalls around the perimeter.

chequer. *Diaper-work* in which the compartments are all square as in late-*Romanesque* and *Gothic* surface-carving.

cherub. Chubby male infant with wings, or an infant's head with wings. *Compare* **putto.**

Cherubim. 1. Figure with wings in the Jewish Temple. **2.** Angel of the *Nine Orders of Angels* with attributes of the knowledge and contemplation of Divine things.

chevet. 1. Apsidal or canted liturgical east end of a large church, with an *ambulatory* (around the curving or canted end of the *choir*) off which *chapels* radiate.

chevron. Ornament resembling a V used in series to form a *dancette* or *zig-zag* in *Romanesque* design, usually on *archivolts* or *string-courses.*

choir or **quire. 1.** Part of a large church appropriated for the singers, with *stalls,* situated to the liturgical east of the *nave,* and partially or fully screened. **2.** In a cruciform church that part east of the *crossing,* including choir, presbytery, and sanctuary around the high altar, wholly or partially screened.

choir-aisle. *Aisle* parallel to and adjoining the *nave* of a *choir,* sometimes joined at right angles or in a semicircle or in a series of cants to its opposite choir-aisle behind the high altar, thus becoming an *ambulatory,* often with *chapels* to the east.

choir-loft. Upper part of *choir-screen* or *pulpitum,* or a balcony in the *choir.*

choir-rail. Rail, low *balustrade,* or *cancelli* separating the *choir* from the *nave.*

choir-screen. Partition, railing, screen, or wall of any sort (pierced or solid) separating the *choir* from the *choir-aisles, ambulatory, retrochoir,* and sometimes the *nave,* although *chancel-screen, jubé, Rood-screen,* or *pulpitum* were formerly preferred to describe the last case.

choir-stall. Raised seat, one of a series of fixed *stalls* in a *choir,* backing on to a *choir-screen* (where there are *choir-aisles*) and on to a *pulpitum* where that exists. Seats were usually hinged, with brackets (*misericords*) underneath, to aid surreptitious partial sitting during the long mediæval offices. In cathedrals, choir-stalls have richly embellished canopies of open-work, enhanced by *pinnacles* and much ornament.

choir-wall. As *choir-screen,* but of masonry between *choir* and *choir-aisles.*

Chrismon. Sacred monogram, an arrangement [☧] composed of the first three Greek letters (*Chi* [X], *Rho* [P], and *Iota* [I] of ΧΡΙΣΤΟΣ, Christ's name, also called a *Christogram,* which suggests the Cross as well as *Pax* (peace). Other symbols associated with Christ are *Alpha* (A) and *Omega* (Ω), the Beginning and the End; INRI (*Jesus Nazarenus Rex Iudæorum* [Jesus of Nazareth King of the Jews], or *In Nobis Regnat Iesus* [Jesus Reigns in Us], or *Igne Natura Renovatur Integra* [Nature is Regenerated by Fire – referring to the Spirit and to Redemption]); IHS (variously explained as the first two and last Greek capital letters of ΙΗΣΟΥΣ, Christ's first name [IHC, the *Iota, Eta,* and *Sigma* (given as S, C, or the Latin S)], an abbreviation of *Iesus Hominum Salvator* [Jesus the Saviour of Man], *In Hoc Signo* [In This Sign (Thou shalt Conquer)], and *In Hac Salus* [in this (Cross) is Salvation]); and the *Fish,* which is a symbol of Christ, Christianity, St Peter, and *Baptism,* as fishes cannot live without water. The first two letters of the Greek for 'fish' (*ιχθύς*) also give the initial I and X (for *Ιησούς Χρίστος* = Jesus Christ), gives ☧ a symbol of Faith and Baptism.

Christmas. Festival of the Nativity of Christ, kept on 25 December.

church. Edifice for public Christian worship, distinguished from a chapel or oratory, which in some respects are not truly public in the wider sense. The simplest type of church-plan consists of an area for the congregation known as the *nave,* and a smaller part (usually divided from the nave by an arch) known as the *chancel,* for use by the officiating clergy and containing the *altar*. The *basilican* form has a clearstoreyed nave, lean-to *aisles*, apsidal east end, and some kind of porch or *narthex*. Centralised church-plans derive from *Byzantine* domed spaces, and from circular or polygonal *mausolea* associated with important tombs and *martyria*. Large, elaborate churches have several chapels, two or more *transepts*, towers, other structures such as *cloisters*, porches, a *baptistry*, and a *chapter-house*.

ciborium (*pl.* **ciboria**). Fixed *domed canopy* over an altar, supported on four columns. Compare **baldacchino**.

Cistercian. Strict monastic Order founded at Cîteaux (1098) as an offshoot of the *Benedictine* rule. Cistercian architecture was international, and plans and elevations were severely simple. *Chancels* had straight, rather than apsidal, east ends, and *chapels* attached to transepts were also squared off.

Classicism. Principles of Greek and Roman art and architecture. *Classical* architecture is derived from precedents drawn from *Antiquity* that were respected as having authoritative excellence.

clearstorey or **clerestorey**. Upper parts of walls carried on *arcades* or *colonnades* in the *nave, choir,* or *transepts* of a church, rising above the lean-to roofs of the *aisles*, and pierced with windows to allow light to enter the nave, choir, and transepts.

cloister. Enclosed court, attached to a monastic or collegiate church, consisting of a roofed *ambulatory* south or north of the *nave* and west of the *transept* around an open *garth*, the walls (*panes*) facing the garth constructed with plain or traceried openings (sometimes wholly or partially glazed). It served as a means of communication between different buildings, and was often equipped with *carrels*, seats, and a *lavatorium* for ablutions. In *Early Christian* churches the cloister was at the west end, and was called an *atrium*, with one side either doubling as, or leading to, the *narthex*.

Close. Enclosed with walls or barriers, e.g. the precinct of a cathedral-church, so *Cathedral Close*.

clustered pier. Compound *pier* with separate *colonnettes* or shafts attached to it and each other by means of *bands of a shaft*, as distinct from a *bundle-pier*. In English *First Pointed Gothic*, shafts were often of dark Purbeck polished marble, contrasting with the lighter stone behind. The Victorians also used detached shafts, often of polished granites.

Collegiate church. Church endowed for a body corporate, or chapter, of dean and canons, attached to it.

Collegiate Gothic. Secular Gothic architecture, e.g. of Oxbridge colleges, as revived in nineteenth-century educational foundations.

colonnade. Series of columns in a straight line supporting an *entablature*. When a colonnade stands in front of a building and carries a roof to create a covered porch, it is called a *portico*, and if it surrounds a building, court, or garden, it is a *peristyle*. *See* **portico**. A colonnade is defined in terms of its number of columns and the spaces between columns.

colonnette. Small column, *baluster*, or slender circular shaft, as in an *annulated pier*.

column. Any relatively slender vertical structural member in compression, supporting a load acting near the direction of its main axis. Sometimes monolithic, it is usually cylindrical (but sometimes square or polygonal on plan), normally carrying an *entablature* or lintel, but sometimes standing on its own. In the *Classical Orders*, a column consists of a *base* (except the Greek Doric Order, which has no base), *shaft*, and *capital*, and the shaft tapers towards the top in a gentle curve called *entasis*. Columns are distinct from *piers, pilasters,* and *pillars*.

Commissioners' churches. Following the Napoleonic Wars, it was feared that England might suffer from upheavals similar to those that had beset France, so, faced with irreligion, an increasing population (much of it restive), and *Nonconformity*,

the authorities decided to build *Anglican* churches, numbers of which (also known as *Waterloo churches*) were erected under the aegis of the Commissioners for Building New Churches appointed under *An Act for Promoting the Building of Additional Churches in Populous Parishes* (58 Geo. III, c. 45), 1818. Most were cheap, utilitarian preaching-boxes, with any architectural pretensions reserved for the west end. Designs were *Classical*, or in a lean, unscholarly *Gothic* style, with low-pitched roofs, galleried interiors, and pointed windows set in *bays* marked by *buttresses*: the latter type was known as *Commissioners' Gothic*.

Commonwealth. The Republican Government established between the execution of King Charles I in 1649 and the Restoration of the *Carolean* Monarchy in 1660.

Communion. **1.** Participation in the *Sacrament* of the Lord's Supper. **2.** The Sacrament itself. *See* **Eucharist**.

Communion-rail. Rail in front of an *altar* at which communicants kneel to receive the elements.

Communion-table. Wooden table in *Protestant* churches, replacing the stone *altar*, introduced as a deliberate denial of the doctrine of *Transubstantiation*.

Composite Order. Grandest of the Roman *Classical Orders of Architecture*, essentially an ornate version of the eight-voluted *Ionic capital* known as the *angular capital*, under which are added two tiers of acanthus-leaves. Its *entablature* is also very ornate.

confessio. Place where the *Relics* of a Martyr or Confessor are kept, or the *crypt* or *shrine* under an *altar*, in which Relics are placed.

confessional. Booth, box, or cubicle in which confessions of penitents are heard in a church.

Confirmation. Rite administered to baptised persons in various Christian Churches: in the *Roman Catholic* and *Orthodox* churches reckoned to be one of the *Seven Sacraments*, and in these and in the *Anglican Church* held to convey Special Grace which confirms or strengthens the recipient in the faith.

Conformity. Compliance with the form of religion legally established, i.e. with the rites, discipline, and doctrines of the *Anglican Established Church*. Anybody who did not *conform* as defined above was a *Nonconformist* or a *Dissenter*.

Congregationalism. Form of *Protestant* Church Government in which each congregation is independent in the management of its own affairs, yet acknowledges itself to be part of the Universal Church, united with other reformed Churches by voluntary ties of fellowship, yet unwilling to submit to external authority.

consecration cross. Cross painted or carved on church walls indicating where *chrism* was to be applied during the consecration of the building. There were twelve in all, and many have survived as permanent interior decoration.

conservation. Retention of existing buildings or groups of buildings, taking care not to alter or destroy character or detail, even though repairs may be necessary.

console. Type of Classical bracket or *corbel* with parallel sides, usually an *ogee* curve surmounted by a horizontal slab, often moulded, fixed upright to a wall with the greater projection at the top. It is commonly found e.g. on each side of the top of a door- or window-*architrave*, supporting the *cornice*. In a horizontal position, the curved part downwards and the bigger scroll at the end fixed to a wall, it appears to carry an element, e.g. a balcony, and thus suggests a *cantilevered* form. Horizontal consoles fixed to the *soffits* of a crowning cornice and appearing to support it are called *modillions*. Wedge-shaped (sides not parallel) consoles are called *ancones*, as used for *keystones*.

Consubstantiation. Doctrine of the *Real Substantial Presence* of the Body and Blood of Christ co-existing together with the bread and wine of the *Eucharist*. *See* **Transubstantiation**.

corbel. Projection from the face of a wall, consisting of a block built into the wall, supporting any superimposed load such as an arch, beam, parapet, truss, etc., so essentially a *cantilever*.

corbel-table. Row of *corbels*, often with carved heads on them, set at intervals, sometimes carrying connecting arches (*Lombardy frieze*), but more often supporting a projecting wall, such as a *parapet* or a *battlement*.

Corinthian Order. *Classical Order* of Architecture, the third of the Greek and fourth of the Roman. Slender and elegant, it consists of a base, a tall shaft (fluted or plain) a capital (the distinguishing feature consisting of two rows of *acanthus*-leaves over the *astragal*, with *caules* rising from the acanthus-leaves and sprouting *helices* or *volutes* from each *calyx* with a bud), with concave-sided *abacus*, and an *entablature*, often of great magnificence.

cornice. Uppermost crowning projecting moulded division of a *Classical entablature*, pedestal, wall, or opening.

corona (*pl.* **coronæ**). **1.** Circlet or loop suspended over an altar, often carrying candles, and called a *corona lucis*. **2.** Part of a *Classical cornice*, above the bed-moulding and below the *cymatium*, with a broad vertical face and underside recessed.

Cosmati-work. Inlaid geometrical polychrome patterns of stone, glass, mosaic, and gilding set in marble. It is associated with *Italian Romanesque* design. Good examples survive in Westminster Abbey (all second half of the thirteenth century). Cosmati patterns were revived in the nineteenth century.

credence. Table or shelf on the south side of the *sanctuary* of a church near the altar, where the Sacred Elements were placed before the *Oblation*. Sometimes associated with the *piscina*, it was often given decorative treatment.

crenel, crenelle. *See* **battlement**.

cress, crest, cresting. **1.** Ornament or series of ornamental elements, often perforated, forming a decorative finish on top of an architectural element, e.g. a *canopy*, *ridge*, *screen*, or *wall*. **2.** A *finial*.

crop, crope. Gothic *knop* of carved leaf-like forms surmounting a *finial*, *gable*, *spire*, etc.

cross. Two straight members set at 90° to each other, one vertical and the other horizontal. It is a symbol of Christianity. The commonest types are: the *Latin* with the three topmost arms of equal length and the bottom arm longer; the *Greek*, with the arms of equal length; and the *clover-leaf* or *bottonée* cross, with three clover-like leaves at the end of each identical arm.

crossette. **1.** *Console* or *truss* set on each flank at the top of an *architrave* around an aperture, supporting a *cornice*. Consoles are also called *ancons, ears, elbows, hawksbills, knees, lugs,* or *prothyrides*. **2.** Type of architrave, the *supercilium* of which projects beyond the *antepagmenta*, forming projections called *ears, elbows, lugs,* or *shoulders*. **3.** Ledged or joggled *voussoir* resting on top of a neighbouring voussoir, as in *rusticated ashlar*.

crossing. Part of a *cruciform* church where the *transepts* cross the east-west *nave*, often with a tower above it.

Crucifixion. Crucifixion groups were set up on *Rood-beams*, and usually featured Christ on the Cross with Sts Mary and John. Sometimes the timber base was carved with skulls, bones, etc., and called a *Golgotha*: a good example survives in the church of St Andrew, Cullompton, Devon.

cruciform. Cross-shaped: e.g. a church with *transepts*.

crypt. **1.** Vaulted chamber, sometimes of considerable size, beneath a church, wholly or partly underground, usually under *chancels* and *chancel-aisles*, often divided into *nave*, *aisles*, and *chapels*. **2.** Space under a church, for the entombment of corpses.

cupola. **1.** Bowl-shaped *vault* on a circular, elliptical, or polygonal plan. **2.** Underside or soffit of a dome. **3.** Bowl-shaped element carved on columns set as a canopy over a tomb, etc., or a

ciborium. **4.** Small dome on the *lantern* over the *eye* of a large dome, or the dome plus lantern, or any diminutive domed form, visible above a roof.

curate. **1.** One entrusted with the care of souls, i.e. any ecclesiastic who has the spiritual charge of a body of laymen. **2.** Clergyman who has the spiritual charge of a parish or parochial district (i.e. the parson of a parish). **3.** Clergyman engaged for a stipend to perform ministerial duties in a parish as a deputy or assistant of the parish-priest or incumbent.

Curvilinear. *Flowing* or *Undulating* tracery of *Second Pointed* or fourteenth-century *Decorated Gothic*. *Ogees* were applied, thus creating elaborate net-like constructions of tracery, often with *dagger, fish-bladder*, and *mouchette* shapes in the lights. Further developments in Europe created the so-called *Flamboyant* tracery, from the flame-like shapes of the lights.

cushion. **1.** Architectural element resembling a bolster, cushion, pad, or *pulvinus*, with convex profiles, such as a *pulvinated frieze*, apparently bulging outwards as if under pressure. **2.** Block on an *impost*, being the springer of an arch. **3.** *Corbel* or pad-stone.

cushion-capital. Also *block* or *cube* capital, it is a *Byzantine* and *Romanesque* form, essentially a cube with its lower corners shaved off and rounded in order to accommodate the transition from square *abacus* to circular *shaft*, its four faces are reduced to semicircular *lunettes*.

cusp. Point formed by the intersection of two curved lines or members, e.g. the projecting point between small arcs or foils in *Gothic* tracery.

cylindrical vault. *Barrel-, cradle, tunnel*, or *wagon-headed* vault, really an elongated or continuous arch like half a cylinder spanning between parallel walls.

cyma (*pl.* **cymæ**). Projecting Classical moulding, with an *ogee* section, usually of equal convex and concave arcs, with a plain *fillet* above and below.

dagger. Light shaped like an *ogee*-ended elongated lozenge resembling a dagger in *Second Pointed* or *Decorated Gothic tracery*.

dansette, *or* **dancette**. *Romanesque chevron* or *zig-zag* moulding.

deacon. In *episcopal* Churches, a member of the third Order of the ministry, ranking below *bishops* and *priests*, and having the functions of assisting the priest in the celebration of the *Eucharist*, visiting the sick, etc.

Decorated. See **Gothic**.

dentil. Small block forming one of a long horizontal series, closely set, under the *cornices*, associated with the bed-mouldings of the *Composite, Corinthian, Ionic*, and (sometimes) *Roman Doric Orders*.

diagonal buttress. *See* **buttress**.

diagonal rib. Rib diagonally crossing a *bay* or compartment of a *vault*.

diaper-work. Decorative pattern on a plain, flat, unbroken surface, consisting of the constant repetition of simple figures (e.g. squares, lozenges, polygons) closely connected with each other, sometimes with embellishments in the form of stylised flowers. It may be lightly carved, painted on a wall, or formed of dark bricks laid in patterns in a lighter brick wall.

diocese. Sphere of jurisdiction of a *bishop*, or the district under the pastoral care of a bishop.

Diocletian window. Semicircular window opening (usually sub-divided by two plain *mullions* into three compartments. Named after its use in the *thermæ* (baths) of Diocletian, Rome (AD 306), its alternative name is *Thermal* window, commonly found in *Palladian* and *Neo-Classical* architecture.

Dissenters. Those who refused to conform to the requirements of the *Established Church* (*see* **Anglican**). In early use Dissenters included *Roman Catholics*, but from *c*.1660 the term came to mean

Protestant Nonconformists who remained separated from the *Anglican* Church, and included Presbyterians, Baptists, Quakers, Independents, Unitarians, and Congregationalists. Later, Methodists and various other Protestant sects were also described as Dissenters. A *Dissenter* is sometimes distinguished from a *Nonconformist* in that the term is restricted to those who not only dissent from the National Established Church as constituted, but who reject any National or State Church.

distyle. Two columns in a portico, often set in a line between the *antæ* of the projecting walls of the buildings, so the portico will be *distyle in antis*.

dog-tooth. 1. Pyramidal ornament consisting of four leaf-like forms radiating from the apex or resembling a pyramid with V-shaped notches pointing towards the apex, forming one of a closely spaced series within a *cavetto* moulding. It is characteristic of *First Pointed* or *Early English Gothic*. 2. Brick laid diagonally with a corner corbelled out and projecting over the wall below, forming one of a series of adjacent similar bricks to create a continuous saw-toothed *band* on a *string-course* or as part of a *cornice*.

dome. Species of *vault* constructed over a circular, elliptical, or polygonal plan, bulbous, segmental, semicircular, or pointed in vertical section.

Domestic Revival. Offshoot of the cult of the *Picturesque* and the *Gothic Revival*, it was a style of domestic architecture that incorporated forms, details, and materials found in English *vernacular* buildings, including steeply-pitched tiled roofs, *dormers*, timber-framing and jettied construction (notably on gables), small-paned mullioned and transomed windows (often with leaded lights), tile-hung walls, tall chimneys (often of the *Tudor* type in carved and moulded brick), and carefully contrived asymmetrical compositions. Associated with the *Arts-and-Crafts* movement, it was also called the *Old English* style.

Doom. Pictorial representation of the Last Judgement. In a church it often took the form of a mural painting over the *chancel-arch*, with Christ in the middle, Hell and the damned on His left (the south or right when viewed from the *nave*), and the Blessed on His right (north). It was also the subject of stained-glass windows and carvings on the *tympana* of doorways.

Doric Order. *Classical Order of Architecture* found in distinct Greek and Roman varieties. In the Greek version it consists of a *stylobate* supporting a baseless column-shaft (normally cut with *flutes* separated by *arrises*, but occasionally unfluted) with a pronounced *entasis* terminating in the *capital* with *annulets* or horizontal *fillets* (from 3 to 5 in number) stopping the vertical lines of the *arrises* and *flutes* of the shaft; an *echinus* or cushion above them; a plain square *abacus*; and an *entablature* with plain *architrave* over which are the *frieze* and *cornice*. The Doric frieze is composed of alternate *metopes* (sometimes ornamented) and *triglyphs* (flat upright slabs, incised with two vertical V-shaped *glyphs* [channels] and two half-glyphs on each side, with a flat band across the top). Triglyphs are normally set over the centre-lines of each column and intercolumniation, except at the corners, where they terminate the frieze, so columns have to be set back. In the *Roman Doric Order* there may be a rudimentary base, but the shaft is generally more slender, and the entablature is only an eighth of the height of the Order: triglyphs at the corners of the building are set over the centre-lines of the columns, leaving a portion of metope at the corner.

dormer. Window inserted vertically in a sloping roof and with its own roof and sides.

dorsal, dossal, dossel. 1. *Reredos*. 2. Cloth suspended at the rear of an altar. 3. Ornamental hanging suspended at the backs of *sedilia* or elsewhere at the sides of a *chancel*. 4. Stall with a back to it, as in a *Collegiate* church or a *cathedral*.

dosseret. 1. Supplementary block or *super-abacus*, often taller than the *capital* itself, placed over an *abacus* of *Early Christian*, *Byzantine*, and *Romanesque* capitals, really an *impost-block* from which arches spring. 2. Block formed like a section of *entablature* over a *column* or *pier*.

double cone. *Romanesque* moulding consisting of a series of truncated cones laid on their sides, with bases joined and truncated tops together, forming a continuous horizontal ornament like a necklace in a *cavetto*.

dove. Symbol of the *Holy Spirit*. With an olive-branch it represents *Peace*.

drop. Type of pointed arch of less height than span, also called a *depressed arch*.

drop-tracery. Fragmental *Gothic tracery* suspended from the *soffit* of an arch.

drum. 1. Nearly cylindrical element from which a column-shaft is formed. 2. Vertical circular or polygonal structure, usually carrying a *cupola* or *dome*, and often pierced with windows. 3. Core of a *Composite* or *Corinthian* capital.

eagle. Symbol of St John the Evangelist, and therefore an important motif in the design of *lecterns*.

ear. 1. *Horn* of an *altar*, *sarcophagus*, or *stele*, etc. 2. *Crossette*. 3. Lug or tab for fixing a pipe to a wall.

Early Christian. Style of architecture that evolved in the Roman Empire from the fourth to the sixth centuries AD, primarily associated with church buildings, usually of brick, and often on the *basilica* plan, with windows and doors treated with semi-circular-headed openings. Early Christian basilicas incorporated colonnaded or arcaded *clearstoreyed naves*, and usually had apsidal east ends. The style was revived in the nineteenth century and was known as the *Rundbogenstil*.

Early English. *See* **Gothic**.

Easter. Festival of the Christian Church commemorating the Resurrection of Christ, corresponding to the Jewish Passover. It is observed on the first Sunday after the calendar full moon, which happens on or after 21 March.

Easter sepulchre. Recess under an arch or canopy associated with a tomb-chest, situated on the north side of a *chancel*, in which Christ was 'buried'. At the end of the liturgy of Good Friday, the priest put off his Mass-vestments and, barefooted, clad in his surplice, carried a *pyx* containing the Third Host (consecrated the day before) and the Cross (which had been kissed by the people during the liturgy) to the north side of the chancel, where the sepulchre was made ready. Both pyx and cross were wrapped in linen and placed in the sepulchre, which was duly censed, covered with a richly embroidered pall, and had numerous candles glowing before it. A watch to protect both the Host and the pyx was kept before the sepulchre until Easter. In the early hours of Easter Sunday all candles in the church were lighted, the clergy processed to the sepulchre (which was censed), the Host was removed to the pyx above the high altar, and the Cross was raised from the sepulchre and carried around the church before being placed on the altar at the north side of the church, where it was venerated. The empty sepulchre remained an object of devotion for days thereafter.

Ecclesiology. The study of churches, church-history, traditions, decorations, and furnishings, followers of which were known as *Ecclesiologists*. *The Ecclesiological Society* was a powerful force in promoting and developing the English *Gothic Revival*, and its journal *The Ecclesiologist* (1841-68), was influential, not least in the making (and breaking) of architectural reputations.

echinus. Plain circular cushion-like convex moulding between the *abacus* and *annulets* of the Greek *Doric capital*, between the abacus and *hypotrachelium* of the *Tuscan* and Roman Doric Orders, and beneath the *pulvinus*, joining the *volutes* of the *Ionic* capital where it is enriched with *egg-and-dart* (so also occurs in the upper part of the *Composite* capital).

eclecticism. 1. Design drawing freely on forms, motifs, and details selected from historical styles and different periods. **2.** The practice of selecting from a wide range of sources what elements, styles, motifs, details, etc., that may appear to be sound, acceptably functional, and beautiful, in order to create a sumptuous architectural effect.

edge-moulding. Mediæval moulding on string-courses, with a convex top and cavetto below, often with a sharp edge at the junction.

edge-shaft. Common *Romanesque* arrangement of an engaged half-shaft attached to a *pier*, usually the element from which an arch springs.

Edwardian. Of the time of King Edward VII (1901-10), often characterised by an opulent *Baroque* revival, but also the period when some of the very finest English Arts-and-Crafts late-Gothic work was created.

Edwardine. Of the period of the reign of King Edward VI (1547-53).

effigy. Sculptured representation of a figure, normally shown clothed or in armour, lying on its back on a tomb-chest.

egg-and-dart. Classical ornament applied to convex rounded mouldings (such as the *echinus* or other *ovolos*) consisting of a series of oviform elements (with their tops cut off) surrounded by a groove and raised rim, between which rims are inserted, one between each pair of 'eggs', a sharply pointed dart-like or anchor form, sometimes resembling a tongue. Thus the egg and dart alternate in series. Also called, depending on the shape of the 'dart', *egg-and-anchor*, *egg-and-tongue*, or *nut-and-husk*.

Egyptian Revival. Style of architecture involving the use of motifs derived from Ancient Egypt (including *obelisks*, *sphinxes*, *pyramids*, *steeply battered* walls, *cavetto* cornices, *pylon* shapes, *lotus-* or *papyrus-headed* columns, Egyptian deities, Canopic jars, and elements [supposedly Egyptian] derived from Piranesi's *Diverse Maniere* of 1769).

elbow. *Crossette.*

Elizabethan. Style prevailing during the reign of Queen Elizabeth I (1558-1603) in which early-Renaissance elements derived from Northern Europe and from published sources were used.

embattled. *See* **battlement.**

embrasure. 1. Space between the *cops* in a *battlement*. **2.** Splayed enlargement of an aperture creating a bigger opening on the inside of a wall than on the outside, thus allowing more light to enter. It is a common motif in church architecture.

encaustic. 1. Fixed by heat, with reference to, e.g., painting with wax colours and fixing them during firing so that the colours are burnt in. **2.** Type of tile decorated with patterns formed with different colours of clay inlaid in the tile made of another colour, then fired, and usually glazed. *Encaustic tiles* with yellowish patterns on a dark red ground were commonly used in mediæval and *Gothic Revival* churches.

engaged. Applied, attached, semi-engaged, inserted, or seemingly partly buried in a wall or pier, such as a column with half or more of its shaft visible, quite distinct from a *pilaster*.

entablature. In *Classical Orders*, the entire horizontal mass of material carried on columns and pilasters above the *abaci*. Normally it consists of three main horizontal divisions: the *architrave* (essentially the *lintel* spanning between the columns; the *frieze* (occasionally omitted, as in certain examples of the *Ionic Order*); and *cornice*. An entablature on top of an *astylar* (without columns or pilasters) façade, as in Florentine Renaissance *palazzo*, is called a *cornicione*.

entasis. In *Classical* architecture shafts of columns are wider at their bases than under the capitals: the transition from base to top is not straight, but curved, and the *diminution* usually begins from

a point about a third of the height from the base. In the *Elizabethan* or *Jacobean* periods, and in the Free-Renaissance Revival of the 1880s and 1890s, entasis was often grossly exaggerated.

épi. *Spire*-shaped termination, as on a hipped roof.

episcopal. 1. Of or pertaining to a *bishop* or bishops. **2.** Constituted on the principle of *episcopacy*, i.e. government of a Church by a system that comprises a hierarchy of *bishops*, *presbyters* or *priests*, and *deacons*.

Epistle side. South side of a church or altar.

Erastianism. Control of the Church by the State. It is named after Thomas Erastus (1524-83), who objected to the tyrannical use of excommunication by Calvinistic Churches, and who did not, in fact, advocate the full subordination of Church jurisdiction to the State. However, from the enactments of the 1820s and 1830s, Churchmen perceived so-called Erastianism to be gaining the upper hand in English Church affairs.

Established Church. The Church as by law established as the public or State-recognised form of religion. In England it was the English branch of the Western Church, which, at the *Reformation*, repudiated the supremacy of the Pope, and asserted that of the Sovereign over all persons and in all causes, ecclesiastical as well as temporal, in his Dominions. *See* **Anglican.**

Eucharist. 1. The *Sacrament* of the Lord's Supper or Communion. **2.** The consecrated elements (the bread and wine), especially the bread. **3.** The box or closed vessel (*pyx*) containing the consecrated bread.

eucharistic window. *Hagioscope* or *lychnoscope*.

Evangelical. 1. A *Protestant*. **2.** Protestant who maintains that the essence of the Gospel consists in the doctrine of Salvation by faith in the Atoning Death of Christ and denies that either Good Works or the *Sacraments* have any saving efficacy. Evangelicals tend to insist: on the depraved state of humanity consequent on the Fall; on the sole authority of the Bible in matters of doctrine (and the denial of the power of the Churches to augment or interpret Scripture); on the denial that any supernatural powers are conferred by the ordination of clergy; and on the view that the Sacraments are merely *allegories*, the value of which lies in their mnemonic aspects. Evangelicals within the *Anglican Church* comprise the *Low Church* party.

Evangelists. Sts Matthew, Mark, Luke, and John, often represented by winged creatures: man (Matthew), lion (Mark), ox (Luke), or eagle (John).

excubitorium. Watching-loft in a church where watch could be kept all night, as on the eve of a Feast-Day, or where an eye could be kept on a Shrine, to prevent theft (an excellent example survives in the Cathedral-church of St Alban, Hertfordshire).

exedra. Large semi-circular niche-like building with seats, sometimes with a hemi-dome over.

exonarthex. *Narthex* outside the main façade of a church, usually part of a colonnaded or arcaded *atrium*.

extrados. Upper curve of each *voussoir* or outer extremity of the *archivolt*.

faïence. Earthenware covered with an opaque coating called *enamel*, usually coloured, and glazed, used for *facings* (finishings to a wall). It is essentially a type of *terracotta*, but coloured and glazed, and usually twice fired.

family pew. Arrangement of seats in a church contained within a high panelled screen around them, also called a *box-pew*, usually rented by one family.

fan-vaulting. Late-*Gothic* form of the *Third-Pointed* or *Perpendicular* style, only known in England during the Middle Ages (though widely copied later). It consists of inverted conoid trumpet-shapes, their rims touching at the top of the vault and their visible surfaces covered with *blind* panel-tracery rising from a *capital* or *corbel* and diverging like the folds of a fan over the entire surface of the distorted cones. The areas between the circular tops of the fans are flat, and form concave-sided lozenge-shapes. At King's College Chapel, Cambridge (1508-15), there are large pendent *bosses* in the centres of the distorted lozenges, and at Henry VII's Chapel, Westminster Abbey (1503-c.1512), the distorted lozenges are covered with blind panelling and there are pendants under the points of each cone as well as in the centres of the lozenges.

fascia (*pl.* **fasciæ**). **1.** One of two or three *bands* on a *Classical architrave*, each projecting slightly beyond the one below. **2.** Any band or belt with a plain vertical face.

femerell. Louvred lantern on a roof for ventilation or to prevent the escape of smoke. It was common before the provision of chimneys.

fenestella. 1. Opening in an altar or shrine affording a view of the *Relics* within. **2.** Niche in the south wall of a *chancel* containing the *piscina* and (sometimes) the *credence-table*. **3.** Opening for a bell in a *bell-cote* over a gable.

fenestration. Pattern formed by windows in a façade.

fereter. 1. Permanent shrine for *Relics*. **2.** Portable shrine containing Relics. **3.** *Bier, catafalque, tomb-chest* or other construction of a similar funerary type.

feretory. Enclosure in a church or chapel, usually defined in some way (e.g. by means of a screen), containing a *fereter*.

fillet. Small, narrow, flat moulding, either a plain band in a group of mouldings, either of projecting rectangular section or simply a flat surface between other mouldings, such as *flutes* of a column-shaft. It is commonly found on *First Pointed piers* to give added verticality to them.

finial. Ornamental termination of *bench-ends, canopies, gables, pinnacles, spires*, etc. Also called *boss, crop, crope, knob*, or *pommel*.

First Pointed. *See* **Gothic.**

fish. *See* **Chrismon.**

fish-bladder. Form of light found in *Second Pointed Curvilinear tracery* looking like a tadpole, with a round or pointed head and a curving pointed tail, also called a *mouchette*.

Five Wounds of Christ. The wounds to the Saviour's hands, feet, and side, caused during the *Crucifixion*, and represented on the *mensa*, or *altar-slab* by five incised crosses, one at each corner and one in the middle.

flambeau. Torch, symbolising life. If reversed, it signifies death.

Flamboyant. Late style of Continental *Gothic* (*c.*1375 – mid-sixteenth century), the name of which derives from the *flame-like* forms of the *tracery lights*. It evolved from *Second Pointed Curvilinear* work, especially the flowing forms of the *tracery*.

flèche. 1. Any *spire*. **2.** *Spirelet* surmounting a roof, especially over the *crossing* of a French *Gothic* cathedral.

fleur-de-lys. Ornament consisting of three leaf-like pointed elements above and one or three below a horizontal cross-bar. Essentially a stylised lily, it is often found in late-*Gothic tracery* and as a *finial* on, e.g., a *bench-end*. It has particular associations with the Blessed Virgin Mary, and occurs as one of her *attributes*.

fleuron. 1. Stylised four-leafed stylan floral ornament, used in late-*Gothic cresting, crockets, cavetto* mouldings, and *tiles*. **2.** Ornamental termination of the apex of a roof, such as a *crop, finial*, or *épi*. **3.** Ornament in the middle of each concave face of the *Corinthian abacus.*

Florentine arch. Semicircular arch with *intrados* and *extrados* struck from different centres, so that the *voussoirs* increase in length towards the top of the arch.

flushwork. Knapped flint, with the split (*spaultered*) dark sides facing outwards, set as flush panels within frames of freestone cut to resemble *tracery*, all the finished faces of flint and stone in the same plane. Spectacular examples occur in the *Perpendicular* churches of East Anglia.

flute. Channel or groove of segmental, partial elliptical, or semi-circular section, one of many set parallel (or nearly so) to each other, as in *Classical* column-shafts, where they occur in all save the *Tuscan Order*. Greek *Doric* flutes are segmental, separated by *arrises* and stopped by *annulets*. Flutes in other Orders are deeper, nearly semicircular in section, separated by *fillets*, and terminate in quarter-spherical forms. Sometimes flutes may have convex mouldings (*cables*) filling them to one-third of the height of the shaft.

foil. In *Gothic tracery* any circular *lobe* tangent to the inner side of a larger arc or arch, meeting other lobes in points termed *cusps* projecting inwards from the arc or arch. Prefixes are used to describe how many foils occur: *trefoil* = 3; *quatrefoil* = 4; *cinquefoil* = 5; *sexfoil* = 6; *multifoil* = with many foils, etc.

foliate. 1. Adorned with *foils*, as in *Gothic tracery*. **2.** Ornament based on plant-leaves, as in certain *Gothic capitals*. *Foliated* therefore means decorated with leaf-ornament, or with foils separated by cusps in apertures or tracery.

font. Basin for the consecrated water used during the *Sacrament* of *Baptism*. It is commonly formed from a large block of stone, hollowed out and carved with Christian symbols, supported on a short *pier* or cluster of *colonnettes* set on a stepped plinth or platform. It may have an elaborate coloured *font-cover* adorned with *finials* and *pinnacles*, etc., capable of being raised on ropes by means of a system of pulleys.

formeret. *Gothic* arch-rib in a *vault engaged* with the wall, called a *wall-rib*, smaller than the rest of the ribs of the vault-compartment.

four-centred arch. *Depressed* arch, the characteristic form of late-*Perpendicular* or *Tudor* arches, with upper central arcs having centres *below* the *springing-line*, flanked by two arcs with centres *on* the springing-line. A *Tudor* arch is a *pseudo-four-centred* late-Perpendicular arch, similar to the four-centred type, but with shanks starting as quarter-circles (their centres on the springing-line), continuing as straight lines to the apex. It is very *depressed* and is often expressed as a single *lintel*.

four-leaf flower. *See* **fleuron.**

Free Classicism. Late nineteenth-century style, essentially a mixture of *Classical, Mannerist, Renaissance*, and *Baroque* motifs.

Free Gothic. 1. Revival of *Gothic* forms and motifs, freely used in an eclectic mix. **2.** Late nineteenth-century style, in which *Arts-and-Crafts* and other references/styles were mingled, creating a non-archaeological, scholarly, yet highly individual style. Examples include work by Caröe, Temple Moore, Charles Nicholson, Sedding, Shaw, and others.

freestone. Stone that can be easily cut and worked in any direction, such as a fine limestone or sandstone.

Free style. Late nineteenth-century style in which *Classical, Domestic Revival, Gothic, Queen Anne*, and *vernacular* themes, motifs, and elements were mingled promiscuously in eclectic compositions, sometimes with additional *Elizabethan* or *Renaissance* allusions.

Free Tudor. Style in which late-*Perpendicular, Tudor*, or *Elizabethan* motifs were mixed in a free manner in the late-nineteenth and early-twentieth centuries.

fresco. Mural painting, carried out while the plaster is still wet and fresh (*buon fresco*). A wall-painting on dry (*secco*) plaster is a poor substitute, for the colours do not seep into the plaster, and the paint may peel and pigments fade.

fret. Complex patterns of ribs in a *Gothic vault*.

frieze. 1. Horizontal central band of a Classical *entablature* below the *cornice* and over the *architrave*, occasionally omitted in the Greek *Ionic Order*. *Tuscan* friezes are flat and unadorned (although *pulvinated* variations may be found); *Doric* friezes are broken up into *metopes* and *triglyphs*; *Ionic, Corinthian*, and

Composite friezes may be plain or enriched, and *pulvinated* varieties are not uncommon in the Ionic and Composite Orders. **2.** *Hypotrachelion* of some Ionic Orders resembling a frieze under the voluted *capital* proper**.**

front. 1. Façade of a building, usually the most important (e.g. street-front). **2.** East end of a church.

frontal. *Antependium* in front of an altar.

frontispiece. 1. Main façade or *front*. **2.** Elaborate entrance, centrepiece, etc., in a main façade.

gable. End-wall of a building or part of a building, closing the end of a pitched roof; it may follow the pitch of the roof behind it. *Romanesque* and *First Pointed* gables are steep (Lincoln Cathedral has gables of 70° pitch or thereabouts), but *Third Pointed* or *Perpendicular* Gothic gables were much lower in pitch, and were coped and sometimes crenellated. A *gable-cross* is one terminating the apex of a gable.

gablet. Small *gable*-shaped top to, e.g., a *buttress*, common in early *Gothic* architecture. It also occurs over *lucarnes*, *niches*, etc.

Galilee. *Narthex* or large room between the exterior and the west end of the *nave*, where penitents and women were admitted, corpses laid out for burial, and where monks collected before or after processions. At Durham Cathedral the Galilee is divided into *aisles*. It is sometimes called a *Paradise*.

gallery. Galleries or *scaffolds* were erected in post-Reformation churches above the aisles and at the west end to accommodate more people. They were detested by *Ecclesiologists*.

gargoyle. Water-spout to take water from a gutter behind a *parapet* away from a wall to spew it on the ground. Mediæval gargoyles (sometimes mere ornaments rather than spouts) are usually of stone, imaginatively carved in the forms of devils, composite animals, etc.

garth. Open area surrounded by the *ambulatory* of a *cloister*.

Georgian. Architecture of the period of the first four King Georges of the House of Hanover (1714-1830).

gesso. Plaster of Paris mixed with glue and whiting (ground chalk) used to prepare a flat surface for painting, or to raise parts of the surface to enhance enrichment of a painting, as in mediæval *chancel-screens*.

Giant Order. *Classical Order* of architecture, the *pilasters* and *columns* of which rise from the ground or plinth through more than one storey. Also called a *Colossal Order*.

Gibbs surround. Banded *architrave* around an aperture, usually with a massive *keystone* and *voussoirs* breaking through the top of the architrave, the whole crowned with a *pediment*. It is named after its inventor, the architect James Gibbs (1682-1754).

Gigantic Order. *Tuscan* Order.

glyph. Channel, *flute*, or groove, normally vertical, as in a *Doric frieze*, where the blocks framing *metopes* are the *triglyphs*, so called because they each have two glyphs and two half-glyphs.

Go. Pejorative term used by some Victorian commentators (e.g. Street) to describe the work of *Rogue Goths* that was restless, too animated or 'acrobatic', and embarrassing. It implied empty fashion, hamfistedness, clumsiness, discord, clashing colours, excessive liveliness, coarseness, loudness, decadence, furious vigour, recklessness, exaggeration, vulgarity, and generally something overdone for the purposes of self-advertisement.

Golgotha. 1. Carved timber base-beam of a *Rood*, above which rise figures of the Crucified Christ, St Mary, and St John. **2.** Burial-ground or charnel-house.

gorge. 1. Shallow part-elliptical *cavetto* moulding. **2.** Neck (*gorgerin*) at the top of column-shafts in the *Tuscan* and *Roman Doric* Orders. **3.** Large cavetto, as in the *gorge-cornice* of Ancient Egyptian architecture.

Gospel side. North side of an altar or church.

Gothic. Architectural style, particularly associated with churches, properly termed *Pointed*, that developed in Europe from the latter part of the twelfth until the sixteenth century, and in certain locations (e.g. Oxford) even continued into the seventeenth century. As its correct name suggests, it is the architecture of the pointed arch, pointed rib-vaults, *piers* with clusters of *shafts*, deep *buttresses* (some of the *flying* type), window-*tracery*, *pinnacles*, *spires*, *battlements*, and a soaring verticality. Gothic is *arcuated* (as opposed to *trabeated*), giving a dynamic impression of thrust and counter-thrust, and is a remarkably coherent style in which forces are expressed and resisted, and non-structural walls were pierced by huge areas of glazed window.

First Pointed (known in England as *Early English* Gothic or the *Lancet* style) evolved and prevailed from the twelfth to the late thirteenth century. Windows were first of all tall and thin, with pointed tops, of the *lancet* type (either with very sharp points, or with tops formed with equilateral arches), set singly or in groups in walls. *Trefoils* and *cinquefoils* occurred over smaller openings, and important doorways (e.g. at the west of a church) were often divided into two by a central shaft (*trumeau*), with a *quatrefoil* or *Vesica Piscis* carved above, associated with sculpture in the *tympanum*. West doorways were usually elaborated with numerous *Orders* and *dog-tooth* enrichments. Mouldings consisted largely of convex and concave rolls, producing strong effects of light and shade, and were deeply cut. Early English ornaments, found on horizontal mouldings, were the *nail-head* (consisting of a repetitive row of small pyramidal forms usually found on the *abaci* of bell-capitals) and the larger, spikier *dog-tooth*. *Foliate* stylised ornament was deeply carved and vigorous, often with the leaves arranged in threes. *Piers* had clusters of shafts (usually of black or dark-grey *Purbeck* marble) around them, held in position by *bands* of freestone, and contrasting with the lighter stone of the pier proper. Ribbed *vaulting* was commonly employed, the pointed arch enabling complex plans to be ceilinged with elegance. *Tracery* seems to have begun as flat masonry slabs pierced with *lights* (known as *plate-tracery*), but towards the end of the thirteenth century *bar-tracery* was used, consisting of moulded *mullions*. These *bars* could intersect at window-heads, forming Y-tracery, but also formed symmetrical patterns involving *circles* and *foils*: this type of arrangement is termed *Geometrical* tracery, for obvious reasons, and reached perfection in the early *Middle Pointed* period of the late thirteenth century, which followed the earliest phase of *First Pointed* or the *Lancet* style. *Capitals* were of the foliate stiff-leaf type, or simple bell-capitals. *Buttresses* were prominent, deep, and narrow, to take the thrust of the stone-vaulted ceilings, and marked the divisions of the length of the church into *bays*: they terminated in *gables* or stepped arrangements (*pinnacles* only came into general use towards the end of the First Pointed style, and were often treated as *bundle-piers*). The use of the pointed arch enabled rib-vaults to be constructed over rectangular spaces without incurring the problems caused when the less flexible geometry of semicircular Romanesque arches had been employed: the pointed arch was rather like a 'hinge', freeing up the geometry of construction and junctions. Roofs, like *Romanesque* structures, were steeply pitched, sometimes dramatically so. By *First Pointed* is meant the period from the end of the twelfth to almost the end of the thirteenth century: it merges with *Middle Pointed*, and there were overlaps with *Second Pointed*.

Second Pointed (known as *Decorated Gothic* in Britain), as the term suggests, has more elaborate enrichment, with decoration (especially *diaper-work*) covering surfaces. Its chief characteristic, however, is the complexity of *tracery* and *vaulting*. At the end of the *First Pointed* period, as noted above, *plate-tracery* evolved, then *bar-tracery* arranged in geometrical patterns. So

Geometrical bar-tracery is usually seen as characteristic of the *Middle* or early *Second Pointed* styles. Nail-head and dog-tooth ornament were superseded by *fleuron*, four-leafed flower, and *ball-flower* enrichment, while *crockets* on *pinnacles* and canopies, and other ornament, multiplied. Floral and foliate decorations tended to be treated more naturalistically. The late phase of Second Pointed saw the development of *Curvilinear* or *Flowing* tracery made possible by use of the *ogee* (or S-shaped) curve: this, in turn, gave rise to the appearance of *fish-bladders*, *daggers*, or *mouchettes* in tracery, and the invention of complex *Reticulated*, or net-like, patterns in windows that became very large. Ogees led to the creation of flame-like shapes in the lights of upper parts of traceried windows: these shapes suggested the term *Flamboyant* to describe later elaborate Gothic on the European Continent. Ogee curves contributed to a sense of remarkable richness and flowing, elegant lines. *Vaulting* became more elaborate, with *intermediate* and *lierne* ribs forming star-shaped patterns. Roofs remained steeply pitched. By *Second Pointed* is meant the style of mediæval architecture as developed from the late thirteenth until the second half of the fourteenth century.

Third Pointed or *Perpendicular Gothic*, which started in the first half of the fourteenth century (*c*.1330), continued into the sixteenth century, even surviving in places like Oxford into the seventeenth century, so it was the longest-lived style of Gothic in England, lasting for about three centuries, and was the first style of Gothic to be revived. Unlike First and Second Pointed, it has no true Continental counterpart, and should really be regarded as the national architectural style of England. It is arguably the greatest contribution England ever made to architecture, although the *Gothic Revival* and aspects of the *Domestic Revival* and *Arts-and-Crafts* movement were also important and original English cultural inventions. It rejected the flowing *ogee* forms (though ogees survived for a time), replacing them with panel-like motifs, which, towards the later phase of the style, acquired very flat, *depressed* arches. So *Perpendicular* is the last of the styles of Gothic which flourished in England in the mediæval period, and its developed characteristics gave it the alternative title of the *Rectilinear* style. It is recognisable because of its delicate patterns of vertical and horizontal bars, especially in *tracery* and *blind tracery* over wall-surfaces. *Transoms* were often ornamented with miniature *battlements*, and *mullions* do not branch out, but rise straight to the undersides of window-openings and are also sometimes carried down over wall-surfaces, thus continuing the rigid panel effects. Arches over openings and spaces became very depressed (of the *four-centred* type). *Vaulting* became more complex, unifying the entire space: at first, vaults were of the *lierne* type, and then evolved into the *fan* pattern, which carried the panel-like motifs on over ceilings as well as walls. There is no parallel to fan-vaulting on the European Continent: it is a power-fully individual English invention. A further important feature of Perpendicular design was the introduction of rectangular frames around apertures: this created *spandrels* (often elaborately ornamented) between the rectangular frames and the four-centred arches, enhancing the disciplined, unifying, panel-like treatment of interiors. The rectangular frames over openings became *hood-moulds* outside terminating in *label-stops* carved as shields or hearts. On occasion windows filled entire walls between buttresses, and the rhythms of window-tracery were repeated as *blind tracery* over internal wall-surfaces: some Perpendicular interiors were so covered with repeated panel-motifs (even over the fan-vaulted ceilings), that a Gothic architecture of tightly-controlled, logical, modular unity was created, as never before. A characteristic of Perpendicular *clearstoreys* is that they contained very large windows, and so were airy, light, and vast: as naves were heightened to accommodate huge ranges of Perpendicular windows, roofs had to be flattened, and disappeared behind parapets decorated with *battlements*. The use of repeated panels over surfaces, in window-tracery, and in fan-vaults; the adoption of rectangular hood-moulds; the flattening of roofs; the adoption of crenellated parapets to conceal those roofs; and the elaboration of *lierne*- and, later, *fan-vaulting* gave the Perpendicular style its chief motifs. During the Perpendicular period, *chancels* were not distinctly compartmented, but were part of the main volume of the church (this influenced architects of late-Victorian churches): they were demarcated by means of sumptuous timber screens, often gloriously coloured, over which was a *Rood*-loft and *Rood*. Such screens were commonly ornamented with *grapevine*, *trail*, *vignette*, *vine-scroll*, or *vinette* running enrichment, often coloured, and crested with *brattishing*. Chancel ceilings were frequently given more elaborate treatment than those of naves and aisles: additional colour was the means usually employed. Some of the most exquisite Perpendicular work may be found in *chantry-chapels* and tombs (e.g. in Tewkesbury Abbey and Winchester Cathedral).

Gothic Revival. Movement that began in England to revive Gothic forms with a full understanding of their original character. Although there is probably an overlap between seventeenth-century *Gothic Survival* (in the sense that it was an unconscious continuation of the late-*Perpendicular* style) and Gothic *Revival*, it is clear that seventeenth-century buildings such as the church of Holy Trinity, Staunton Harold, Leicestershire (1653-6), and the Cathedral-church of St Columb, Londonderry (1628-33), were erected in Gothic because Holy Trinity's founder wished to make a stand against the Republican-Puritan regime of Cromwell, and the builders of St Columb's (the City of London) desired to distance themselves from the Palladian style favoured by the Stuart Court. They are therefore *Gothic Revival*.

Wren and his team used Gothic for some City churches, as well as in Tom Tower, Oxford. Hawksmoor used Gothic at Westminster Abbey (1734) and All Souls College, Oxford (1716-35), and these were followed by Gibbs's Gothic Temple, Stowe, Buckingham-shire (1741-4), Sanderson Miller's works in Warwickshire (1740s), and Keene's designs (1760s). Miller and Keene advised Sir Roger Newdigate, Bt., on Gothic works at Arbury Hall in the 1750s. Horace Walpole's Strawberry Hill, Twickenham (*c*.1760-76), helped to make 'Gothick' fashionable.

In the early nineteenth century many 'Gothic' churches were built that were often unconvincing in terms of archaeology and scholarship, and did not resemble mediæval buildings. Simple *Georgian Commissioners' Gothic* churches with rudimentary *First Pointed* or *Perpendicular* windows often purported to be Gothic. What became the scholarly Gothic Revival in which real mediæval exemplars provided the precedents for design really began with the works of Rickman in the second decade of the nineteenth century, with the publications of Bloxam in the third and fourth decades, and with the polemics of A. W. N. Pugin in the fourth and fifth decades. *Ecclesiology* and the religious debates of the 1830s and '40s also helped to promote the Revival, as did the popular success of the Palace of Westminster (from 1836) by Barry and Pugin. There can also be little doubt that the Romantic movement in which ecclesiastical antiquities, ruins, and irrationalism had rôles, together with a growing taste for 'Gothic' novels, helped to create a climate in which mediæval buildings could play their parts within a *Picturesque* or even *Sublime* landscape. A growing body of scholarship began to inform the nineteenth-century Gothic Revival, and the ambitious programme of church-building was increasingly served by architects thoroughly immersed in the style. The building industry had to adapt too, craftsmen trained, and the lost language of Gothic learned anew. In England the Revival began with *Perpendicular*; turned to

Second Pointed (English first, then Continental), largely due to the arguments of Pugin and the Ecclesiologists who perceived fourteenth-century Gothic as fully developed with advantages over the '*undeveloped*' *Lancet* style of *First Pointed* and the supposedly 'decadent' Perpendicular; then embraced Continental Gothic (especially that of Italy, in which possibilities of *structural polychromy* had attracted commentators including Street and Ruskin). The mid-Victorian Gothic Revival of the 1850s and early 1860s was thus often coloured, incorporating polished granites, marbles, many-coloured brick-and-tile-work, becoming more free in expression and less archæologically derivative in the process. Gothic Revivalists then sought a more robust and 'primitive' Gothic, and so turned to the powerful First Pointed Burgundian precedents of the thirteenth century: this produced the so-called 'muscular Gothic' of Brooks, Pearson, Street, and others.

Some practitioners, such as Sir George Gilbert Scott, settled for *Middle Pointed* as the ideal: it was more sophisticated than the Lancet style and les fussy than Curvilinear Second Pointed. Lastly, however, architects such as Bodley turned to late Second Pointed and Perpendicular sources, producing exquisitely delicate work such as the church of the Holy Angels, Hoar Cross, Staffordshire (1872-1900). A feature of English late Gothic Revival was its eclecticism and its close connection with the Arts-and-Crafts movement, as in Sedding's Holy Trinity, Sloane Street, London (1888-90).

Grace. 1. Free favour of God manifest in the *Salvation* of sinners and the bestowing of Blessings. **2.** Divine influence which operates to regenerate and sanctify, to inspire virtue, and to impart strength to endure trials and resist temptation.

gradin, gradine. 1. One of a series of low steps or seats raised one above the other. **2.** Raised shelf set above an altar and at its back, usually as long as the *mensa* (the stone slab or other piece forming the top of the altar), a third or a quarter as deep, and having the front (often painted) closed in. The narrow strip of pictures is called the *predella*. **3.** Platform, *foot-pace*, or *predella* on which an altar stands, projecting about a metre and a half in front of the altar and about a third of a metre on either side, approached by at least two generously sized steps. Some Victorian writers seem to use the term to describe the *whole* raised area of a *chancel* in which an altar stands.

grapevine. *See* **pampre, trail, vignette.**

Greek Revival. Style of architecture in which accurate copies of Ancient Greek motifs were incorporated into the design of buildings from the 1750s. It was part of the *Neo-Classical* movement, and drew on scholarly studies of Antique buildings, especially *The Antiquities of Athens* (1762-1816). Application of Greek elements to ecclesiastical architecture required imagination and flair: there were no Greek precedents for towers and spires, for examples, so forms drawn from the Tower of the Winds and the Choragic monument of Lysicrates (both in Athens) were used to create steeples, and fenestration had to be provided above and below galleries (Greek temples had few openings). Thus Greek motifs had to be applied to a form of building evolved from the times of Wren, Hawksmoor, Gibbs and Archer.

grid-tracery. A type of late-*Perpendicular* (*see* **Gothic**) tracery in large windows, consisting of a grid of mullions and transoms without any depressed arches over the *lights*.

groin. Arris formed by the salient between two intersecting *vaults*, as in two barrel-vaults crossing each other at right angles.

grotesque. Capricious Classical ornament consisting of animals, figures, flowers, foliage, sphinxes, etc., all connected together, distinct from *arabesques* which do not have animal or humanoid representations. They are so called after the Antique decorations discovered in buried Roman ruins (*grotte*) in 1488.

grouped columns. More than two columns closely placed on one *base*, *pedestal*, or *plinth*. If two columns only are similarly placed, they are *coupled*.

guild. Craft fraternity particularly involved in protecting the interests of the brethren and sisters. Guilds erected and maintained guild- or chantry-chapels for the care of the souls of departed brothers and sisters.

hagioscope. *Squint*, *loricula*, or aperture, cut obliquely in a wall (usually of a *chancel*), affording a visual connection between the high altar and *aisles* or side-chapels.

hall-church. Church with *nave*, *aisles*, and no *clearstorey*, the interior of which is of approximately uniform height throughout. It is a characteristic German type (*Hallenkirche*).

halo. *Disc of radiance* or *nimbus* around a head. Compare **aureole**.

hatchment. *Achievement of Arms* represented on a square panel hung diagonally in a church after the funeral of a gentleman.

haunch. Indefinite approximately triangular portion or *flank* between the *crown* and *abutments* of an arch, i.e. between the crown and the *springing* on the *piers*. A *haunched arch* is one with the crown on a different curvature from that immediately above the springing, as in a *four-centred-arch*.

hearse, herse. 1. Open metal framework over a sepulchral memorial to support the *pall*. **2.** Portcullis. **3.** Horizontal grille with *prickets* for candles.

helm roof. *Spire* on a square tower, each side of which is crowned with a *gable*.

Henrician. Of the period of the reign of King Henry VIII (1509-47), sometimes also applied to the reign of Henry VII (1485-1509).

heraldic. Decoration derived from heraldic motifs and/or colours, found on ceilings, screens, floor-tiles, etc.

Hertfordshire spike. *Flèche* or short needle-spire rising from a church-tower, its base concealed by a *parapet*, common in Hertfordshire.

Hiberno-Romanesque. Nineteenth- and twentieth-century *Romanesque* revival, with round arches, round towers, Celtic crosses etc., based on Irish exemplars.

high altar. Main altar of a church sited on the principal east-west axis at the east end of the *choir* or *chancel*.

High Church. Party or principles of the *High Churchmen* who hold views that give a high place: to the claims of the episcopate and the priesthood; to the saving *Grace* of the *Sacraments*; and to those points of doctrine, discipline, and ritual by which the *Anglican Church* is distinguished from *Calvinistic Protestant* and *Nonconformist* Churches. The High Church party emphasises the *Catholic* aspects of the *Church of England*, its continuity with the *pre-Reformation*, *pre-Tridentine* Church *in* England, and the beauty of ceremonial. It is associated with the *Oxford Movement*, *Tractarianism*, *Ritualism*, and *Anglo-Catholicism*.

High Gothic. *Second Pointed* style of the fourteenth century.

High Victorian Gothic. Unsatisfactory term used by some to describe the style of the somewhat harsh *polychrome* structures of the *Gothic Revival* in the 1850s and 1860s when Ruskin presided as the arbiter of taste through his writings. Its gritty 'muscularity' owed much to Continental Gothic, but use of the term poses a question as to what might constitute Low Victorian Gothic, and there is no satisfactory answer to that.

Historicism. Architecture strongly influenced by the past, especially Revivalist architecture (*Greek*, *Gothic*, *Early Christian*, *Romanesque*, *Italianate*, *Renaissance*, *Rundbogenstil*, *Jacobethan*, *Tudor*, etc.). It has been facilitated by many lavish and scholarly publications, notably those including measured drawings. The term has been used pejoratively by some, who also employ *pastiche* as a term of abuse, but Historicism draws on precedents, and requires care and learning, so has been rejected by Modernists.

holy loft. *Rood-Loft*, *-beam*, or *-screen*.

honeysuckle. Common Ancient Greek enrichment resembling a honeysuckle flower, called *anthemion* or *palmette*.

hood. *Drip-stone* or *label-moulding* over the heads of apertures, arched, or rectangular, usually with *label-stops* at each end.

horn. 1. *Ionic*, *Composite*, or *Corinthian volute*. 2. Strong-stemmed projection ending in stiff leaves common on thirteenth-century *Gothic* capitals. 3. Projection at each corner of a *Classical altar*, *ash-chest*, *pediment*, *sarcophagus*, or *stele*, also called *acroterium* or *ear*. 4. Each of four projecting portions of any *abacus* curved on plan. 5. Side of an altar.

horseshoe arch. Semicircular or pointed arch narrower towards the base below the *springing-line*. It is associated with Islamic styles, but is sometimes found in nineteenth-century *synagogues*.

housing. *Niche*, *tabernacle*, or similar.

hypotrachelion. In *Classical* architecture that part of a column between the *shaft* and the *capital*, especially the *frieze* or *neck* of *Tuscan*, *Roman Doric*, and *Greek Doric Orders*. In *Greek Doric* it refers to the horizontal grooves encircling the column just below the capital proper.

iconostasis. In Greek and Russian *Orthodox* churches, a screen between the *sanctuary* and the body of the church, with three doorways. It is often hung with icons and other images, hence its name.

IHS. *See* **Chrismon**.

impost. Projecting member, often moulded, from which an arch springs, e.g. a *block*, *bracket*, *corbel*, or *dosseret*.

in antis. Between *antæ*.

Incarnation. God becoming Man in the person of Christ, i.e. the investiture or embodiment in flesh. It is represented in art either as the *Annunciation* or the *Nativity*.

incised slab. Slab of stone with a design cut into its surface, commonly a funerary monument with representations of *effigies*, emblems, etc., and with inscriptions. The incised work is often enhanced with black or coloured filling. A variation is a more comprehensive series of indents filled with *brass* or *latten* sheets cut to fit and themselves incised and inlaid.

INRI. *See* **Chrismon** .

Instruments of the Passion. Thirty Pieces of Silver, Scourge with Thongs, Column and Cord, Sceptre of Reeds, Crown of Thorns, Dice, Lance, Ladder, Nails, Robe, Sponge, and Shroud, carried by Angels. If represented on a Shield they are called *Arma Christi*.

intercolumniation. Space between the lower parts of the shafts of adjacent columns in a *Classical colonnade* or *portico* defined by modules the same size as the shaft diameters.

interlacing arches. *Intersecting* semicircular *Romanesque* arches in a *blind arcade*, overlapping and forming pointed arches. Each arch springs from centres from which adjacent arches are struck.

intersecting. 1. Overlapping arcades, e.g. as *interlacing arches* producing a series of pointed arches. 2. *Intersecting tracery* of *c*.1300 is created by forks spring from *mullions* and intersecting to describe Y-forms (*see* **tracery**).

intersticium. Where the transepts cross the *nave* of a church, a space is defined between the nave proper and the chancel called *intersticium*.

intrados. Lower or under-curve of each *voussoir* forming the arch: it coincides with the *soffit* of the arch.

Ionic Order. *Classical Order* of architecture, the second Greek and the third Roman. It is identified by its *capital*, with its rolled-up cushion-like forms on either side creating the distinctive *volutes*.

iris. Symbol of the Virgin Mary and of Chastity, representing Reconciliation between Man and God.

Irvingite. A member of the *Holy Catholic Apostolic Church* founded (*c*.1835) by disciples of Edward Irving (1792-1834): it was a strange mixture of *Presbyterianism*, *Ritualism*, and arcane

beliefs, but prompted the erection of some fine works of architecture.

Italianate. Style of architecture modelled on astylar palazzi, e.g. Barry's Traveller's Club, London (1829-32). In churches it tended to draw on further Italian precedents, including *Early Christian campanili*, and was related to the *Rundbogenstil*.

Jacobean. Architecture and decoration of the period of King James I and VI (1603-25).

Jacobethan. Revivalist architecture of the late-nineteenth and early-twentieth centuries in which *Elizabethan* and *Jacobean* elements were freely mixed.

Jerusalem. 1. *Jerusalem* or *Crusader's cross* is a Greek or *potent* cross (with each arm terminating in a T), with a small Greek cross in each of the four areas bounded by the arms. 2. Centre of a maze cut in turf or inlaid in a church floor used for symbolic pilgrimages in the Middle Ages.

Jesse. Genealogical tree depicting Christ's ancestry, called *Tree of Life*. It is usually in the form of a tree or vine springing from the recumbent body of Jesse, with figures denoting his descendants standing on the ends of the branches, the Virgin and Child forming the fruit at the top. It occurs in *reredoses*, paintings, stained-glass windows, and in *tracery* (e.g. the Abbey-church of Sts Peter and Paul, Dorchester, Oxfordshire (*c*.1340).

jubé. 1. *Pulpitum*, or screen at the west end of a *choir* in a French church. 2. *Rood*-loft or gallery in the same position.

keel. Common *First* and *Second Pointed* moulding on vault-ribs and elsewhere, resembling the keel of a ship, in section consisting of two *ogees* meeting at an *arris* or a *fillet*.

Kentish rag. Very hard compact grey-white limestone used in polygonal rubble rough or close-pitched walling, often on *Gothic Revival* churches in London. Its irregular forms create a network of mortar-joints.

Kentish tracery. *Tracery* with split *cusps* forming barbs between the *foils*.

knapped. Split. Usually applied to flint, it was a means by which the smooth dark surfaces were exposed and laid *flush* with *freestone tracery*-like patterns in mediæval *flushwork*.

kneeler. 1. Large, approximately triangular stone at the foot of a *gable*, cut to have a horizontal bed and a top conforming to the slope of the gable. This *foot-stone*, *gable-springer*, or *skew-table* provides a securely anchored stop for the *raked* slope. 2. Stone securely bedded, with one side cut at an angle or *skew*, forming the *springing* of an arch or vault. 3. *Cop* or *merlon* in a *battlement*.

knop. *Boss* or *finial*.

label. Hood-moulding extending horizontally over the top of a late-*Gothic Perpendicular* or *Tudor* aperture, returning vertically downwards on each side and terminating in *label-stops*, often enriched with carving. The term may also be applied to certain curved hood-mouldings.

Lady Chapel. Chapel in a larger church, expressly for veneration of the Virgin Mary, often situated east of the chancel or choir, but in smaller churches usually to the east of one or other chancel-aisle.

Lamb. Symbol of Christ. If it is with a flag or banner, it represents John the Baptist. If depicted on a hill with four rivulets, it signifies the Church and the Gospels.

lancet. *First Pointed Gothic* tall, narrow window-opening with a pointed arched head, either a single insert in a wall or one of several *lights* of similar shape in a larger window. The *Lancet Style* is an archaic term for the *First Pointed* style (*see* **Gothic**) before the development of *tracery*.

lantern. 1. Any structure above the roof of a building having apertures to admit light. 2. Upper structure above a *cupola*, such as the lantern on top of St Paul's Cathedral, London. 3. Upper stage of a church-tower, usually octagonal, treated in a very light and graceful way, and pierced with tracery, as at the church of St Mary and All Saints, Fotheringhay, Northamptonshire.

Last Judgement. *See* **Doom**.

Last Supper. The subject is usually depicted on the *reredos* behind altars, either carved or painted.

Latin Cross. Cross with three topmost arms of equal length (though sometimes the head is shorter than the arms), and a much longer lower arm. It is the basic plan-form of Western *cruciform* churches.

lattice. **1.** A *came*. **2.** System of small, light bars, crossing each other at intervals, forming regular squares or lozenge-shaped openings, as in *leaded lights*, so a *light* filled with leaded lights would be termed a *lattice-window*.

Laudian rail. Altar- or Communion-rail, often with *balusters*, and usually of oak, dating from the time (1633-40) when William Laud (1573-1645) was Archbishop of Canterbury.

leaded lights. Any windows in which the *panes* or *quarrels* of glass, often arranged in *lattice* patterns (usually lozenges), are secured in lead *cames*.

lean-to. Structure with a roof pitching away from a taller building or wall against which it is erected, such as an *aisle* of a church, leaving the *clearstorey* rising above.

lectern. **1.** High, sloping reading-desk, especially in a church, placed on the *Epistle* side, usually consisting of a column or pedestal carrying a globe on which perches an eagle with outstretched wings (a symbol of St John the Evangelist). **2.** An *ambo*.

ledger. Large flat stone slab used as the top of a structure (e.g. an *altar-tomb*), or covering a brick-lined grave, sometimes *incised* or *inlaid* with *brasses*.

Lent. Period of forty weekdays from Ash Wednesday to the eve of Easter, observed as a time of fasting and penitence, in commemoration of Our Lord's fasting in the Wilderness.

Lenten veil. Cloth concealing statuary and other images during Lent.

lich-gate. *See* **lych-gate**.

lierne. Rib in a *vaulted* ceiling (not a *ridge-rib*) that does not rise from one of the main springing-points, but runs from rib to rib, usually joined to them at *bosses*.

light. **1.** Aperture, or *day*, through which daylight may pass. **2.** An area or compartment in a window around which are *mullions* or *transoms* (or both), or an opening defined by the *bars* of *tracery*.

lily. The *fleur-de-lys*, an *attribute* of the Blessed Virgin Mary.

linenfold. *Parchemin plié*, or *linen-pattern*, a late-*Gothic* ornamental finish to a panel, resembling linen with loose vertical folds. It is common in *Tudor* interiors.

lintel. Beam spanning between *jambs* over an aperture carrying a wall above.

lion. **1.** Emblem of St Mark. It is associated with the Resurrection. **2.** Carved representations of lions' masks occur on Classical *cornices*.

liturgy. Form of public worship in the Christian Church, conducted in accordance with a prescribed form, especially the service of the Holy *Eucharist*. Thus *liturgiology* is the study of liturgies.

lobe. Small *arch*, *arc*, or *foil* in mediæval architecture, separated by a *cusp* from another lobe or foil.

loft. Elevated *platform*, *staging*, or *gallery*, within a larger room or hall, such as an *excubitorium*, or *watching-loft* (e.g. to guard a shrine, such as that of St Alban in Hertfordshire), a *Rood-loft*, or *organ-loft* in a church.

Lombard style. Style of architecture, essentially an amalgam of *Early Christian* and *Romanesque*, that flourished in Northern Italy in and around Como. It was revived in the nineteenth century as part of the *Rundbogenstil*.

Lombardy frieze. Arched *corbel-table* or series of small arches under *eaves* and supported on *corbels*.

louvre, luffer. One of several boards sloping downwards and outwards, each board lapping over the one below, with a space between to exclude rain but allow the sound of bells to be heard, as in a *belfry*.

Low Church. Party of the *Church of England* holding opinions that give a low place: to the claims of the episcopate and priest-hood; to the inherent *Grace* of the *Sacraments*; and to matters of ecclesiastical organisation. Low Churchmen hold much in common with *Protestant Nonconformists*. *See* **Evangelical**.

lozenge. Diamond-shaped equilateral parallelogram with two opposite angles more acute then the other two. It occurs in mouldings, on *diaper-patterns*, in *strapwork*, in *window-lights*, and as small lights over *Gothic lancet-lights* in *tracery*, in *net-vaults*, and in many other instances.

lucarne. Window or gabled aperture on the sloping sides of a *Gothic spire*.

lug. **1.** *Crossette*. **2.** Projecting *ear* or *tab* for fixing a pipe to a wall.

lunette. **1.** Vertical wall-plane beneath a segmental or semicircular *vault* running into it, bounded by the *intrados* and *springing-line*. **2.** Similar-shaped aperture bounded by an arch or vault, e.g. in a wall at the end of a *barrel-vault* or over a door set in an arched opening, where it may be a *fanlight*. **3.** *Tympanum* in a semicircular or segmental *pediment*. **4.** Semicircular face of a *Romanesque cushion-capital* formed by cutting its lower part to fit the circular shaft.

Lutheranism. Body of doctrine taught by the German Reformer Martin Luther (1483-1546) and his followers. It is mostly found in Germany, Scandinavia, and North America. Lutherans accepted the *Augsburg Confession* and Luther's doctrine on *Consubstantiation*.

lych-gate. Gateway with a wide-spreading pitched roof sited at the main entrance of a burial-ground.

Magi. Three Kings or Wise Men: *Balthasar* (black, with myrrh), *Caspar* (yellow, with frankincense), and *Melchior* (white, with gold). Their *Relics* are in Cologne Cathedral: their translation is celebrated in the carol *I saw three ships*.

mandala. Also *mandorla*, *mandoral*. Almond-shaped figure composed of two vertical arcs each passing through the other's centre, enclosing a panel, called *aureole* or *vesica piscis*, often found on *tympana* of *Gothic* doorways. It often contains the figure of Christ in Majesty.

manse. Residence of a parson, especially a Presbyterian minister.

marigold. **1.** Formal, stylised floral decoration, resembling a *rosette*, but more like a *chrysanthemum* or *marigold*, repeated in series, e.g. on the *architrave* of *Greek Revival* churches. **2.** Mediæval circular window subdivided by radiating *bars* or *tracery*, sometimes resembling a marigold and sometimes a *rose* (if more complicated in geometry).

martyrium (*pl.* **martyria**). **1.** Building, usually circular or polygonal, built over the tomb of a Christian martyr, so essentially a *mausoleum*. Hundreds of Christian churches owe their existence to martyria. **2.** Place in a church where *Relics* are deposited.

Mass. The *Eucharistic* service, especially as doctrinally viewed and administered by the Roman Catholic Church, but also used to describe the liturgy used by *Anglo-Catholics*.

Mass-bell. *Sanctus*-bell, hung in a *Sancte-cote*, so called because it was rung during *Mass* so that those outside would be reminded of what was going on inside the church.

mensa. **1.** Slab of stone forming the top of an altar in a church. **2.** The upper surface of the same.

merlon. *See* **battlement**.

Methodism. Protestant denomination originating in the eighteenth-century evangelistic movement of Charles (1707-88) and John (1703-91) Wesley. The term probably derives from the idea of following a specific 'method' of Bible study, or a correct attitude to fear.

metope. Plain or enriched slab on the *frieze* of the *Doric Order* between *triglyphs*.

metropolitan. *Bishop* having the oversight of the *bishops* of a *province*. In the West the term approximates to an *archbishop*, but in the *Orthodox* Churches a metropolitan ranks above an archbishop and below a *patriarch*.

Middle Pointed. Style of *Gothic* architecture immediately after the *Lancet Style* and before the *Curvilinear* phase of *Second Pointed*. It saw the introduction of *bar-tracery* in *Geometrical* patterns, and flourished in the second half of the thirteenth and the beginning of the fourteenth century.

millefleurs. Decorative pattern of stylised flowers. It was used in the late mediæval period, and so was a feature of the *Perpendicular* style.

minister. General designation of a person charged with spiritual functions in the Christian Church. It came into use after the *Reformation*, but today is associated with *Evangelicals, Low Churchmen*, or *Nonconformists*, the term *priest* being used by *Anglo-Catholics, High Churchmen, Roman Catholics*, and members of the *Orthodox* churches.

minster. **1**. Abbey- or priory-church, or, more usually, a large *collegiate* church, distinguished from a parish-church or a cathedral. **2**. A monastery or its church.

misericord. *Mercy-seat, subsellium*, or small ledge on the under-side of hinged mediæval choir-stall seats. When the seats were upright, the misericords could give some surreptitious support to a person standing up during the long services. It had a carved *corbel*-like element under the ledge, frequently representing scenes from everyday life, fables, comic episodes, and caricatures.

mitre-head. *Ogee*-headed bulbous top of a *pinnacle* or *turret* of late *Perpendicular* or *Tudor Gothic*, as in Henry VII's Chapel at Westminster Abbey. Its shape resembles a *bishop's* head-dress.

modillion. Projecting bracket resembling a horizontal *console* fixed in series under the *soffit* of the *cornice* of the *Composite, Corinthian* and (occasionally) the *Roman Ionic Order*, expressive of a *cantilever*. Compare **mutule**.

monstrance. Open or transparent vessel in which the *Host* is exposed or *Relics* are displayed. If it displays the *Eucharistic* wafer it is called an *ostensory*.

monument. Building or memorial to perpetuate the memory of an event or an individual, e.g. a public memorial or a funerary monument. The *Gothic Revival* re-introduced memorial *brasses*, tomb-chests, and mural monuments with Gothic detail.

Moresque. Style derived from Islamic architecture of North Africa and the Iberian peninsula.

mortuary-chapel. **1**. Chapel in a cemetery or attached to a building where coffined corpses lie briefly before disposal. **2**. Free-standing building, or one attached to a church, under which is a space used for entombment by one family. Post-Reformation mortuary-chapels as extensions to churches replaced pre-Reformation *chantry-chapels*.

mosaic. Pattern created by rectangular squares of glass, marble, pottery, stone, etc., embedded in a cement or plaster matrix.

mosque. Islamic building for communal prayer, usually with at least one minaret, and often domed.

mouchette. Fourteenth-century light (often *ogee* on at least one side) resembling a curving dagger-like form with *foils* at one end in *Second Pointed Curvilinear tracery*. It resembles a tadpole.

mourners. See **weeper**.

Mozarabic. Style of Spanish Christian architecture incorporating horseshoe arches and other *Moresque* elements, judiciously mixed with *Romanesque* motifs.

mullion. Vertical post of stone, timber, or brick, usually moulded, between the *lights* of a window or screen.

multifoil. Arch or arc with several *foils* and *cusps*.

mural. **1**. Of or pertaining to a wall. **2**. A painting on a wall.

mural monument. Commemorative memorial or tablet fixed to a wall.

muscular Gothic. Phase of the *Gothic Revival* that drew on *First Pointed* precedents from thirteenth-century Burgundy. It featured brickwork (often polychrome), massive cylindrical *piers*, and chunky elements: it was bold, strong, stern, and robust.

mutule. Flat, inclined block on the *soffit* of a Doric cornice, with several *guttæ* on its underside, placed in line with *triglyphs* and centres of *metopes* in the *frieze* below. *Tuscan* mutules are plain and horizontal. Compare **modillion**.

narthex. **1**. Church vestibule, in *Byzantine* churches of two kinds: an *esonarthex* or inner narthex, between the outer porch and the body of the church proper separated from the *nave* and *aisles* by a wall, *arcade, colonnade*, or screen; and an *exonarthex* or outer narthex outside the main wall, sometimes also serving as a *portico* or part of the cloistered *atrium*. **2**. Mediæval *ante-church*, often with a nave and aisles, sometimes called a *Galilee* porch, as at Durham Cathedral.

Nativity. Representation of the newly-born Christ and His family in paintings, carvings, etc.

nave. Central clearstoreyed *aisle* of a *basilican* church, or the main body of the church, aisled or not, between the western wall and the *chancel*. It is used by the laity. It was often separated from the *choir* or chancel by a screen, and from the aisles by *nave-arcades*.

nebule. *Romanesque* ornament, the lower edge of which forms a continuous waving overhang. It is found in *corbel-tables* and *archivolts*.

needle-spire. Tall, slender spire rising from a tower behind a *parapet*. Like a *Hertfordshire spike*, but taller and finer.

Neo-Baroque. Revival of Baroque architecture, or of motifs drawn from such architecture, e.g. Brompton Oratory, London.

Neo-Byzantine *Byzantine Revival*, a style incorporating certain *Byzantine* features, as in the nineteenth-century *Rundbogenstil*. A good example is S. H. Barnsley's church of St Sophia, Lower Kingswood, Surrey (1891).

Neo-Classicism. Dominant style in European and American architecture in the late-eighteenth and early-nineteenth centuries, essentially a return to the *Classicism* of *Antiquity*. It embraces the *Greek* and *Egyptian Revivals*, and drew on archæological investigations and measured drawings. In its more extreme manifestations it sought stereometrical purity of form, clarity of expression, and the elision of all superfluous ornament.

Neo-Grec. **1**. Greek Revival. **2**. Style of the Second Empire in France (1852-70) in which Græco-Roman, Louis Quinze, Louis Seize, Pompeian, Egyptian Revival, and other motifs were disposed in a richly eclectic polychromatic mélange.

Neo-Norman. *Romanesque Revival*, especially from *c*.1820.

net-tracery. *Second Pointed Curvilinear tracery* forming net-like shapes, so said to be *Reticulated*.

niche. Shallow ornamental recess in a wall, *pier*, or *buttress*, usually to contain a statue or other ornament. *Gothic* niches (called tabernacles) have *gablets* or canopies over them. *Classical* niches are usually arched, with quarter-spherical heads, and some are set within *ædicules*.

nimbus. See **aureole**.

nine altars. *Nine Choirs of Angels* are held to mediate between God and Man, nine squaring the *Trinity*. This is reflected in the design of certain *retrochoirs*, e.g. that at Fountains Abbey, Yorkshire (*c*.1205-47).

nodding ogee. Ogee canopy-head, the apex of which projects beyond the springing-line of the canopy: it is an ogee in section as well as elevation.

Nonconformists. See **Dissenters**.

Norman. See **Romanesque**.

obelisk. Lofty, four-sided, often monolithic shaft, on a square plan, tapering (i.e. diminishing) upwards, with a pyramidal top.

Oblate. Person devoted to a monastery or to religious work, especially a member of the Roman Catholic secular *priests* of the Order of St Charles Borromeo (*Oblate of St Charles*).

Oblation. Act of offering something to God, as in the sacrifice of the *Mass* or *Eucharist*.

oculus (*pl. oculi*). **1.** *Roundel*, circular opening or recess, bull's-eye, or *œil-bœuf*, as in a window in the *tympanum* of a *pediment* or at the top of a dome (e.g. the Pantheon, Rome). **2.** Button, disc, or eye from which the spirals of an *Ionic volute* progress.

œil-de-bœuf (*pl. œils-de-bœuf*). Elliptical 'ox-eye' window, often with four keystones. As *oculus*, but usually applied to elliptical, not circular, examples.

offset. Top of a wall, *buttress*, etc., where the wall or buttress above is smaller, usually appearing as a sloping ledge in mediæval buttresses or plinths.

ogee. Upright double curve, concave at the top and convex at the bottom (or the other way round). Double ogees appear in canopies, and are characteristic of the *Second Pointed* style, especially in *funerary monuments*, *niches*, *sedilia*, *shrines*, and *tracery*. They occur in the *Perpendicular* style as well. *See* **nodding ogee**.

Old English. Architectural style involving the revival of *vernacular* elements from Sussex and the Kent Weald, one of the threads of the nineteenth-century *Domestic Revival*, *Queen Anne* style, and the *Arts-and-Crafts* movement. It was characterised by tile-hung walls, *diaper* patterns on brickwork, leaded windows of the case-ment type, timber-framing of gables and jettied elements, fretted barge-boards, rubbed-brick dressings, steep tiled roofs, and tall ornamented chimneys of moulded brick or terracotta. Certain aspects of the style are occasionally found in church architecture (e.g. St Chad's, Hopwas, Staffordshire [1881]).

oratory. **1.** Small chapel for solitary prayer, such as one in a private house. **2.** Church and buildings of the Congregation of St Philip Neri, constituted in *c*.1550.

orb. **1.** Circular *boss* at the intersection of ribs in a *Gothic vault*, concealing the junction of the ribs and acting as an *abutment* for them. **2.** *Blind* panel in *tracery*, especially in *Perpendicular* work.

Order. **1.** In *Classical* architecture, the elements making up the expression of a *columnar* and *trabeated* structure, including a *column* with (usually) a *base* and *capital*, and *entablature*. There are *eight* distinct Classical Orders: *Greek Doric*, *Roman Doric*, *Greek Ionic*, *Roman Ionic*, *Greek Corinthian*, *Roman Corinthian*, *Tuscan* (also known as the *Gigantic Order*), and *Composite*. An Order may also include a *pedestal*, *plinth*, or *podium*. Greek Doric columns have no bases, and the Tuscan shaft is unfluted. **2.** *Romanesque* and *Gothic* arched opening consisting of several layers of arched openings usually with *colonnettes*, each smaller than the layer in front, and collectively forming an *Order-Arch*.

organ-case. Decorative case around the organ-pipes in a church.

orientation. Planning, siting, and arrangement of a building in relation to the points of the compass. Churches in Western Europe were usually orientated with the altars set at the east. Churches sited without regard to this are nevertheless described in terms of *liturgical orientation*.

Orthodox. Epithet of the Eastern Church, which recognises the leadership of the *Patriarch* of Constantinople, and of the various national Churches of Russia, Serbia, Romania, etc., recognising each other as of the same Communion. It is also called the *Greek Church*. The *Orthodox Church* now consists of the four ancient Patriarchates of Constantinople, Antioch, Alexandria, and Jerusalem, with several other self-governing Churches, the most important of which are the Greek and Russian Churches. All Orthodox Churches use the *Byzantine* liturgy in archaic forms of vernacular languages (especially Greek and Russian). The Eastern church separated from the Western by the Schism of 1054, but the fall of Constantinople to the Ottoman Turks in 1453 was probably the defining event in the isolation of the Eastern from the Western Church. Intensely conservative in liturgy and ecclesiastical art, the Orthodox Churches have remained aloof from modernising tendencies in ritual and theology.

ovolo. Convex moulding, often enriched with *egg-and-dart* or similar motifs.

Oxford Movement. Movement for the revival of *Catholic* doctrine and ceremonial in the *Church of England*, which is generally reckoned to have begun in Oxford with John Keble's sermon on *National Apostasy* in 1833, but which probably began stirring a few years earlier. It is also called *Tractarian*, after the *Tracts for the Times* issued between 1833 and 1841 in advocacy of *High Church* principles.

pace. *Daïs*. A stepped *podium* or *plinth*. See **gradin**.

Palladian window. See **Venetian window**.

pampre. **1.** Grapes, leaves, and vine-stems as running undercut ornament in *cavettos* and continuous hollows at the tops of *Perpendicular Gothic* screens. Also called *grapevine trail*, *vine*, or *vignette*. **2.** Representation of vines draped in spirals around Classical column-shafts.

Papist. **1.** A *Roman Catholic*, *Romanist*, or member of the Roman Catholic church. **2.** Advocate of papal supremacy. The term is often used pejoratively, but it also has an historical basis that has no demeaning overtones.

Paradise. **1.** Cloistered *atrium*, or court, before the west end of a church. **2.** West or south porch of a church, including any room over it, corruptly called a *parvise*. **3.** A *cloister garth*. **4.** Burial-ground of a conventual establishment, usually to the east of a church. **5.** *Jerusalem*, or innermost part of a *labyrinth* or *maze*.

parapet. Low wall or barrier at the edge of a balcony, bridge, roof, terrace, or anywhere there is a drop. It may be found with *battlements* on many *Perpendicular Gothic* churches.

parchemin plié. *Linenfold* panelling.

parclose. **1.** *Screen* defining a chapel, etc., or between a chancel and a chapel beside it, in a church. **2.** Front of a gallery.

parish-church. Church of the smallest area in a division of a diocese under the jurisdiction of a *rector* or *vicar*.

Particularism. Calvinistic doctrine of *particular election* or *particular redemption* by which divine *Grace* is provided for or offered to a selected part, not the whole, of the human race.

parvise. See **Paradise**.

pastiche. **1.** Composition made up of fragments or elements derived from various sources, e.g. parts of a building copied from earlier buildings, or influenced by them. **2.** Eclectic architecture quoting motifs from various designs, often displaying great originality, wit, and inventiveness. **3.** Term of abuse used by those who denounce as mere copyists those who employ historical references as mnemonics to trigger resonances not perceived as desirable or necessary.

patriarch. Official title of the *bishops* of the *sees* of Con-stantinople, Alexandria, Antioch, and Jerusalem in the *Orthodox* Church, the Patriarch of Constantinople being the head, or *Œcumenical Patriarch*, of the Church. The term *patriarch* is also given to the heads of other Churches (e.g. the Abyssinian, Armenian, Jacobite, and Coptic). In the *Roman Catholic Church* a patriarch is a bishop second only to the Pope in *episcopal*, and to the Pope and Cardinals in *hierarchical*, rank, and above *primates* and *metropolitans*. The Roman Catholic bishops of Constantinople, Alexandria, Antioch, and Jerusalem, as well as those of the Indies, Lisbon, and Venice, were also called patriarchs.

patristic. Pertaining to the writings and doctrines of the Fathers of the Church.

Pax. Representation of the Crucifixion.

pedestal. 1. Substructure consisting of a *plinth*, *dado* (or *die*), and *cornice*, beneath a column-base in *Classical* architecture. 2. Part of a *balustrade*, terminating a row of *balusters*.

pediment. Low-pitched triangular gable following the roof-slopes over a *portico* or façade in *Classical architecture*, formed with *raked cornices* on the slopes and a horizontal cornice at the bottom, often containing sculpture in the *tympanum*. Pediments may also crown subordinate features such as doorways, niches, windows, etc. Although triangular pediments are the most usual (sometimes fully or partially *broken* (i.e. with the centre omitted), *segmental* and *scrolled* pediments also occur..

pelican. The bird is shown piercing her breast with her beak to draw blood (*vulning* herself) to feed her young. The image is symbolic of piety and the *Eucharist*.

pellet. Band enriched with a series of closely-spaced discs or half-balls in *Romanesque* architecture.

pendant. Fixed hanging ornament, resembling an elongated *boss* suspended from *Perpendicular fan-vaulting*, *Jacobean* ceilings, etc.

pendentive. A dome over a square compartment requires a structure to effect the transition between the corner of the square and the circular form over it. This is achieved by forming a fragment of a sail-vault (resembling a concave, distorted, almost triangular *spandrel*) in each corner: this is called a *pendentive*.

pentacle. Five-pointed star shape in *Gothic tracery*.

peristlye. *Colonnade* surrounding a building or a court.

Perpendicular. See **Gothic**.

pew. Fixed wooden seat with a back and *bench-ends* (the last often elaborately carved with *blind tracery* and finished with *poppy-head finials*) in use in churches from around the thirteenth century. *Box-pews* were enclosed with high panelled partitions and a door, and (where they have survived at all) usually date from the late-seventeenth or eighteenth century.

phoenix. Mythical bird, a symbol of Immortality and of the Resurrection.

Picturesque. *Æsthetic category*, a standard of taste, largely concerned with landscapes, and with emotional responses to associations evocative of passions or events. Essentially anti-urban, it was concerned with sensibility, linked to notions of pleasing the eye with compositions reminiscent of those in paintings by, e.g., Claude, Salvator Rosa, and the two Poussins. Picturesque scenes were full of variety, interesting detail, and elements drawn from many sources, so were neither serene (like the **Beautiful**) nor awe-inspiring (like the **Sublime**). In architecture, the Picturesque encouraged asymmetrical composition, and the freeing of architectural design from the tyranny of symmetry was undoubtedly due to the Picturesque, a term that suggested variety, smallness, irregularity, roughness of texture, and an association with the power to stimulate the imagination. Thus the Picturesque led to *eclecticism*, and, by its appreciation of variety and asymmetry, to the *Gothic* and other *Revivals*.

pier. 1. Detached mass of construction, generally acting as a support, such as the solid part of a wall between windows, or a massive element from which arches spring, as in a bridge. 2. Support, such as a pier in a repetitive mediæval *nave-arcade* varying from sturdy, oversized *Romanesque* examples to the lighter, taller, more slender, multi-moulded *Perpendicular* types. Piers are generally more massive than columns.

pierced. Describes any wall that has apertures, such as windows.

pila. *Font* on a free-standing shaft.

pilaster. Rectangular projection attached to a wall that conforms to the column of an *Order*, carrying an *entablature*. It should not be confused with an *anta* (which has parallel vertical sides and does not conform to the Order used for columns) nor with an *engaged column* (which is like a column partly buried in a wall). In most cases the shafts of pilasters also have *entasis*. Pilasters, unlike columns or piers, have no structural purpose, and are used to respond to columns or to the design of the *soffit* of a ceiling for purely architectural or decorative reasons.

pilier cantonné. *Gothic pier* consisting of a large central core, with four attached *colonnettes* associated with the springing of the *nave arcade* and the *vaults* over the *aisle* and *nave*.

pillow-capital. Capital resembling a cushion, or a cubic capital with the lower angles rounded off, as in *Romanesque* architecture.

pinnacle. Ornamental pyramidal or conic form, the terminating feature of a *buttress*, *parapet-angle*, *spire*, *turret*, etc., often ornamented with *crockets*.

piscina (*pl.* **piscinæ**). Stone basin connected with a drainage-channel for carrying away the water used in rinsing the vessels employed at *Mass* and washing the hands of the *priest*. It was usually set in a *niche* in the south wall of the *chancel* in a church to be near the *altar*, and was often given decorative treatment. Sometimes it was incorporated with the *sedilia*. Piscinæ are also found in chapels and in aisle-walls where there were altars before the *Reformation*.

pix, pyx. Box, casket, shrine, or tabernacle to hold the consecrated bread in a church.

plaque. Plate, stone slab, or any kind of tablet, usually inscribed, fixed to or inserted in a wall-surface, pavement, etc., as a memorial, ornament, etc.

plate-tracery. (*See* **tracery**). Early *First Pointed tracery* consisting of a thin flat panel of *ashlar* pierced, like simple fretwork, with *lights*. It had no projecting mouldings, and is quite distinct from *bar-tracery*.

plinth. 1. In the *Classical Orders*, the low plain block under the base-mouldings of a *column*, *pedestal*, or *pilaster*. 2. Plain, continuous, projecting surface under the base-mouldings of a wall, pedestal, or podium, connecting the architectural member to the ground. 3. Any monumental support for a statue etc.

pointed. A pointed arch may be formed by a radius equal to the width of the opening, struck from both sides of the springing-line, or by striking the radius from any point on a line projected through the springing-lines, in which case the arch can be sharply pointed. With a capital 'P', *Pointed* refers to the *Gothic* style, divided into *First*, *Middle*, *Second*, and *Third Pointed* (the last most commonly called *Perpendicular* in England). See **Gothic**.

polychromy. Enrichment of exteriors and interiors of buildings by means of the application of several colours. *Structural polychromy* is achieved by using differently coloured materials (e.g. bricks, stones, tiles, etc.) in the construction, rather than by applying colour using paints.

polyfoil. With many *foils*, also *multifoil*.

pommel. 1. As *crop*. 2. Ball, boss, knob, or knot terminal used as a *finial* for *pinnacles*, etc.

pontifical altar. Altar placed in a central position in a church, such as the great Bernini altar in St Peter's, Rome.

Popery. 1. Hostile term for the doctrines, practices, and ceremonial associated with the *Roman Catholic Church*, and especially with the Pope as its head. 2. Anything savouring of adherence to the Roman Catholic religion.

poppy-head. Carved top of, e.g., a *bench-end*, resembling the *fleur-de-lys*, but often richly decorated with figures, flowers, fruit, and foliage. The term is a corruption of *poupée*, meaning a bunch of hemp or flax tied to a staff, and has nothing to do with poppies.

portico. Roofed space forming a porch-like element in front of a church, consisting of a series of columns placed at regular intervals supporting the roof. The volume so created can be open or partly enclosed at the sides: if it has a *pediment* over it, it is

referred to as a *temple-front*. Classical porticos are of several types:
engaged: with the ensemble of columns, entablature, and pediment embedded in the front wall, so not forming a covered space, and intended purely for architectural effect;
in antis: with the columns set in a line between the projecting walls enclosing the sides of the portico, i.e. between the *antæ* of the walls;
prostyle: with the columns set in a line standing before and detached from the front wall of the building behind.
In both *in antis* and *prostyle* porticoes the design is further defined by the number of columns visible on the front elevation. The commonest varieties are: *distyle* (2, usually *in antis*); *tetrastyle* (4); *hexastyle* (6); *octastyle* (8); *decastyle* (10); and *dodecastyle* (12). Even numbers are more usual in order to ensure a void on the central axis, but odd numbers (*tristyle* [3], *pentastyle* [5], *heptastyle* [7], and *enneastyle* [9]) are not unknown. A portico with four columns standing in front of the main wall of the body of a church is *prostyle tetrastyle* (or *tetraprostyle*), and if it has two set between the *antæ* of the flanking walls it is *distyle in antis*.

powdered. Wall, ceiling, etc., embellished with repetitive patterns of crossed flowers, stars, etc., usually stencilled on a painted coloured background. It is found in many fine *polychrome* interiors of the *Gothic Revival*.

predella. **1.** Platform or step on which an altar stands, synonymous with **gradine**. **2.** *Gradino*, or front of a step at the top and back of an altar, supporting the *altar-piece*. It may have panels depicting events in the lives of Saints, and be associated with a *triptych* or *reredos*.

presbyter. In *episcopal* Churches, a *priest* ranking below a *bishop* and above a *deacon*.

Presbyterianism. System of government in a *Protestant* Church in which no higher order than that of *elder* is recognised. Each congregation is governed by its *Session*, consisting of the minister and other elders, but each Session is subordinate to the *Presbytery*, each Presbytery to the *Synod*, and (in most Presbyterian Churches) the Synods to the *General Assembly* of the Church. There are various seceding congregations of Presbyterians, some independent, some 'Free', but the history of Presbyterianism is too vast and complex to be covered here.

presbytery. **1.** Part of a church (*presbyterium*) in which the high altar stands, at the east of the *choir*. It is used exclusively by those who minister in services and at the altar. **2.** A Church-Court consisting of the minister and one elder from each church within a certain district, in the *Presbyterian* system. **3.** Priest's or minister's house.

pricket. **1.** Metal spike on which a candle may be impaled, e.g. as on a *hearse*, with a rimmed plate fixed below it into which the wax would run. **2.** Uppermost part of a *spire*.

priest. Clergyman in the second of Holy Orders, above a *deacon* and below a *bishop*, with the authority to administer the *Sacraments* and pronounce *Absolution*. In the *Anglican Church* the term would not be applied to a *minister* of *Low Church* or *Evangelical* views.

priest's door. Entrance to the *chancel* of a church, usually on the south side.

primate. *Archbishop* holding first place among all the bishops of a *province*. In the Anglican Church the Archbishops of York and Canterbury are both primates, but the Archbishop of Canterbury is the primate of all England.

prismatic billet. Billet-moulding consisting of rows of prisms in series, usually found in association with another series of billets in a row above or below, the billets of one row alternating with those of another (i.e. staggered), in *Romanesque* architecture.

prismatory. *Sedilia* in a chancel, sometimes including the *piscina*.

procession path. **1.** Line of paving for the marshalling of those participating in processions associated with church services. **2.** *Ambulatory*, or *aisle* to the east of the high altar and its *reredos* in cathedrals and larger churches.

prostyle. With columns of a *portico* erected in front of the enclosed building. *See* **portico**.

Protestant. Originally one of those who *protested*, i.e. made a declaration of dissent from the decision of the Diet of Speier (1529) which re-affirmed the Edict of the Diet of Worms against the Reformation, it is a general designation of an adherent to the reformed doctrines or Churches that repudiated papal authority: a member of a Christian Church outside the *Roman Catholic* communion in the West.

prothesis. **1.** Recess in the north side of a *bema* or *apse* of a *basilican* church out of which the bread and wine were taken for Consecration. **2.** A chapel containing such a recess.

proudwork. Similar to *flushwork*, but with the freestone tracery in higher relief than the flint panels, which are set back rather than flush with the stone.

province. District within the jurisdiction of an *archbishop* or *metropolitan*, e.g. Canterbury and York.

pulpit. Partially enclosed elevated desk of masonry or wood in a church (usually on the north-east side of the *nave*) for a preacher. Often decorated, it may have a canopy (*tester*) over it, functioning partly as a sound-reflector. The *Anglican three-decker pulpit* contains at the bottom level a clerk's stall, a reading-desk above, and at the top a pulpit proper, designed as a whole.

pulpitum. Stone *screen* set between the *nave* and the *choir*, acting as the back of the *choir-stalls*, over which is a *gallery*, *Rood*, or organ.

pulvin, pulvinus (*pl.* **pulvins, pulvini**). **1.** Form resembling a cushion, such as the *baluster*-like side of an *Ionic volute*. **2.** *Impost-block* or *dosseret* between the *capital* and arch in a *Byzantine* or *Rundbogenstil* arcade.

pulvination. A swelling, as though a cushion was being squashed. Roman *friezes* are occasionally *pulvinated*, or bulging outwards with a convex profile.

Purbeck marble. Dark grey or grey-greenish hard limestone, called a marble, originating in the Isle of Purbeck, Dorset, and almost entirely composed of univalve and bivalve remains fossilised and bound together. Capable of taking a spectacular polish, it was used by English mediæval architects for *colonnettes*, shafts, monuments, effigies, and tombs because of its attractive properties: the dark shiny shafts set against lighter limestone contribute to the richness of *First Pointed Gothic* interiors such as those of Lincoln and Salisbury Cathedrals. In the *Victorian* period coloured marbles and granites were used to create similar effects on *piers*, etc.

Puritan. English Protestant who regarded the Reformation of the Church under Queen Elizabeth I (1558-1603) as incomplete, and called for its further 'purification' from what was considered unscriptural and corrupt forms and ceremonial retained from before the Reformation. The term was later applied to those who separated from the Established Church on points of ritual, doctrine, or polity, holding these to be at variance with a 'pure' reading of the New Testament. Essentially anti-episcopal, Puritanism veered towards *Presbyterianism*, and gained the upper hand politically during the *Commonwealth* (1649-60), when a grim joylessness seems to have prevailed.

purlin. Horizontal structural beam carried on the *principal rafters* of *roof-trusses* to give intermediate support to the *common rafters*.

Puseyite. Name given by opponents to the theological and ecclesiastical principles and doctrine of Dr E. B. Pusey (1800-82), and those with whom he was associated in the

Oxford Movement for the revival of *Catholic* doctrine and observance in the *Church of England*, more formally (and courteously) called *Tractarian*.

pyx. See **pix**.

quadripartite. Divided by the system of construction used into four parts, e.g. a *Gothic* vault over a rectangular compartment, with the vault divided into four parts by means of intersecting diagonal ribs.

Quaker. Member of the Society of Friends founded (1648-50) by George Fox (1624-91). Quakerism is distinguished by peaceful principles, plainness of dress, unassuming manners, and gatherings of extreme simplicity in which egalitarianism prevails. Buildings for Quaker religious observance are modest too.

quarrel, quarry. 1. Lozenge- or square-shaped *light* in *Gothic* *tracery*. 2. Similarly-shaped piece of glass held in the *cames* of leaded lights. 3. Any floor-tile, lozenge-shaped or square.

quarter. *See* **foil**, **quatrefoil**.

quatrefoil. *See* **foil**. The form, resembling a stylised plant with four leaves, is composed of four *foils* separated by *cusps*. Bands of quatrefoils in series were favoured during the *Perpendicular* period, with the *lobes* or *foils* arranged at the top, bottom, and either side: when set diagonally (i.e. with the foils set in the corners of square panels), quatrefoils are referred to as *cross-quarters*, *quarter* being another name for a quatrefoil.

Queen Anne. The *Queen Anne style* or *Revival* evolved from the 1860s, and had only tenuous connections with the style of architecture of the reign of Queen Anne (1702-14). It was a style largely used in domestic architecture: some motifs were derived from English and Dutch domestic architecture of the late-seventeenth and early-eighteenth centuries, but it was an eclectic mélange that included tall small-paned sash-windows, rubbed-brick arches and dressings over and around openings, *terracotta* embellishments, *vernacular* features such as tile-hanging, open-bed and broken pediments, steeply-pitched roofs (often rising from eaves-cornices), massive chimneys, shaped and Dutch *gables*, and white-painted balustrades, balconies, and bay-windows. Such elements were combined with asymmetrical and informal planning derived from the *Gothic Revival* and the ideas of A. W. N. Pugin. Although mostly found in domestic work, the style occasionally surfaced in some ecclesiastical architecture.

quoin. 1. External angle or corner of a building. 2. Angular course of stone, etc., at the corner of a building, usually laid as alternate *quoin-headers* and *-stretchers*. 3. One of such stones.

radiating chapels. In a large church, projecting chapels grouped radially around the *ambulatory* of a semicircular or polygonal liturgical east end. See *chevet*.

rag. Piece of hard, coarse-textured stone, capable of being broken into thick, flattish pieces, the commonest being *Kentish rag* (tough, hard limestone, readily fragmented into usable pieces). *Rag-stones* are mostly used as *facings* to brick or other types of stone wall. A rag-stone wall will be covered with a pattern of approximate polygons with the mortar joints coarse (*rough picked*) or fine (*close picked*). Kentish rag is commonly found in nineteenth-century *Gothic Revival* churches in London and the south-east of England.

Rageur. Nineteenth-century style of French architecture in which motifs are over-stated, over-emphatic, and outlandishly proportioned, e.g. tomb of the Duc de Morny (1865-6) in Père-Lachaise cemetery, Paris, by Viollet-le-Duc. It had parallels in a few *muscular Gothic* examples in England. *Raguer* is the French for to chafe or to irritate, so it is applied to a phase of the mid-nineteenth-century *Gothic Revival* in France characterised by perversity, discordant originality, and aggressiveness not unlike aspects of English and American *Rogue Gothic*. See also **Go**.

rake. Inclination or slope of anything, e.g. a roof. A *raking*

coping is one on, e.g., a *gable*, and a *raking cornice* is a cornice on the inclined top of a triangular *pediment*.

rampant arch. Arch with one *impost* set higher than the other, also called a *raking arch*.

ratchement. Curved member resembling a variety of *flying buttress* rising from the corner uprights of a *hearse*, meeting a similar member at a central upright. Ratchements supported the hangings, valancing, and palls, and often carried *prickets*.

Rayonnant. Style of *Gothic* prevailing in France from *c.*1227 to the middle of the fourteenth century. It takes its name from the shapes formed by *tracery-bars* and from *vault-ribs* radiating from *piers* shaped with masses of shafts corresponding to the ribs.

Real Presence. Actual presence of Christ's Body and Blood in the *Sacrament* of the *Eucharist*. In the *Roman Catholic* and *Lutheran* Churches it implies the presence by means of *Transubstantiation* or *Consubstantiation* of the actual Body and Blood. A more Protestant view would be that the Body and Blood are present only in a 'heavenly and spiritual manner', or that the *Eucharistic* Elements are 'only' *allegories*. See **allegory**, **symbol**.

Rectilinear style. Late phase of *Perpendicular Gothic* in which panel-like *lights* and *blind tracery* predominant.

rectory. Province or residence of the parson (*rector*) serving the parochial or common church, who had the right to the great *tithes*, and who was the holder of a perpetual *curacy*.

recusant. One who refused to attend services of the *Established Anglican Church* or conform (*see* **Conformity**) to its beliefs and practices. The term became synonymous with *Roman Catholics* even though it could theoretically be applied to all *Dissenters*.

Reformation. The sixteenth-century religious movement that led to the establishment of the various *Reformed* and *Protestant* Churches of Central and North-Western Europe which broke with the *Roman Catholic Church*.

Regency. Style of English architecture fashionable during the incapacity of King George III between 1810 and 1820, when the Prince of Wales (1762-1830) was Regent, but loosely applied to the period from the late 1790s to the accession of King William IV in 1830.

Relic. Some object, such as a bone-fragment, skull, or part of the body or clothing, or any article, remaining as a memorial of a Saint, Martyr, etc., carefully preserved and venerated.

reliquary. Container holding *Relics*.

repeating ornament. Pattern capable of being infinitely extended, e.g. *chequer-board* designs and *diaper-work*.

reredos. Ornamental facing or *screen* behind an altar in a church, free-standing or forming part of the *retable*. It is often enriched with statues in niches, pinnacles, etc., but could take the form of a *triptych*. In larger churches the reredos separates the *choir* from the *retrochoir* and other parts to the liturgical east.

Reservation of the Sacrament. Practice of reserving part of the *Eucharistic* elements for the Communion of the sick. The presence of such elements is usually signified by a *sanctuary-lamp*.

respond. 1. Corbel, half-pier, or other architectural element engaged to a wall at the end of an *arcade* from which the first arch springs. 2. In *Classical* architecture, an *anta* or *pilaster*-like motif where *arcades* or *colonnades* engage with a wall.

Resurrection. 1. The Rising of Christ after His Death and Burial 2. Commemoration of this event at Easter.

retable. 1. *Screen* to the rear of an altar, rising up behind it. Often richly decorated, and including the *reredos*. 2. Shelf or setting for ornamental panels or pictures behind an altar. 3. Frame around the paintings or decorative panels of a reredos.

reticulated. 1. Arranged to resemble a net, with the repetition of the same figure all over the surface or plane, e.g. in a *screen* or *lattice*, or in a wall made of *ragstone*. 2. With a capital R (*Reticulated*), the term refers to a type of *Curvilinear Gothic* *tracery* consisting of a net-like mesh of interweaving *ogees*.

retrochoir. Portion of a large church behind the *retable* or *reredos* of the high altar, essentially the volume bounded by the *sanctuary* and the *chapels* to the east, as in Winchester Cathedral. In apsidal arrangements the retrochoir would include parts of the north and south chancel-aisles as well as the area to the east and the *radiating chapels*.

rib. Moulding on a flat or vaulted ceiling. In mediæval work a raised moulding forming part of the *vault*, framing the panels or *webs*, often with elaborate sections, and with their crowning intersections adorned with sculptured *bosses*.

ribbon. 1. Any ribbon-like strip of decoration. 2. Lead *came* around the pieces of glass in a leaded *light*.

riddell. In a church, the curtains suspended around an altar, sometimes from rods fixed into the wall behind, but more often from some means of hanging that spans between *riddell-posts*: there were normally four of the last, polygonal on plan, coloured and gilded, and crowned by angels, often supporting *candelabra*. Arrangements of riddells behind and around altars seem to have been not uncommon in England and Flanders towards the end of the Middle Ages, and were revived during the late flowering of the *Gothic Revival*, especially by Ninian Comper and Temple Moore, and popularised by Percy Dearmer.

ridge. 1. Apex of a pitched roof, where two angles meet, especially the horizontal edge formed thus, often decorated with a *ridge-crest*. 2. Internal apex of a *Gothic vault*, often covered with a horizontal *ridge-rib*.

rinceau. Classical ornament on a *band*, consisting of a continuous wave of scrolling foliage, often vine. *See* **pampre, trail, vine, vignette**.

rising arch. As *rampant* arch.

Ritualism. The study, practice, or system of ritual observances and ceremonial revived in the *Anglican Church* by the *High Church* party and by *Anglo-Catholics* within the *Church of England*. It had a profound effect on the planning and detail of many Anglican churches, especially in relation to altars.

rock-faced. Quarry-faced ashlar, with a dressed, rough, projecting face, as though recently taken from the quarry, also called *rock-faced* or quarry-faced work.

Rogue. *Gothic Revival* architecture unmarked by scholarship, serenity, or tact. It was characterised by repetitive notchings and chamferings of woodwork and *arcades*, frantic roof structures, saw-toothed arrises, scissor-shaped trusses, and harsh, barbaric, polychrome decorations (much of them structural). The somewhat debauched acrobatic Gothic and elephantine compositions earned opprobrium from Ecclesiologists. *Rogue Goths* tended to be in the *Evangelical* camp. *See* **Go** and **Rageur**.

Roman Catholic. Adherent of the *Roman Catholic Church* recognising the spiritual supremacy of the Pope and accepting the doctrines and teachings of that Church.

Romanesque. Architectural style in Romanised Western Europe having certain characteristics similar to those in *Early Christian*, late-*Roman*, and *Byzantine* work, notably the semicircular-headed arch set in massive walls, the *basilica* form for churches, and the survival of design elements such as the *Classical capital* (though much coarsened and transformed). Some would hold that the Romanesque style evolved from the seventh century, drawing *Carolingian* and *Anglo-Saxon* architecture within the Romanesque umbrella. Others argue that it began with the Ottonian Empire in Germany (tenth century) and the evolution of architecture at Cluny in Burgundy (from 910). Mature Romanesque church architecture had thick walls and sturdy *piers* (often cylindrical); semicircular-headed openings; vaults based on semicircles (often barrel-vaults, but frequently groin- and rib- vaults); plans that were simple in their geometry, including apses and circular buildings;

and clearly defined *bays*, square or rectangular on plan, and delineated by means of *pilaster*-like *lesenes* outside and shafts inside rising up to the tops of the walls, or associated with the springing of arches. The Romanesque style dominated Western Europe from the tenth to the end of the twelfth century, and is known as *Norman* in Northern France and the British Isles (where it was prevalent from the mid-eleventh to the end of the twelfth century). Detail was distinctive but limited in range. Doorways were often deeply recessed, often of several *Orders*; capitals were often clearly derived from Byzantine and Roman prototypes, but also included examples of the *cushion* and *scalloped* type; and mouldings and ornaments were simple and straightforward, including the *beak-head*, *billet*, *cable*, *chevron* (in various permutations), *double-cone*, *nebule*, and reversed *zig-zag*. The style enjoyed a nineteenth-century revival connected with a general trend towards *Historicism*, and it was merged with Early Christian and Byzantine elements in the *Rundbogenstil*.

Romanticism. Late-eighteenth and early-nineteenth-century artistic movement, commonly perceived as a reaction against the rationalism of the Enlightenment, *Classicism*, and *Neo-Classicism*. In architecture it is allied with *Historicism*, the *Gothic Revival*, the *Picturesque*, and the *Sublime*, and so with the study of mediæval styles and the use of asymmetrical compositions.

Rood. 1. Cross. 2. Large *Crucifixion* set above the entrance to the *chancel* of a church, sometimes suspended, sometimes supported on a *Rood-beam* spanning from wall to wall, and sometimes rising from a *Rood-loft* over a *Rood-screen*. The Crucifixion group often includes the figures of the Blessed Virgin Mary and St John on either side of the Cross. A *Rood-altar* is one under a Rood, or an altar physically attached to a Rood-screen, facing the nave. A *Rood-spire* or *Rood-tower* stands over the *crossing* of a church.

rose. 1. Conventional representation of a flower in architectural ornament. Roses are sometimes found carved on *confessionals* (*sub rosa* [under the rose] implies secrecy and silence). 2. *Attribute* of the Blessed Virgin Mary. 3. Type of *Gothic* window, circular, subdivided by complex *tracery* radiating from the centre to form a stylised floral design of great beauty. It should be distinguished from a *Catherine-wheel*, *marigold*-, or *wheel-window*. 4. Ceiling-ornament from which chandeliers, etc., may be suspended.

roundel. 1. Small circular panel or window. 2. Bull's eye or *oculus* (see *œil-de-bœuf*). 3. *Astragal* or large *bead*.

rubric. Direction for the conduct of Divine Service in *liturgical books*, properly printed in red to distinguish it from the text proper.

rudenture. *See* **cable**.

Rundbogenstil. German for 'round-arched style', meaning an eclectic mix of *Byzantine*, *Early Christian*, *Italian Romanesque*, and *Florentine Renaissance* elements. It was promoted by Heinrich Hübsch (1795-1863), Leo von Klenze (1784-1864), Friedrich von Gärtner (1792-1847), and others, and found favour in England under the aegis of Prince Albert and his artistic adviser, Ludwig Grüner (1801-82).

Sabbatarianism. *Protestant* principle of prohibiting any recreation on Sundays, and attempts to apply the Fourth Commandment relating to the keeping of the Jewish *Sabbath* to the Christian Sunday. Sabbatarians were usually *Nonconformists* or *Evangelicals*, whose opinions and practices with regard to Sunday were unusually strict, rigid, and joyless.

sacellum. *Chantry*-, *mortuary*-, or other small roofless *chapel* in a church defined by a screen.

Sacrament. Religious rite regarded as a channel to and from God, or as a sign of *Grace*. Among *Protestants* the two signs ordained by Christ (*Baptism* and the *Lord's Supper* [or *Eucharist*]) are recognised, and among *Roman Catholics* and members of the

Orthodox Church, the Sacraments of *Confirmation, Extreme Unction, Holy Orders, Matrimony,* and *Penance* are accepted in addition to Baptism and the Eucharist.

sacrarium. 1. Part of a *chancel* or *choir* in the vicinity of the high *altar,* usually defined by altar-rails (i.e. the *sanctuary*). **2.** A shrine. **3.** Piscina. **4.** Sacristy.

sacristy, sacrist. Church *vestry* near the *chancel* in which ecclesiastical garments, utensils used in services, etc., are stored.

Saint. Person recognised by the Church as having, by his or her exceptional holiness of life, attained an exalted station in Heaven, and therefore entitled to veneration. A *Saint's Day* is the date identified with a particular Saint, called a *Feast*: St Patrick's Day, for example, is 17 March, and St George's Day is 23 April.

saltire. Diagonal or St Andrew's *cross.*

Sancte-bell. *See* **bell-cote.**

sanctuary. 1. *Sacrarium.* **2.** *Chancel* or *presbytery.*

sanctuary-lamp. Lamp (usually with coloured glass) suspended in a chapel near an altar, indicating that the consecrated Host or Element (*Reserved Sacrament*) *is* present.

sarcophagus (*pl.* **sarcophagi**). Stone or terracotta sepulchral chest, often enriched, to contain a corpse, or simply used as an architectural motif (e.g. in funerary architecture).

scallop. 1. *Romanesque* moulding consisting of a series of convex *lobes* resembling the edge of an apron. A variety of it occurs in *Classical friezes.* **2.** Type of Romanesque *capital,* like a *cushion*-capital, with the curved lower part further carved with conical forms resembling trumpets, so that the *lunette* element has three curved lower edges instead of one semicircular edge. **3.** *Classical* enrichment derived from the shell of a scallop, with many applications, including enrichment of the quarter-spherical heads of arched *apses* and *niches.* **4.** Badge of pilgrims who had been to the shrine of St James at Compostella in Spain, or to the Holy Land. **5.** Holy-water stoup, often in the form of a large scallop-shell.

scissor-truss. *Truss* with *braces* crossing and fixed to each other, thus tying pairs of principal rafters together.

Scrape. To remove something especially an outer layer. The word was used disparagingly to describe a process by which all accretions were removed from the fabric of a church during drastic 'restorations' by ruthless architects who showed little sensitivity to the historical development of the building. Thus the movement founded by William Morris to protect ancient buildings (the Society for the Protection of Ancient Buildings, or S.P.A.B.) was called *Anti-Scrape.*

screen. 1. Partition of metal, timber, or stone, not part of the main structure of a church, separating the *choir* from the *nave* (also called variously *chancel-, choir-, Rood*-screen, or *pulpitum*), *choir* from *chancel-* or *choir-aisle* (called *parclose* screen), or defining a *chantry-* or *mortuary-chapel,* etc. **2.** Open *colonnade* around a *court,* e.g. in a *cloister.*

seaweed. Decorative carved foliage and *crockets* in *Second Pointed* architecture.

Second Pointed. *See* **Gothic.**

sedile (*pl.* **sedilia**). Seat. The plural term describes the series of stone seats (usually three) set in the south wall of *chancels,* often crowned with elaborate canopies and pinnacles, used by officiating clergy. Sedilia, collectively known as the *prismatory,* may include the *piscina* within its series of arched niches.

see. 1. *Seat* or a *daïs.* **2.** *Diocese* under the jurisdiction of a *bishop.* **3.** *Cathedra.*

serliana. *See* **Venetian window.**

seven lamps. Lamps suspended in front of an altar, signifying the *Sacraments.*

severy. 1. Structural *bay.* **2.** Top of a *ciborium.*

sexfoil. Aperture or panel with six *foils, lobes,* or *leaves,* separated by *cusps.*

sexpartite. Divided into six parts. The term is usually applied to *Gothic* vaults.

shaft. 1. *Body, fust,* or *trunk* of a *colonnette* or *column* extending from the top of the *base* to the bottom of the *capital,* in the *Classical Orders* diminishing in diameter as it rises (*see* **entasis**). **2.** Slim, cylindrical, tall element (one of several around a *Gothic pier* and tied to it by *shaft-rings* or *bands of a shaft*), often made of *Purbeck marble* or some other material (such as granite) capable of taking a high polish to contrast with the lighter stone of the pier proper. **3.** *Colonnette* set at an angle of a building, e.g. a junction of a *jamb* with a wall, or one of a pair framing a *reveal.*

shrine. 1. *Fereter,* often of sumptuous magnificence, for *Relics.* **2.** Building, *feretory,* or *shrine-chapel* in which the Relics are deposited.

side. *Horn* of an altar, that on the south being the *Epistle* side and that on the north the *Gospel* side.

side-chapel. Chapel to the side of an *aisle* or *choir* in a church.

skew. Anything that slopes or is set obliquely, e.g. the top of a *Gothic* buttress or the *cope* of a *gable.* A *skew-block, skew-butt, skew-corbel, skew-put,* or *skew-table* is a large stone at the bottom end of a raking top of a gable to hold the cope in place and stop it sliding off, also called a *gable-springer, kneeler, springer,* or *summer-stone.*

Solomonic column. *Barley-sugar, Salomonic, spiral, torso,* or *twisted* column, with a contorted or twisted shaft like a corkscrew, unlike the *Antonine, triumphal,* or *Trajanic* column with its spiral band of sculpture wound around the shaft. The form was based on *Antique* precedents from the Herodian Temple in Jerusalem, said to be from the Temple of Solomon, brought to Rome in the first century AD.

Sondergotik. German late *Gothic* from *c.*1380, characterised by *hall-churches* of immense height, complicated vaults, and highly complex *tracery.* Although contemporary with English *Perpendicular,* it is quite unlike that style.

south door. 1. *Priest's door* **2.** Door on the south side of the nave, often associated with a porch.

spandrel. 1. Quasi-triangular plane framed by the *extrados* of an arch, a horizontal line projected from the crown of the arch, and a vertical line rising from the *springing,* often embellished in some way, as in a *nave arcade.* **2.** *Web* of a *vault* between its *ribs.*

spiral column. *See* **Solomonic column.**

spire. Tall structure, circular, polygonal, or square on plan, rising from a roof, tower, etc., terminating in a point, especially the tapering part of a church-*steeple.* Types of spire include:
> *broach*: octagonal spire on a square tower, that part of the tower not occupied by the spire covered by a structure (resembling part of a *pyramid* sloping towards one of the faces of the spire) known as a *broach,* forming a transition between the square and the octagon;
> *crown*: carried on *buttress*-like elements resembling the arched forms at the top of a royal or imperial crown;
> *Hertfordshire spike*: small *needle-spire* set on a tower behind a *parapet*;
> *needle-spire*: very tall slender spire rising from a tower behind a parapet, like a *Hertfordshire spike,* but much taller, more acute, and finer;
> *spike*: short spire, *flèche,* or *spirelet*;
> *splay-foot*: spire with a base opening out at a flatter pitch and forming *eaves* over the tower.

spire-light. Gabled *lucarne,* or opening, set on the acutely sloping sides of a *spire.*

squinch. Small arch, series of parallel arches of increasing radius, or corbelled elements built out course by course, spanning the angles of a square compartment to support the alternate sides of octagonal *spires* on square towers, or to carry a drum or dome in place of a *pendentive*.

squint. See **hagioscope**.

stage. *Storey* of a tower, usually defined in some way, by means of *buttresses*, *string-courses*, etc.

stall. Fixed seat in a *chancel* or *choir*, one of a number, generally elevated, enclosed at the back and sides, arranged in rows on the north and south sides, and, in grander churches, surmounted by high canopies of *tabernacle-work*. Seats were often hinged with *misericords* on the undersides. In major churches the choir-stalls returned at the west, parallel to the *choir-screen* or *pulpitum*.

stanchion.**1**. Vertical support or post, e.g. a *stud* in a timber-framed wall. **2**. *Mullion*. **3**. Vertical iron bar between stone mullions in a *Gothic* window, sometimes used to support the stained glass.

Stations of the Cross. Series of pictures or sculptures (usually fourteen in number) representing successive incidents of the Passion (i.e. the narrative of the sufferings of Christ from His Judgement to the Cross and Entombment), placed in churches (or sometimes in the open) to be visited in order for meditation and prayer.

steeple. A *church-tower* and *spire* together.

stiff-leaf. Late-twelfth- and thirteenth-century stylised three-lobed carved foliage, usually on capitals and bosses.

stilted arch. One with its springing-line above the impost, so having straight sides before the curves of the arch begin.

stop. Termination of any moulding, e.g. architrave, hood-moulding, label, string-course, etc. A *Gothic label* over an opening, for example, terminates in a *label-stop*.

stoup. Fixed basin for Holy Water in a niche, corbelled out from a pier or wall, or free-standing on a pedestal, near the entrance to a church. It may be shaped like a scallop-shell.

structural polychromy. Architectural decoration in which the colour is not applied after construction, but is provided by the brick, stones, or tiles used in the building: it was a feature of the mature *Gothic Revival*.

Stuart. Architecture of the early-seventeenth century, otherwise *Jacobean* or *Caroline*, but also loosely applied to the period 1603 to 1714.

Sublime. Eighteenth-century *æsthetic category* (*see* **Beautiful, Picturesque**) associated with ideas of awe, intensity, power, ruggedness, terror, and vastness emphasising Man's relative insignificance in the face of Nature, arousing strong emotions, and stimulating the imagination. In architecture the Sublime was associated with great size, overwhelming scale, primitive, powerful, unornamented fabric, repetition (e.g. as in a vast colonnade or viaduct), and gloomy, cavernous interiors.

sun. Representations of the sun are found on the heraldic right of Christ's head, with the moon on the heraldic left, in depictions of the Crucifixion: they suggest Good and Day, Evil and Night.

super-altar. **1**. Shelf above an altar, or to the east of it, on which are placed objects not allowed on the altar itself. **2**. Consecrated altar-stone, -slab, or *mensa*.

symbol. **1**. Authoritative statement of the belief of the Christian Church; a confession of faith or a creed. **2**. Representation of something sacred, such as either of the elements of the *Eucharist*. **3**. A representation of something that it is. See **allegory**.

synagogue. Building for Jewish religious observances and instruction. Nineteenth-century synagogues tended to favour a round-arched *Byzantine Romanesque* style.

tabernacle. **1**. Cupboard with doors to contain the consecrated Host on an altar. **2**. *Pyx*. **3**. Canopied *niche* containing an image. **4**. Shrine or canopied tomb. **5**. *Baldacchino*, *ciborium*, or any free-standing canopy. **6**. Place of worship distinguished from a

church, e.g. a meeting-house for *Nonconformist Protestants*.

tabernacle-work. **1**. Ornate *Gothic* canopy over a funerary monument. **2**. Openwork canopy over *niches*, *sedilia*, *shrines*, *choir-stalls*, or a *cathedra*.

tegurium. Cover with pitched sides over a *sarcophagus* or *tomb-chest*, supported on *colonnettes*.

temple-front. See **portico**.

terracotta. Hard unglazed pottery of which architectural enrichment, decorative tiles, statuary, urns, etc., are made.

tester. Canopy over a pulpit (called *abat-voix*) or tomb.

Third Pointed. See **Gothic**.

tierceron. In a *Gothic* vault, a rib that rises from one of the main springing-points, between main diagonal and transverse ribs, to a position on the ridge-rib.

tithe. A tenth part of annual produce or earnings, formerly taken as a tax for the support of the Church and clergy.

tomb-canopy. Canopy, often forming a grandly decorative ensemble, over an altar-tomb or tomb-chest, as though protecting the effigies below.

tomb-chest. Rectangular stone funerary monument above a tomb, often with effigies on top or suggested by figures incised on the top slab or cut into inserts of metal ('brasses'). The sides were often enriched with quatrefoils, etc., or with niches containing *weepers* (upright or kneeling figures).

torus (*pl.* **tori**). Bold projecting convex moulding of semi-circular section, enriched or plain.

town canopy. Structure resembling an arched gabled opening, with elaborate crocketed pinnacles, finials, etc., like a miniature building, set over a niche or protecting a statue: it was common in funerary architecture, set horizontal (i.e. 90° from the usual vertical position as a protection from the weather), on tomb-chests over the heads of effigies, and was depicted in two dimensions on incised slabs and funerary 'brasses'.

trabeated. Construction on the *column-* and *–lintel* system, as opposed to *arcuated* structures.

tracery. Arrangement by which panels, screens, vaults, or windows are divided into parts or *lights* of different shapes and sizes by means of moulded stone *bars* or *ribs*. Early Gothic windows with more than one light did not have bars, but had the flat stone *spandrel* above the main lights (usually two) pierced with a *quatrefoil*, *roundel*, or other figure: this type of tracery is the *First Pointed plate* variety, consisting of a thin flat panel of ashlar pierced, like simple fretwork, with *lights*. Starting with early thirteenth-century French examples, the flat plate was abandoned, the large lights were divided by moulded *mullions*, the section of which continued at the heads of the window-openings to describe circular and other lights, leaving the *spandrels* open and divided into small lights of various shapes and sizes: this type of subdivision is termed *bar-tracery*, and it was one of the most important elements of *Gothic* architecture, with definite stylistic connotations. Simple bar-tracery formed patterns of *Middle Pointed Geometrical* tracery, which consisted of circles and foiled circles, with roughly triangular lights between the major elements. Mullions in *Geometrical* tracery usually had *capitals* from which the curved bars sprang. After the late-thirteenth-century *Geometrical* tracery came *Intersecting* tracery in which each mullion of the window branched (without capitals) into curved bars: as the window proper had a head formed of two equal curves, the forms of the *Intersecting* tracery were also equal. The mullions therefore continued in curved Y-shaped branches to meet the window-opening, thus forming a series of lozenge-shaped lights at the top. *Intersecting* tracery had bars and the main window opening all described from the same centres, but with different radii, so that such windows were subdivided into two or (usually) more main lights, each forming a pointed, lancet-shaped arch. *Intersecting* tracery occurred around 1300. *Curvilinear, Flowing*, or *Undulating* tracery of *Second Pointed* work dominated the fourteenth century, when *ogees* were applied to the basic arrangement of *Intersecting* tracery, thus creating a net-like construction of bars at the tops of windows: this type of tracery is called *Reticulated*, because it looks like a net, and was commonly found in work of the first half of the fourteenth century. *Curvilinear* or *Flowing* tracery then developed further and more freely, using the *ogee* curves to create *daggers, fish-bladders*, or flame-shaped lights called *mouchettes*: such designs evolved further throughout the fifteenth century in Europe, and became known as *Flamboyant* because of the flame-like forms enclosed by the tracery-bars. From the late fourteenth century, England began to develop *Perpendicular* or *Third Pointed* tracery, in which the main mullions (often joined by transoms) ran straight up to the underside of the main window-arch head, with some mullions branching to form subsidiary arches: this system created panel-like lights, and so the style became known as *Rectilinear* or *panel*-tracery. Later still, from the end of the fourteenth century, but mostly fifteenth- and early sixteenth-century work, the window-heads became much flatter *four-centred* arches, divided into panels, with *crenellated transoms*, and the windows filled the whole wall between buttresses. *See* **Gothic.**

Tractarianism. Tenets or principles of the *High Church Anglican Tractarians*, who maintained the doctrines and practices set forth in the *Tracts for the Times* (1833-41), a series of pamphlets on theological and ecclesiastical topics published in Oxford. Tractarianism aimed to arrest the advance of liberalism in religious thought, and to revive what its adherents held to be the true conception of the relation of the *Church of England* to the *Catholic Church* at large. It is intimately linked with the *Oxford Movement*, the adherents of which are called *Tractarians, Puseyites*, or even *crypto-Papists*.

trail, trayle. Continuous horizontal *running enrichment* of vine-leaves, tendrils, stalks, and grapes, called also *grapevine, vignette, vine-scroll*, or *vinette*, often found enriching *Perpendicular* canopies and screens, e.g. in funerary architecture and chancel-screens. It is essentially a late *Gothic* ornament.

Trajan column. Commemorative single free-standing column, essentially of the *Tuscan Order*, with spiral bands of relief sculpture winding around the shaft, a large pedestal-base, and a commemorative statue on top.

transenna. Lattice-work of marble or metal enclosing a shrine.

transept. Any large division of a building lying across its main axis at 90°. In a *cruciform* church the transept is often of the same section as the nave, and may have aisles: eastern transept-aisles were usually subdivided into chapels. The position where the transepts branched on either side of the *crossing* was often marked by a *crossing-tower*, a *flèche*, or a *lantern*. Larger mediæval cathedrals (e.g. Lincoln) sometimes had secondary transepts at the west end of the nave (really a type of *narthex*), and to the east of the crossing, on either side of the *sanctuary* and *choir-aisles*: in both cases they would have had eastern chapels.

Transition. Denotes the merging of one style with another, especially the twelfth-century transition from *Romanesque* to *Gothic*, but is sometimes applied to other styles.

transom, transome. 1. Horizontal element framed across a window, generally used during the *Perpendicular* period, and commonly found in the *grid-tracery* of Elizabethan and *Jacobean* houses, dividing the window-aperture into lights framed by *bars* forming the *mullions* and *transoms*. 2. Horizontal element in a doorway forming part of the frame, above which is a *fanlight*.

Transubstantiation. Conversion, in the *Eucharist*, of the whole *substance* of the bread into the Body and wine into Blood of Christ,

only the *appearances* (and other 'accidents') of bread and wine remaining. It is a doctrine of the *Roman Catholic Church*, as opposed to *Consubstantiation*, in which the bread and wine are held to co-exist with the Body and Blood.

transverse. A *transverse arch* or *rib* separates one bay of a vault from another, and is set at 90° to the main axis of the vaulted space and outside wall.

Tree of Life. *See* **Jesse.**

trefoil. Gothic ornament, light, panel, or opening of three foils set in a circle, meeting in *cusps* projecting inwards.

trellis moulding. *Romanesque* ornament resembling a band of overlapping *chevrons* set between two horizontal framing mouldings.

tribune. 1. Apsidal part of a *basilica*. 2. Eastern part of a church, especially if apsidal. 3. *Pulpitum* or *ambo*, and therefore, by extension, a *pulpit*. 4. Gallery in a church, usually for seating, supported on columns. 5. Raised platform or seat in a basilican church.

Tridentine. The adjective from the nineteenth Ecumenical Council held at Trent in the Tirol, between 1545 and 1563. That Council defined differences between the *Roman Catholic* and *Protestant Churches*, established certain forms of worship (especially that of the *Mass*), and reconfirmed attitudes towards iconoclasm and the legitimacy of images in churches for the purpose of reinforcing faith, among other matters. It also reinforced discipline and the authority of the Papacy. It follows, therefore, that the Church *in* England before the Reformation was *pre-Tridentine*, and that forms of worship and traditions differed greatly from *post-Tridentine* practices (which appeared very foreign to Englishmen no matter what their religious persuasion might be).

triforium. In larger *Romanesque* and *Gothic* churches, an arcaded wall-passage facing on to the *nave*, above the *aisle* and *nave-arcade*. Its own arcade forms an important part of the elevation of a nave-interior above the nave-arcade and below the *clearstorey*.

triglyph. One of the upright blocks in series in a *Doric frieze* separated by *metopes*: each face of the triglyph has two vertical V-shaped channels cut in it, called *glyphs*, and the edges are chamfered with half-glyphs, hence the three glyphs in all. Triglyphs occur over the centre-lines of columns and over *intercolumniations*, except at the corners of buildings of the Greek Doric Order, where the triglyphs join, so the corner-columns are set closer to their immediate neighbours.

Trinitarianism. The doctrine of Trinitarians, i.e. those who accept the Father, Son, and Holy Spirit as Three in One.

Trinity. The three 'persons' or modes of being as conceived in orthodox Christian belief, the Father, Son, and Holy Spirit as constituting one God.

triptych. Pictures or carvings in three compartments side by side, the lateral ones usually subordinate (though connected in subject-matter) and hinged to enable them to be folded over the central compartment. A triptych was often a late-mediæval altar-piece, called in German a *Flügelaltar*. When closed, the part visible (i.e. the backs of the folding leaves) often displayed *grisaille* paintings.

trumeau. Stone *mullion, pier*, or *shaft* supporting the *tympanum* of a wide *Gothic* doorway.

truss. 1. Rigid structural framework of timber bridging a space, each end resting on supports at regular intervals, carrying longitudinal timbers (e.g. *purlins*) that in turn support the *common rafters* and roof-covering. Its stability also prevents the roof from spreading. 2. Element projecting from a wall, e.g. *console*.

Tudor. English architecture during the Tudor monarchy of Kings Henry VII and VIII (1485-1547), primarily associated with late *Perpendicular Gothic*, very flat four-centred or Tudor arches, domestic architecture of brick with *diaper-patterns*, elaborate chimneys of carved and moulded brick, and square-headed *mullioned* windows with *hood-moulds* and *label-stops*.

Tudor arch. *Pseudo-four-centred* late-*Perpendicular* arch, with shanks starting as quarter-circles (with centres on the springing-lines) continuing as straight lines to the apex. It is very *depressed*, and often expressed as a single carved *lintel*.

Tudor flower. Late *Gothic* ornament resembling a flattish trefoil diamond-shaped stylised ivy-leaf or flower rising on a stalk. It was commonly used as *brattishing* or *cresting* on *Perpendicular choir-screens*, *tomb-canopies*, etc.

Tudor Revival. Nineteenth-century revival of *Tudor* architecture.

tumbling-courses. Courses of brickwork laid at 90° to the slope of a *buttress*, *chimney*, *gable*, etc., and tapering into the horizontal courses. It was often employed during the 'muscular' phase of the nineteenth-century *Gothic Revival*.

Tuscan Order. One of the five *Roman Orders* of *Classical* architecture, and the simplest. It resembles *Roman Doric*, but has no *triglyphs* on its unadorned *frieze*. Its base is plain, with a square plinth-block supporting a large *torus* over which is the *fillet* and *apophyge* creating the transition to the unfluted shaft.

tympanum (*pl. tympana*). **1.** Triangular or segmental face of a *pediment* contained between the horizontal and raking cornices or horizontal and segmental cornices, often enriched. **2.** Area above a *lintel* over an opening contained by the arch set above it, or over two openings carried on a *trumeau* in a *Gothic* doorway.

undercroft. Crypt or vaulted space under a church or other building, wholly or partly underground.

Ultramontanism. An *Ultramontane* was a representative of the *Roman Catholic Church* north of the Alps as opposed to an ecclesiastic in Italy (literally *beyond the mountain*). *Ultramontanism*, therefore, was the principle and practice of the Ultramontane party in the Church advocating absolute papal supremacy outside Italy (especially in France, Germany, Northern Europe generally, and the British Isles).

Unitarianism. Belief in or affirmation of the unity of God. Unitarians (a *Protestant* sect) rejected the doctrine of *Trinitarianism*.

vault. Arched structure constructed of stone or brick, and sometimes of wood or plaster in imitation of a stone vault, forming a ceiling over a space.

Venetian arch. Semicircular arch framing two semicircular-headed *lights* separated by a *colonnette* over which is a *roundel* in the space between the tops of the smaller lights and the main arch.

Venetian Gothic. Prompted by Street's *Brick and Marble in the Middle Ages* (1855, 1874), and Ruskin's *Stones of Venice* (1851-3), it featured *polychrome* brick and masonry, elaborately patterned arcades, and other elements taken from Italian Gothic. It was particularly associated with *structural polychromy*.

Venetian window. Tripartite window, door, or blind architectural feature consisting of a central opening with a semicircular arch over it springing from two *entablatures* each supported by two *columns* or *pilasters* flanking narrower flat-topped openings on either side. Called a *Palladian window* or a *Serliana*, it was a common motif in Palladian architecture.

vernacular architecture. Unpretentious, simple, indigenous, traditional structures made of local materials and following well-tried forms and types, e.g. country cottages, farm-buildings, etc. It provided precedents for the *Domestic Revival*.

vesica piscis. **1.** *Light* in *Second Pointed Curvilinear* or *Flowing tracery* resembling a tadpole or air-bladder of a fish. **2.** *Almond*, *aureole*, *glory*, or *mandala* of the upright almond-shaped variety, produced by placing two equilateral triangles above and below a base-line as mirror images and striking arcs from each end of the base-line passing through the other points of the triangle: this

creates two pointed arches base-to-base, commonly found as a vertical aureole enclosing a figure of, e.g., Christ in Majesty. The shape is found in windows, e.g. the rose-window in the south transept of Lincoln Cathedral. *See* **Chrismon**.

vestry. **1.** Room adjoining the *chancel* in a church where vestments are stored and the clergy are *vested*. **2.** *Sacristy* where sacred vessels, books, and vestments are stored, and meetings can be held.

vicar. **1.** Earthly representative of Christ, so the Pope or the Patriarch of Jerusalem. **2.** Incumbent of a parish of which tithes were impropriated or appropriated, in contrast to a *rector*. A *vicarage* is the *benefice* or *living* of a vicar, or the house or residence of a vicar, or the position, office, or duties of a vicar.

vignette. Running ornament of leaves and tendrils (usually of *vines*) in a *cavetto* moulding in *Gothic* work, also called a *trail* or *vinette*.

vine. Grapevine, *trail*, *trayle*, *vine-scroll*, or *vignette*.

volute. Spiral *scroll*, of which there are normally four on the *Ionic* capital, eight on the *angular* and *Composite* capitals, and smaller types, sometimes called *helix*, on the *Corinthian* capital. It is also a distinctive element of the *ancon*, *console*, and *modillion*.

votive. Dedicated, consecrated, offered, erected, etc., in consequence of, or in fulfilment of, a vow, e.g. a church, altar, or statue.

voussoir. *Cuneus*, or block of stone or brick, its long sides coinciding with the radii of the arch of which it forms part of the wedge-shaped structure.

wall-pier. Internal *buttress* forming the walls of side-chapels or pierced to form *passage-aisles*.

watching-loft. Elevated gallery or chamber in a church from which a holy shrine could be guarded or watched over.

water-leaf. *Transitional* early *Gothic* twelfth-century carved ornament on each angle of a capital, essentially a large, broad, plain leaf resembling a water-lily or lily-pad, flowing out from above the *astragal* in a concave curve, then returning upwards in a convex curve, turning inwards at each angle under the *abacus*.

web. *Cell*, *compartment*, *infill*, or *severy* between the *ribs* of a *Gothic vault*.

weeper. One of a series of mourning-figures set around a *tomb-chest*, usually in niches, in funerary architecture, common in mediæval work.

Wesleyanism. System of *Arminian* theology as taught by John Wesley. It was the kernel of *Methodism*.

wheel-window. **1.** Circular window with spoke-like *colonnettes* or *bars* radiating from the centre. **2.** Circular part of an early *Middle Pointed Geometrical* window with *bar-tracery*.

Whig. **1.** Adherent of the *Presbyterian* cause in seventeenth-century Scotland. **2.** Extreme anti-Royalist Nonconformist. **3.** Exclusioner opposed to the succession of James, Duke of York, as King James II and VII (1685-8), on the ground of his being a Roman Catholic. **4.** From 1689 an adherent of one of the two main political parties in England, and, eventually, in Great Britain. From around 1840 the term was superseded by *Liberal*.

Whitefieldian, Whitfieldian. A follower of George Whitefield (1714-70), the leader of the *Calvinistic Methodists*.

Y-tracery. In *intersecting* tracery, the *mullions* form Y-shaped branches that intersect: this is called *Y-tracery*.

zig-zag. *Romanesque* decorative Z- or V- and inverted V (Λ)-shaped device (*chevron* or *dancette*), either incised or in relief, occurring as a continuous *band* or *string*, as an ornament around an arch or series of arches, or cut into the drum of a *pier*.

Select Bibliography

The renewal, in this country, of a taste for Mediæval architecture, and the reapplication of those principles which regulate its design, represent one of the most interesting and remarkable phases in the history of art.
CHARLES LOCKE EASTLAKE (1836-1906): *A History of the Gothic Revival*
(London: Longmans, Green, & Co., 1872), 1.

The Author acknowledges the generous assistance of Mrs Karen Latimer, Mr Roger Towe, and Mrs Kay Woollen in the compilation of this Bibliography.

ACLAND, HENRY, and RUSKIN, JOHN (1859): *The Oxford Museum* (London: Smith, Elder).

ALDRICH, MEGAN (1994): *Gothic Revival* (London: Phaidon).

ALLIBONE, JILL (1988): *Anthony Salvin 1799-1881: Pioneer of Gothic Revival Architecture* (Columbia, Mo.: University of Missouri Press, and Cambridge: The Lutterworth Press).

——— (1991): *George Devey, Architect, 1820-1886* (Cambridge: The Lutterworth Press).

ALLSOPP, BRUCE (*Ed.*) (1967): *Historic Architecture of Newcastle upon Tyne* (Newcastle upon Tyne: Oriel Press).

AMERY, COLIN (1980): *See* STAMP, GAVIN.

ANSELL, PETER F. (1960): *Fashions in Church Furnishings 1840-1940* (London: Faith Press).

ASLIN, ELIZABETH (1969): *The Æsthetic Movement* (London: Paul Elek).

AUZAS, P.M. (*Ed.*) (1965): *Eugène Viollet-le-Duc 1814-1879* (Paris: Caisse Nationale des Monuments Historiques).

BERESFORD-HOPE, ALEXANDER JAMES (1861): *See* HOPE, ALEXANDER JAMES BERESFORD.

BETJEMAN, JOHN (*Ed.*) (1980): *Collins Guide to English Parish Churches* (London: Collins).

BINFIELD, CLYDE (2001): *James Cubitt 1836-1912* (Stowmarket: The Chapels Society).

BISHOP, REV. H. H. (1886): *Architecture in Relation to Our Parish Churches* (London: S.P.C.K.).

BLAU, E. (1982): *Ruskinian Gothic: The Architecture of Deane and Woodward (1845-61)* (Princeton: Princeton University Press).

BLOXAM, JOHN ROUSE (*Ed.*) (1842): *The Book of Fragments* (Oxford: printed by W. Baxter).

BLOXAM, MATTHEW HOLBECHE (1882): *The Principles of Gothic Ecclesiastical Architecture, with an explanation of technical terms, and a centenary of ancient terms. Together also with Notices of the internal arrangement of churches prior to, and the changes therein in and from, the reign of Edward VI* (London: George Bell & Sons).

BOND, FRANCIS (1914): *Dedications of English Churches* (London: Humphrey Milford, for Oxford University Press).

——— (1916): *The Chancel in English Churches* (London: Humphrey Milford, for Oxford University Press).

BRANDWOOD, GEOFFREY K. (1997): *Temple Moore. An Architect of the Late Gothic Revival* (Stamford: Paul Watkins).

BROCKMAN, H.A.N. (1974): *The British Architect and Industry, 1841-1940* (London: Allen & Unwin).

BRODIE, ANTONIA, FELSTEAD, ALISON, FRANKLIN, JONATHAN, PINFIELD, LESLIE, and OLDFIELD, JANE (2001): *Directory of British Architects 1834-1914* (London and New York: Continuum).

BROOKS, CHRIS (1995): *See* SYMONDSON, ANTHONY.

——— (1999): *The Gothic Revival* (London: Phaidon Press Ltd.).

——— , and SAINT, ANDREW (*Eds.*) (1995): *The Victorian Church. Architecture and Society* (Manchester and New York: Manchester University Press).

BURY, S. (1967): *Copy or Creation? Victorian Treasures from English Churches* (London: Goldsmith's Company).

CAMBRIDGE CAMDEN SOCIETY (later THE ECCLESIOLOGICAL SOCIETY) (1843): *Church Enlargement and Church Arrangement* (Cambridge: Cambridge University Press).

——— (1842-68): *The Ecclesiologist.*

——— (1847): *A Hand-Book of English Ecclesiology* (London: J. Masters).

CHADWICK, OWEN (1987a): *Victorian Church: 1829-59* (London: S.C.M.P.).

——— (1987b): *Victorian Church: 1860-1901* (London: S.C.M.P.).

CHURCH, R. W. (1891): *The Oxford Movement: Twelve Years, 1833-1845* (London: Methuen & Co.).

CHURCH BUILDER, THE: 1862-1901.

CLARK, KENNETH (1962): *The Gothic Revival* (London: John Murray).

CLARKE, BASIL FULFORD LOWTHER (1958): *Anglican Cathedrals outside the British Isles* (London: S.P.C.K.).

—————— (1966): *Parish Churches of London* (London: B. T. Batsford Ltd.).

—————— (1969): *Church Builders of the Nineteenth Century: A Study of the Gothic Revival in England* (Newton Abbot: David & Charles).

COLE, DAVID (1980): *The Work of Sir George Gilbert Scott* (London: Architectural Press).

COMPER, JOHN NINIAN (1947): *Of the Atmosphere of a Church* (London: Sheldon Press).

COOMBS, JOYCE (1975): *One Aim. Edward Stuart 1820-1877* (London: The Stanhope Press).

CROOK, J. MORDAUNT (1970): See EASTLAKE, CHARLES LOCKE.

—————— (1971): *Victorian Architecture: A Visual Anthology* (New York: Johnson Reprint).

—————— (1981): *William Burges and the High Victorian Dream* (London: John Murray).

CUBITT, JAMES (1870): *Church Design for Congregations: its Development and Possibilities* (London: Smith, Elder, & Co.).

CURL, JAMES STEVENS (1983): *The Life and Work of Henry Roberts (1803-76)* (Chichester: Phillimore & Co. Ltd.).

—————— (1990): 'All Saints', Margaret Street' in the *Masters of Building* series in *The Architects' Journal*, **cxci**, 25 (20 June), 36-55.

—————— (1990 and 1992): *Victorian Architecture* (Newton Abbot: David & Charles).

—————— (2000): *Oxford Dictionary of Architecture* (Oxford: Oxford University Press).

——————, and SAMBROOK, JOHN (1973): 'E. Bassett Keeling, Architect' in *Architectural History*, **xvi**, 60-69, and Figs. 26-32.

—————— (1999): ' E. Bassett Keeling – A Postscript' in *Architectural History*, **xlii**, 307-315.

DEARMER, PERCY (1911): *The Chancel and the Altar* (London: A. R. Mowbray & Co. Ltd.).

—————— (1931): *The parson's handbook; containing practical directions both for parsons and others as to the management of the parish church and its services according to the Anglican use* (London and New York: H. Milford).

DICKINSON, GILLIAN (*Ed.*) (1983): *Rutland Churches before Restoration: An Early Victorian Album of Watercolours and Drawings – with Commentaries and Photographs* (Rutland: Barrowden Books).

DIXON, ROGER, and MUTHESIUS, STEFAN (1985): *Victorian Architecture* (London: Thames & Hudson).

DUFFY, EAMON (1992): *The Stripping of the Altars. Traditional Religion in England c.1400- c.1580* (New Haven and London: Yale University Press).

—————— (2001): *The Voices of Morebath: reformation and rebellion in an English village* (New Haven and London: Yale University Press).

DYKES BOWER, STEPHEN ERNEST (1973): 'The Importance of Style' in *The Architect* (December), 54-7.

DYOS, H.J., and WOLFF, MICHAEL (*Eds.*) (1973): *The Victorian City: Images and Realities* (London: Routledge & Kegan Paul).

EASTLAKE, CHARLES LOCKE (1970): *A History of the Gothic Revival: An attempt to show how the Taste for Mediæval Architecture which lingered in England during the last two Centuries has since been encouraged and developed*, with an Introduction by J. MORDAUNT CROOK (Leicester: Leicester University Press).

ELLERAY, D. ROBERT (1981): *The Victorian Churches of Sussex, with illustrations and a Check-List of Churches and Chapels erected during the years 1810-1914* (Chichester: Phillimore & Co. Ltd.).

ELLIOTT, JOHN (1996): 'Lancing College Chapel: A Question of Attribution' in *Architectural History*, **xxxix**, 114-123.

—————— (*Ed.*) (2001): *See* WEBSTER, CHRISTOPHER.

FAWCETT, JANE (*Ed.*) (1976): *Seven Victorian Architects* (London: Thames & Hudson).

FELSTEAD, ALISON (2001): *See* BRODIE, ANTONIA.

FERREY, BENJAMIN (1861): *Recollections of A.N. Welby Pugin, and His Father Augustus Pugin* (London: E. Stanford).

FERRIDAY, PETER (*Ed.*) (1963): *Victorian Architecture* (London: Jonathan Cape).

FORTESCUE, ADRIAN (1917): *The Mass; a Study of the Roman Liturgy* (London and New York: Longmans, Green, & Co.).

FRANKLIN, JONATHAN (2001): *See* BRODIE, ANTONIA.

GARRIGAN, K. (1973): *Ruskin and Architecture: His Thought and Influence* (Madison: University of Wisconsin Press).

GERMANN, GEORG (1972): *Gothic Revival in Europe and Britain: Sources, Influences, and Ideas* (London: Lund Humphries).

GOODHART-RENDEL, H.S. (1949): 'Rogue Architects of the Victorian Era' in *Journal of the R.I.B.A.*, Third Series, **lvi**/6, 251-9.

—————— (1989): *English Architecture Since the Regency: An Interpretation* (London: Century, first published by Constable in 1953).

GRAY, A. STUART (1985): *Edwardian Architecture. A Biographical Dictionary* (London: Duckworth).

GWYNN, DENNIS R (1946): *Lord Shrewsbury, Pugin, and the Catholic Revival* (London: Hollins & Carter).

HAGUE, GRAHAM, and JUDY (1986): *The Unitarian Heritage. An Architectural Survey of Chapels and Churches in the Unitarian Tradition in the British Isles* (Sheffield: P.B. Godfrey).

HALL, MICHAEL (1993): 'The rise of refinement: G. F. Bodley's All Saints, Cambridge, and the return to

English models in Gothic architecture' in *Architectural History*, **xxxvi**, 103-126.

HARBISON, ROBERT (1992): *The Shell Guide to English Parish Churches* (London: André Deutsch).

HARPER, ROGER H. (1983): *Victorian Architectural Competitions: an Index to British and Irish Architectural Competitions in* The Builder, *1843-1900* (London: Mansell).

HARRIES, J.G. (1973): *Pugin: an Illustrated Life of Augustus Welby Northmore Pugin, 1812-52* (Aylesbury: Shire Publications).

HARRIS, CHARLES (*Ed.*) (1933): *See* WILLIAMS, NORMAN POWELL.

HARRIS, THOMAS (1860): *Victorian Architecture: A Few Words to Show that a National Architecture Adapted to the Wants of the Nineteenth Century is Attainable* (London: s.n.).

HEATHCOTE, EDWIN, and SPENS, IONA (1997): *Church Builders* (Chichester: Academy Editions).

HERSEY, GEORGE L. (1972): *High Victorian Gothic. A Study in Associationism* (Baltimore & London: The Johns Hopkins University Press).

HITCHCOCK, HENRY-RUSSELL (1954): *Early Victorian Architecture in Britain* (New Haven: Yale University Press).

————— (1968): *Architecture: Nineteenth and Twentieth Centuries* (Harmondsworth: Penguin).

HOBHOUSE, HERMIONE (*Ed.*) (1986): *The Survey of London*, **xlii** (London: Athlone Press).

HOMAN, R (1984): *Victorian Churches of Kent* (Chichester: Phillimore & Co. Ltd.).

HOPE, ALEXANDER JAMES BERESFORD- (1861): *The English Cathedral of the Nineteenth Century* (London: John Murray).

————— (1863): *The Conditions and Prospects of Architectural Art* (London: Architectural Museum).

HOWELL, PETER (1968): *Victorian Churches* (Feltham: Country Life Books).

————— and SUTTON, IAN (*Eds.*) in conjunction with The Victorian Society (1989): *The Faber Guide to Victorian Churches* (London: Faber & Faber).

HUBBARD, EDWARD (1991): *The Work of John Douglas* (London: The Victorian Society).

HUMPHREY, STEPHEN C. (*Ed.*) (1991a): *Blue Guide Churches and Chapels of Northern England* (London: A.& C. Black, and New York: W. W. Norton & Company, Inc.).

————— (1991b): *Blue Guide Churches and Chapels of Southern England* (London: A. & C. Black, and New York: W. W. Norton & Company, Inc.).

INGLIS, KENNETH STANLEY (1963): *Churches of the Working Classes in Victorian England* (London: Routledge & Kegan Paul).

JACKSON, NEIL (1980): 'The Un-Englishness of G. E. Street's Church of St James-the-Less' in *Architectural History*, **xxiii**, 86-94.

————— (2000): 'Christ Church, Streatham, and the Rise of Constructional Polychromy' in *Architectural History*, **xliii**, 219-252.

JACKSON, T.G. (1950): *Recollections of Thomas Graham Jackson 1835-1924*. Arranged and Edited by BASIL H. JACKSON (London: Geoffrey Cumberlege, Oxford University Press).

JENKINS, SIMON (1999): *England's Thousand Best Churches*, with photographs by PAUL BARKER from the *Country Life* archive (London: Allen Lane, The Penguin Press).

JERVIS, SIMON (1983): *High Victorian Design* (Woodbridge: Boydell Press).

JONES, RONALD P. (1914): *Nonconformist Church Architecture* (London: Lindsey Press).

LEE, FREDERICK GEORGE (1866): *See* PURCHAS, JOHN.

LITTLE, BRYAN (1966): *Catholic Churches since 1623: a Study of Roman Catholic churches in England and Wales from Penal Times to the Present Day* (London: Robert Hale).

————— (1971): *Birmingham Buildings: The Architectural Story of a Midland City* (Newton Abbot: David & Charles).

MACAULAY, JAMES (1975): *The Gothic Revival 1745-1845* (Glasgow: Blackie).

McCARTHY, MICHAEL (1987): *The Origins of the Gothic Revival* (New Haven: Yale University Press).

MacLEOD, R.(1971): *Style and Society: Architectural Ideology in Britain 1840-1914* (London: R.I.B.A.).

MASKELL, WILLIAM (*Ed.*) (1846-7): *Monumenta ritualia ecclesiæ Anglicanæ; or, Occasional offices of the Church of England according to the ancient use of Salisbury, the Prymer in English, and other prayers and forms, with dissertations and notes by THE REV. WILLIAM MASKELL* (London: W. Pickering).

————— (1882): *The Ancient Liturgy of the Church of England, according to the uses of Sarum, York, Hereford, and Bangor, and the Roman Liturgy arranged in parallel columns with Preface and Notes* (Oxford: The Clarendon Press). Originally published in 1844.

METCALF, PRISCILLA (1972): *Victorian London* (London: Cassell).

MICKLETHWAITE, J. T. (1874): *Modern Parish Churches* (London: H. S. King).

MITCHELL, ANTHONY (1990): *Thomas Earp: Master of Stone. The Life and Work of this noted sculptor of the Victorian era* (Birmingham: Barracuda Books Ltd.).

MUTHESIUS, STEFAN (1970): 'The "Iron Problem" in the 1850s' in *Architectural History*, **xiii**, 58-63 and Figs. 36-39.

————— (1972): *The High Victorian Movement in Architecture, 1850-70* (London: Routledge & Kegan Paul).

————— (1985): *See* DIXON, ROGER.

OLDFIELD, JANE (2001): *See* BRODIE, ANTONIA.

O'REILLY, SEÁN (1997): 'Roman *versus* Romantic: Classical Roots in the Origins of a Roman Catholic Ecclesiology' in *Architectural History*, **xl**, 222-240.

ORBACH, JULIAN (1987): *Blue Guide: Victorian Architecture in Britain* (London: A. & C. Black [Publishers] Ltd., and New York: W. W. Norton & Co. Inc.).

PALMER, WILLIAM (1845): *Origines liturgicæ; or Antiquities of the English Ritual, and a Dissertation on Primitive Liturgies* (London: Francis & John Rivington).

PARKER, JOHN HENRY (1850): *A Glossary of Terms used in Grecian, Roman, Italian, and Gothic Architecture* (Oxford: John Henry Parker).

————— (1898): *ABC of Gothic Architecture* (London: James Parker & Co.).

————— (1902): *An Introduction to the Study of Gothic Architecture* (London: James Parker & Co.).

PAWLEY, MARGARET (1994): *Faith and Family. The Life and Circle of Ambrose Phillipps de Lisle* (Norwich: Canterbury Press).

PEPPERELL, REV. WILLIAM (1872): *The Church Index. A Book of Metropolitan Churches and Church Enterprise [in Kensington]* (London: W. Wells Gardner).

PEVSNER, NIKOLAUS (1968): *Studies in Art, Architecture, and Design* (London: Thames & Hudson).

————— (1969): *Ruskin and Viollet-le-Duc: Englishness and Frenchness in the Appreciation of Gothic Architecture* (London: Thames & Hudson).

————— (1972): *Some Architectural Writers of the Nineteenth Century* (Oxford: The Clarendon Press).

—————, *ET AL.* (from 1951): *The Buildings of England* Series (Harmondsworth and London: Penguin).

PICTON-SEYMOUR, DESIREE (1977): *Victorian Buildings in South Africa, including Edwardian and Transvaal Republican Styles 1850-1910: a Survey of Houses, Churches, Schools, Public and Commercial Buildings,... and the Influence of European Styles* (Cape Town and Rotterdam: Balkema).

PINFIELD, LESLIE (2001): *See* BRODIE, ANTONIA.

PORT, M.H.(1961): *Six Hundred New Churches: A Study of The Church Building Commission 1818-56* (London: S.P.C.K.).

PUGIN, AUGUSTUS WELBY NORTHMORE (1843*a*): *An Apology for the Revival of Christian Architecture in England* (London: John Weale).

————— (1843*b*): *The Present State of Ecclesiastical Architecture in England* (London: Dolman).

————— (1851): *A Treatise on Chancel Screens* (London: Dolman).

————— (1853): *The True Principles of Pointed or Christian Architecture: Set forth in Two Lectures delivered at St. Marie's, Oscott* (London: Henry G. Bohn).

————— (1973): *Contrasts: Or, a Parallel between the Noble Edifices of the Middle Ages, and Corresponding Buildings of the Present Day; Shewing the Present Decay of Taste*, originally published in 1841 in London by Charles Dolman (Leicester: Leicester University Press). An earlier version, with a slightly different title, came out in 1836.

PURCHAS, JOHN (1866): *The Directorium Anglicanum; being a manual of Directions for the Right Celebration of the Holy Communion, for the saying of Matins and Evensong, and for the Performance of other Rites and Ceremonies of the Church according to the Ancient Uses of the Church of England. With Plan of Chancel and Illustrations* (London: T. Bosworth). Originally published in 1858, the second edition was revised by FREDERICK GEORGE LEE.

QUINEY, ANTHONY (1979): *John Loughborough Pearson* (New Haven and London: Yale University Press).

————— (1988): 'The Door Marked "Pull": J. L. Pearson and His First Clients in the East Riding of Yorkshire' in *Architectural History*, **xli**, 208-219.

————— (1995): '"Altogether a Capital Fellow and a Serious Fellow Too": A Brief Account of the Life and Work of Henry Woodyer, 1816-1896' in *Architectural History*, **xxxviii**, 192-219.

RICHES, ANNE (1982): *Victorian Church Building and Restoration in Suffolk. A supplement to H. Munro Cautley's* Suffolk Churches (Woodbridge: The Boydell Press).

RICKMAN, THOMAS (1848): *An Attempt to Discriminate the Styles of Architecture in England, from the Conquest to the Reformation* (London: John Henry Parker).

ROCK, DANIEL (1849-53): *The Church of Our Fathers, as seen in St Osmund's rite for the Cathedral of Salisbury* (London: C. Dolman).

ROYAL INSTITUTE OF BRITISH ARCHITECTS (2001): *See* BRODIE, ANTONIA, *ET AL.*

RUSKIN, JOHN (1859): *See* ACLAND, HENRY.

————— (1903-12): *Works* (London: Longmans Green). *See* especially *The Seven Lamps of Architecture* (1849) and *The Stones of Venice* (1851-3).

SAINT, ANDREW (1976): *Richard Norman Shaw* (New Haven and London: Yale University Press).

————— (1995): *See* SYMONDSON, ANTHONY.

————— (1995) (*Ed.*) *See* BROOKS, CHRIS.

SAUNDERS, MATTHEW (1982): *The Churches of S.S. Teulon* (London: The Ecclesiological Society).

SCOTT, GEORGE GILBERT (1850): *A Plea for the Faithful Restoration of our Ancient Churches* (London: J.H. Parker).

————— (1879): *Personal and Professional Recollections* (London: Sampson, Low, Marston, Searle and Rivington). *See also* the new edition, edited by GAVIN STAMP (1995): (Stamford: Paul Watkins).

SCOTT, GEORGE GILBERT, JR. (1881): *An essay on the history of English church architecture prior to the separation of England from the Roman obedience* (London: Simpkin, Marshall, & Co.).

SERVICE, ALASTAIR (1977): *Edwardian Architecture* (London: Thames & Hudson).

SHEPPARD, F.W.H. (*Ed.*) (1973): *The Survey of London* (**xxxvii**) (London: Athlone Press for the G.L.C.).

SMART, C.M. (1990): *Muscular Churches: Ecclesiastical Architecture of the High Victorian Period* (Arkansas: University of Arkansas Press).

SPENS, IONA (1997): *See* HEATHCOTE, EDWIN.

STAMP, GAVIN (1995): *See* SCOTT, GEORGE GILBERT.

——————, and AMERY, COLIN (1980): *Victorian Buildings of London, 1837-1887: an Illustrated Guide* (London: Architectural Press).

STANTON, PHOEBE B. (1971): *Pugin* (London: Thames & Hudson).

STEPHENS, W.R.W (1879): *The Life and Letters of Walter Farquhar Hook* (London: Bentley).

STEWART, CECIL (1956): *The Stones of Manchester* (London: Edward Arnold).

STREET, GEORGE EDMUND (1850): 'On the Proper Characteristics of a Town Church' in *The Ecclesiologist*, **xi**, 227-33.

—————— (1853): *An Urgent Plea for the Revival of the True Principles of Architecture in the Public Buildings of the University of Oxford* (Oxford: J.H. Parker).

—————— (1855): *Brick and Mortar in the Middle Ages: Notes of a Tour in the North of Italy* (London: John Murray).

SUMMERSON, JOHN (1963): *Heavenly Mansions and other Essays on Architecture* (New York: W. W. Norton).

—————— (1970): *Victorian Architecture: Four Studies in Evaluation* (New York and London: Columbia University Press).

—————— (1976): *The Architecture of Victorian London* (Charlottesville, Va.: University Press of Virginia).

SURVEY OF LONDON, THE: From 1900. *See* SHEPPARD, and *See* HOBHOUSE (*Eds.*)

SYMONDSON, ANTHONY (1995): 'Theology, worship, and the late Victorian church' in *The Victorian Church* edited by CHRIS BROOKS and ANDREW SAINT (Manchester: Manchester University Press), 192-222.

—————— (1997): 'Look With Your Ears: Some 20th-century Attitudes to the Late Gothic Revival' in *The Victorian Society Annual 1996*, edited by SARAH WHITTINGHAM (London: The Victorian Society), 37-49.

THOMPSON, PAUL (1971): *William Butterfield* (London: Routledge & Kegan Paul, and Cambridge, Mass.: M.I.T. Press).

TWENTIETH CENTURY SOCIETY, THE (1998): *The Twentieth Century Church. Twentieth Century Architecture 3* (London: The Twentieth Century Society).

UNWIN, FRANCIS SYDNEY (1912): *The Decorative Arts in the Service of the Church* (London: A. R. Mowbray & Co. Ltd.).

VICTORIA AND ALBERT MUSEUM (1971): *Victorian Church Art. Catalogue of an Exhibition. November 1971-January 1972* (London: H.M.S.O.).

WATKIN, DAVID (1974): *The Life and Works of C.R. Cockerell* (London: Zwemmer).

—————— (1977): *Morality and Architecture: Development of a Theme in Architectural History and Theory from the Gothic Revival to the Modern Movement* (Oxford: The Clarendon Press). *See also* the same author's (2001): *Morality and Architecture Revisited* (London: John Murray).

WEBB, BENJAMIN (1848): *Sketches of Continental Ecclesiology, or, Church Notes in Belgium, Germany, and Italy* (London: J. Masters).

WEBSTER, CHRISTOPHER, and ELLIOTT, JOHN (*Eds.*) (2001): 'A Church as it Should Be': the Cambridge Camden Society and its Influence (Donington: Shaun Tyas/Paul Watkins Publishing).

WHITE: JAMES F.(1962): *The Cambridge Movement: The Ecclesiologists and the Gothic Revival* (Cambridge: Cambridge University Press).

WHITTINGHAM, SARAH (1997): *See* SYMONDSON, ANTHONY.

WILLIAMS, NORMAN POWELL, and HARRIS, CHARLES (*Eds.*) (1933): *Northern Catholicism; centenary studies in the Oxford and parallel movements* (London: S.P.C.K., and New York: The Macmillan Company).

WOLFF, MICHAEL (*Ed.*) (1973): *See* DYOS, H.J.

Index

(Compiled by Frances Mather)

Asterisks indicate illustration or caption; *SIG* indicates that the item appears in the Glossary *pp.157-181*